UNCERTAINTY MANAGEMENT IN INFORMATION SYSTEMS

FROM NEEDS TO SOLUTIONS

UNCERTAINTY MANAGEMENT IN INFORMATION SYSTEMS

FROM NEEDS TO SOLUTIONS

EDITED BY

Amihai Motro
George Mason University
Fairfax, VA, USA

Philippe Smets
Université Libre de Bruxelles
Brussels, Belgium

KLUWER ACADEMIC PUBLISHERS
Boston/London/Dordrecht

Distributors for North America:
Kluwer Academic Publishers
101 Philip Drive
Assinippi Park
Norwell, Massachusetts 02061 USA

Distributors for all other countries:
Kluwer Academic Publishers Group
Distribution Centre
Post Office Box 322
3300 AH Dordrecht, THE NETHERLANDS

Library of Congress Cataloging-in-Publication Data

A C.I.P. Catalogue record for this book is available
from the Library of Congress.

Printed on acid-free paper.

Printed in the United States of America

To my parents, Ram and Elisheva
A.M.

In memory of my father and to my family
P.S.

CONTENTS

CONTRIBUTORS

Philippe Besnard
IRISA
Rennes, France

Piero P. Bonissone
General Electric Corporate R&D
Schenectady, NY, USA

Patric Bosc
Université de Rennes
Lannion, France

W. Bruce Croft
University of Massachusetts
Amherst, MA, USA

Robert Demolombe
ONERA/CERT
Toulouse, France

Curtis E. Dyreson
James Cook University
Townsville, Australia

Luis Fariñas del Cerro
Université Paul Sabatier
Toulouse, France

Dov Gabbay
Imperial College
London, UK

David E. Heckerman
Microsoft Research Laboratories
Redmond, WA, USA

Max Henrion
Institute for Decision Systems Research
Los Altos, CA, USA

Anthony Hunter
Imperial College
London, UK

Rudolf Kruse
University of Magdeburg
Magdeburg, Germany

Stephen Kwan
San Jose State University
San Jose, CA, USA

E. H. Mamdani
Imperial College
London, UK

Amihai Motro
George Mason University
Fairfax, VA, USA

Frank Olken
Lawrence Berkeley Laboratory
Berkeley, CA, USA

Gregory Piatetsky-Shapiro
GTE Laboratories Incorporated
Waltham, MA, USA

Alain Pirotte
Université de Louvain
Louvain-la-Neuve, Belgium

Henri Prade
Université Paul Sabatier
Toulouse, France

Doron Rotem
Lawrence Berkeley Laboratory
Berkeley, CA, USA

Philippe Smets
Université Libre de Bruxelles
Brussels, Belgium

Henri J. Suermondt
Hewlett-Packard Laboratories
Palo Alto, CA, USA

Howard R. Turtle
West Publishing Company
Eagan, MN, USA

Esteban Zimányi
Université de Bruxelles
Brussels, Belgium

PREFACE

As its title suggests, "Uncertainty Management in Information Systems" is a book about how information systems can be made to manage information permeated with uncertainty. This subject is at the intersection of two areas of knowledge: *information systems* is an area that concentrates on the design of practical systems that can store and retrieve information; *uncertainty modeling* is an area in artificial intelligence concerned with accurate representation of uncertain information and with inference and decision-making under conditions infused with uncertainty.

New applications of information systems require stronger capabilities in the area of uncertainty management. Our hope is that lasting interaction between these two areas would facilitate a new generation of information systems that will be capable of servicing these applications. Although there are researchers in information systems who have addressed themselves to issues of uncertainty, as well as researchers in uncertainty modeling who have considered the pragmatic demands and constraints of information systems, to a large extent there has been only limited interaction between these two areas.

As the subtitle, "From Needs to Solutions," indicates, this book presents viewpoints of information systems experts on the needs that challenge the uncertainty capabilities of present information systems, and it provides a forum to researchers in uncertainty modeling to describe models and systems that can address these needs.

This book comprises 15 chapters. Except for the introductory chapter and the final chapter, which provides a bibliography, the core of the book is divided roughly into two parts. The first part (Chapters 2–7) was authored by researchers who work in information systems, and the second part (Chapters 8–14) was authored by researchers in uncertainty modeling.

The purpose of the first part is twofold: (1) To describe the issues and challenges in the area of imperfect information that confront information systems. (2) To describe the state of the art with respect to this area; that is, the solutions that have already been applied and the experience that has been gained from these solutions. The purpose of the second part is twofold as well: (1) To describe the principal theories for modeling imperfect information. (2) To show how these theories may be adapted to information systems, responding to their particular challenges, and, in some cases, to discuss actual experimentation with prototype systems that demonstrate these theories.

Hence, this book is not a collection of research papers, in which researchers describe the results of their recent work; such collections, as excellent as they may be, do not necessarily cover an area methodically, and individual papers are often inaccessible to nonexperts. Rather, we first outlined the structure of a book that will cover the entire spectrum of uncertainty modeling in information systems, and then solicited from experts in each field authoritative tutorials and surveys that would fit the outline. We are delighted to have been able to assemble such a fine selection of experts, and we hope that this collective effort will prove useful to its readers.

Acknowledgments

This book is the culmination of a joint USA-EU project that brought together in two workshops researchers in the scientific communities of information systems and uncertainty modeling. The workshops were attended by most of the 24 contributors to this book, and by ten additional participants: Alex Borgida, Alessandro D'Atri, Christos Faloutsos, Hector Garcia-Molina, Guy Hulin, Werner Kiessling, Judea Pearl, Avi Silberschatz, Maria Zemankova, and Roberto Zicari. The chapters of this book are outgrowth of the papers that appeared in the proceedings of these workshops. We wish to thank all the authors for their outstanding contributions and dedication to this effort. Thanks are also due to the other participants for the comments and reviews, which have helped shape this final product. We also thank the agencies that recognized the importance of this subject and provided the financial support for the workshops: (1) The National Science Foundation—Division of Information, Robotics, and Intelligent Systems (specifically, the Database and Expert Systems Program, and the Knowledge Models and Cognitive Systems Program) in the USA, and (2) The ESPRIT II program (Basic Research Action) of the Commission of the European Communities in the EU.

Amihai Motro
Philippe Smets

1

INTRODUCTION

Amihai Motro

Department of Information and Software Systems Engineering
George Mason University
Fairfax, VA 22030, USA

1 SCOPE

As its title suggests, "Uncertainty Management in Information Systems" is a book about how information systems can be made to manage information permeated with uncertainty. This subject is at the intersection of two areas of knowledge: *information systems* is an area that concentrates on the design of practical systems that can store and retrieve information; *uncertainty modeling* is an area in artificial intelligence concerned with accurate representation of uncertain information and with inference and decision-making under conditions infused with uncertainty.

New applications of information systems require stronger capabilities in the area of uncertainty management. Our hope is that lasting interaction between these two areas would facilitate a new generation of information systems that will be capable of servicing these applications. Although there are researchers in information systems who have addressed themselves to issues of uncertainty, as well as researchers in uncertainty modeling who have considered the pragmatic demands and constraints of information systems, to a large extent there has been only limited interaction between these two areas.

As the subtitle, "From Needs to Solutions," indicates, this book presents viewpoints of information systems experts on the needs that challenge the uncertainty capabilities of present information systems, and it provides a forum to researchers in uncertainty modeling to describe models and systems that can address these needs.

The following subsections describe somewhat more formally the scope of this book. It should be noted that the term *uncertainty* has been in use as both a *broad* term covering any number of situations in which the information available is short of perfection (and we use it in this interpretation in the title of this book), and to describe a *specific* kind of imperfection (where the correctness of the available information is in doubt). In general, we try to use *imperfect information* for the broad term; otherwise, it should be clear from the context whether uncertainty is used in its broad or specific meaning.

1.1   Imperfect Information

Consider an information system D that attempts to represent some part of the real world W, and assume that both D and W are denoted in the same modeling formalism; for instance, both D and W could be relational databases.[1] We may consider W as the perfect information, and D as its *approximation*. This information D is *complete*, if D "contains" W; that is, the stored information includes *all* the information that the system presumes to model. D is *sound*, if D is "contained" in W; that is, the stored information includes *only* true information. Roughly speaking, an information system is perfect if it includes the *whole* truth and *nothing but* the truth.

In most practical situations, information systems rarely meet this standard of perfection. When an information system is not sound and complete, the common practice is to *ignore* the imperfections; that is, to continue operation as if the system were sound and complete. This implies that queries might be answered inaccurately: answers might exclude correct information, and some of the information they include might be incorrect.

Often, however, the negative consequences of inaccurate answers can be reduced by improving the modeling techniques used in the approximation of W.

Assume an initial model without any features for representing anything but sound and complete information. An example of such a model is this simple binary data model, in which, a database of employees is a set of employee numbers, each identifying a unique employee, and several two-column tables that store information about employees; for instance, *(Employee_number, Name)*, *(Employee_number, Department)*, and *(Employee_number, Age)*. The semantics of this database are that the set of employee numbers is sound and complete (i.e., it agrees perfectly with the employee numbers of the actual set of employ-

---

[1]Of course, only D is available; W is only hypothetical.

ees), and that each database pair provides accurate and reliable information about a specific employee. Thus, the pair (9128,30) in the table *Age* indicates that the age of the employee whose number is 9128 is indeed 30.

Consider now these examples.

- Assume that the age of a particular employee is not known precisely, only that it is in the range 25–40. In the model just described, the corresponding age pair would be excluded from the database. Yet, if the model is extended to allow such imprecise information, the available information could be stored. A query that lists all the employees older than 40 could be answered perfectly, and a query to list the age of this employee could provide this range. In both cases, the answers are more informative.

- Assume now that the age of an employee is given as 35, but there are some doubts about this information. For example, it might be estimated that with probability 0.8 the age is 35, but with probability 0.2 it is some other value. If the model is extended to include such uncertain information, the available information could be stored, and a query regarding the age of this employee could be answered more informatively.

- Finally, assume that the age of the male employees is known precisely, but the age of the female employees is correct only in an estimated 75% of the cases. Moreover, it is known that an estimated 5% percent of the temporary employees are not even recorded in the database. Again, if the model is extended to include such quality information, then many queries could be answered more informatively.

These examples illustrate three situations in which the information that is available is not sound or complete. Yet, rather than completely exclude all information that is short of perfection, it is advantageous to include in the system whatever relevant knowledge is available.

In the first example, the model extensions would enable the system to represent *imprecise* information; in the second, the system would be extended to represent *uncertain* information; and in the third, the system would take into consideration the *quality* of the information (statements that *qualify* the soundness and completeness of D).

These three kinds of extensions, respectively address three major kinds of imperfect information. Yet, there are various other flavors of imperfect information, and Chapter 8 provides a thorough analysis of the subject. In fact, many other chapters begin with a classification, simple or intricate, of the various kinds of imperfections that are addressed.

1.2   Manipulating Imperfect Information

Of course, once an information model provides structures for *representing* imperfect information, it must also show how to process *retrieval requests* against such information.

Returning to our abstract representation with D and W, we may define a retrieval request as a function m that derives from the description D, another description D', which is the answer to the request. Then, the definition of m must be extended to the case where D describes imperfect information.

In our simple binary model, assume that retrieval requests are issued with this simple statement: **retrieve** *attribute* **where** *attribute condition value*, where both attributes are from the same two-column table. For example, **retrieve** *Age* **where** *Employee_number* $= 9128$, or **retrieve** *Employee_number* **where** *Age* ≥ 45. If the model is extended to allow imprecise or uncertain information, then the processing of such queries would have to be extended as well. For example, in the latter query, would employee number 6310 be returned, if the age is given as in the range 40–50? Would it be returned, if the age is given as 35 with probability 0.8 and some other value with probability 0.2? And if the model is extended with quality information, then the processing of queries must be extended to determine the quality of the answers it issues.

1.3   Imperfect Retrieval Requests

Most information systems provide retrieval languages for formulating precise, well-understood queries. Once information systems are capable of storing imperfect information, it is only natural to extend their query languages to allow "imperfect" queries as well. Consider these examples.

- Retrieve the employees who are *certain* to have a given skill.

- Retrieve the five employees who match *most closely* a given qualification.

- Retrieve all the employees who are *young and well paid.*

Note the difference between extensions that allow conventional query languages to work with more general kinds of information (discussed earlier) and extensions that allow more general kinds of queries (discussed here).

Altogether, the scope of this book includes the representation and manipulation of imperfect information, and the definition and execution of imperfect retrieval requests.

2 STRUCTURE

This book comprises 15 chapters. Except for this introductory chapter and the final chapter, which provides a bibliography, the core of the book is divided roughly into two parts. The first part (Chapters 2–7) was authored by researchers who work in information systems, and the second part (Chapters 8–14) was authored by researchers in uncertainty modeling in artificial intelligence.

The purpose of the first part is twofold:

1. To describe the issues and challenges in the area of imperfect information that confront information systems.

2. To describe the state of the art with respect to this area; that is, the solutions that have already been applied and the experience that has been gained from these solutions.

The purpose of the second part is twofold as well:

1. To describe the principal theories for modeling imperfect information.

2. To show how these theories may be adapted to information systems, responding to their particular challenges, and, in some cases, to discuss actual experimentation with prototype systems that demonstrate these theories.

The discussion in the first part is divided mostly by specific kinds of information systems. Chapter 2 is a general introduction to the problems and issues of imperfect information in information systems. Using an abstract model of an information system it classifies the various kinds of imperfection in information systems, and it provides a quick survey of the most notable solutions that have been attempted or suggested. Chapters 3–7 focus, respectively, on relational databases, intelligent databases, scientific and statistical databases, expert systems, and information-retrieval systems.

The most common type of information system are databases, and the most popular kind of databases are relational databases. Consequently, considerable attention has already been paid to various types of imperfect information in relational databases; mostly, missing information. Chapter 3 provides a thorough survey of this subject. The term *intelligent databases* is used in Chapter 4 to describe extensions to the relational model within the framework of mathematical logic. Essentially, these models introduce rules into the relational framework, thereby providing abilities to capture "knowledge." Whereas the discussion in Chapters 3 and 4 is, for the most part, independent of specific applications, Chapter 5 focuses on databases that are used in scientific and statistical applications. These two areas are a source for a variety of challenging problems of imperfect information.

Chapter 6 considers a second kind of information systems: expert systems. More accurately, it considers problems of imperfect information that are encountered in acquired knowledge: whether this knowledge is *declared* by human experts, as in most expert systems, or *discovered* in databases, by means of mostly automatic knowledge mining techniques.

Finally, Chapter 7 focuses on a third kind of information system: information-retrieval systems. Such systems, for example, systems for storing and retrieving documents, were early to develop models for representing objects whose contents are often open to subjective interpretations, and then develop retrieval techniques that "neutralize" this subjectiveness. This enables users to request documents on a specified subject, and retrieve relevant documents even when they have been classified under "close" subjects.

We note that both knowledge discovery and information retrieval are receiving much attention these days, with the explosive growth of databases and document repositories on the Internet and the World Wide Web. In their different ways, knowledge discovery and information retrieval both attempt to help us tame the enormous amount of information now available.

The discussion in the second part of this book is centered around the different theories that have been developed to manage imperfect information. Chapter 8 is an introduction to these theories. It provides a thorough classification of the various kinds of imperfect information, and it presents the various approaches that have been proposed to model imperfect information. Chapters 9–12 are devoted to models that are based, respectively, on probability theory, fuzzy set and possibility theory, mathematical logic, and belief functions. All but the logic-based models may be classified as *quantitative* models; logic-based models are *qualitative*.

Chapter 9 discusses uncertainty models that use probabilistic methods. The emphasis is on pragmatic issues. It is observed that there are a variety of probabilistic and Bayesian methods, each requiring different effort and providing different benefits, and the approach is to choose a model so that its costs will be commensurate with its benefits. Chapter 10 is devoted to uncertainty models that are based on fuzzy set theory and its associated theory of possibility. These theories offer a unified framework for managing a wide range of imperfect information, as well as for formulating retrieval requests of the kind discussed in Section 1.3. Various nonclassical logics have been proposed for modeling imperfect information, and Chapter 11 focuses on two such logics. Paraconsistent logic can represent and manipulate inconsistent information, and default logic can manage default information, such as rules that are usually true but are allowed to have exceptions. Chapter 12 concludes the discussion of uncertainty models with its transferable belief model. In the transferable belief model agents express their subjective opinions that a subset of the universe of possible values indeed contains the correct value. As in the Bayesian approach, this degree of belief is usually quantified by a probability measure, except that it does not rely on probabilistic quantification but on belief functions.

The uncertainty modeling part concludes with chapters 13 and 14, which survey the area of uncertainty modeling from personal perspectives. Chapter 13 discusses progress made in the field of approximate reasoning systems and their relevance and applicability to information systems. It considers mostly quantitative models, such as those based on probability theory, fuzzy set theory, or belief functions. Chapter 14 considers the question of whether it is possible to classify the different uncertainty techniques by the application needing uncertainty management; i.e., whether it is feasible to construct a matrix, whose columns are the different uncertainty models, and whose rows are the different kinds of applications, and whose values will indicate the suitability of the model to the application.

Chapter 15 concludes this book with an extensive, classified bibliography on the subject of imperfect information.

This book is the culmination of a project that brought together researchers in the scientific communities of information systems and uncertainty modeling to study the needs of the information systems community and to tap the expertise of the uncertainty modeling community for solutions that respond to these needs [1, 2].

REFERENCES

[1] A. Motro and P. Smets, editors. *Proceedings of Workshop on Uncertainty Management in Information Systems: From Needs to Solutions* (Puerto de Andraitx, Mallorca, Spain, September 23–26), 1992.

[2] P. Smets and A. Motro, editors. *Proceedings of Workshop on Uncertainty Management in Information Systems: From Needs to Solutions* (Avalon, California, April 2–5), 1993.

2

SOURCES OF UNCERTAINTY, IMPRECISION, AND INCONSISTENCY IN INFORMATION SYSTEMS

Amihai Motro

Department of Information and Software Systems Engineering
George Mason University
Fairfax, VA 22030, USA

1 INTRODUCTION

An information system is a computer model of the real world. Like any other model, it captures an abstracted version of the real world, using a level of abstraction that is implied by the expected applications. As with any other model, the most important consideration is the integrity of the model; i.e., the accuracy of the representation. Unfortunately, our knowledge of the real world is often imperfect, thus challenging our ability to create and maintain information systems of integrity.

There are two solutions for upholding the integrity of an information systems in situations in which knowledge of the real world is imperfect.

The first solution is to *restrict* the model to that portion of the real world about which perfect information is available. Assume, for example, that the information model being used describes each employee with a record of several fields. Then, only the employees for whom perfect information is available in each of these fields would be included in the information system.

The second solution is to develop information models that allow the representation of imperfect information. Assume that the available information about the age of a particular employee is imperfect; for example, the age is only known to be within a specific range. If the information model had features for specifying and manipulating ranges, then this imperfect information could be captured in a system that still maintains its integrity.

Because the second solution often permits additional applications, most information systems adhere to information models that include at least some features for capturing imperfect information. For example, database systems can represent missing values, information-retrieval systems can match information to requests using a "weak" matching algorithm, and expert systems can represent rules that are known to be true only most or some of the time.

Yet, these capabilities are weak, in comparison with the variety and the degree of imperfection that is encountered in practice. Although the research community has shown persistent interest in this subject (see the extensive bibliography in Chapter 15), most of these efforts have yet to transcend experimental prototypes. By and large, commercial information systems have been slow to incorporate capabilities for handling imperfect information.

Nevertheless, many new applications require such capabilities (see Section 5). Without general systems that possess capabilities for handling imperfect information, such applications must be dealt with in an ad-hoc manner; this usually means that specific algorithms must be designed and specific systems must be built for each application that cannot be satisfied by the present generation of information systems.

This chapter is intended as a general introduction to the issues of imperfect information in information systems. Our goals are to *classify* the various kinds of imperfect information that are encountered in information systems (this fundamental task is undertaken in several other chapters as well), and to *survey* the basic solutions that have been proposed. Our treatment is *comprehensive*, in that we consider imperfections in all aspects of information systems, including the representation of imperfect information, imperfections in the specification of transactions, and imperfections in the processing of transactions. At the same time, our treatment is *abstract*, in that our classification and survey attempt to identify principles that are common to different kinds of information systems.

In our examples we consider three popular types of information systems: database systems, information-retrieval systems, and expert systems; databases are considered in more detail in Chapters 3, 4, and 5; expert systems are covered in Chapter 6, and information-retrieval systems are covered in Chapter 7.

For our goal of comprehensive and abstract treatment of the issues of imperfect information, we define here a simple, general model of an information system.

An information system includes a declarative component for *describing* the real world, and an operational component for *manipulating* this description. Typical manipulations are of two different kinds: (1) *modifications* of the description, either to refine the model or to track any changes that may have occurred in the real world, and (2) *transformations* of the description, to derive implied descriptions. Thus, an information system can be abstracted as a description D of the real world, a stream of modifications, and a stream of transformations. Each modification m replaces the present description with a new description; each transformation t computes a new description from the present description (without changing the present description).

As an example, in a relational database system a description is a set of tables (i.e., a database); a modification can affect either the definition or the contents of tables (i.e., restructuring or update); and a transformation reduces the set of tables into a single table (i.e., query evaluation).

The objective of information systems is to provide their users with the information they need. In our terminology, such information is always the result $t(D)$ of transforming a description D with a transformation t. Thus, it is the quality of $t(D)$, rather than the quality of D, that should concern the designers and users of information systems. A result $t(D)$ may be imperfect, because either

- the initial description D is imperfect,

- the specification of a later modification m of the description is imperfect,

- the specification of the transformation t is imperfect, or

- the processing of t against D is imperfect.

Whereas most treatments of this subject focus exclusively on imperfect descriptions, in this chapter we shall examine all these disparate sources of imperfection. Sections 2 and 3 are devoted to imperfect descriptions: in Section 2 we classify the various kinds of imperfect descriptions, and in Section 3 we survey the basic solutions that have been proposed. Section 4 is devoted to imperfections in modifications, transformations, and processing. Finally, in Section 5 we speculate on the reasons commercial information systems have been slow to incorporate capabilities for dealing with imperfect information. We then describe several applications that challenge present database systems by requiring more powerful methods for dealing with imperfection, and we point to some promising areas of research; in particular, we postulate that suitable solutions could come from fusing information systems technology with various theories of artificial intelligence.

2　IMPERFECT DESCRIPTIONS: CLASSIFICATION

A basic assumption that we adopt is that imperfections permeate our *models* of the real world, not the real world itself. Hence, we assume that a perfect description of the real world does exist but may be unavailable. The stored description is therefore an *approximation* of an ideal description (this assumption is further elaborated upon in Section 3.6).

In this section we examine several basic issues regarding description imperfection; namely, the different *kinds* of imperfection, the different *elements* of descriptions that could be affected with imperfection, the different *causes* for imperfection, and the different *degrees* of imperfection.

2.1　The Basic Kinds of Imperfect Information

There have been many attempts to classify the various possible kinds of imperfect information. In this chapter we concern ourselves with three basic kinds: error, imprecision, and uncertainty. We note that other kinds of imperfection have been observed, including vagueness and ambiguity (see Chapter 8), but they are not as important for information systems.

Error. Erroneous information is the simplest kind of imperfect information. Stored information is erroneous when it is different from the true information. We take the approach that all errors, large or smalls, compromise the integrity of an information system, and should not be tolerated. An important kind of erroneous information is *inconsistency*. Occasionally, the same aspect of the real world is represented more than once (this could be in the same information system, or in different information systems that are considered together). When the different representations are irreconcilable, the information is inconsistent. Issues of information inconsistency are of particular relevance, given the present interest in information integration [20, 32].

Imprecision. Stored information is imprecise when it denotes a *set* of possible values, and the real value is one of the elements of this set. Thus, imprecise information is not erroneous and does not compromise the integrity of an information system. Specific kinds of imprecise information include *disjunctive* information (e.g., John's age is either 31 or 32), *negative* information (e.g., John's age is not 30), *range* information (e.g., John's age is between 30 and 35, or John's age is over 30), and information with *error margins* (e.g., John's age is 34 ± 1 year). The two extreme kinds of imprecision are *precise* values and *null values*: a value is precise when the set of possibilities is a singleton; a null value usually denotes that no information is available, yet could be regarded as imprecise information where the set of possible values encompasses the entire domain of legal values.

Uncertainty. At times, our knowledge of the real world (precise or imprecise) cannot be stated with absolute confidence. This requires that we qualify our confidence in the information stated. Again, information with qualified certainty is not erroneous and does not compromise the integrity of an information system. Whereas the statement "John's age is either 31 or 32" denoted imprecision, the statement "John is probably 32" denotes uncertainty. At times, precision can be traded for certainty and vice-versa. A precise value may entail low certainty, but as this value is substituted by values that are progressively less precise, certainty increases gradually, until finally it is maximal for a value that is minimally precise; i.e., a null value (see also the hypothesis about an Information Maximality Principle in Chapter 8).

2.2   What Might Be Imperfect?

Depending on the model used, descriptions may take different forms, and imperfection can affect each of them.

Consider, for example, relational databases. The structures of the relational model admit different kinds of imperfection. The first kind involves imperfection at the level of data values; for example, the values of *Salary* in the relation *Earn (Employee, Salary)* might be imprecise. The second kind involves imperfection at the level of the tuple; for example, the values of each of the attributes of the relation *Assign (Employee, Project)* may be certain and precise, but there might be uncertainty about the exact assignment of employees to projects. A third kind involves imperfection at the level of the relation scheme (the structure); for example, there might be uncertainty whether employees may belong to more than one department, and hence what should be the proper description of this relationship [5].

As another example, consider an information-retrieval system that models each document with an identifier and a vector of keywords. There might be uncertainty at the level of a keyword; i.e., the appropriateness of a specific keyword to a given document may be questionable. In addition, there might be uncertainty at the level of an entire document; i.e., the existence of some documents may be in doubt.

As a third example, consider an expert system that models real-world knowledge with facts and rules expressed in logic. There might be uncertainty about specific facts (similar to the tuple uncertainty in relational databases), and there might be uncertainty about specific rules; i.e., a rule might be only an approximation of the behavior of the real world.

2.3   Why Is It Imperfect?

Having excluded the possibility that reality itself is subject to imperfection, we can assume that a perfect description of any real-world object always exists. Thus, imperfect descriptions are solely due to the *unavailability* of these perfect descriptions. For example, the precise salary of Tom might be unknown, or the true relationship between Bordeaux wine and good health might be unclear. Yet, within this generic unavailability, we observe several specific causes (refer also to Chapter 5 for a more detailed survey of the sources of imperfect information).

Imperfect information might result from using *unreliable information sources*, such as faulty reading instruments, or input forms that have been filled out incorrectly (intentionally or inadvertently). In other cases, imperfect descriptions are a result of *system errors*, including input errors, transmission noise, delays in processing update transactions, imperfections of the system software, and corrupted data owing to failure or sabotage.

At times, the imperfect information is the unavoidable result of information gathering methods that require *estimation* or *judgment*. Examples include the determination of the subject of a document, the digital representation of a continuous phenomenon, and the representation of a phenomenon that is constantly varying.

In other cases, imperfections are the result of restrictions imposed by the *model*. For example, if the database schema permits storing at most two occupations per employee, descriptions of occupation would be incomplete. Similarly, the sheer *volume* of the information that is necessary to describe a real-world object might force the modeler to turn to approximation and sampling techniques.

2.4 How Imperfect Is It?

The relevant information that is available in the absence of perfect information may take different forms, each exhibiting a different *level* of imperfection. The amount of relevant information available offers an alternative classification of imperfections. The following discussion is independent of the particular structure affected by imperfection. It assumes an element e of the description models an object o of the real world. The element e might be a value, a tuple, a fact, a rule, and so on.

The least informative case (this is often referred to as *ignorance*) is when the mere *existence* of some real-world object o is in doubt. The simplest solution is to ignore such objects altogether. This solution, however, is unacceptable if the model claims to be *closed world* (i.e., the model guarantees that objects not modeled do not exist).

Ignorance is reduced somewhat when each element e of the description is assigned a value in a prescribed range, to indicate the likelihood that the modeled object exists. When the element is a fact, this value can be interpreted as the *confidence* that the fact holds; when it is a rule, this value can be interpreted as the *strength* of the rule (e.g., the proportion of cases in which the rule applies).

Assume now that existence is assured, but some of or all the information with which the model describes an object is *unknown*. Such information has also been referred to as *incomplete*, *missing*, or *unavailable*.

The quality of the information increases when the description of an object is known to come from a limited set of alternatives (possibly a range of values). This information is referred to as *disjunctive* information. Note that when a set of alternatives is simply the entire universe of possible values, this case reverts to the previous (less informative) case. When this set contains a single value, the available information is perfect.

The quality increases even further when each alternative is accompanied by a number describing the likelihood that it is indeed the true description. When these numbers indicate probabilities, the information is *probabilistic*, and when they indicate possibilities, the information is *possibilistic*. Again, when these numbers are unavailable, this case reverts to disjunctive information.

3   IMPERFECT DESCRIPTIONS: SOLUTIONS

Space considerations forbid discussion of all the different solutions that have been attempted for accommodating imperfections in descriptions. We sketch here five approaches that are significantly different from each other; they also exhibit sufficient generality to be applicable in different information systems. Of course, any approach for *describing* imperfect information must also address the *manipulation* (transformation and modification) of imperfect descriptions (e.g., querying and updating).[1]

3.1   Null and Disjunctive Values

Most data models insist that similar real-world objects be modeled with similar descriptions. The simplest example of this approach are models that use tabular descriptions. Each such table models a set of similar real-world objects: each row describes a different object, and the columns provide the different components of the description. Often, some elements of a particular description cannot be stated with precision and certainty. Occasionally, this problem may be evaded simply by not modeling any object whose description is imperfect. Often, however, the consequences of this approach are unacceptable, and imperfect descriptions must be admitted.

The least ambitious approach to admitting imperfect descriptions is to ignore all partial information that may be available about the imperfect parts of a description, and to model them with a pseudo-description, called *null*, that denotes unavailability [25, 11, 23].[2] The semantics of a null value is that *any* value from the corresponding domain of legal values is an equally probable candidate for the true value.

Once null values are admitted into descriptions, the model must define the behavior of transformations and modifications in the presence of nulls. This is not a simple task. For example, an extension to the relational calculus that is founded on a three-valued logic [10] has been the subject of criticism [12].

---

[1] Note the difference between manipulations of imperfect descriptions, which are discussed in this section, and imperfect manipulations, which are the subject of Section 4.

[2] Null values have also been used to denote *inapplicability*; i.e., that a specific attribute is inapplicable to a specific object. Such null values do not indicate imperfection of information. Hence, the term *null* will be used here to denote applicability but unavailability.

Inference in incomplete databases is discussed in [14], and updates of incomplete databases are discussed in [1].

Null values model the ultimate lack of information about a value (except that it exists). Other kinds of null values have been suggested that express some additional information. For example, two values in a database may be unavailable but are known to be identical. Such partial information may be modeled by using distinguishable instances of nulls (*marked nulls*) throughout the database in general, but the same null instance for these two values. Recording this partial information proves to be useful in the performance of joins.

At times, it is known that a missing value belongs to a more limited set of values (possibly, a range of values). This partial information has been modeled by *disjunctive values*. A disjunctive value is a set of values that includes the true value. Hence, disjunctive values are more informative than nulls (a null value is a specific kind of disjunctive value, in which the set of possible values is the entire domain). Disjunctive databases are discussed in [24, 26].

Clearly, null and disjunctive values both express *imprecision*. More on these kinds of imprecision can be found in Chapters 3 and 4.

3.2   Confidence Factors

Confidence factors denote confidence in various elements of the description. Hence, they offer a simple tool for representing *uncertainty*. Confidence factors have been applied in both information-retrieval systems and in expert systems but not in database systems proper.

In information-retrieval systems, confidence factors (often called *weights* or *relevance coefficients*) have been used to denote confidence that a specific keyword describes a given document (or alternatively, to denote the strength with which this keyword applies to the document) [45, 41]. Methods have even been developed for computing confidence factors automatically, by scanning documents and applying keyword counting techniques. The manipulation of these confidence factors is relatively simple, as they are easily accommodated in the vector space models that are often used in information retrieval. Refer to Chapter 7 for the use of relevance coefficients in information retrieval.

In expert systems, confidence factors have been used to denote confidence that stated facts and rules indeed describe real-world objects [18]. Such factors are

usually declared by the knowledge engineers as part of the knowledge acquisition process but can also be derived automatically as part of a knowledge
discovery process [35]. The manipulation of confidence factors in expert systems is often straightforward; for example, assuming confidence factors in the
range [0,1], when a rule with confidence p is applied to a fact with confidence
q, the generated fact is assigned a confidence factor $p \cdot q$. Pragmatic considerations may have been the reason that commercial expert systems often prefer this
mostly informal representation of uncertainty over more formal approaches that
are based on probability theory. However, many objections have been raised
against confidence factors, showing that the lack of firm semantics may lead to
unintuitive results [34].

3.3   Probability Theory

Probabilistic information systems represent information with variables and
their probability distributions. In a relational framework, the value of a particular attribute A for a specific tuple t is a variable $A(t)$, and this variable has an
associated *probability distribution* $P_{A(t)}$. $P_{A(t)}$ assigns values in the range $[0, 1]$
to the elements of the domain of attribute A, with the provision that the sum
of all values assigned is 1. An example of a probabilistic value is the variable
$Age(john)$ and this probability distribution:[3]

$$P_{Age(john)} = \left\{ \begin{array}{ll} 32 & 0.6 \\ 33 & 0.4 \end{array} \right.$$

The interpretation of this information is that with probability 0.6 the age of
John is 32, with probability 0.4 it is 33, and the probability that John's age is
some other value is 0.

A probabilistic relational model based on this approach and a suitable set of
operators are defined in [3]. The model allows probability distributions that
are incompletely specified: each such distribution is completed with a special
null value, which is assigned the balance of the probability. It is also possible to
define probability distributions for combinations of interdependent attributes.
A somewhat different (but equivalent) model is given in [8]. In this model
a database is a collection of objects in which each object has an associated
set of attributes (a scheme), a set of tuples over that scheme (a domain), and
a probability distribution function that assigns each tuple of the domain a
probability (the sum of the probabilities for the entire domain of an object is
1).

---

[3]We use the key value *john* to identify a specific tuple.

We have observed that disjunctive information; e.g., "32 or 33" is a form of imprecise information, whereas "32 with confidence 0.6" is a form of uncertain information. Consider now this statement "32 with probability 0.6 and 33 with probability 0.4." In many ways, such probabilistic information is a combination of both imprecision and uncertainty. It is imprecise because it denotes several different alternatives, and it is uncertain because every alternative is associated with a likelihood. Our conclusion is that the distinction between imprecision and uncertainty is often useful, but is not a "partitioning" classification. A similar conclusion is reached in Chapter 9, which offers more details on the use of probability theory for modeling imperfect information.

3.4 Fuzziness and Possibility Theory

The basic concept of fuzzy set theory is the *fuzzy set*. A fuzzy set F is a set of elements in which each element has an associated value in the interval [0,1] that denotes the *grade* of its membership in the set. An example of a fuzzy set (using a common notation) is $F = \{30/1.0, 31/1.0, 32/1.0, 33/0.7, 34/0.5, 35/0.2\}$. The elements 30, 31, and 32 are in this set with grade of membership 1.0, the elements 33, 34, and 35 have corresponding grades of membership 0.7, 0.5, and 0.2, and all elements not shown have grade of membership 0.

Several different models of databases have been based on fuzzy set theory. The simplest model extends relations, which are subsets of a Cartesian product of domains, to fuzzy relations; i.e., fuzzy subsets of the product of domains [7, 37]. Thus, each tuple in a relation is associated with a membership grade. For example, the tuple *(john, pascal)* belongs to the relation *Proficiency(Programmer, Language)* with membership grade 0.9. Associating a membership grade with each tuple may be regarded as a statement of *uncertainty*.

Alternatively, the same tuple may be interpreted as stating that John's proficiency in Pascal is 0.9. In this interpretation, the membership grades indicate the strength of the association between the components of the tuple (in this case, a programmer and a programming language). These different interpretations should not be confused, and must be taken into account when defining operations for manipulating fuzzy relations.

The theory of possibility is based on fuzzy set theory. In a relational framework, the value of a particular attribute A for a specific tuple t is a variable t_A, and this variable has an associated *possibility distribution* $\pi_{A(t)}$. $\pi_{A(t)}$ assigns values in the range [0, 1] to the elements of the domain of attribute A. Using the same variable $Age(john)$, an example of a possibilistic distribution is

$$\pi_{Age(john)} = \begin{cases} 30 & 1.0 \\ 31 & 1.0 \\ 32 & 1.0 \\ 33 & 0.7 \\ 34 & 0.5 \\ 35 & 0.2 \end{cases}$$

The interpretation of this information is that it is completely possible that the age of John is 30, 31, or 32, it is very possible that it is 33, it is somewhat possible that it is 34, it is remotely possible that it is 35, and it is completely impossible that it is any other age. If this individual possibility distribution is assigned a name; e.g., *early_thirties*, then it is also possible to interpret it as a definition of the linguistic term *early thirties*: it is a term that refers to 30–32 year olds with possibility 1.0, to 33 year olds with possibility 0.7, etc. Thus, possibility distributions may be used to describe vague linguistic terms.

Consider now standard relations, but assume that the elements of the domains are not values but possibility distributions [48, 36]. This provides the basis for an alternative fuzzy database model. Having possibility distributions for values permits specific cases where a value is one of several kinds: (1) A vague term, for example, a value of *Age* can be *early_thirties*; (2) a disjunctive value, for example, a value of *Department* can be {*shipping, receiving*}, or a value of *Salary* can be *40,000–50,000*; (3) a null value; (4) a simple value. Our earlier observation that probabilistic information expresses both uncertainty and imprecision applies to possibilistic information as well.

To manipulate fuzzy databases, the standard relational algebra operators must be extended to fuzzy relations. The first approach, in which relations are fuzzy sets but elements of domains are crisp, requires simple extensions to these operators. The second approach, where relations are crisp but elements of domains are fuzzy, introduces more complexity because the softness of the values in the tuples creates problems of value identification (e.g., in the join, or in the removal of replications after projections). Also, in analogy with standard mathematical comparators such as = or <, which are defined via sets of pairs, the second approach introduces fuzzy comparators such as *similar-to* or *much-greater-than*, which are defined via fuzzy sets of pairs. These fuzzy operators offer the capability of expressing fuzzy (vague) retrieval requests.

The use of fuzzy set and possibility theory to represent and manipulate imperfect information is discussed in more detail in Chapter 10. Fuzziness in databases and information-retrieval systems is also the subject of [6]. Although their basic axioms and much of their semantics are very different, probability theory, possibility theory, and confidence factors share a common intuitive concept, namely, they all *qualify* database values with numbers that attempt to describe the likelihood that these specific values are indeed the correct ones.

3.5   Information Distances

An approach to imprecision that has been applied successfully to both database systems and information-retrieval systems handles imprecise information with *distance*. The basic idea is to model the real world with apparently precise descriptions, to define the notion of distance between any two descriptions, and thus to create *neighborhoods* of descriptions.

Thus, any imprecision about a real-world object *o* is ignored, and an apparently precise description of it *e* is stored. It is then hoped that this "negligence" would be compensated for by having *e* somewhere in the neighborhood of the true description. When a request for information specifies this true description, *e* would be retrieved along with the other neighbors of the true description.

As an example, consider an information-retrieval system that describes documents with sets of keywords [41, 45]. Such systems often represent keyword sets with vectors: the dimension of each vector is the number of possible keywords, and a specific vector position is 1 if a particular keyword is in the set and 0 otherwise. Often, there is uncertainty about whether a specific vector is the true description of a given document. By establishing a distance among document descriptions, usually with some vector metric, and retrieving all the information in the neighborhood of a request vector, the negative effects of imprecisions in the description are diminished. Refer to Chapter 7 for a more detailed discussion of information-retrieval models.

As another example, consider relational database systems. Such systems describe objects with tuples, and often there is uncertainty regarding the value of some attribute in a given tuple. It is possible to establish a distance among the elements of the domain of this attribute. Then, when a query specifies a value of this attribute, all the tuples would be retrieved whose values for that attribute are in the neighborhood of the specified value [28].

We assumed here that descriptions are subject to imprecision (which is ignored) and requests are precise. The same solution applies when descriptions are precise and requests are imprecise. Such requests would be specified with apparent-precision and would be answered with the neighborhood of the request. Again, the negative effects of imprecision in the request would be moderated. Imprecise requests are discussed in more detail in Section 4.1.

A refinement of this general method is to admit confidence factors (Section 3.2) in the descriptions and in the requests. For example, vectors describing keyword sets use values in the range [0,1] to denote the confidence that a specific keyword is relevant to the given document (or, alternatively, to denote the degree of relevance of this keyword). Similarly, request vectors use such values to denote the relative weights of various keywords in the overall request.

3.6   Soundness and Completeness

The final approach that we discuss [29] does not attempt to model imperfect information; instead, declarations are made of the portions of the database (i.e., *views*) that are prefect models of the real world (and thereby the portions that are possibly imperfect).

Thus, like distances (Section 3.5) and unlike disjunctive values (Section 3.1), confidence factors (Section 3.2), probabilistic values (Section 3.3) or possibilistic values (Section 3.4), the descriptions themselves have no special features for representing imperfection (i.e., they appear perfect). However, meta-information provides the distinction between perfect and imperfect information.

This approach interprets perfectness, which it terms *integrity*, as a combination of *soundness* and *completeness*. A description is sound if it includes *only* information that occurs in the real world; a description is complete if it includes *all* the information that occurs in the real world. Hence, a description has integrity if it includes the whole truth (completeness) and nothing but the truth (soundness).

With this information included in the database, the database system can *qualify* the perfectness of the answers it issues in response to queries: each answer is accompanied by statements that define the portions (i.e., views) that are guaranteed to be perfect. A technique is described in [29] for inferring the views of individual answers that are guaranteed to have integrity, from the views of the entire database that are known to have integrity.

The notion of view completeness is similar to an assumption that a certain view of the database is *closed world* [38]. Also, *open nulls* [16] are actually declarations of views that are incomplete. The notion of view soundness is shown to be a generalization of standard database integrity constraints.

View soundness and view completeness have been extended in [33] to measure *relative* soundness and completeness of views (with respect to the real world). Let v denote the extension of some view in the database and let v_0 denote the real-world extension of the same view. Let $|v|$ denote the number of tuples in v. Then

$$\frac{|v \cap v_0|}{|v|}$$

expresses the proportion of the database answer that appears in the true answer. Hence, it is a measure of the soundness of v. Similarly,

$$\frac{|v \cap v_0|}{|v_0|}$$

expresses the proportion of the true answer that appears in the database answer. Hence, it is a measure of the completeness of v. Relative soundness and completeness are similar to the *precision* and *recall* measures used in information retrieval [41, 45], but whereas precision and recall measure the goodness of retrieved information relative to the stored information, soundness and completeness measure the goodness of stored information relative to the real information. In other words, they measure the *quality* of information sources. These measures are used to guide the *harmonization* of inconsistent answers in a multidatabase environment [32, 33].

4 IMPERFECT MANIPULATION AND PROCESSING

Although most of the work on imperfect information has focused on description imperfection, transaction and processing imperfection also have important impact on the quality of the information delivered to users. In this section we discuss briefly issues and solutions that concern imperfections in the definition of transformations (e.g., queries), in the definition of modifications (e.g., updates or restructuring operations), and in the processing of such transactions.

4.1   Transformations

Transformations are operations that derive new descriptions from stored descriptions. The most frequent type of transformation are queries. Imperfect queries may occur for different reasons.

At times, users of information systems have insufficient knowledge of the information system they are using: they might not have a clear idea of the information available in the system (or how it is organized), or they might not know how to formulate their requests using the tools provided by the system.

Requests for information formulated by such naive users often exhibit a high level of imperfection. They range from requests that cannot be interpreted by the system (for reasons that are either syntactical or semantical) to requests that do not achieve correctly the intentions of the users (or achieve them only in part).

Regardless of their level of expertise, occasionally users may try to access an information system with only a *vague* idea of the information they seek. For example, a user may be accessing an electronic catalogue for a product that would be "interesting" or "exceptional." Alternatively, users could have a clear idea of the information they want but might lack the information necessary to specify it to the system. An example is a user who wishes to look up the meaning of a word in a dictionary but cannot provide its correct spelling.

To summarize, we distinguish among (1) insufficient knowledge of the *information available* (or how it is organized), (2) vagueness with respect to the *information needed* (or how to denote it in terms acceptable to the system), and (3) insufficient knowledge of the *system languages and tools* that are used to formulate requests.

To address all these, the approach has been to develop alternative access tools. Browsers allow users to access information in either situation discussed above [27, 39, 2, 13]. Interactive query constructors conduct user-system dialogues to arrive at satisfactory formulations of user requests [47]. Vague query processors allow users to embed imprecise specifications in their requests (e.g., neighborhood queries, as described in Section 3.5) [21, 28]. Error-tolerant interfaces use relaxed formalisms in their interpretation of requests [30].

As previously mentioned, even after a request for information had been accepted by the system and its answer delivered to the user, uncertainty might still persist because it is not always possible to verify that the request indeed achieved correctly the intention of the user. Often, the only assurance that the information delivered is the information needed is that the user is somewhat familiar with it. In the absence of such familiarity, uncertainty will persist.

Hence, one must accept that there are frequent instances where the answer that is delivered is imperfect, yet both the system and the user are unaware of this imperfection. Often, the imperfection of apparently perfect answers is revealed only when a conflicting answer to the same request is received from another information system.

4.2   Modifications

Modifications (update and restructuring) are operations that affect the descriptions stored in information systems. Like transformations (queries), modifications are defined by users, and we identify three similar main sources of imperfection: (1) insufficient knowledge of the system and its tools, (2) insufficient knowledge of the contents and organization of information stored in the system, and (3) uncertainty or imprecision concerning the information embedded in a modification.

Many of the approaches aimed at alleviating the problems of transformation imperfections (Section 4.1) are also applicable to modification imperfections. However, fewer tools have been developed to address modification imperfections. A possible explanation is that, whereas modifications may be attempted by users at all levels of expertise, it is often assumed that users who modify information should have good familiarity with the system.

The third source of imperfection, uncertain or imprecise information, is unrelated to expertise. One example is a request to add imprecise information; for example, "the new manager is either Paul or John." Another example is an imprecisely-specified request to delete information; for example, "some of the telephone numbers are no longer valid."

However, this kind of imperfection is not any different from the description imperfections that were the subject of Sections 2 and 3. Thus, the first request would be accommodated as any information of the kind "exactly one of the following values holds," and the second request would be accommodated as any information of the kind "some of the following values hold." (Of course, if the system cannot model these kinds of imperfection, then it would not be able to handle these modifications.)

4.3 Processing

Even when a description D and a transformation t are free of imperfections, the result $t(D)$ may be imperfect because of the methods used by the system to process requests. In certain applications, an information system might allocate only limited computational resources to process a request [22]. For example, a recursive query to a genealogical database to list all the ancestors of a specific individual might be terminated after a predetermined period of time (presumably the number of ancestors retrieved by then would be sufficient). A query processor that provides monotonically improving partial answers under constraints of time or unavailability is described in [46]. In other applications, query processing might involve randomizations, sampling, or other estimation techniques (see Chapter 5). For example, a statistical database system might introduce perturbations into its answers deliberately, for reasons of security. In each case, the answers would exhibit imperfections.

Finally, it is sometime considered advantageous to sacrifice accuracy for the sake of *simplicity*. Recent research on *intensional answers* [31] has focused on the generation of abstract answers that describe the exhaustive answers compactly, albeit imperfectly. For example, a query to list the employees who earn over $50,000 might be answered simply and compactly "engineers," even when the set of engineers and the set of employees who earn over $50,000 are not exactly the same (e.g., when the two sets overlap substantially, or when one set contains the other).

5 CHALLENGES

Commercial information systems have been slow to incorporate capabilities for managing imperfect information. While solutions based on fuzzy set theory (Section 3.4) are gaining acceptance in several technologies, commercial information systems have not embraced this solution yet. In database systems, the only capabilities widely available are for handling null values (Section 3.1), and for specifying imprecise queries with regular expressions. Most commercial information-retrieval systems do not have the capabilities that come with the definition of distances (Section 3.5). The situation is somewhat better in expert systems, in which commercial systems often permit certainty factors in their facts and rules (Section 3.2).

Examining the reasons for this slow acceptance may suggest directions for further research, and we offer here several possible reasons. First, information systems practitioners are concerned primarily with the *performance* of their systems. Here, many of the algorithms for matching uncertain data or for processing imprecise requests are extremely complex and inefficient.

Practitioners are also concerned with *compatibility*. This dictates that capabilities for managing uncertainty and imprecision should be offered as strict extensions of existing standards. Additionally, database practitioners have often been dissatisfied with various *idiosyncratic implementations* of such capabilities (minor examples are the inability to specify an incomplete date value, or the inability to sort answers with null values flexibly). This may have had a chilling effect on further implementations.

Another hindrance for database systems with capabilities for managing imperfect data may lie in the *expectations of users*. A fundamental principle of database systems has been that queries and answers are never open to subjective interpretations, and users of database systems have come to expect their queries to be interpreted unambiguously and answered with complete accuracy. In contrast, users of information-retrieval systems would be pleased with a system that delivers high rates of recall (proportion of relevant material retrieved) and precision (proportion of retrieved material that is relevant). Similarly, users of expert systems are aware that conclusions offered by automated experts are often questionable and would be satisfied with systems that were shown to have high rates of success. A database system that must adhere to the principles of unambiguity and complete accuracy cannot accommodate the full range of imperfect information; for example, it can accommodate null values or disjunctive data but not (because of its more subjective nature) probabilistic or possibilistic data.

Recently, new applications have emerged that require information systems with capabilities for managing imperfect information. Several of these challenging applications are described next. Their description is followed by a discussion of a possible source of suitable technology, and the challenges involved in adapting it for information systems.

5.1 Heterogeneous Database Environments

In recent years, the integration and interchange of information among heterogeneous database systems has been recognized as an important area of database system research and development. Multidatabase environments present a
strong case for having uncertainty management capabilities. Even though individual database systems are usually careful to avoid internal inconsistencies
(mostly with methodical design that avoids repeating the same information in
multiple locations in the system), when information from independent systems
with overlapping information is integrated, inconsistencies often surface. Thus,
even when individual answers are free from imperfections, their integration in
a global answer would introduce inconsistency. Therefore, database systems in
a multidatabase environment should be capable of combining conflicting answers into a single, consistent answer, and then store and manipulate such
information [32, 33].

5.2 Multimedia Databases

As discussed in Section 3, retrieval from traditional databases is usually based
on *exact matching*, where a request for data establishes a specific retrieval goal,
and the database system retrieves the data that match it exactly. Presently, the
management of image databases largely follows the same paradigm: images are
stored (in digitized form) in large databases but retrieval is performed on *textual
descriptions* of these images that are stored along with the images themselves.

A more ambitious approach, such as IBM's Query By Image Content (QBIC)
[15], is to retrieve images that match a given *image*. Image matching techniques
are usually based on algorithms of *best matching*. As with the information-
retrieval systems discussed earlier, the use of uncertainty formalisms is essential.
A similar problem is to match handwritten addresses against a database of
addresses.

5.3 Imputation and Knowledge Discovery

In various applications, notably in scientific and statistical projects, it is necessary to estimate missing data (nulls) from other data that are available. For
example, a missing measurement is estimated by other measurements made by
the same instrument at other times as well as by measurements made by other
instruments at the same time. This process, usually referred to as *imputation*,

yields information of varying degrees of uncertainty. The management of this information cannot be done by traditional database techniques and requires the use of uncertainty techniques.

The inference of missing values from their contexts is related to the more general issue of discovering new knowledge in large databases. Database knowledge is usually *declared*: rules and constraints are assumed to be definite and accurate and to hold in any database instance (exceptions, if any, must be stated). In contrast, *discovered* knowledge is always subject to uncertainty: the patterns and rules are often tenuous and could be refuted by future data. Again, the management of such information requires uncertainty techniques.

5.4 Information Systems and Artificial Intelligence

Modeling imperfect information in information systems involves a classical dilemma. On one hand, we want a model as rich and powerful as possible; for example, a single concept of information that is capable of representing elegantly all known kinds of imperfect information as well as perfect information. On the other hand, database systems must abide by crucial constraints of simplicity and efficiency, both of their descriptions and of the manipulations of their descriptions.

Like information systems, the field of artificial intelligence too has been concerned with modeling accurately our knowledge of the real world. Numerous uncertainty theories have been developed. Mostly they are founded on nonclassical logics, on probability theory, on belief functions, or on possibility theory [4, 42].

It might be said that, traditionally, research in artificial intelligence has been emphasizing rich and powerful models, striving to model accurately all the minute nuances of reality. On the other hand, research in information systems has been emphasizing economical representations with lower expressiveness but with small representational overhead and high processing efficiency.

A notable case in point are the so-called *semantic data models* that were defined in the late 1970s to enhance the modeling capabilities of early database systems [17, 19]. These models incorporated modeling features, such as generalization and aggregation hierarchies, that had been adapted from research in artificial intelligence. An even earlier example is the adaptation of *semantic networks* for databases [40]. A third and more recent example are *knowledge-rich database systems*, that incorporate inference rules expressed in mathematical logic [43, 44, 9]. Not surprisingly, a major research thrust among database researchers that have been working in this area has been the development of *highly efficient* inference techniques for a *limited* class of rules.

Thus, information systems may be said to have embraced "poor-person's AI," or, more graciously put, to have adapted AI concepts to work under the strict constraints of information systems. The adaptation of uncertainty theories that have been developed for artificial intelligence to operational techniques for information systems is an important challenge for information systems researchers. This challenge is the subject of Chapters 8–14.

Acknowledgments

This work was supported in part by NSF grant No. IRI-9007106 and by ARPA grant, administered by the Office of Naval Research under grant No. N0014-92-J-4038.

REFERENCES

[1] S. Abiteboul and G. Grahne. Update semantics for incomplete databases. In *Proceedings of the Eleventh International Conference on Very Large Data Bases* (Stockholm, Sweden, August 21–23), pages 1–12. Morgan Kaufmann, Los Altos, California, 1985.

[2] R. Agrawal, N. H. Gehani, and J. Srinivasan. OdeView: The graphical interface to Ode. In *Proceedings of ACM-SIGMOD International Conference on Management of Data* (Atlantic City, New Jersey, May 23–25), pages 34–43. ACM, New York, New York, 1990.

[3] D. Barbara, H. Garcia-Molina, and D. Porter. The management of probabilistic data. *IEEE Transactions on Knowledge and Data Engineering*, 4(5): 487–502, October 1992.

[4] Lea Sombe (P. Besnard, M.-O. Cordier, D. Dubois, L. Farinas del Cerro, C. Froidevaux, Y. Moinard, H. Prade, C. Schwind, and P. Siegel). Special issue, Reasoning under incomplete information in artificial intelligence. *International Journal of Intelligent Systems*, 5(4), September 1991.

[5] A. Borgida. Language features for flexible handling of exceptions in information systems. *ACM Transactions on Database Systems*, 10(4): 565–603, December 1985.

[6] P. Bosc and J. Kacprzyk, editors. *Fuzziness in Database Management Systems*. Physica-Verlag, Heidelberg, Germany, 1995.

[7] B. P. Buckles and F. E. Petry. A fuzzy representation of data for relational databases. *Fuzzy Sets and Systems*, 7(3): 213–226, May 1982.

[8] R. Cavallo and M. Pittarelli. The theory of probabilistic databases. In *Proceedings of the Thirteenth International Conference on Very Large Data Bases* (Brighton, England, September 1–4), pages 71–81. Morgan Kaufmann, Los Altos, California, 1987.

[9] S. Ceri, G. Gottlob, and L. Tanka. *Logic Programming and Databases*. Springer-Verlag, Berlin, Germany, 1990.

[10] E. F. Codd. Extending the database relational model to capture more meaning. *ACM Transactions on Database Systems*, 4(4): 397–434, December 1979.

[11] C. J. Date. *Relational Database: Selected Writings*. Addison Wesley, Reading, Massachusetts, 1986.

[12] C. J. Date. NOT is not "not"! In *Relational Database Writings 1985–1989*. Addison Wesley, Reading, Massachusetts, 1990.

[13] A. D'Atri, A. Motro, and L. Tarantino. ViewFinder: an object browser. Technical report 95-115, Department of Information and Software Systems Engineering, George Mason University, February 1995.

[14] R. Demolombe and L. Farinas del Cerro. An algebraic evaluation method for deduction in incomplete data bases. *Journal of Logic Programming*, 5: 183–205, 1988.

[15] C. Faloutsos, W. Equitz, M. Flickner, W. Niblack, D. Petkovic, and R. Barber. Efficient and effective querying by image content. *Journal of Intelligent Information Systems*, 3(3/4), July 1994.

[16] G. Gottlob and R. Zicari. Closed world assumption opened through null values. In *Proceedings of the Fourteenth International Conference on Very Large Data Bases* (Los Angeles, California, August 25–28), pages 50–61. Morgan Kaufmann, Los Altos, California, 1988.

[17] M. Hammer and D. McLeod. Database description with SDM: A semantic database model. *ACM Transactions on Database Systems*, 6(3): 351–386, September 1981.

[18] P. Harmon and D. King. *Expert Systems—Artificial Intelligence in Business*. John Wiley & Sons, New York, New York, 1985.

[19] R. Hull and R. King. Semantic database modeling: Survey, applications and research issues. *Computing Surveys*, 19(3): 201–260, September 1987.

[20] A. R. Hurson, M. W. Bright, and S. H. Pakzad, editors. *Multidatabase Systems: An Advanced Solution for Global Information Sharing*. IEEE Computer Society Press, Los Alamitos, California, 1994.

[21] T. Ichikawa and M. Hirakawa. ARES: A relational database with the capability of performing flexible interpretation of queries. *IEEE Transactions on Software Engineering*, SE-12(5): 624–634, May 1986.

[22] T. Imielinski. Intelligent query answering in rule based systems. *Journal of Logic Programming*, 4(3): 229–257, September 1987.

[23] T. Imielinski. Incomplete information in logical databases. *Data Engineering*, 12(2): 29–40, June 1989.

[24] T. Imielinski and K. Vadaparty. Complexity of query processing in databases with or-objects. In *Proceedings of PODS-89, the 8th Symposium on Principles of Database Systems* (Philadelphia, PA, March 29–31), pages 51–65, 1989.

[25] D. Maier. *The Theory of Relational Databases*. Computer Science Press, Rockville, Maryland, 1983.

[26] J. Minker. On indefinite databases and the closed world assumption. In *Lecture Notes in Computer Science No. 138*, pages 292–308. Springer-Verlag, Berlin, Germany, 1982.

[27] A. Motro. BAROQUE: A browser for relational databases. *ACM Transactions on Office Information Systems*, 4(2): 164–181, April 1986.

[28] A. Motro. VAGUE: A user interface to relational databases that permits vague queries. *ACM Transactions on Office Information Systems*, 6(3): 187–214, July 1988.

[29] A. Motro. Integrity = validity + completeness. *ACM Transactions on Database Systems*, 14(4): 480–502, December 1989.

[30] A. Motro. FLEX: A tolerant and cooperative user interface to databases. *IEEE Transactions on Knowledge and Data Engineering*, 2(2): 231–246, June 1990.

[31] A. Motro. Intensional answers to database queries. *IEEE Transactions on Knowledge and Data Engineering*, 6(3): 444–454, June 1994.

[32] A. Motro. Multiplex: A formal model for multidatabases and its implementation. Technical Report ISSE-TR-95-103, Department of Information and Software Systems Engineering, George Mason University, March 1995.

[33] A. Motro and I. Rakov. Estimating the quality of data in relational databases. In *Proceedings of the 1996 Conference on Information Quality* Cambridge, Massachusetts, October 25–26, 1996.

[34] J. Pearl. *Probabilistic Reasoning in Intelligent Systems: Networks of Plausible Inference*. Morgan Kaufmann, San Mateo, California, 1988.

[35] G. Piatetsky-Shapiro. Discovery, analysis and presentation of strong rules. In G. Piatetsky-Shapiro and W. Frawley, editors, *Knowledge Discovery in Databases*, pages 229–248. AAAI Press/MIT Press, Menlo Park, California, 1991.

[36] H. Prade and C. Testemale. Generalizing database relational algebra for the treatment of incomplete or uncertain information and vague queries. *Information Sciences*, 34(2): 115–143, November 1984.

[37] K. V. S. V. N. Raju and A. Majumdar. Fuzzy functional dependencies and lossless join decomposition of fuzzy relational database systems. *ACM Transactions on Database Systems*, 13(2): 129–166, June 1988.

[38] R. Reiter. On closed world data bases. In *Logic and Databases*, pages 55–76. Plenum Press, New York, New York, 1978.

[39] T. R. Rogers and R. G. G. Cattell. Object-oriented database user interfaces. Technical report, Information Management Group, Sun Microsystems, 1987.

[40] N. Roussopoulos and J. Mylopoulos. Using semantic networks for data base management. In *Proceedings of the First International Conference on Very Large Data Bases* (Framingham, Massachusetts, September 22–24), pages 144–172. ACM, New York, New York, 1975.

[41] G. Salton and M. J. McGill. *Introduction to Modern Information Retrieval*. McGraw-Hill, New York, New York, 1983.

[42] P. Smets and M. R. B. Clarke (Guest Editors). Special issue, Uncertainty, conditionals and non-monotonicity. *Journal of Applied Non-Classical Logics*, 1(2), 1991.

[43] J. D. Ullman. *Database and Knowledge-Base Systems, Volume I.* Computer Science Press, Rockville, Maryland, 1988.

[44] J. D. Ullman. *Database and Knowledge-Base Systems, Volume II.* Computer Science Press, Rockville, Maryland, 1989.

[45] C. J. van Rijsbergen. *Information Retrieval (Second Edition).* Butterworths, London, 1979.

[46] S. V. Vrbsky and J. W. S Liu. APPROXIMATE: a query processor that produces monotonically improving approximate answers. *IEEE Transactions on Knowledge and Data Engineering*, 5(6): 1056–1068, December 1993.

[47] M. D. Williams. What makes RABBIT run? *International Journal of Man-Machine Studies*, 21(4): 333–352, October 1984.

[48] M. Zemankova and A. Kandel. Implementing imprecision in information systems. *Information Sciences*, 37(1, 2, 3): 107–141, December 1985.

3

IMPERFECT INFORMATION IN RELATIONAL DATABASES

Esteban Zimányi
Alain Pirotte*

Department of Information and Documentation
Université de Bruxelles
Brussels, Belgium

* IAG Management School
Université de Louvain
Louvain-la-Neuve, Belgium

1   INTRODUCTION

Databases model the real world at two levels: the database schema specifies the structure of the database, and the database extension represents a set of facts or events of the real world. The *Appropriate Scheme Assumption* [10] expresses that this two-level description is a valid view of the world. Such a distinction between schema and extension is often blurred in artificial intelligence.

The information contained in a database is *complete* and *certain* if it represents an accurate and adequate picture of the corresponding application domain in the real world. However, in real life, information is often *imperfect* in several ways. Giving a precise characterization of imperfectness is not easy, and possible definitions follow. An item of information in a database is *uncertain* if the corresponding information in the real world is known only imperfectly. An item of information in a database is *imprecise* if it approximates the corresponding piece of information in the real world. With these definitions, vagueness is similar to imprecision, whereas incompleteness is an extreme case of imprecision, where an item of information is missing entirely.

Often, uncertainty and imprecision are two facets of the same phenomenon. Also, a characterization of what is uncertain and what is imprecise is relative to the pragmatics of database usage or simply to the way of phrasing the imperfect information.

For example, the fact "John is between 34 and 40 years of age" may be seen as certain but imprecise. For the same reality, the fact "John is between 35 and 37 years of age" would be less certain but more precise.

Data manipulation (that is, query answering, integrity constraints checking, and database updates) must be redefined to take the imperfect knowledge into account. The choice of which incompleteness and uncertainty to introduce in the database depends on the availability of mechanisms and algorithms for manipulating such information in a semantically correct way. Another concern is the complexity of manipulating incompleteness or uncertainty, which must not prevent its application to practical situations. Thus, the treatment of incompleteness and uncertainty is a trade-off between richness of representation and efficiency of manipulation.

Null values have been most widely used to model incomplete information. There are many possible nuances of nulls (the ANSI/X3/SPARC study [4] listed 14 of them). This chapter reviews the most important ones in addition to other approaches to incomplete and uncertain information listed next

Existential null values express that the existence of an attribute value is known but the specific value is not. If the attribute is single-valued, the null value is called *atomic* existential value; an example is when the age of a person is unknown. When the attribute is multivalued, the null value is called *set* existential value; an example is when it is known that a student is registered in at least one course without knowing which one(s). *Or-sets* are particular kinds of existential null values in which the unknown attribute takes its value from a specified subset of a database domain. *Inexistent* or *inapplicable null values* are used when an attribute cannot have a value. For example, for a single person, the name of the spouse is inapplicable. *Universal null values* represent that a property is satisfied for all the possible values of an attribute. For example, a professor may teach the same unknown course in all departments. *Default null values* one allow to represent that an object has a predetermined value, unless explicitly specified otherwise. For example, all employees will receive a 5% salary raise, except those working in a specific department. *No-information* or *open null values* correspond to the case in which it is not known whether a value exists. For example, if the marital status of a person is unknown, the name of the spouse is a no-information null value. As for existential values, there are two possible interpretations: *atomic* and *set*. Incomplete information in a database may also take the form of general *disjunctive information*, as in "John teaches Physics or Mary teaches Algebra." *Maybe information* is uncertain information, as in "Jean possibly teaches Physics." As will be shown, maybe information is related to disjunctive information. Uncertainty can also take the form of *probabilistic databases.* An example is "John teaches Physics with probability 0.8."

This chapter is organized as follows. Section 2 introduces the important semantics of possible worlds. Section 3 is a motivating section presenting the basic manipulation mechanisms for an imperfect database and illustrating them with or-sets and null values. This section can be omitted on a first reading as it uses concepts presented in more detail in subsequent sections. Section 4 is devoted to a systematic presentation of existential null values and their generalizations as or-sets. Section 5 treats inexistent values, and Section 6 discusses open databases. Section 7 briefly considers the combination of null values, an area in which many questions remain open. Section 8 considers the universal relation model. Section 9 addresses nested relational databases. Section 10 addresses maybe information. Section 11 is devoted to general disjunctive databases. Finally, Section 12 is devoted to probabilistic databases.

2   POSSIBLE WORLDS

A database models some part of the real world. If the information available is complete and certain, then there is a clear correspondence between the database and the real world. However, when knowledge about the world is incomplete or uncertain, several scenarios or states with complete and certain knowledge may be possible, but it is not known which of them represents the real state of the world.

Thus, a database containing incomplete or uncertain information implicitly represents a set of possible states or worlds. A *possible world* is a hypothetical state of the world that may be represented by an ordinary database with complete and certain information. If the knowledge about the world is represented with a logical theory, each possible world corresponds to a model of the theory.

Consider, for example, the relations *teaches(professor,course)* and *takes(student, course)* shown in Figure 1, where the variables x and y represent unknown values or, more precisely, *null values* of the type "value exists, but is unknown." As we shall see in future sections, there are different ways of interpreting these relations depending on how the null values and the relations are interpreted.

The semantics of a database with incomplete or uncertain information assign to each relation R, the value of a representation function $REP(R)$, which is a

teaches			takes	
professor	*course*		*student*	*course*
Martin	Physics		Paul	Physics
x	Algebra		Peter	*y*

Figure 1   Incomplete relations *teaches* and *takes*.

set of possible worlds. More generally, the representation function associates with a database (i.e., a set of relations) a set of classical relational databases, which are its possible worlds.

For example, suppose that for the relations *teaches* and *takes* above, the null values x and y represent, respectively, the or-sets {Martin, Anne} and {Algebra, Calculus} and that the or-sets are exclusive (i.e., either Martin or Anne, but not both, teaches Algebra). In addition, suppose that the relations are interpreted under the *Closed World Assumption* [58], stating that all facts not explicitly represented in the relations are false. The possible worlds $REP(\langle teaches, takes \rangle)$ are as in Figure 2.

M_1 : *teaches* = {(Martin,Physics),(Martin,Algebra)},
   takes = {(Paul,Physics),(Peter,Algebra)}
M_2 : *teaches* = {(Martin,Physics),(Martin,Algebra)},
   takes = {(Paul,Physics),(Peter,Calculus)}
M_3 : *teaches* = {(Martin,Physics),(Anne,Algebra)},
   takes = {(Paul,Physics),(Peter,Algebra)}
M_4 : *teaches* = {(Martin,Physics),(Anne,Algebra)},
   takes = {(Paul,Physics),(Peter,Calculus)}

Figure 2 $REP(\langle teaches, takes \rangle)$.

If the relations are considered with other interpretation of nulls, or under another closure assumption, $REP(\langle teaches, takes \rangle)$ may yield another set of possible worlds.

The notion of possible worlds provides a convenient tool that we use throughout this paper to investigate the semantics of both the representation and the manipulation of imperfect information.

3 MANIPULATING AN IMPERFECT DATABASE

This section illustrates the basic mechanisms for defining, with the help of possible worlds, the manipulation of an imperfect database. Two different points of view must be considered. Under a *semantical* point of view, the transformation of a database represented by a set of possible worlds $\mathcal{X}$ produces another set of possible worlds $\mathcal{Y}$, representing the intuitive meaning of the operation. Under a *syntactical* point of view, database relations are extended to represent imperfect information by null values, disjunctions, probabilities, etc., and a set of extended relations $\mathbf{R}$ yields another set of extended relations $\mathbf{R}'$. However, so that the manipulation will be faithful, the set of relations $\mathbf{R}'$ must capture the meaning represented by the set of possible worlds $\mathcal{Y}$.

3.1 Queries

With complete and certain information, every assertion is either true or false in the model of the world that is described by the database, and queries have a result made of a list of sure assertions. However, when only partial or uncertain information is available, each assertion may have a different truth value in each of the possible worlds. Thus, the mechanisms for database manipulation must be adapted accordingly.

To process queries on such extended relations, the relational algebra operators have to be generalized while remaining faithful to the underlying semantics defined by the representation function *REP* based on possible worlds.

Consider again the relations *teaches* and *takes* of Figure 1 and the associated set of possible worlds $REP(\langle teaches, takes \rangle)$ of Figure 2. Suppose we want to obtain, through a generalized join of *teaches* and *takes*, a relation representing professors teaching courses to students. The possible worlds $REP(\langle teaches, takes \rangle)$ are the basis for the meaning of the generalized join. Since all the possible worlds are equally likely, the possible results for the join are obtained by performing a classical join in each possible world of $REP(\langle teaches, takes \rangle)$, as shown in Figure 3. The relation obtained as result of the generalized join of *teaches* and *takes* should have these relations as its set of possible worlds.

Formally, let f be an arbitrary relational expression over a multirelation $\mathbf{R}$, i.e., over a collection $\mathbf{R} = \langle R_1, \ldots, R_k \rangle$ of extended relations. The best way to

$$
\begin{aligned}
M_1 &= \{(\text{Martin,Physics,Paul}),(\text{Martin,Algebra,Peter})\} \\
M_2 &= \{(\text{Martin,Physics,Paul})\} \\
M_3 &= \{(\text{Martin,Physics,Paul}),(\text{Anne,Algebra,Peter})\}
\end{aligned}
$$

Figure 3   *teaches* ⋈ *teaches* in the possible worlds.

define the extension $\bar{f}(\mathbf{R})$ of f over $\mathbf{R}$ is

$$
REP(\bar{f}(\mathbf{R})) = f(REP(\mathbf{R})) = \{f(\mathbf{r}) \mid \mathbf{r} \in REP(\mathbf{R})\}. \tag{3.1}
$$

This definition [37] is the strongest requirement that can be made, since it states that the expressive power of a given type of extended relation $\mathbf{R}$ is sufficient to exactly represent the results of all relational algebra expressions as extended relations $\bar{f}(\mathbf{R})$ of the same kind as $\mathbf{R}$.

Condition (3.1), referred to as *strong correctness criterion*, is schematized in Figure 4: both paths from the upper-left corner to the lower-right corner must produce the same result (in this figure *PW* stands for Possible Worlds).

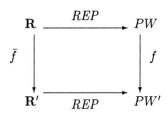

Figure 4   Strong correctness of f.

This requirement, however, is too strong for some extensions [36, 44], even when $\bar{f}$ is restricted to a subset of the relational algebra. This means that the desired result $f(REP(\mathbf{R}))$ of some expressions is not representable by any extended relation of the same kind as $\mathbf{R}$. There are two ways to cope with this problem: further generalize the relations to enhance their expressive power, or abandon strong correctness and define weaker correctness criteria.

For example, it can be shown that the possible worlds of Figure 3 cannot be represented by a relation with existential null values. They are represented by this relation:

professor	course	student
Martin	Physics	Paul
z	Algebra	Peter

where the null value z represents the or-set $\{\text{Anne}, \text{Martin}, \emptyset\}$ (see Section 4.3).

When a particular kind of relations is too weak to represent results of arbitrary expressions f, an alternative to further generalization is to accept approximations. The semantics of possible worlds may be used to specify *weaker correctness criteria* and to measure the information loss. One such weak correctness criterion could be that expressions $\bar{f}$ capture everything in $f(REP(\mathbf{R}))$ and as little extra as possible [47]. This can be stated as

$$REP(\bar{f}(\mathbf{R})) \supseteq f(REP(\mathbf{R}))$$

with the additional condition that there is no multirelation $\mathbf{R}'$ such that

$$REP(\bar{f}(\mathbf{R})) \supset REP(\mathbf{R}') \supseteq f(REP(\mathbf{R})).$$

Clearly, if an operator satisfies the strong correctness criterion, it also satisfies this weak criterion.

As another approximation, suppose that instead of defining the semantics of a query f as $\{f(\mathbf{r}) \mid \mathbf{r} \in REP(\mathbf{R})\}$, we define it as $\bigcap_{\mathbf{r} \in REP(\mathbf{R})} f(\mathbf{r})$, i.e., the information that is true in all possible worlds. For example, in Figure 3, Martin teaches Physics to Paul in all possible worlds. This motivates the notion of *true sets*.

Given a set of possible worlds $\mathcal{X}$, the true set $\cap \mathcal{X}$ is the set of tuples belonging to all worlds in $\mathcal{X}$. The requirements for a faithful extension of relational operations on a multirelation $\mathbf{R}$ then reduce to [34]:

(1) *Preservation of true sets*: any relational algebra expression f must satisfy

$$\cap REP(\bar{f}(\mathbf{R})) = \cap f(REP(\mathbf{R})),$$

i.e., the relation $\bar{f}(\mathbf{R})$ should preserve information about all the tuples that surely belong to $f(REP(\mathbf{R}))$.

(2) *Recursiveness*: $\bar{f}(\bar{g}(\mathbf{R})) = (\bar{f}\bar{g})(\mathbf{R})$. This states that, as in the usual relational algebra, intermediate results of subexpressions can be saved and used for computing the full expression.

Requirements (1) and (2) are truly minimal for any reasonable extension of the relational algebra. They are still restrictive, i.e., extensions of some operations operating on some type of relations will be impossible. A common mistake in extending the relational algebra is to consider the correctness of each operation separately and ignore their interaction. These interactions are captured by the recursiveness requirement.

3.2 Integrity Constraints

Integrity constraints express properties that any database instance must satisfy to be a legal state of the database schema. We consider here two of the more common constraints: *functional* and *multivalued dependencies*. Given a relation scheme $R(A, B, C)$, the functional dependency $A \rightarrow B$ can be expressed by the formula

$$\forall x \ \forall y \ \forall z \ \forall y_1 \ \forall z_1 \ r(x, y, z) \wedge r(x, y_1, z_1) \rightarrow y = y_1.$$

The multivalued dependency $A \rightarrow\rightarrow B$ can be expressed by the formula

$$\forall x \ \forall y \ \forall z \ \forall y_1 \ \forall z_1 \ r(x, y, z_1) \wedge r(x, y_1, z) \rightarrow r(x, y, z).$$

A relation r satisfies a dependency δ if r is a model of δ (in the sense of mathematical logic). A relation r satisfies a set of dependencies Σ if it satisfies every δ in Σ. Given a set of dependencies Σ defined over a scheme R, $Sat(\Sigma)$ is the set of relations on R that satisfy Σ.

The meaning of a database specified by a multirelation $\mathbf{r} = \langle r_1, \ldots, r_k \rangle$ and a set Σ of dependencies is called the *completion of* $\mathbf{r}$ *with respect to* Σ and is denoted by $comp_\Sigma(\mathbf{r})$. The completion $\mathbf{s} = \langle s_1, \ldots, s_k \rangle$ of $\mathbf{r}$ should satisfy [47]:

1. $r_i \subseteq s_i$ for all i,

2. $\mathbf{s} \in Sat(\Sigma)$,

3. for any $\mathbf{s}'$ that satisfy (1) and (2), $s_i \subset s_i'$ for at least one i.

The intuition is that (1) the original information should be maintained; (2) the completion should satisfy the dependencies; and (3) the additional information should be minimal. If the database is consistent, then the completion exists and is unique.

In the case of an imperfect database, a meaning must be assigned to a set of possible worlds $\mathcal{X}$ in the presence of a set of dependencies Σ. Since each possible world represents a conventional relational database, the notion of satisfaction of a set of dependencies generalizes to $\mathcal{X} \subseteq Sat(\Sigma)$. Let $\mathcal{X}$ be the following set of possible worlds of a relation *teaches(professor,course,department)*

$$
\begin{aligned}
M_1 &= \{(\text{Paul,Calculus,Zoology}),(\text{Paul,Algebra,Botany})\} \\
M_2 &= \{(\text{Thomas,Calculus,Zoology}),(\text{Anne,Calculus,Botany})\} \\
M_3 &= \{(\text{Anne,Calculus,Zoology}),(\text{Anne,Calculus,Botany}), \\
&\quad (\text{Anne,Algebra,Zoology}),(\text{Anne,Algebra,Botany})\}
\end{aligned}
$$

and $\Sigma = \{\delta_1 = prof \rightarrow\rightarrow course, \delta_2 = course \rightarrow prof\}$. $\mathcal{X}$ should be changed in order to satisfy Σ. To satisfy δ_1, the tuples (Paul, Calculus, Botany) and (Paul, Algebra, Zoology) should be added to M_1. M_2 violates δ_2 and the only possibility is to drop it from the completion. M_3 satisfies both δ_1 and δ_2.

Thus, the completion of a set of possible worlds $\mathcal{X}$ with respect to a set Σ of dependencies is obtained by replacing each multirelation in $\mathcal{X}$ by its completion, provided that it exists [26]:

$$Comp_\Sigma(\mathcal{X}) = \{comp_\Sigma(\mathbf{r}) \mid \mathbf{r} \in \mathcal{X}\}.$$

Consider now the syntactical point of view. Given a multirelation $\mathbf{R}$ containing imperfect knowledge, the natural interpretation that $\mathbf{R}$ satisfies Σ is

$$REP(\mathbf{R}) \subseteq Sat(\Sigma).$$

Thus we need to define a function $\overline{Comp}$ for transforming $\mathbf{R}$ in order to reduce $REP(\mathbf{R})$ to $REP(\mathbf{R}) \cap Sat(\Sigma)$ for any multirelation $\mathbf{R}$ and set of dependencies Σ.

Furthermore, $\overline{Comp}$ should be defined so that the possible worlds of the transformed multirelation are the same as those obtained by completing the possible worlds individually, as schematized in Figure 5.

Consider a relation *teaches*

prof.	*course*	*dept.*
Anne	Calculus	Zoology
x	Algebra	Botany

and the functional dependency $\delta_2 = prof \rightarrow course$. To represent the function $\overline{Comp}_{\delta_2}(teaches)$ we must be able to express the fact that x cannot be

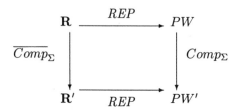

Figure 5 Completion with respect to dependencies Σ.

equal to Anne. Now consider the same relation with the multivalued dependency $\delta_1 = prof \rightarrow\rightarrow course$. Any relation in $Comp_{\delta_1}(REP(teaches))$ should include two or four tuples depending on the value of x. Thus, in order to define $\overline{Comp}_{\delta_1}(teaches)$, we need a C-relation [36]:

prof.	course	dept.	Con
Anne	Calculus	Zoology	
x	Algebra	Botany	
x	Calculus	Botany	$x = $ Anne
x	Algebra	Zoology	$x = $ Anne

This relation states that the last two tuples belong to the relation only in the case that condition $x = $ Anne is verified. C-relations are presented in Section 4.

3.3   Updates

An update to an imperfect database is correct if the possible worlds of the updated database are the same as those obtained by applying the update separately to each possible world of the original database. This is schematized in Figure 6. Thus, for example, the semantics for inserting a tuple t into a database **R** is given by inserting t into each possible world of **R**.

Consider a relation *teaches*

professor	course
Tom	Physics
Luc	x
y	Algebra

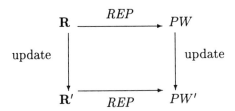

Figure 6 Update of an imperfect database.

in which the domains for attributes *professor* and *course* are, respectively, {Tom, Luc, Anne} and {Physics, Algebra}. The possible worlds of the relation are given in Figure 7.

$$M_1 = \{(\text{Tom,Physics}),(\text{Luc,Physics}),(\text{Tom,Algebra})\}$$
$$M_2 = \{(\text{Tom,Physics}),(\text{Luc,Physics}),(\text{Luc,Algebra})\}$$
$$M_3 = \{(\text{Tom,Physics}),(\text{Luc,Physics}),(\text{Anne,Algebra})\}$$
$$M_4 = \{(\text{Tom,Physics}),(\text{Luc,Algebra}),(\text{Tom,Algebra})\}$$
$$M_5 = \{(\text{Tom,Physics}),(\text{Luc,Algebra})\}$$
$$M_6 = \{(\text{Tom,Physics}),(\text{Luc,Algebra}),(\text{Anne,Algebra})\}$$

Figure 7 Possible worlds of *teaches*.

Updates can be incompletely specified as well. For example, the information that "Anne teaches an unknown course" is represented by a pair of one-tuple possible worlds $\mathcal{Y} = \{\{(\text{Anne}, \text{Physics})\}, \{(\text{Anne}, \text{Algebra})\}\}$. Thus, in general, update operations must be viewed as set-theoretical operations involving sets of possible worlds.

Ordinary relational updates are not sufficiently powerful to express all desirable transformations on a set of possible worlds. For example, with ordinary updates, there is no way to add new possible worlds or to eliminate possible worlds when they become inappropriate. We will now describe several types of updates to incomplete databases, as defined in [2].

Given two sets of possible worlds $\mathcal{X}$ and $\mathcal{Y}$, the *insertion* of $\mathcal{Y}$ into $\mathcal{X}$ is given by the pairwise union

$$\mathcal{X}(\cup)\mathcal{Y} = \{x \cup y \mid x \in \mathcal{X} \wedge y \in \mathcal{Y}\},$$

i.e., a possibility for the result is obtained by inserting a possibility of $\mathcal{Y}$ into a possibility of $\mathcal{X}$. For example, inserting into the database $\mathcal{X}$ of Figure 7 the set of possible words $\mathcal{Y}$ representing the fact "Anne teaches an unknown course" yields a set of 12 possible worlds.

The *deletion* of $\mathcal{Y}$ from $\mathcal{X}$ is accomplished by the pairwise difference

$$\mathcal{X}(-)\mathcal{Y} = \{x - y \mid x \in \mathcal{X} \wedge y \in \mathcal{Y}\}.$$

For example, the result of deleting all facts about Tom from database $\mathcal{X}$ of Figure 7 can be defined by $\mathcal{X}(-)\mathcal{Y}_2$ where $\mathcal{Y}_2 = \{\{(\text{Tom}, \text{Physics}), (\text{Tom}, \text{Algebra})\}\}$.

The knowledge contained in two databases $\mathcal{X}$ and $\mathcal{Y}$ can be integrated into one database by taking the tuples common to a possible state in $\mathcal{X}$ and a possible state in $\mathcal{Y}$ as one possible state of the new database. This *integration* update is defined by the pairwise intersection

$$\mathcal{X}(\cap)\mathcal{Y} = \{x \cap y \mid x \in \mathcal{X} \wedge y \in \mathcal{Y}\}.$$

The *subjection* update is used when our knowledge of the world has increased so that only some specific states of a database $\mathcal{X}$ remain possible. If, for instance, Tom is now known to teach only one course and if $\mathcal{Y}_3$ are all states satisfying this fact, the database must keep only those states in $\mathcal{X}$ that are also in $\mathcal{Y}_3$, i.e., $\mathcal{X} \cap \mathcal{Y}_3$ must replace $\mathcal{X}$.

Similarly, negative knowledge can be incorporated into a database. If we know that Luc does not teach algebra and $\mathcal{Y}_4$ is the set of all states in which Luc teaches algebra, the database $\mathcal{X}$ must be replaced by $\mathcal{X} - \mathcal{Y}_4$. Notice the implicit use of the Closed World Assumption, since the absence of a fact in a possible state means that the fact is false in that state.

Notice also that, unlike updates based on pairwise operations, the subjection updates only restrict the set of possible states of the database: the true state of the database is not modified, it is our knowledge of it that becomes more precise.

The *augmentation* of $\mathcal{X}$ with $\mathcal{Y}$ is defined as $\mathcal{X} \cup \mathcal{Y}$. The intuitive meaning is that, in addition to the set $\mathcal{X}$ of possible worlds already known, other possible worlds $\mathcal{Y}$ are also plausible. Hence, the new set of possible worlds are those that are either in $\mathcal{X}$ or in $\mathcal{Y}$.

Finally, the *modification* update applies a transformation f to each possible world. For instance, f could modify Anne's course to Physics in the set of possible worlds $\mathcal{X}$ of Figure 7.

Notice that the modification can be incompletely specified. If we want to modify either Anne's course or Luc's course to Physics, this is accomplished by a modification F which is a set of two modification functions: one is like the previous one and the other modifies Luc's course to Physics. The result of the modification is thus defined as

$$F(\mathcal{X}) = \{f(x) \mid f \in F \wedge x \in \mathcal{X}\}.$$

So far, we have considered the desired semantics of updates in the form of general operations on sets of possible worlds. As for query evaluation and dependency checking, we need a syntactical way of updating an imperfect database so that the update captures the semantics of the operation in the possible worlds.

Consider these relations *teaches* and *takes*

professor	course
Anne	Calculus

student	course	dept.
John	Calculus	Chemistry
Martin	x	Botany
Peter	y	Physics

and suppose one wishes to update the database so that all students taking Calculus are in the Botany department. While (John, Calculus, Botany) surely belongs to the updated relation, the problem for Peter is that his department depends on the values of the unknown value y. The update is captured by the C-relation

student	course	dept.	Con
John	Calculus	Chemistry	
Martin	x	Botany	
Peter	y	Physics	$y \neq$ Calculus
Peter	y	Botany	$y =$ Calculus

Notice that every possible world of this relation contains exactly three tuples.

Consider now the update that Peter's professor also teaches Algebra. Then, Anne's courses in relation *teaches* depend on an unknown null value in a different relation. The update is represented by the C-relation

professor	*course*	*Con*
Anne	Calculus	
Anne	Algebra	$y = $ Calculus

The two updates considered were completely specified. Consider now an update so that either Martin or Peter is deleted from the first relation *takes* above. Intuitively, this means that, in each possible world of *REP(takes)*, one of the tuples can be deleted. Such an update can be represented with the C-relation

student	*course*	*dept.*	*Con*
John	Calculus	Chemistry	
Martin	x	Botany	$v \neq$ Martin
Peter	y	Botany	$v \neq$ Peter

in addition to a global condition stating that $v = $ Martin $\vee$ $v = $ Peter. It can be verified that, in any possible world, either the second or the third tuple is discarded.

3.4 Summary

In this section, we introduced mechanisms for defining the manipulation of imperfect databases in a semantically correct way. The different types of imperfect information are studied in detail in the next sections. However, as we will see, manipulating imperfect information is not an easy task. A negative result typical of this complex field is that the simplest ideas do not work very far. For example, the intuitively appealing existential null values do not support a satisfactory definition of the relational join. An existential null value on a finite domain can be represented as an or-set, but or-sets do not permit a correct join either; relations with or-sets represented by variables are the next step, but still unsatisfactory for the algebra. Only conditional relations and general disjunctive databases, fairly more complex than databases with existential null values, are flexible and powerful enough to support a definition of the algebra.

4 EXISTENTIAL VALUES

4.1 Atomic Existential Values

Existential null values model a situation in which the value of an attribute exists, but the specific value is unknown. An existential value is *atomic* when the unknown attribute has exactly one possible value. *Set* existential values are studied in the next section.

We describe now several types of relations having null values. In the relation *teaches*

professor	course	classroom
Marc	Databases	AX210
Pierre	x	H1309
Thomas	Mechanics	y
Thomas	Languages	z

variables represent null values, where two different variables may or may not represent the same constant. Thus, the course taught by Pierre in classroom H1309 and the rooms in which Thomas teaches his two courses are unknown.

Such relations can be supplemented with global conditions composed of equalities and inequalities, as in this example:

professor	course	classroom
Marc	Databases	AX210
Pierre	x	H1309
Thomas	Mechanics	y
Thomas	Languages	y

$$\boxed{x \neq y \land y \neq \text{H3322}}$$

The fact that y appears twice means that Thomas teaches both his courses in the same room. The global condition gives additional information about the values of x and y. Notice that $x \neq y$ can be deduced from the database since the domains of *course* and *classroom* are disjoint.

Finally, *conditional relations* (or *C-relations*) are obtained by adding to the relations a column containing local conditions composed of equalities and inequalities. An example is

professor	course	classroom	cond
Marc	Databases	AX210	
Pierre	x	H1309	
Thomas	Mechanics	y	$x = \text{Physics}$
Thomas	Languages	y	$x \neq \text{Physics}$

$$x \neq y \wedge y \neq \text{H3322}$$

In this example, Thomas teaches Mechanics if Pierre teaches Physics; otherwise he teaches Languages. Notice that, unlike the previous example, Thomas teaches only one course. *Horn tables* are conditional tables in which only restricted types of local and global conditions are allowed [26].

Existential values in relational databases have been an active area of research after their introduction by Codd [12, 13]. Codd studied the introduction of a unique null value and proposed a three-valued logic based on the truth values $\{true, false, unknown\}$ and a so-called null substitution principle. Later, Codd [14, 15] generalized the approach to inapplicable null values in a four-valued logic with an additional truth value *inapplicable*. However, as pointed out by various researchers [27, 70, 9, 10], Codd's approach suffers from several drawbacks (for example, in the treatment of tautologies and in not providing for several unknown values).

An aspect of the existential null values was pointed out by Lipski [42, 43], who defined information that *surely*, alternatively *possibly*, can be extracted from a database in the presence of unknown values, and proposed a query language containing these modal operators. Notice that such considerations apply in general to all types of incomplete information.

An important step in the understanding of the unknown null values was achieved by Imieliński and Lipski [36]. Unlike Codd, they introduced several unknown values for obtaining more modeling power, and they generalized the relational algebra operators. Their most important contribution was the definition of the correctness criteria presented in Section 3 and the methodology for generalizing relational operators. These ideas can be applied to a much wider range of databases than was initially expected. Another major result was to prove that to obtain all the answers to arbitrary relational queries, the expressive power of conditional relations was needed.

Grahne [26] defined the semantics of incomplete databases as sets of possible worlds and showed that two different lattices can be defined in incomplete databases. He studied query evaluation, integrity constraint satisfaction, and database updates as operations on these lattices. Grahne also studied the manipulation of different types of relations containing unknown null values and, following [3], established the complexity of query evaluation, integrity constraint satisfaction, and database updates in this context.

On the other hand, from a logical standpoint, the information content of a database can be formalized by means of *extended relational theories* [60, 61, 32]. In these theories an *extension axiom* is associated with each relation of the database to specify the precise set of tuples of constants belonging to the relation.

Extended relational theories also contain a set of *unique name axioms*, specifying which distinct constants represent different objects (for example Marc $\neq$ Pierre). In extended theories, existential null values are represented by constants of the same type as ordinary constants. It is the absence of some unique name axioms that expresses the incompleteness of knowledge.

For example, given the previous conditional relation, the extension axiom of predicate *teaches* is

$$\forall x \,\forall y \,\forall z \; teaches(x, y, z) \leftrightarrow (x = \text{Marc} \land y = \text{Databases} \land z = \text{AX210}) \lor$$
$$(x = \text{Pierre} \land y = \omega_1 \land z = \text{H1309}) \lor$$
$$(\omega_1 = \text{Physics} \to x = \text{Thomas} \land y = \text{Mechanics} \land z = \omega_2) \lor$$
$$(\omega_1 \neq \text{Physics} \to x = \text{Thomas} \land y = \text{Languages} \land z = \omega_2).$$

Constants ω_1 and ω_2 represent existential values. In addition to unique name axioms like Marc $\neq$ Pierre or Marc $\neq$ Thomas for ordinary constants, the extended theory contains unique name axioms for the existential null values $\omega_2 \neq$ H3322, and $\omega_1 \neq \omega_2$.

Reiter gave an algorithm to answer queries in extended relational theories and proved that his algorithm is *sound*, in the sense that all the answers retrieved are correct, but is *incomplete*, since some correct answers are not obtained by the algorithm. In [17], Reiter's approach is extended to theories containing constraints on the existential null values.

With respect to dependencies in relations containing existential values, after the early works of [71, 35], Grahne [25, 26] introduced the notion of general conditions and proved that conditional relations with general conditions are powerful enough for enforcing a set of functional and full join dependencies. Query evaluation and dependency satisfaction were also studied in [39, 40] using Reiter's logical framework.

Updates in relations containing existential values were studied by Abiteboul and Grahne [2, 26]. They defined the semantics of updates and the different set-theoretic operators that can be used for updating a database containing existential values, as presented in Section 3.3. In addition, they highlighted the ability of different relations to support update operations. In particular they showed that conditional relations fully support all updates operations whereas other types of relations are well suited for only some types of update operations. Using a logical approach, Wilkins [72, 74, 73] studied updates with null values and disjunctive information in restricted theories of first-order logic with equality.

Figure 8 summarizes the successive generalizations needed to support correct manipulations of null values, together with the problems that justify the next richer version.

Extended Relations	*Problem*
relations with one null value	tautologies
relations with marked null values	complete algebra and integrity constraints
conditional relations with null values	updates
conditional relations with null values and global conditions	complexity of manipulation

Figure 8   Enrichment of expressive power for null values.

4.2   Set Existential Values

Consider a relation *optional_course*, stating the optional courses taken by students, given by

student	*optional_course*
Dominique	Languages
Anne-Marie	$\{x\}$
Martin	$\{y\}$
Jean-Pierre	z

Databases $\notin \{x\}$

Here, $\{x\}$ and $\{y\}$ denote set existential values, meaning that Anne-Marie and Martin take *at least one* course while Jean-Pierre takes *exactly* one. In addition, it is known that Databases is not among the courses of Anne-Marie.

Set existential values have been studied by Hulin [31]. Representing them in first-order logic leads to *two-sorted extended theories*, with a sort $\mathcal{C}$ for ordinary constants and atomic existential values, and a sort $\mathcal{D}$ for sets. Variables are sorted and each n-ary relational predicate is defined as being of sort $(\mathcal{C}, \ldots, \mathcal{C})$. In addition, the binary predicate $\in$ (belongs), of sort $(\mathcal{C}, \mathcal{D})$, is included.

In the previous example, variables $\{x\}$ and $\{y\}$ are represented by constants ϵ_1 and ϵ_2 of sort $\mathcal{D}$. To specify that these constants do not represent the empty set, the *nonemptiness axioms* $\exists x\ x \in \epsilon_1$, and $\exists x\ x \in \epsilon_2$ are introduced in the theory, where variable x is of sort $\mathcal{C}$.

Another type of information that can be introduced in the theory is that two sets are disjoint. This is represented with this *disjointness axiom*:

$$\neg(\exists x\ x \in \epsilon_1 \wedge x \in \epsilon_2) \text{ or, equivalently, } \forall x\ x \notin \epsilon_1 \vee x \notin \epsilon_2.$$

Finally, the extension axiom for predicate *optional_course* is

$$\forall x\ \forall y\ optional\_course(x, y) \leftrightarrow (x = \text{Dominique} \wedge y = \text{Languages}) \vee$$
$$(x = \text{Anne-Marie} \wedge y \in \epsilon_1) \vee (x = \text{Martin} \wedge y \in \epsilon_2) \vee$$
$$(x = \text{Jean-Pierre} \wedge y = \omega).$$

In addition to unique name axioms, the *nonmembership axiom* Databases $\notin \epsilon_1$ is needed.

As remarked by Imieliński [33], incomplete information is often introduced in relational databases by updates on views. Set existential values are important in this context because they allow to reflect more accurately our knowledge of the world.

For example, given the predicates *teaches(professor,course)* and *takes(student, course)*, a view v defined by

$$\forall x\ \forall y\ v(x, y) \leftrightarrow (\exists z\ teaches(x, z) \wedge takes(y, z))$$

may be used for obtaining the (*professor,student*) pairs for professors giving at least one course to a student. To add to view v the pair (Peter,Anne), stating that Peter teaches one (or several) courses to Anne, the classical approach is to use an existential value, or a Skolem constant ω, and assert the facts *teaches*(Peter, ω) and *takes*(Anne, ω).

Thus, existential values are often the result of Skolemizing existentially quantified conjunctive views. Yet Skolemization preserves satisfiability but not derivability, i.e., Skolemizing views may make true formulas that were false before. Hulin [31] gives several examples of Skolemized theories that lead to anomalous answers when evaluating queries. Such anomalous answers, derived from Reiter's axiomatization of null values, are not discovered by his evaluation algorithm because of its incompleteness. However, other anomalous answers are derived by his algorithm that cannot be justified in the non-Skolemized theory. Hulin showed that the anomalous answers generated with the extended relational theories disappear with two-sorted relational theories.

4.3   Or-sets and Restricted Cardinality Sets

Or-sets (or disjunctive sets) [42, 67, 76, 37, 34] generalize existential null values. An existential value represents an attribute whose actual value is in a database domain. An or-set represents an attribute whose value is an explicit, smaller set.

When an or-set appears in a relation tuple, the actual value of the attribute is one element of the or-set. An ordinary atomic value can be viewed as an or-set with the value as single element. An existential value corresponds to an or-set containing the entire attribute domain. Or-sets can also contain a special value $\emptyset$ to represent the possibility of there being no value.

In the following relation *teaches(professor,course)*, the second tuple represents that Thomas teaches one of the courses of the set {Physics, Chemistry, Biology}. The third tuple represents that either Susan teaches Algebra or that Martha does or that the course is not taught.

professor	course
Marc	Databases
Thomas	{Physics, Chemistry, Biology}
{Susan, Martha, $\emptyset$}	Algebra

Or-sets are not powerful enough to represent some useful varieties of incomplete information. For this reason, Michalewicz and Groves [52] proposed the *generalized or-sets*, in which the actual value is understood to be some nonempty subset of the stored set. If the actual value may be empty, the special value $\emptyset$ is included in the stored set. For example, interpreting in the relation above

{Susan, Martha, $\emptyset$} as a generalized or-set means that Algebra may be taught by either Susan or Martha, or both, or may not be offered.

Michalewicz and Groves [52] also studied the combination of or-sets, generalized or-sets, as well as and-sets. An *and-set* in an attribute A of a tuple t represents that the actual value of the attribute is precisely the specified set of values. And-sets are those used in the context of nested or nonfirst normal form relations, which are studied in Section 9.

In addition, another kind of sets are defined in [51], the *restricted cardinality sets* (*rc-sets*). An rc-set $S_{p,q}$ defines a set S of values from the attribute's domain such that $0 \leq p \leq q \leq n$, where n is the number of elements in S. The meaning of an rc-set is that the actual value of the attribute is some subset s of the stored set of candidates S, such that $p \leq \text{card}(s) \leq q$. If $q = 0$, the actual value is the empty set.

For example, a tuple (Thomas, {Physics, Chemistry, Biology}$_{1,2}$) in a relation *teaches* means that Thomas will teach between one and two of the courses represented in the set. Notice that rc-sets allow to represent ordinary atomic values, or-sets, generalized or-sets, and and-sets.

Generalized operators on relations containing rc-sets as defined in [51] suffer from one important drawback. As shown in [34], it is not possible to define algebraic operators over relations having or-sets (and, consequently, having generalized or-sets and rc-sets) that satisfy the requirements stated in Section 3.1 for a correct generalization of the relational algebra.

For this reason, Imieliński and Vadaparty [37, 34] represented or-sets by variables, in what they called *or-relations*. These relations contain variables, with a set of values associated with each variable. An example of or-relation is

professor	*course*	*classroom*
Marc	Databases	AX210
Pierre	x	H1309
Thomas	Mechanics	y

where x and y represent or-sets with $\text{dom}(x) = \{\text{Physics, Materials}\}$ and $\text{dom}(y) = \{\text{H1309, H1310}\}$. In this example, Pierre teaches either Physics or Materials, and Thomas teaches Mechanics either in room H1309 or in room H1310.

However, as shown by Imieliński, the expressive power of relations with or-sets (even when represented with variables) is not sufficient to support both projection and join. In fact, to support both operators, or-sets must be extended to general disjunctions like *teaches*(Marc, Calculus) ∨ *teaches*(Anne, Algebra). This leads to the disjunctive databases presented in Section 11. Furthermore, since Imieliński and Vadaparty used the true sets for stating the semantics of queries, they did not consider "possible" or "maybe" information, which can be derived from the database. Maybe information is studied in Section 10.

Similar to Figure 8, Figure 9 summarizes the successive generalizations of or-sets. The problem listed with each one justifies the definition of the next one.

Extended Relations	*Problem*
relations with or-sets	unable to represent that the attribute takes no value
relations with extended or-sets having a special value ∅	unable to represent that two or-sets are the same
relations with extended or-sets represented by variables	unable to represent or-sets over several attributes
disjunctive databases	definition of full algebra

Figure 9   Enrichment of expressive power for or-sets.

5   INEXISTENT VALUES

Inexistent null values, denoted by ⊥, allow one to represent that an attribute is inapplicable. For example, consider this relation *takes*(*student*, *department*, *course*):

student	*department*	*course*
Pierre	Physics	Calculus
Jean	⊥	Probability

The second tuple represents that Jean takes Probability without being registered in any department.

Representing inexistent null values in mathematical logic is not straightforward. In particular, the following are incorrect representations:

$$\neg(\exists x) takes(\text{Jean}, x, \text{Probability}) \text{ or } (\forall x)\neg takes(\text{Jean}, x, \text{Probability})$$

because they prevent obtaining Probability as an answer to the query "in which courses is Jean registered?"

The same problem arises when representing inexistent values as empty-set existential values in a two-sorted theory. As stated by Hulin [31], inapplicable null values probably require three-valued and two-sorted logic theories.

Another solution is to represent inexistent values with a special constant $\perp$ of the same type as other constants, leaving their interpretation to extra-logical notions. The extension axiom of predicate of predicate *takes* becomes

$$\forall x \, \forall y \, \forall z \, takes(x, y, z) \leftrightarrow (x = \text{Pierre} \wedge y = \text{Physics} \wedge z = \text{Calculus})\vee$$
$$(x = \text{Jean} \wedge y = \perp \wedge z = \text{Probability}).$$

To respect the meaning of the inexistent null value, the following constraint must be introduced in the theory:

$$\forall x \, takes(\text{Jean}, x, \text{Probability}) \leftrightarrow x = \perp .$$

As shown by this constraint, it is necessary to introduce in the database a different constant for each inexistent value. In fact, representing that "Marie is registered in Algebra without being registered in any department" by adding the tuple (Marie, $\perp$, Algebra) would result in considering both persons as belonging to the same department, which is not correct.

Therefore, the constants of the database must be divided in two subsets: a set C containing the ordinary constants and a set $\perp = \{\perp_1, \ldots, \perp_n\}$ that contains all the inexistent values appearing in the database. Of course, appropriate unique name axioms have to be introduced in the theory for stating that inexistent values are different from each other and from every other constant.

Inapplicable values were studied by various researchers. As already mentioned, Codd proposed a four-valued logic for the manipulation of existential as well as inapplicable null values. Vassiliou [70] used a denotational semantics approach. In addition, inexistent null values were studied by Zaniolo [78] and by Gottlob and Zicari [24] in conjunction with other kinds of null values to be presented in later sections.

6   OPEN DATABASES AND NULL VALUES

6.1   Closure Assumptions

With the *Closed World Assumption* (CWA), all the information not explicitly represented in the database is supposed to be false. Thus, for a relation
teaches(professor, course, department), the CWA amounts to saying that there
are no other professors, no other courses, and no other departments than those
appearing in the relation.

With the *Open World Assumption* (OWA), the previous assumption does not
hold, since there may be other tuples in the relation. In addition, with the
OWA, the negative information must be explicitly stated, contrary to closed
databases. For instance, in the relation

	professor	*course*	*department*
positive component $\{$	Pierre	Calculus	Physics
	Marc	Calculus	Chemistry
negative component $\{$	Marc	Algebra	Physics

it is represented that "Marc does not teach Algebra in the Physics department."

This relation is represented by these formulas:

$$\forall x \, \forall y \, \forall z \; teaches(x, y, z) \leftarrow (x = \text{Pierre} \land y = \text{Calculus} \land z = \text{Physics}) \lor$$
$$(x = \text{Marc} \land y = \text{Calculus} \land z = \text{Chemistry}),$$
$$\neg teaches(\text{Marc,Algebra,Physics}).$$

Open and closed databases have some properties in common. For instance,
a relational expression not containing the difference operator yields the same
result for both open or closed databases. The difference operator implicitly
assumes the Closed World Assumption. Thus, a difference operator that takes
into account the negative component of relations is needed.

Another difference between open and closed databases pointed out by Reiter [62] deals with integrity constraint checking when constraints are expressed
as formulas in epistemic logic. Much work remains to be done to establish relationships between open and closed databases, and to define query answering,
integrity checking, and updates in open databases.

6.2   Universal and Default Values

Under the OWA, two other categories of null values naturally arise: the *universal* and the *default values.*

Suppose that "Jean teaches Biology in all departments," and "Brigitte teaches no course in the Chemistry department" must be represented in relation *teaches* of the previous section.

If the relation is interpreted under the CWA, the first fact can be represented by adding to the relation a set of tuples of the form (Jean, *dept*, Biology), one for each department *dept* of the database. In addition, if the information present in the relation is consistent with the second fact, the CWA implies that Brigitte teaches no course in the Chemistry department.

The situation is completely different under the OWA. Since not all the departments are necessarily known, the first fact cannot be represented by introducing tuples of the form (Jean, *dept*, Biology). The situation is still different when representing the second fact, because the negative information must be explicitly introduced in open databases. Therefore, the previous facts must be represented with a *universal null value*, denoted by $\forall$:

	professor	*course*	*department*
positive component	Pierre	Calculus	Physics
	Marc	Calculus	Chemistry
	Jean	Biology	$\forall$
negative component	Marc	Algebra	Physics
	Brigitte	$\forall$	Chemistry

Under the OWA, this relation is represented as

$$\forall x\, \forall y\, \forall z\; teaches(x,y,z) \leftarrow (x = \text{Pierre} \wedge y = \text{Calculus} \wedge z = \text{Physics}) \vee$$
$$(x = \text{Marc} \wedge y = \text{Calculus} \wedge z = \text{Chemistry}) \vee$$
$$(x = \text{Jean} \wedge y = \text{Biology}),$$

in addition to the formulas

$$\neg teaches(\text{Marc,Algebra,Physics}),$$
$$\forall x\; \neg teaches(\text{Brigitte}, x, \text{Chemistry}).$$

Although universal values were introduced by Biskup in [10], to our knowledge, no work has formally studied the manipulation of such values in relational databases.

Default null values are another category of nulls needed when the OWA is applied to a database. Suppose that the income of university professors is represented by the relation

year	professor	income
1990	Jean	19,000
1990	Marc	20,000

Without more information, suppose that it is estimated by default that every professor not explicitly represented earned \$22,000 in 1990. Under the OWA, since not all professors are known, we need to introduce in the relation the tuple $\langle 1990, *, 22,000 \rangle$, where $*$ denotes a default null value.

Thus, the relation can be represented in first-order logic by this extension axiom:

$$\forall x, y, z \; income(x, y, z) \leftarrow (x = 1990 \wedge y = \text{Jean} \wedge z = 19,000) \vee$$
$$(x = 1990 \wedge y = \text{Marc} \wedge z = 20,000) \vee$$
$$(x = 1990 \wedge y \neq \text{Jean} \wedge y \neq \text{Marc} \wedge z = 22,000),$$

in addition to the constraint

$$(\forall x, y, z)(income(x, y, z) \wedge x = 1990 \wedge y \neq \text{Jean} \wedge y \neq \text{Marc} \rightarrow z = 22,000).$$

It is also possible to represent default values in first-order logic with a set-theoretical notation. The default information can be represented by defining a set $\epsilon_1 = \{\text{Jean}, \text{Marc}\}$, by replacing the last disjunct in the extension axiom of *income* by the formula

$$x = 1990 \wedge y \notin \epsilon_1 \wedge z = 22,000,$$

and by replacing the constraint with

$$\forall x, y, z \; income(x, y, z) \wedge x = 1990 \wedge y \notin \epsilon_1 \rightarrow z = 22,000.$$

The introduction of default information in databases is very important. Because many applications have to deal with great number of unknown parameters; for example, in economical environments it is necessary to make estimations and decisions based on these estimations. Default information provides an extra capability for handling uncertainty, because it states common or average values that are likely to be true in the absence of evidence proving the contrary.

Nevertheless, little work has been realized on defaults in databases. Some basic issues are discussed in [16] for relational databases and in [38] for deductive databases. Notice that systems like SYNTEL [63], a programming system used for financial risk assessment, includes default information, as well as unknown and uncertain values. For manipulating such information, SYNTEL includes an ad-hoc *default join* operator.

Research in this context has to be based on the definition of precise semantics for default values. All the work on default logics (e.g., [59]) is relevant.

6.3 Open Values

Thus far, we have considered databases that are totally open or totally closed. Another possibility is to use a mixed approach, where each relation of the database is interpreted either under the Open or under the Closed World Assumption. This is the approach followed by Gelfond and Przymusinska for the definition of the *Careful Closure Assumption* [23].

The *Locally Open World Assumption* [24] enables to partially or entirely relax the closure assumption inside a relation. An *open null value* expresses that an attribute of a tuple must be interpreted under the Open World Assumption: the attribute value may not exist, it may take exactly one value, or it may take several values. In other words, no assumption is made about the attribute's value. In the following relation, the open null value Ω expresses that the relation is closed, except for attribute *student*:

student	*department*	*course*
Pierre	Biology	Calculus
Ω	Chemistry	Algebra

The following facts can be inferred: (1) the only departments are Biology and Chemistry; (2) the only courses are Calculus and Algebra; (3) the only student in Biology who takes Calculus is Pierre; and (4) there may be zero, one, or several students registered in the Chemistry department taking Algebra. No other fact is true in this relation.

Suppose now that $(\Omega_1, \Omega_2, \Omega_3)$ replaces the second tuple of the above relation. The open values express that the relation is interpreted under the Open World Assumption. All the attributes of the second tuple are open, meaning that that

Pierre is registered in Biology and takes Calculus, but nothing else is known and, in particular, there are no negated facts.

The no-information nulls of Zaniolo [78] can be seen as open null values taking at most one value from the attribute domain. As remarked by Zaniolo, open null values are less informative than existential (either atomic or set) and inexistent null values. They can approximate both when it is not known whether or not values exist for the attribute.

The semantics for relations containing open null values can be specified as follows. Consider the first relation *takes* above and suppose that the domain for *student* is {Pierre, Anne}. Then, the relation represents this set of possible worlds

$$
\begin{aligned}
M_1 &= \{(\text{Pierre,Biology,Calculus}),(\bot,\text{Chemistry,Algebra})\} \\
M_2 &= \{(\text{Pierre,Biology,Calculus}),(\text{Pierre,Chemistry,Algebra})\} \\
M_3 &= \{(\text{Pierre,Biology,Calculus}),(\text{Anne,Chemistry,Algebra})\} \\
M_4 &= \{(\text{Pierre,Biology,Calculus}),(\text{Pierre,Chemistry,Algebra}), \\
    &\qquad (\text{Anne,Chemistry,Algebra})\}
\end{aligned}
$$

Open null values can be modeled in first-order logic with two-sorted relational theories, in which each open value is represented by a set. As noted by Hulin [31], the only difference between the set existential values and the open values is that the open null values do not have nonemptiness axioms. For example, the above relation is represented in a two-sorted relational theory with the axiom

$$
\forall x \ \forall y \ \forall z \ takes(x,y,z) \leftrightarrow (x = \text{Pierre} \land y = \text{Biology} \land z = \text{Calculus}) \lor \\
(x \in \epsilon_1 \land y = \text{Chemistry} \land z = \text{Algebra}).
$$

Gottlob and Zicari [24] studied the manipulation of open values in conjunction with existential and inexistent values. This study is presented in the next section.

7 COMBINATION OF NULL VALUES

Consider the relation *takes*

student	department	course
Pierre	Botany	Calculus
Ω_1	Ω_2	Calculus
Marie	Physics	$\perp$
Jean	Physics	$\{x\}$
Paul	Biology	Ω_3
$\forall$	Chemistry	Calculus
Paul	Biology	Statistics
*	Botany	Calculus

positive component: rows Pierre through Paul; negative component: rows $\forall$, Paul, *.

Interpreted under the Locally Open World Assumption, it models these facts:

- Pierre is registered in Botany and takes Calculus;

- students, explicitly known or not, registered in departments, explicitly known or not, may take Calculus;

- Marie is registered in Physics and takes no course;

- Jean is registered in Physics and takes one or several courses, but it is not known which ones;

- Paul may take courses in Biology, but Statistics is not among them;

- no student registered in Chemistry takes Calculus;

- no student registered in Botany, except Pierre, takes Calculus.

The relation is represented in first-order logic by the extension axiom

$$\forall x \ \forall y \ \forall z \ takes(x, y, z) \leftrightarrow$$
$$(x = \text{Pierre} \wedge y = \text{Botany} \wedge z = \text{Calculus}) \vee$$
$$(x \in \epsilon_1 \wedge y \in \epsilon_2 \wedge z = \text{Calculus}) \vee$$
$$(x = \text{Marie} \wedge y = \text{Physics} \wedge z = \perp) \vee$$
$$(x = \text{Jean} \wedge y = \text{Physics} \wedge z \in \epsilon_3) \vee$$
$$(x = \text{Paul} \wedge y = \text{Biology} \wedge z \in \epsilon_4),$$

and the axioms

$$\exists x \ x \in \epsilon_3,$$
$$\forall x \ takes(\text{Marie}, \text{Physics}, x) \leftrightarrow x = \perp,$$
$$\forall x \ x = \text{Statistics} \rightarrow x \notin \epsilon_4,$$
$$\forall x \ \neg takes(x, \text{Chemistry}, \text{Calculus}),$$
$$\forall x \ x \notin \{Pierre\} \rightarrow \neg takes(x, \text{Botany}, \text{Calculus}).$$

The semantics of relations combining several types of nulls can be derived from the possible worlds semantics of the individual nulls. However, as pointed out by Gottlob and Zicari [24], combining nulls raises the question of consistency and redundancy.

If $\mathbf{t} = (\text{Pierre}, \text{Botany}, \perp)$ is added to the relation *takes* above, it becomes inconsistent, since $\mathbf{t}$ contradicts the first tuple stating that Pierre is registered in Botany and takes Calculus.

Consider now redundancy. Intuitively, a tuple $\mathbf{t}$ is redundant in a relation R iff $\mathbf{t}$ can be removed without changing the semantics of the relation, that is, iff the possible worlds of R are the same as those of $R - \{\mathbf{t}\}$. For instance, $(\text{Jean}, \text{Physics}, y)$, where y is an existential value is redundant, since it does not add any information to $(\text{Jean}, \text{Physics}, \{x\})$. Similarly, $(\text{Marie}, \text{Physics}, \Omega)$ is redundant with respect to $(\text{Marie}, \text{Physics}, \perp)$, the second tuple constraining Marie to take no course.

The relational operators have to be generalized for manipulating the different types of null values. In addition, integrity checking and database updates must also take into account the semantics expressed by all types of nulls. Much work remains to be done in this context.

8 UNIVERSAL RELATION DATABASES AND NULL VALUES

The *Universal Relation model* (UR model) [68, 69, 48, 49] allows users to view a relational database as if it were composed of a single relation. Thus the UR model provides logical data independence by freeing users from navigating among the relations in a given database. The most fundamental assumption of the model is that there is a universal set of attributes $U = \{A_1, \ldots, A_k\}$ for the application being modeled, each attribute having a unique meaning. It is also assumed that every set of attributes $X \subseteq U$ has a basic relationship, that is, in the user's mind there is a unique semantic relationship amongst the attributes of X. The theory of the universal relation model was firmly established with the introduction of the *weak instance approach* [30].

Given a database schema $\mathbf{R} = \langle \mathbf{R_1}, \dots, \mathbf{R_n} \rangle$, each relation scheme R_i is a subset of U. Constants and variables are allowed in tuples. A *tableau* on a relation scheme $\mathbf{R}$ is a set of tuples on $\mathbf{R}$, whereas a *relation* on $\mathbf{R}$ is a set of total tuples (i.e., tuples without variables) on $\mathbf{R}$.

The underlying data structure of the UR model is the *representative instance*, which is suitable for storing all the data of the database in a single relation. The representative instance is a tableau over the universe U of attributes, defined for each database state $\mathbf{r}$ as follows. First, a tableau over U (called the *state tableau* for $\mathbf{r}$ and denoted by $T_\mathbf{r}$) is the union of all the relations in $\mathbf{r}$ extended to U by means of variables, initially different from each other. Then, a chase procedure is applied to $T_\mathbf{r}$ to satisfy the dependencies specified for the database.

Consider this database with the functional dependency *professor* $\rightarrow$ *department*:

professor	*course*
John	Algebra
Bob	Calculus

professor	*department*
John	Physics
Tom	Chemistry

The corresponding representative instance is

professor	*course*	*department*
John	Algebra	Physics
Bob	Calculus	v_1
John	v_2	Physics
Tom	v_3	Chemistry

Given a state $\mathbf{r}$ for a database scheme $\mathbf{R} = \langle \mathbf{R_1}, \dots, \mathbf{R_n} \rangle$, a relation u over the universe U is a *containing instance* for $\mathbf{r}$ if its projections on the relation schemes of $\mathbf{R}$ contain the corresponding relations of $\mathbf{r}$; formally, $\pi_{R_i}(u) \supseteq r_i$, for $i = 1, \dots, n$. Given a set of dependencies F, a relation w is a *weak instance* for $\mathbf{r}$ with respect to F if w is a containing instance for $\mathbf{r}$ and w satisfies F.

The database $\mathbf{r}$ is in general an incomplete description of a weak instance w. There are infinitely many weak instances for $\mathbf{r}$ that satisfy F (or a very large number if all attribute domains are finite). Thus, the only facts that can be deduced from the UR model, given the relations in the database **r** are those that hold in all weak instances. Note that weak instances may be obtained by replacing variables by constants of the appropriate domain in the representative instance.

The weak instance model was formalized in [49]. However, as shown in [5], the weak instance model has one drawback: it considers all the tuples for which incomplete information is available as existentially quantified with respect to the missing values. This fact is apparent from the way in which weak and representative instances are built, and especially, from the definition of the logical theories associated with them. In the example above, the usual definition of the weak instance model assumes that, for each professor, there is exactly one department and at least one course. For this reason, the values v_i stand for actual, unknown values. Therefore, it would be conceptually wrong to use this database to model an application in which professors do not necessarily teach courses.

An alternative definition of the weak instance model is presented in [5]. The main difference is that, in weak instances, inexistent null values are allowed together with constants from the domain. Thus, a weak instance for a state is an extended relation (i.e., a set of tuples with constants and inexistent values) that satisfies the constraints and contains the base relations in its projections. Two possible weak instances for the database above are

professor	course	department		professor	course	department
John	Algebra	Physics		John	Algebra	Physics
Bob	Calculus	Biology		Bob	Calculus	$\perp$
Tom	Calculus	Chemistry		Tom	$\perp$	Chemistry

The first one is a weak instance according to the classic definition, whereas the second is not, since it contains inexistent values. Since each weak instance represents a possible world compatible with the data in the database, with the extended definition, the possibility that Tom teaches a course is open. For this reason, under the extended definition, variables in the representative instance are no-information or open null values, depending on the functional dependencies of the database.

The alternative definition of the weak instance model can be formalized as follows [5]. A first-order language is defined with a predicate symbol for each nonempty subset of the universe U. A first-order theory with four kinds of axioms is associated with every database state $\mathbf{r} = \langle r_1, \ldots, r_n \rangle$.

(1) A set DB of atomic sentences describing the relations in the database: for every relation $r \in \mathbf{r}$ and every tuple $t \in r$, there is the sentence $R(t)$. In the database discussed above, there are four sentences: $PC(\text{John}, \text{Algebra})$, $PC(\text{Bob}, \text{Calculus})$, $PD(\text{John}, \text{Physics})$, and $PD(\text{Tom}, \text{Chemistry})$.

(2) A set CON of sentences stating that, for every tuple t satisfying a predicate X, for every subset Y of X, the subtuple $t[Y]$ satisfies the predicate associated with Y. In the example, there are 12 sentences:

$$\forall p \, \forall c \, \forall d \; PCD(p,c,d) \rightarrow PC(p,c) \qquad \forall p \, \forall c \; PC(p,c) \rightarrow P(p)$$
$$\forall p \, \forall c \, \forall d \; PCD(p,c,d) \rightarrow PD(p,d) \qquad \forall p \, \forall c \; PC(p,c) \rightarrow C(c)$$
$$\vdots \qquad\qquad\qquad\qquad\qquad \vdots$$

(3) A set DIS of sentences stating that all constants are distinct.

(4) A set DEP of first-order sentences representing the set F of dependencies. The functional dependency *professor* $\rightarrow$ *department* of the example above is represented by

$$\forall p \, \forall d_1 \, \forall d_2 \; PC(p,d_1) \wedge PC(p,d_2) \rightarrow d_1 = d_2,$$
$$\forall p \, \forall c \, \forall d \; PD(p,d) \wedge PC(p,c) \rightarrow PCD(p,c,d).$$

The first sentence enforces the dependencies with respect to nonnull values. The second sentence formalizes the requirement that if tuples t and t' take the same values on P and $t[D]$ is not null, then $t'[D]$ is not null either, and it is equal to $t[D]$.

The results in [5] showed that the main properties of the original weak instance model are preserved. Several approaches to updating weak instances are studied in [6].

9 NULL VALUES IN NESTED RELATIONAL DATABASES

In recent years there has been increasing interest in *nonfirst normal form* or *nested relations* in which attributes can take values which are sets, ordered lists, or relations.

Consider this example of a nested relation:

student	dept.	(course	(exam)*	(project)*)*
		course	(exam)*	(project)*
			exam	project
Iris	CS	Databases	mid final	1NF
		Programming	final	ADA
Noam	languages	French	mid	Cyrano
		German	mid	Faust
		English	final	Othello

In this relation each student is registered in one department and takes a set of courses. For each course there is a set of exams and a set of projects.

The nested relational model, in addition to the usual algebraic operators, has two restructuring operators: *nest* (ν) and *unnest* (μ). Intuitively, nesting transforms a nested relation into one that is more deeply nested, while unnesting flattens one level of a nested relation. The operator unnest* (μ^*) transforms a nested relation r^* into a flat relation r.

Since in the nested relational model, an attribute can be a relation as well (that is, a set of tuples), the domain of a complex attribute includes the empty set as a legal value. Suppose that in the nested relation of the example above we want to represent the tuple

David	EE	VLSI	mid final	∅

where the attribute (*project*)* for the course VLSI takes as value the empty set, meaning that there are no projects for the course. The empty set is in a sense a particular type of null value: indeed, unnesting a relation that contains an empty set introduces nulls into the resulting first normal form relation. For the tuple above, applying the operator μ^* causes no loss of information if explicit null values are allowed in the relation as follows:

student	dept.	course	exam	project
David	EE	VLSI	mid	⊥
David	EE	VLSI	final	⊥

Incorporating the empty set into nested relations has been a controversial issue, as it is not clear what the result of unnesting the empty set should be. Several authors state that unnesting the empty set produces "undefined value" and "unnatural value." In [1], when the empty set is unnested the resulting tuples are removed; however, such an approach is unsatisfactory since information is lost. Several researchers have assigned the *inexistent* interpretation of null values to the empty set [50, 1, 66, 24]. Others [65], in the context of the OWA, considered the semantics of the empty set to be the "no information" null.

The need for nulls is even more critical in a nested database than in a classical relational database. Since nested relations allows to represent multiple relationships in a single nested relation, we must also deal with the fact that one or more of those relationships may be unknown or inexistent at some time. Notice that similar considerations apply when considering the database under the universal relation model, which is discussed in Section 8.

To ascertain if an extended algebra for nested relations is reasonable, the notions of *faithfulness* and *preciseness* are used [47, 65]. An extended operator is *faithful* if it gives the same result on flat relations as the corresponding standard operator. For *preciseness*, let γ be a classical operator, $\bar{\gamma}$ be the operator for nested relations, and let α be another operator. Then $\bar{\gamma}$ is said to be a precise generalization of γ relative to α if one of the following conditions holds:

$$\alpha(\bar{\gamma}(r)) = \gamma(\alpha(r)) \text{ if } \gamma \text{ is an unary operator} \tag{3.2}$$

$$\alpha(r_1 \bar{\gamma} r_2) = \alpha(r_1)\gamma\alpha(r_2) \text{ if } \gamma \text{ is a binary operator} \tag{3.3}$$

If α is taken to be the μ^* operator, the above conditions say that unnesting* the result of $\bar{\gamma}$ yields the flat relation obtained by applying the classical operator γ to the argument relations previously flattened.

However, for some choices of α, not all relational operators have a precise generalization. In this case, it is considered a weaker notion of an *adequate* and *restricted* generalization, which captures $\gamma(\alpha(r))$ or $\alpha(r_1)\gamma\alpha(r_2)$ and as little extra as is possible.

Now consider the introduction of null values into the nested relations. As for classical relations, it is necessary to determine semantically the sets of possible worlds represented by a nested relation. For this reason a mapping REP^* has to be defined for associating with a nested relation containing nulls r^* the set of nested relations without nulls it represents.

When generalizing the algebra for nested relations with null values, there are two possible ways of establishing whether the operators are reasonable. The first one, which is used for example in [65], is equivalent to the strong correctness criterion for relational databases given in Section 3.1. It is stated by conditions (3.2)–(3.3) when α is taken to be the REP^* operator. As in the relational case, not all operators have a precise generalization relative to REP^* and the weaker notions of adequate and restricted are needed.

The second way of establishing if the operators are reasonable, which is used in Levene [41], is based on the definitions of the operators γ for flat relations with nulls. Therefore, taking α as the μ^* operator, and $\bar{\gamma}$ as the operator on nested relations with null values, (3.2)–(3.3) state that $\bar{\gamma}$ correctly extends the operator γ. Levene uses Zaniolo's operators for flat relations with null values [78].

The study of null values in nested relations has been based on the work of Zaniolo [78], which used existential, inexistent, and no information null values. However, Zaniolo considered unmarked nulls, and thus the equality relationship is modified so that two null values or a constant and a null value are not equated. This approach is not always adequate for representing incomplete information, especially in the presence of dependencies. Therefore, there is a need to extend the results of [65] and [41] for marked null values.

10 MAYBE TUPLES

One of the extensions of the relational model proposed by Codd [13, 14, 15] to manipulate existential null values was the *maybe tuples*. This approach was formalized by Biskup [10].

Maybe tuples represent information that is possibly true, such as "it is possible that Jean takes Calculus." To represent maybe tuples in a relational database, each relation must be composed of a *sure component* and a *maybe component*. Consider the relation *takes*

student	*course*
Pierre	Calculus
Marc	Algebra
Jean	Calculus

sure component { Pierre Calculus, Marc Algebra }
maybe component { Jean Calculus }

The third tuple is a maybe tuple: it represents an assertion that may or may not hold. Under the Closed World Assumption, relation *takes* represents the following set of possible worlds, where in each situation every tuple is certain.

$$M_1 = \{(\text{Pierre},\text{Calculus}),(\text{Marc},\text{Algebra})\}$$
$$M_2 = \{(\text{Pierre},\text{Calculus}),(\text{Marc},\text{Algebra}),(\text{Jean},\text{Calculus})\}$$

The relation is expressed in first-order logic as

$$\forall x \, \forall y \, takes(x,y) \rightarrow (x = \text{Pierre} \wedge y = \text{Calculus}) \vee$$
$$(x = \text{Marc} \wedge y = \text{Algebra}) \vee (x = \text{Jean} \wedge y = \text{Calculus}),$$
$$\forall x \, \forall y (x = \text{Pierre} \wedge y = \text{Calculus}) \vee$$
$$(x = \text{Marc} \wedge y = \text{Algebra}) \rightarrow takes(x,y).$$

Straightforward generalizations of relational operators were proposed by several researchers (e.g., [9, 10]). However, to our knowledge, no study was done on integrity constraint checking and updates for databases containing maybe information.

11 DISJUNCTIVE DATABASES

Multiple efforts have been made since the 1970s to manipulate disjunctive information, especially in recent years. We cover here disjunctive information in relational databases. The fields of disjunctive logic programming and disjunctive deductive databases are beyond the scope of this chapter. They are discussed in Chapter 4, and, for example, in [54, 20].

To introduce general disjunctive facts in the relations, the definition of tuple has to be generalized. Given a relation scheme $R(A_1, \ldots, A_n)$, tuples of the form $\mathbf{t} = \mathbf{t}_1 \vee \ldots \vee \mathbf{t}_m$, where each $\mathbf{t}_i \in \text{dom}(A_1) \times \ldots \times \text{dom}(A_n)$, are called *disjunctive tuples*. Classical tuples are then called *definite tuples*. An example of a disjunctive relation *takes* is given next.

(*student, course*)
(Anne,Calculus)
(Marc,Algebra)∨(Marc,Physics)
(Paul,Algebra)∨(Martha,Algebra)

The first tuple is a definite tuple, and the other two are disjunctive tuples.

Disjunctive information is closely related to maybe information. A first idea is to represent a disjunctive tuple such as (Marc, Algebra) ∨ (Marc, Physics) by introducing its literals (Marc,Algebra) and (Marc,Physics) as maybe tuples. However, this entails a loss of information. Indeed, from the disjunctive tuple, it can be inferred that Marc takes at least one course; such certain information is lost when representing the fact with two maybe tuples.

Maybe tuples can be produced from disjunctive tuples when the database evolves. Suppose that in the relation above it becomes known that Paul takes Algebra. If we replace (Paul, Algebra) ∨ (Martha, Algebra) by (Paul, Algebra), the information that Martha could take Algebra is lost. Therefore, (Martha, Algebra) must be introduced as a maybe tuple as shown in Figure 10. In addition, maybe information is also obtained from disjunctive information by applying relational operators.

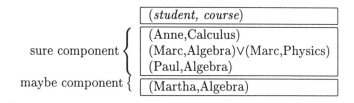

Figure 10   Disjunctive relation *takes*

Consider now the semantics of disjunctive relations, that is, their set of possible worlds. For the relation of Figure 10, if disjunctions are interpreted as inclusive, the tuple (Marc, Algebra) ∨ (Marc, Physics) represents three possible cases: Marc only takes Calculus, Marc only takes Physics, or Marc takes both courses. For the maybe component, either Martha takes Algebra or she does not. Therefore, under a closed world interpretation, the relation has six models.

A revised closure assumption is needed for disjunctive relations, to infer negative information, without having to store it explicitly. As is well known, the CWA is inconsistent with disjunctive information. For this reason, Minker [53] proposed the *Generalized Closed World Assumption* (GCWA). The semantic definition of the GCWA is that a ground fact can be assumed false if it appears in no minimal model.

However, it is not possible to represent maybe information if the GCWA is applied to the database. Furthermore, the GCWA interprets disjunctions as exclusive, not as inclusive [64]. As noted by Przymusinsky [56], every closure assumption based on minimal models interprets disjunctions as exclusive. Several extensions of the GCWA have appeared in the literature [75, 22, 23] but they are all based on minimal models.

Ross and Topor [64] defined the Disjunctive Database Rule (DDR). When applying this rule to disjunctive relations, all tuples not explicitly represented either as definite tuples, as literals of disjunctive tuples, or as maybe tuples are assumed false, and disjunctions are interpreted inclusively. Rajasekar, Lobo and Minker [57] defined the *Weak Generalized Closed World Assumption* (WGCWA), and they proved its equivalence with the DDR.

The WGCWA applied to the relation above can be represented with this first-order formula:

$$\forall x\ \forall y\ takes(x,y) \rightarrow (x = \text{Anne} \land y = \text{Calculus}) \lor$$
$$(x = \text{Marc} \land y = \text{Algebra}) \lor (x = \text{Marc} \land y = \text{Physics}) \lor$$
$$(x = \text{Paul} \land y = \text{Algebra}) \lor (x = \text{Martha} \land y = \text{Algebra}).$$

Consider now the representation of disjunctive relations in first-order theories. The disjunctive relation of Figure 10 is represented with the above formula, in addition to these two axioms:

$$\forall x\ \forall y\ (x = \text{Anne} \land y = \text{Calculus}) \rightarrow takes(x,y),$$
$$takes(\text{Marc}, \text{Algebra}) \lor takes(\text{Marc}, \text{Physics}).$$

The first formula indicates those tuples that are definite, i.e., the tuples surely belonging to the relation. The second formula represents the disjunctive fact.

Query evaluation in disjunctive relational databases was first addressed in [28]. This work defined an algorithm to compute all minimal answers to a query; however, the main disadvantage of their algorithm is its complexity.

Disjunctive relations are used in [77] for obtaining complete query evaluation in databases containing unknown null values. Although a generalization of the relational algebra to disjunctive relations is given, several of the results are incorrect. Further, using disjunctive information to obtain completeness in query evaluation with unknown values is impractical because of the complexity of the algorithms. Indeed, methods for manipulating existential values such as conditional relations are far more efficient than increasing the complexity of manipulating disjunctive databases with the addition of existential values.

Liu and Sunderraman [45, 46] also extended the relational algebra for disjunctive relations. They proposed a semantics for disjunctive relations different from ours in that it is based on minimal models. As discussed in [79], this implies that their semantics treat disjunctions as exclusive. Although they state that their interpretation of disjunction is inclusive, several of their results are correct only in the exclusive case.

However, they do not give a correct definition of the intersection and join operators: they are defined as a selection on the Cartesian product. This definition is totally impractical since computing in the general case the Cartesian product of two disjunctive relations R_1 and R_2 amounts to computing the product of each possible world of R_1 with each possible world of R_2, i.e., to computing $REP(R_1) \times REP(R_2)$ and to obtaining the disjunctive normal form of $REP(R_1) \times REP(R_2)$. In addition, they do not define the division operator.

We have argued [79] that it is not always adequate to interpret disjunctions as exclusive. Using our semantics, we generalize the relational operators for disjunctive relations, and prove their correctness. In particular, we give new correct definitions of intersection, join, and division operators.

Disjunctive relations can be generalized a step further by introducing negative clauses. Suppose we want to add to the relation of Figure 10 the disjunction

$$takes(\text{Paul}, \text{Physics}) \vee takes(\text{Helen}, \text{Physics}) \vee takes(\text{Lula}, \text{Physics})$$

and suppose in addition that these assertions hold:

Marc takes either Algebra or Physics but not both; and
if Paul takes Physics then Helen and Lula also take Physics.

To model such assertions, we must introduce disjunctive tuples containing negative literals. Therefore, disjunctive relations are extended with an extra *negative component*.

These assertions can be represented with the formulas

$$\neg takes(\text{Marc}, \text{Algebra}) \vee \neg takes(\text{Marc}, \text{Algebra}), \quad (3.4)$$

$$\neg takes(\text{Paul}, \text{Physics}) \vee takes(\text{Helen}, \text{Physics}), \quad (3.5)$$

$$\neg takes(\text{Paul}, \text{Physics}) \vee takes(\text{Lula}, \text{Physics}). \quad (3.6)$$

Therefore, the relation becomes

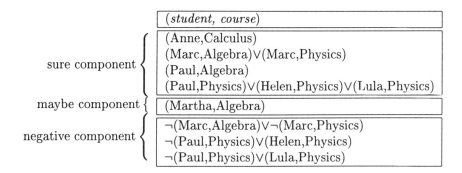

The semantics defined above can be extended to take into account negative tuples. These tuples act as integrity constraints excluding the models in which Marc takes both Algebra and Physics, and the models in which Paul takes Physics and Helen or Lula do not. Thus, the relation *takes* has 16 models, while the relation without the negative component has 42 models.

To represent in logic these generalized disjunctive relations, negative tuples must be introduced as clauses of the theory. For example, relation *takes* above can be represented with the axioms for the sure and maybe components as defined above, in addition to the formulas (3.4)–(3.6).

Introducing negative tuples in disjunctive relations raises the question of consistency. Consider the relation *takes*(*student, course*)

(*student, course*)
(Peter,Algebra)∨(Peter,Physics)
(Peter,Algebra)∨(Peter,Calculus)
(Peter,Physics)∨(Peter,Calculus)
¬(Peter,Algebra)∨¬(Peter,Physics)
¬(Peter,Algebra)∨¬(Peter,Calculus)
¬(Peter,Physics)∨¬(Peter,Calculus)

in which the negative component represents the constraint that Peter takes at most one course. This relation is inconsistent because it has no model.

The expressive power of disjunctive relations containing negative tuples is significant. Indeed, these relations allow one to model every set of ground formulas from first-order logic, since the formulas can be transformed into disjunctive normal form and treated as a disjunctive database. In particular, for each disjunction in the database, it can be chosen whether it is exclusive or inclusive, removing the restriction of an *a priori* choice between these two interpretations. Moreover, the relational operators can be generalized to treat the negative component of the relations without increasing their complexity. To our knowledge, no study has addressed the introduction of negative tuples in disjunctive relations.

12   PROBABILISTIC DATABASES

Two different types of probabilistic data can be introduced in a relation: probabilistic information about the association of values and probabilistic information about data values. These two kinds of informations are respectively represented with *type-1* and *type-2 probabilistic* relations.

Type-1 probabilistic relations generalize classical relations with a supplementary attribute $w_R(\mathbf{t})$ indicating the probability that tuple $\mathbf{t}$ belong to relation R. The probability attached to a tuple is supposed to be independent from that of other tuples. Figure 11 shows an example of a type-1 relation. This relation states, for example, that Martin surely takes Physics, and that the probability that he takes Biology is 0.9. Thus, the probability that he does not take Biology is 0.1. Under the CWA, every pair (student,course) not explicitly represented in the relation has probability 0.

student	course	w_R
Martin	Physics	1.0
Martin	Biology	0.9
John	Physics	0.6

Figure 11   A type-1 probabilistic relation *takes*.

Relation *takes* represents four different possible worlds, which are classical relations with an associated probability, computed as the product of the probabilities for the presence or absence of each tuple of relation *takes*. These possible worlds are

$M_1 = \{(\text{Martin,Physics}),(\text{Martin,Biology}),(\text{John,Physics})\}$ $\mathcal{P}(M_1) = 0.54$
$M_2 = \{(\text{Martin,Physics}),(\text{Martin,Biology})\}$ $\mathcal{P}(M_2) = 0.36$
$M_3 = \{(\text{Martin,Physics}),(\text{John,Physics})\}$ $\mathcal{P}(M_6) = 0.06$
$M_4 = \{(\text{Martin,Physics})\}$ $\mathcal{P}(M_8) = 0.04$

Note that the probabilities add up to 1.

Although type-1 relations enable us to represent uncertainties about the association of data values, their role to capture uncertainties in data values is limited. For this reason the notion of a probabilistic set is needed. A *probabilistic set* in a universe of discourse U is defined with a probability distribution $w_F : U \rightarrow [0, 1]$ satisfying $\sum_{u \in U} w_F(u) \leq 1$. A probabilistic set F is written as follows:

$$F = \{u_1/w(u_1), u_2/w(u_2), \ldots, u_n/w(u_n)\},$$

where $u_i \in U$, for $i = 1, \ldots, n$. It is always assumed that the values in a probabilistic set are mutually exclusive, i.e., an attribute represented by a probabilistic set can take only one value.

For example, if a course taken by John is represented by the probabilistic set Courses $= \{\text{Algebra}/0.5, \text{Calculus}/0.4\}$, then John is registered in Algebra with probability 0.5 and in Calculus with probability 0.4. Since the probabilities add up to 0.9, with probability 0.1 John is not registered in any courses.

Type-2 probabilistic relations have key attributes that are deterministic, as in classical relations. Thus, each tuple represents a known entity or relationship. The other attributes may be deterministic or stochastic. The latter are described with the help of probabilistic sets. Thus, the domain for a key attribute is a classical set, whereas the domain for a nonkey attribute is either a classical set or a set of probabilistic sets. An example of a type-2 probabilistic relation *takes* is shown in Figure 12.

The semantics of type-2 probabilistic relations can be expressed in terms of possible worlds as follows. In Figure 12, the first tuple represents three possibilities: John takes Algebra, John takes Calculus, or John takes no course. For the second tuple, since the probabilities of the course taken by Anne add up to 1.0, there are only two possibilities. Therefore, the relation has these six possible worlds.

student	course
John	Algebra/0.5
	Calculus/0.4
Anne	Physics/0.5
	Calculus/0.5

Figure 12 A type-2 probabilistic relation *takes*.

$$M_1 = \{(\text{John,Algebra}),(\text{Anne,Physics}))\} \quad \mathcal{P}(M_1) = 0.25$$
$$M_2 = \{(\text{John,Calculus}),(\text{Anne,Physics})\} \quad \mathcal{P}(M_2) = 0.20$$
$$M_3 = \{(\text{John},\bot),(\text{Anne,Physics})\} \quad \mathcal{P}(M_3) = 0.05$$
$$M_4 = \{(\text{John,Algebra}),(\text{Anne,Calculus})\} \quad \mathcal{P}(M_4) = 0.25$$
$$M_5 = \{(\text{John,Calculus}),(\text{Anne,Calculus})\} \quad \mathcal{P}(M_5) = 0.20$$
$$M_6 = \{(\text{John},\bot),(\text{Anne,Calculus})\} \quad \mathcal{P}(M_6) = 0.05$$

Note that we represent that John takes no course with the inexistent null value $\bot$.

To understand the differences between type-1 and type-2 relations, compare the first tuple of the relation in Figure 12 with this:

student	course	μ_R
John	Algebra	0.5
John	Calculus	0.4

Here, tuples are unrelated or independent, i.e., John takes Algebra with probability 0.5 and the probability that he does not take Algebra is 0.5, but this is unrelated to his probability of taking or not taking Calculus. In contradistinction, in Figure 12, John takes only one course among Algebra and Calculus.

Type-2 probabilistic relations are further generalized by allowing several attributes to have dependent probability distributions. Consider, for example, a relation representing the probability distribution of course grades:

course	marks
Algebra	0–14/0.7
	15–18/0.2
	19–20/0.1
Physics	0–18/0.7
	19–20/0.3
Calculus	19–20/1

The probability of propositions such as "student x takes course y and obtains grade z," can be obtained through a probabilistic join:

student	(course, grade)
John	(Algebra,0–14)/0.35
	(Algebra,15–18)/0.10
	(Algebra,19–20)/0.05
	(Calculus,19–20)/0.4
Anne	(Physics,0–18)/0.35
	(Physics,19–20)/0.15
	(Calculus,19–20)/0.5

For example, since Anne takes Physics with probability 0.5, she will obtain a grade 0–18 with probability 0.35 and 19–20 with probability 0.15.

The development of a formal logical system for reasoning about probability is recent. After the pioneering work by Nilsson [55], the main development in probabilistic logics was achieved by Fagin, Halpern, and Meggido [19, 18] and by Halpern [29].

To formalize probabilistic databases, we use one of Halpern's probabilistic logics. Given a first-order language for reasoning about a domain and a formula ϕ of this logic, probabilistic logic allows formulas of the form $w(\phi) \geq 0.5$, which can be interpreted as "the probability that ϕ is satisfied is greater than or equal to 0.5."

To distinguish between probabilities and objects of the domain, Fagin, Halpern and Meggido use a two-sorted logic, where a sort $\mathcal{O}$ describes objects of the domain and a sort $\mathcal{F}$ describes probabilities. In addition, to represent probabilistic sets, we introduce a supplementary sort $\mathcal{S}$ describing sets of objects. Variables of sorts $\mathcal{O}$, $\mathcal{S}$, and $\mathcal{F}$ are denoted respectively by x, x^s, and x^f.

Probabilistic databases are formalized with probabilistic theories. As in relational theories, each relation is associated with an object predicate for which there is a set of *extension axioms*. Also, probabilistic theories contain a non-empty set of simple types, modeling different domains for the variables.

For example, the type-1 relation *takes* of Figure 11 can be represented with these extension axioms:

$$\forall x \, \forall y \; takes(x,y) \rightarrow (x = \text{Martin} \wedge y = \text{Physics}) \vee$$
$$(x = \text{Martin} \wedge y = \text{Biology}) \vee (x = \text{John} \wedge y = \text{Physics}),$$
$$\forall x \, \forall y \; (x = \text{Martin} \wedge y = \text{Physics}) \rightarrow takes(x,y),$$
$$\forall x \, \forall y \, \forall z^f \; w(takes(x,y)) = z^f \wedge 0 < z^f < 1 \leftrightarrow$$
$$(x = \text{Martin} \wedge y = \text{Biology} \wedge z^f = 0.9) \vee$$
$$(x = \text{John} \wedge y = \text{Physics} \wedge z^f = 0.6).$$

The first extension axiom realizes the closure of the relation by stating all the tuples that belong to it. With this axiom we can deduce, for example, that Anne does not take Physics. The second extension axiom states the tuples that surely belong to the relation, i.e., the tuples that have probability 1.0. Finally, the third extension axiom specifies the tuples that belong to the relation with probability greater than 0 and less than 1.0.

Further, in probabilistic theories we need axioms for stating the independence of events. For example,

$$w(takes(\text{Martin}, \text{Biology}) \wedge takes(\text{John}, \text{Physics})) =$$
$$w(takes(\text{Martin}, \text{Biology})) \times w(takes(\text{John}, \text{Physics})),$$

states that the Martin taking Biology and John taking Physics are independent events. Still, other axioms could impose other conditions. For example,

$$w(takes(\text{Martin}, \text{Biology}) \leftrightarrow takes(\text{Anne}, \text{Biology})) = 0.9$$

states that, with 0.9 probability, Martin takes Biology iff Anne does.

Consider now the type-2 probabilistic relation given in Figure 12. First, the probabilities of the course taken by John are represented defining a probabilistic set ϵ_1:

$$\forall x \; x \in \epsilon_1 \rightarrow x = \text{Algebra} \vee x = \text{Calculus},$$
$$\forall x \, \forall z^f \; w(x \in \epsilon_1) = z^f \wedge 0 < z^f < 1 \leftrightarrow$$
$$(x = \text{Algebra} \wedge z^f = 0.2) \vee (x = \text{Calculus} \wedge z^f = 0.4),$$
$$\forall x \, \forall y \; x \in \epsilon_1 \wedge y \in \epsilon_1 \rightarrow x = y.$$

Notice that the last axiom represents that John takes only one course. The probabilistic set ϵ_2 representing the probabilities of the course taken by Anne is defined in similar way. Finally, relation *takes* is represented with this extension axioms:

$$\forall x \; \forall y \; takes(x, y) \rightarrow (x = \text{John} \land y \in \epsilon_1) \lor (x = \text{Anne} \land y \in \epsilon_2),$$
$$\forall x \; \forall y \; \forall z^f \; w(takes(x,y)) = z^f \land 0 < z^f < 1 \leftrightarrow$$
$$(x = \text{John} \land y \in \epsilon_1 \land z^f = w(y \in \epsilon_1)) \lor$$
$$(x = \text{Anne} \land y \in \epsilon_2 \land z^f = w(y \in \epsilon_2)).$$

The probabilistic approach for modeling uncertainty in relational databases has not been deeply studied so far. Preliminary models for probabilistic relational databases have been proposed in [21, 11]. The probabilistic database model defined in [7, 8] studies probabilistic relations similar to our type-2 probabilistic relations, although they considered a different semantics. We studied in [79, 81, 80] the manipulation of type-1 probabilistic relations from an algebraic point of view, extending the relational operators and proving their correctness. Also, type-1 probabilistic relations are formalized in a logical framework with probabilistic theories, and we give a sound and complete query evaluation algorithm for such theories. The corresponding studies for type-2 probabilistic relations suggest an open area of research.

REFERENCES

[1] S. Abiteboul and N. Bidoit. Non first normal form relations: An algebra allowing data restructuring. *Journal of Computer and System Sciences*, 33: 361–393, 1986.

[2] S. Abiteboul and G. Grahne. Update semantics for incomplete databases. In *Proceedings of the 11th International Conference on Very Large Databases*, pages 1–12, Stockholm, Sweden, 1985.

[3] S. Abiteboul, P. Kanellakis, and G. Grahne. On the representation and querying of sets of possible worlds. *Theoretical Computer Science*, 78(1): 159–187, Jan. 1991.

[4] ANSI/X3/SPARC. Study group on Data Base Management Systems Interim Report. *SIGMOD FDT Bulletin*, 7(2), 1975.

[5] P. Atzeni and M. C. De Bernardis. A new interpretation for null values in the weak instance model. *Journal of Computer and System Sciences*, 41(1): 25–43, 1990.

[6] P. Atzeni and R. Torlone. Approaches to updates over weak instances. In *Proceedings of the 2nd Symposium on Mathematical Fundamentals of Database Systems, Lecture Notes in Computer Science No. 364*. Springer-Verlag, Berlin, 1989.

[7] D. Barbará, H. García-Molina, and D. Porter. A probabilistic relational data model. In F. Bancilhon, C. Thanos, and D. Tsichritzis, editors, *Proceedings of EDBT 90, the International Conference on Extending Database Technology, Lecture Notes in Computer Science No. 416*, pages 60–74. Springer-Verlag, Berlin, 1990.

[8] D. Barbará, H. García-Molina, and D. Porter. The management of probabilistic data. *IEEE Transactions on Knowledge and Data Engineering*, 4(5): 487–502, 1992.

[9] J. Biskup. A formal approach to null values in database relations. In H. Gallaire, J. M., and J.-M. Nicolas, editors, *Advances in Data Base Theory*, volume 1, pages 299–341. Plenum Press, 1981.

[10] J. Biskup. A foundation of Codd's relational maybe-operations. *ACM Transactions on Database Systems*, 8(4): 608–636, Dec. 1983.

[11] R. Cavallo and M. Pittarelli. The theory of probabilistic databases. In *Proceedings 13th International Conference on Very Large Databases*, pages 71–81, Brighton, UK, 1987.

[12] E. F. Codd. Understanding relations (installment No. 7). *FDT Bulletin of ACM SIGMOD*, 7(3–4): 23–2, 1975.

[13] E. F. Codd. Extending the database relational model to capture more meaning. *ACM Transactions on Database Systems*, 4(4): 397–434, Dec. 1979.

[14] E. F. Codd. Missing information (applicable and inapplicable) in relational databases. *SIGMOD Record*, 15(4): 53–78, Dec. 1986.

[15] E. F. Codd. More commentary on missing information in (applicable and inapplicable) relational databases. *SIGMOD Record*, 16(1): 42–50, Mar. 1987.

[16] C. J. Date. *Relational Databases: Selected Writings*. Addison-Wesley, Reading, MA, 1986.

[17] R. Demolombe and L. Fariñas Del Cerro. An algebraic evaluation method for deduction in incomplete databases. *Journal of Logic Programming*, 5(3): 183–205, Sep. 1988.

[18] R. Fagin, J. Halpern, and N. Meggido. A logic for reasoning about probabilities. *Information and Computation*, 87: 78–128, 1990.

[19] R. Fagin and J. Y. Halpern. Uncertainty, belief and probability. In *Proceedings of the 1989 International Joint Conference on Artificial Intelligence*, pages 1375–1381, 1989.

[20] J. A. Fernandez and J. Minker. Disjunctive deductive databases. In *Proceedings of the International Conference on Logic Programming and Automated Reasoning*, pages 332–356, St. Petersburg, Russia, 1992.

[21] E. Gelenbe and G. Hebrail. A probability model of uncertainty in databases. In *Proceedings of the International Conference on Data Engineering*, pages 328–333, 1986.

[22] M. Gelfond and H. Przymusinska. Negation as failure: Careful closure procedure. *Artificial Intelligence*, 30: 273–287, 1986.

[23] M. Gelfond, H. Przymusinska, and T. C. Przymusinsky. The extended closed world assumption and its relationship to parallel circumscription. In *Proceedings of the 5th ACM SIGACT-SIGMOD Symposium on Principles of Database Systems*, pages 133–139, 1986.

[24] G. Gottlob and R. Zicari. Closed world databases opened through null values. In *Proceedings of the 14th International Conference on Very Large Databases*, pages 50–61, Los Angeles, CA, 1988.

[25] G. Grahne. Dependency satisfaction in databases with incomplete information. In *Proceedings of the 10th International Conference on Very Large Databases*, pages 37–45, Singapore, 1984.

[26] G. Grahne. *The Problem of Incomplete Information in Relational Databases*. Lecture Notes in Computer Science No. 554. Springer-Verlag, Berlin, 1991.

[27] J. Grant. Null values in a relational data base. *Information Processing Letters*, 6(5): 156–157, Oct. 1977.

[28] J. Grant and J. Minker. Answering queries in indefinite databases and the null value problem. In B. Buchanan and B. & E. Shortliffe, editors, *Advances in Computing Research*, volume 3, pages 247–267. JAI Press, 1986.

[29] J. Y. Halpern. An analysis of first–order logics of probability. *Artificial Intelligence*, 46(3): 311–350, June 1990.

[30] P. Honeyman. Testing satisfaction of functional dependencies. *Journal of the ACM*, 29(3): 668–667, 1982.

[31] G. Hulin. Relational databases with marked null values: A new approach. Manuscript M333, Philips Research Laboratory, Belgium, Jan. 1990.

[32] G. Hulin, A. Pirotte, D. Roelants, and M. Vauclair. Logic and databases. In A. Thayse, editor, *From Modal Logic to Deductive Databases*, pages 279–350. Wiley, 1989.

[33] T. Imieliński. Query processing in deductive databases with incomplete information. In *Proceedings of ACM-SIGMOD International Conference on Management of Data*, pages 268–280, Washington, DC, 1986.

[34] T. Imieliński. Incomplete information in logical databases. *IEEE Data Engineering*, 12(2): 29–40, 1989.

[35] T. Imieliński and W. Lipski, Jr. Incomplete information and dependencies in relational databases. In *Proceedings of ACM-SIGMOD International Conference on Management of Data*, pages 178–184, San Jose, CA, May 1983.

[36] T. Imieliński and W. Lipski, Jr. Incomplete information in relational databases. *Journal of the ACM*, 31(4): 761–791, Oct. 1984.

[37] T. Imielinski and K. Vadaparty. Complexity of query processing in databases with or-objects. In *Proceedings of the 8th ACM SIGACT-SIGMOD Symposium on Principles of Database Systems*, 1989.

[38] P. King and C. Small. Default databases and incomplete information. *The Computer Journal*, 34(3): 239–244, 1991.

[39] N. Lerat. Evaluation de requêtes sur une base de données logique satifaisant un ensemble de dépendances. In *2èmes Journées Bases de Données Avancées*, pages 233–243, Giens, Apr. 1986.

[40] N. Lerat. Query processing in incomplete logical databases. In G. Ausiello and P. Atzeni, editors, *Proceedings of the International Conference on Database Theory, Lecture Notes in Computer Science No. 243*, pages 261–277. Springer-Verlag, Berlin, 1986.

[41] M. Levene. *The Nested Universal Relation Database Model. Lecture Notes in Computer Science No. 595*. Springer-Verlag, Berlin, 1992.

[42] W. Lipski, Jr. On semantic issues connected with incomplete information databases. *ACM Transactions on Database Systems*, 4(3): 262–296, Sep. 1979.

[43] W. Lipski, Jr. On databases with incomplete information. *Journal of the ACM*, 28(1): 41–70, Jan. 1981.

[44] W. Lipski, Jr. On relational algebra with marked nulls. In *Proceedings of the 3rd ACM SIGACT-SIGMOD Symposium on Principles of Database Systems*, pages 201–203, Warterloo, Canada, 1984.

[45] K.-C. Liu and R. Sunderraman. Indefinite and maybe information in relational databases. *ACM Transactions on Database Systems*, 15(1): 1–39, Mar. 1990.

[46] K.-C. Liu and R. Sunderraman. On representing indefinite and maybe information in relational databases: a generalization. In *Proceedings of the 6th IEEE International Conference on Data Engineering*, pages 495–502, Los Angeles, CA, 1990.

[47] D. Maier. *The Theory of Relational Databases*. Pitman, London, 1983.

[48] D. Maier and J. Ullman. Maximal objects and the semantics of the universal relation databases. *ACM Transactions on Database Systems*, 8(1): 1–14, 1983.

[49] D. Maier, J. D. Ullman, and M. Vardi. On the foundations of the universal relation model. *ACM Transactions on Database Systems*, 9(2): 283–308, 1984.

[50] A. Makinouchi. A consideration on normal form of not-necessarily-normalized relation in the relational data model. In *Proceedings of the 3rd International Conference on Very Large Databases*, pages 447–453, Tokyo, Japan, 1977.

[51] Z. Michalewicz and L. J. Groves. Sets and uncertainty in relational databases. In B. Bouchon, L. Saitta, and R. R. Yager, editors, *Uncertainty and Intelligent Systems, IPMU'88, Lecture Notes in Computer Science No. 313*, pages 127–137, Springer-Verlag, Berlin, 1988.

[52] Z. Michalewicz and A. Yeo. Sets in relational databases. In *Proceedings of the Canadian Information Processing Society*, pages 237–245, Edmonton, Canada, 1987.

[53] J. Minker. On indefinite databases and the closed world assumption. In D. W. Loveland, editor, *Proceedings of the 6th Conference on Automated Deduction, Lecture Notes in Computer Science No. 138*, pages 292–308. Springer-Verlag, Berlin, 1982.

[54] J. Minker. Toward a foundation of disjunctive logic programming. In E. L. Lusk and R. A. Overbeek, editors, *Proceedings of the North American Logic Programming Conference*, pages 1215–1235. MIT Press, 1989.

[55] N.J. Nilsson. Probabilistic logic. *Artificial Intelligence*, 28(1): 71–87, 1986.

[56] T. C. Przymusinsky. On the declarative semantics of deductive databases and logic programs. In J. Minker, editor, *Foundations of Deductive Databases and Logic Programming*. Morgan Kaufmann, Los Altos, CA, 1988.

[57] A. Rajasekar, J. Lobo, and J. Minker. Weak generalized closed world assumption. *Journal of Automated Reasoning*, 5(3): 293–307, 1989.

[58] R. Reiter. On closed world data bases. In H. Gallaire and J. Minker, editors, *Logic and Databases*, pages 55–76. Plenum Press, 1978.

[59] R. Reiter. A logic for default reasoning. *Artificial Intelligence*, 13(1, 2): 81–132, 1980.

[60] R. Reiter. Towards a logical reconstruction of relational database theory. In M. Brodie, J. Mylopoulos, and J. Schmidt, editors, *On Conceptual Modelling*, pages 191–238. Springer-Verlag, Berlin, 1984.

[61] R. Reiter. A sound and sometimes complete query evaluation algorithm for relational databases with null values. *Journal of the ACM*, 33(2): 349–370, Apr. 1986.

[62] R. Reiter. What should a database know? In *Proceedings of the Symposium on Computational Logic*, pages 96–113, Brussels, Belgium, 1990.

[63] T. Risch, R. Reboh, P. Hart, and R. Duda. A functional approach to integrating database and expert systems. *Communications of the ACM*, 31(12): 1424–1437, Feb. 1988.

[64] K. Ross and R. Topor. Inferring negative information from disjunctive databases. *Journal of Automated Reasoning*, 4: 397–424, 1988.

[65] M. A. Roth, H. F. Korth, and A. Silberschatz. Null values in nested relational databases. *Acta Informatica*, 26: 615–642, 1989.

[66] H.-J. Schek and M. H. Scholl. The relational model with relation-valued attributes. *Information Systems*, 11(2): 137–147, 1986.

[67] J. F. Sowa. *Conceptual Structures*. Addison-Wesley, 1984.

[68] J. Ullman. The U.R. strikes back. In *Proceedings of the ACM Symposium on Principles of Database Systems*, pages 10–22, Los Angeles, CA, 1982.

[69] J. Ullman. Universal relation interfaces for database systems. In *Proceedings of the 9th IFIP World Computer Congress*, pages 243–252, Paris, France, 1983.

[70] Y. Vassiliou. Null values in data base management: A denotational approach. In P. A. Bernstein, editor, *Proceedings of ACM-SIGMOD International Conference on Management of Data*, pages 162–169, 1979.

[71] Y. Vassiliou. Functional dependencies and incomplete information. In *Proceedings of the 6th International Conference on Very Large Databases*, pages 260–269, Montreal, Canada, 1980.

[72] M. W. Wilkins. Updating logical databases containing null values. In Giorgio Ausiello and Paolo Atzeni, editors, *Proceedings of the International Conference on Database Theory, Lecture Notes in Computer Science No. 243*, pages 421–435. Springer-Verlag, Berlin, 1986.

[73] M. W. Wilkins. A framework for comparison of update semantics. In *Proceedings of the ACM Symposium on Principles of Database Systems*, pages 315–324, Austin, TX, 1988.

[74] M. W. Wilkins. A model-based approach to updating databases with incomplete information. *ACM Transactions on Database Systems*, 13(2): 167–196, 1988.

[75] A. Yahya and L. Henschen. Deduction in non-Horn databases. *Journal of Automated Reasoning*, 1: 141–160, 1985.

[76] A. Yeo. Sets in relational databases. Master's Thesis, Department of Computer Science, Victoria University, Wellington, New Zealand, 1987.

[77] L. Y. Yuan and D.-A. Chiang. A sound and complete query evaluation algorithm for relational databases with null values. In *Proceedings of ACM-SIGMOD International Conference on Management of Data*, pages 74–81, Chicago, IL, 1988.

[78] C. Zaniolo. Database relations with null values. *Journal of Computer and System Sciences*, 28: 142–166, 1984.

[79] E. Zimányi. *Incomplete and Uncertain Information in Relational Databases*. Ph.D. Dissertation, Université Libre de Bruxelles, Belgium, 1992.

[80] E. Zimányi. Probabilistic relational databases. Technical Report RR 92-02, INFODOC, Université Libre de Bruxelles, Belgium, Oct. 1992.

[81] E. Zimányi. Query evaluation in probabilistic databases. *Theoretical Computer Science*, 1996 (forthcoming).

4

UNCERTAINTY IN INTELLIGENT DATABASES
Robert Demolombe

ONERA/CERT
Toulouse, France

1 INTRODUCTION

By an *intelligent database* we mean a traditional relational database with additional functionalities to represent either (1) general rules, as in deductive databases, or (2) some kind of incomplete information, like marked null values or disjunctive facts, or (3) additional meta-information, like information validity, uncertainty factors, or some kind of modality.

We shall assume first that such a database can be represented by a first-order theory DB. This theory is intended to represent a part of the world, called W, that is formally represented by an interpretation of the same language used to represent the theory DB. Subsequently, we shall see that first-order theories are not enough to represent certain kinds of additional information.

The subject of uncertainty in intelligent databases is broad and covers many different approaches and interpretations. The following discussion distinguishes among several different kinds of uncertainty.

Incompleteness[1]

The first kind of uncertainty refers to a situation in which we know that $A \vee B$ holds, but we are uncertain which of the two (A or B) holds. For example, we may know that "John teaches Mathematics or Logic," represented by

---

[1]In this chapter the terms *incompleteness* and *validity* are used in the sense defined by Motro in [22, 23]. They do not refer to properties of a formal system about the links between syntax and semantics, as is the case in logic.

Teach(John, Mathematics)∨ *Teach(John, Logic)*, but not which of these courses he actually teaches. The uncertainty is about what is true in the world.

More generally, incompleteness is a form of uncertainty in the sense that if the theory *DB* has several distinct (up to an isomorphism) models $M_1, M_2, \ldots, M_n$, we are not certain whether W is (up to an isomorphism) M_1, or M_2, or $\ldots$ or M_n. This can be expressed by

$$W = M_1 \quad \text{or} \quad W = M_2 \quad \text{or} \quad \ldots \quad \text{or} \quad W = M_n.$$

Validity

Even if the information A, say *Teach(John, ComputerScience)*, is in *DB*, we are not always certain that A holds in the world. In this case uncertainty is about whether A is true or false in W. This type of uncertainty refers to information validity.

This notion of uncertainty is unrelated to the former one, and it can be defined whether or not *DB* is a complete theory. If we call $M(DB)$ the set of *DB* models, it expresses lack of knowledge about whether W is a model of *DB* or not. This can be expressed by

$$W \in M(DB) \quad \text{or} \quad W \notin M(DB).$$

Inconsistency

If inconsistent data like A and $\neg A$ can be derived from a database *DB*, in most cases it is because these data have been inserted by different agents that have different beliefs about the world. For example, in the context of distributed databases, if each database is considered an agent, it may happen that A is derivable from the database DB_1, and $\neg A$ is derivable from the database DB_2.

For example, DB_1 might have $\{Male(Jane), \forall x \ (Male(x) \wedge Female(x) \ \rightarrow)\}$, and therefore $\neg Female(Jane)$ is derivable from DB_1, whereas DB_2 might have *Female(Jane)*. In this case uncertainty is about the database that contains the correct information.

The mutual inconsistency of DB_1 and DB_2, that is, their lack of common model, can be expressed by

$$W \in M(DB_1) \quad \text{or} \quad W \in M(DB_2).$$

Vagueness

A predicate used to represent information in a database might not have a precise definition, with the result that we are not certain whether or not a given object satisfies the predicate. This uncertainty does not come from lack of information about the world; it comes from the vagueness of the language itself.

If we consider, for example, the predicate $Tall(x)$, and the person John, it may be uncertain whether John is a tall person. In this situation one can assign a value in $[0, 1]$, say 0.75, to a fact such as $Tall(John)$. The intuitive interpretation of such a value is somewhat controversial, as we can propose at least two interpretations.

The first interpretation is that the value represents a distance between the properties of a perfectly tall person, and John's properties. However, in many cases, the perfect properties are not explicitly defined, and there is no definition of a distance measure over these properties; consider, for example, the vague predicate "good restaurant."

Another interpretation is that each agent has his own definition of what is a tall person. That is, each agent can define the extension of the predicate $Tall(x)$, but these extensions are not the same for all the agents. In other words, each agent has a precise definition of the predicate, but there is no consensus about this definition. In this case the coefficient 0.75 can be interpreted as the percentage of agents that agree on the fact that $Tall(John)$ is true.

This chapter surveys only the first two kinds of uncertainty: *incompleteness* and *validity*. We shall try to reformulate in a logical framework the different formalisms presented by the different authors. At times, we shall change some aspects of the original works, for the sake of a simplified and uniform presentation. We hope that this will not significantly alter the intentions of the authors. Our survey is presented according to the kind of uncertainty; for each kind we consider how information is represented, techniques for reasoning with this information in order to compute answers to queries, the sources of the uncertainty, and the kind of constraints that can be defined to limit uncertainty. Our survey discusses representative works in these areas, and it does not attempt to be exhaustive.

2 INCOMPLETENESS

2.1 Representation of Uncertainty

We consider here how incompleteness is represented, starting from standard relational databases, and ending with more sophisticated types of intelligent databases.

Relational Databases

In standard relational databases, information is represented by a set of tables. Each table contains a set of facts of one predicate. The column names, called *attributes*, allow easy reference to the predicate arguments. As an example, consider the table *Teach*, below:

Teach	
Teacher	Course
John	Mathematics
Peter	Logic

The associated first-order theory DB_1 is quite simple. It contains as many ground facts as there are lines in the table:

$$DB_1 = \{\,Teach(John, Mathematics),\, Teach(Peter, Logic)\}$$

The language associated with this theory is formed with the predicate *Teach* (x, y), and the set of constants $\{John, Peter, Mathematics, Logic\}$.

An implicit assumption in relational databases is that each constant name refers to a distinct element. This assumption is represented in the theory by *Unique Name Axioms (UNA)*, as defined by Reiter [27]. In this section we shall assume that the theory associated with a database always contains unique name axioms, although, for simplicity, they will not be specified explicitly.

The standard definitions of the relational model also implicitly assume that the domain of each predicate argument is known. This assumption can be represented in logic by a *Domain Closure Axiom (DCA)* as defined by Reiter [27] (see next section). However, in practical situations the definition of these domains is problematic because the set of elements that may occur in a column may be unknown. For example, in the table *Teach*, we know the set of teachers that appear in that state of the table, but we might not know the set of teachers that may appear in future states. Therefore, in this chapter, the *DB* theories will not contain the DCA.

An interpretation of the language is defined by a domain D and a meaning function m, that assigns to each predicate a set of tuples formed with elements of the domain. We assume that to each constant in the language, i.e., to each constant that appears in a table, a distinct element of the domain is assigned, which has the same name as the constant. For example, the constant *John* is interpreted by an element of the domain also named *John*.

Examples of models of the theory *DB* include

- $M_1 = <D_1, m_1>$ where

$$\begin{aligned} D_1 &= \{John, Peter, Mathematics, Logic\} \\ m_1(Teach) &= \{<John, Mathematics>, <Peter, Logic>\} \end{aligned}$$

- $M_2 = <D_2, m_2>$ where

$$\begin{aligned} D_2 &= \{John, Peter, Mathematics, Logic\} \\ m_2(Teach) &= \{<John, Mathematics>, <Peter, Logic>, \\ &\quad <Peter, Mathematics>\} \end{aligned}$$

- $M_3 = <D_3, m_3>$ where

$$\begin{aligned} D_3 &= \{John, Peter, Mathematics, Logic, Programming\} \\ m_3(Teach) &= \{<John, Mathematics>, <Peter, Logic>, \\ &\quad <John, Programming>\} \end{aligned}$$

In this example, the representation W of the world might be, for example, M_3.

Except for the UNA, this logical representation of a relational database corresponds to what Reiter called the *Open World Assumption (OWA)*. This means that there is no assumption about the truth value of facts that are not present in a table. For example, $<Peter, Mathematics>$ is not in the table *Teach*, so we make no assumption about whether or not W contains *Teach(Peter, Mathematics)*.

Relational Databases with Null Values

Null values have been added to the relational model by Codd [4]. Null values can have many different meanings. The meaning we consider here corresponds to a value that exists but is unknown. All the occurrences of null values are represented by the symbol $-$, but it is not assumed that all these unknown values are identical. As an example, consider the following table:

Teach	
Teacher	Course
John	Mathematics
Peter	Logic
Paul	$-$
$-$	Programming

In the associated first-order theory null values are represented by existentially quantified variables:

$$DB_2 = \{Teach(John, Mathematics), Teach(Peter, Logic), \\ \exists x\ Teach(Paul, x), \exists y\ Teach(y, Programming)\}$$

Null values represent a special kind of uncertainty. For example, if we know the fact $\exists x\ Teach(Paul, x)$, then we know that x is an element in the extension of $Teach(Paul, x)$, but are unaware which element it is.

Relational Databases with Marked Null Values

Marked null values are a refinement of "simple" null values. Reiter [27] and Imielinski and Lipski [15] (and see also [32, 31, 1, 16]) introduced special symbols, called *variables*, to represent marked null values. The same variable may have several occurrences in a database, and each occurrence refers to the same value, though this value is unknown. An example is the following table:

Teach	
Teacher	Course
John	Mathematics
Paul	ω_1
ω_2	Logic
ω_2	Programming

Such tables are called V-tables in [15]. The associated first-order theory is

$$DB_3 = \{Teach(John, Mathematics), \exists x\, Teach(Paul, x),$$
$$\exists y\, (Teach(y, Logic) \land Teach(y, Programming))\}$$

In fact, marked null values are, in the logical framework, Skolem constants. The Skolemization of DB_3 leads to

$$DB_3' = \{Teach(John, Mathematics), Teach(Paul, \omega_1),$$
$$Teach(\omega_2, Logic), Teach(\omega_2, Programming)\}$$

From a practical point of view, the only difference between these Skolem constants and standard constants is that Skolem constants are not covered by unique name axioms like $\neg(\omega_1 = Mathematics)$ or $\neg(\omega_1 = \omega_2)$.

Nevertheless, Demolombe and Fariñas del Cerro [10] have extended the marked null values approach to represent constraints on marked null values of the form $\neg(\omega_1 = Mathematics)$. This extension allows to represent, for example, the information $\exists x\, (Teach(Paul, x) \land \neg(x = Mathematics))$.

Relational Databases with Conditional Tuples

Imielinski and Lipski [15] introduced tables with conditional tuples. To each table, an additional column is added that contains Boolean expressions formed only with the equality predicate. The intuitive interpretation is that a tuple corresponding to a line in the table satisfies the corresponding predicate if, for a given interpretation of the Skolem constants, the Boolean expression takes the value *true*. These tables are called *conditional tables*, or *C-tables* for short. For example,

Teach		
Teacher	Course	con
John	Mathematics	true
Paul	ω_1	$\neg(\omega_1 = Mathematics)$
ω_2	Logic	$(\omega_2 = Peter) \lor (\omega_2 = Paul)$

The information captured in this table, denoted *Rep(Teach)*, is a *set* of relations defined in the following way. For each interpretation of the marked null values ω_1 and ω_2, the conditions take the value *true* or *false*, and all the relations that contain the lines for which the condition is true are in *Rep(Teach)*.

Notice that, in the interpretation, when ω_2 is interpreted by *John*, the condition $(\omega_2 = Peter) \vee (\omega_2 = Paul)$ takes the value *false*. In this case, we notice that (1) relations in *Rep*(*Teach*) may or may not contain the tuple $< John, Logic >$, and (2) there are relations in *Rep*(*Teach*) that contain neither $< Peter, Logic >$ nor $< Paul, Logic >$; therefore, the last line in the table cannot be interpreted as *Teach*(*Peter*, *Logic*)$\vee$*Teach*(*Paul*, *Logic*). However, it is possible to represent this disjunctive information with the C-table *Teach'*,

Teach'		
Teacher	Course	con
ω_2	Logic	$\omega_2 = Peter$
Paul	Logic	$\neg(\omega_2 = Peter)$

Indeed, if ω_2 is interpreted by *Peter*, then relations in *Rep*(*Teach'*) must contain the tuple $< Peter, Logic >$, and if ω_2 is not interpreted by *Peter*, then corresponding relations in *Rep*(*Teach'*) must contain the tuple $< Paul, Logic >$. Thus, every relation in *Rep*(*Teach'*) must contain either $< Peter, Logic >$ or $< Paul, Logic >$. Of course, they may also contain both.

The first-order theory associated with the table *Teach* is

$$DB_4 = \{Teach(John, Mathematics),$$
$$\exists x \, (\neg(x = Mathematics) \to Teach(Paul, x)),$$
$$\exists y \, ((y = Peter) \vee (y = Paul) \to Teach(y, Logic))\}.$$

The Skolemized theory that corresponds to DB_4 is

$$DB_4' = \{Teach(John, Mathematics),$$
$$\neg(\omega_1 = Mathematics) \to Teach(Paul, \omega_1),$$
$$(\omega_2 = Peter) \vee (\omega_2 = Paul) \to Teach(\omega_2, Logic)\}.$$

And the first-order theory associated with *Teach'* is

$$DB_4' = \{\exists x \, ((x = Peter) \to Teach(x, Logic) \wedge$$
$$(\neg(x = Peter) \to Teach(Paul, Logic)))\}.$$

First-Order Deductive Databases

Relational databases have been extended to deductive databases containing rules, represented by first-order Horn clauses [13]. Although this extension increased the expressive power of relational databases, it had no significant implications on the aspect of uncertainty arising from incompleteness.

A more significant change, from the point of view of uncertainty, was the extension to *Disjunctive Deductive Databases (DDDB)*, as defined by Minker *et al* [17, 20, 21].

A DDDB is defined as a first-order theory with two kinds of information: ground facts, that are positive ground clauses, and rules, that are non-Horn clauses. As usual in deductive databases, these clauses do not contain function symbols. The following is an example of a DDDB.

$$DB_5 = \{Teach(John, Mathematics), Teach(Peter, Logic),$$
$$Permanent(John),$$
$$\forall x \forall y \ (Teach(x, y) \land Permanent(x) \to Professor(x) \lor$$
$$Assistant(x)),$$
$$\forall x \ (Professor(x) \to PhD(x)), \forall x \ (Assistant(x) \to PhD(x))\}$$

2.2 Reasoning with Uncertain Information

Reasoning techniques are needed to compute answers to queries. The answer to a query represented by the first-order formula $q(x)$, where x is the free variable in q, is defined as the set of constants in the language whose substitutions for x in $q(x)$ gives a logical consequence of the theory DB. More formally, the answer is defined by

$$\{a \mid DB \vdash q(a)\}.$$

This definition can easily be extended to queries that have more than one free variable.

In principle, any theorem proving technique may be used to compute answers. However, for efficiency, special techniques must be designed for the specific kind of theories encountered in intelligent databases. For this reason, researchers in relational databases proposed at first using the relational algebra to compute answers. Relational Algebra (RA) is very efficient because it computes all the tuples that satisfy a given formula at the same time. Nevertheless, problems arise with RA.

The first problem is mainly theoretical: not all first-order formulas can be translated to RA. For example, the query $\neg Teach(x, Mathematics)$ cannot be translated. In fact, only *domain independent* formulas can be translated to RA (see [7]). Fortunately, queries that cannot be translated have little practical interest.

Relational Databases

The second problem, a more serious one, is that in the context of the OWA, the relational algebra is not always sound. Consider, for example, the query

$$q_1(x) = \exists y \ (Teach(x, y) \wedge \neg Teach(x, Mathematics)).$$

Its translation to RA is

$$Q_1 = \pi_{Teacher}(Teach - \sigma_{Course=Mathematics}(Teach)).$$

Evaluating Q_1 in the first table $Teach$ of Section 2.1 results in $\{Peter\}$, while we do not have

$$DB_1 \vdash \exists y(Teach(Peter, y) \wedge \neg Teach(Peter, Mathematics))$$

because $\neg Teach(Peter, Mathematics))$ is not derivable from DB_1.

To get a sound and complete answer we should evaluate Q_1 in every model of DB_1 and retain in the answer only tuples that are in the intersection of all these evaluations. This, of course, is intractable in general.

In fact, a relational table can be considered a representative of all the models only for a certain kind of queries; intuitively, these are the queries whose predicate calculus expressions do not contain negations.[2] This corresponds, in RA, to queries that involve neither differences nor negative selections. For these queries, evaluation on the tables indeed gives the same result as the intersection of all the evaluations in all the models.

Relational Databases with Null Values

It was shown in [15] that RA operators can be extended to evaluate "correctly" certain kinds of queries on tables with null values.

To define a "correct" evaluation we must first define Ω-equivalence between the representations of two tables T and U, where Ω is a set of RA operators; for

---

[2]This characterization is somewhat informal, since a query like $\neg\neg Teach(x, Mathematics)$ can, of course, be evaluated correctly on a table.

example, projection and union. T and U are Ω-equivalent if, for RA expressions formed with operators in Ω, $Rep(T)$ and $Rep(U)$ are indiscernible, in the sense that the intersection of the evaluations of such expressions on relations in $Rep(T)$ or in $Rep(U)$ are identical. This equivalence relation is denoted by

$$Rep(T) \equiv_{\Omega} Rep(U)$$

It is possible to "correctly" evaluate a RA expression *exp* on a table T, if it is possible to define a corresponding expression *exp'*, with specific extended RA operators for this type of table, in such a way that the representation of the evaluation of *exp'* on T, $Rep(exp'(T))$, contains the same information, with respect to Ω-operators, as the result of the evaluation of *exp* on all the relations in $Rep(T)$; i.e.,[3]

$$Rep(exp'(T)) \equiv_{\Omega} exp(Rep(T))$$

Imielinski and Lipski showed that for tables with null values, queries formed with projection and selection can be "correctly" evaluated.

The projections in *exp'* are evaluated as usual. A selection of the form $\sigma_{sel}(T)$ is evaluated as follows: a tuple t in T is in the result *iff* $sel(t)$ is true for any substitution of all the nulls in $sel(t)$ by any element of the domain. Notice that this definition does not require a three-valued logic. In particular, if *sel* is a tautology such as $(Teacher = Peter) \vee \neg(Teacher = Peter)$, it will be evaluated to *true* even if, for a given tuple t, the value of *Teacher* is $-$. As an example, the query

$$q_2(x, y) = Teach(x, y) \wedge \neg(x = Peter)$$

whose translation to RA is

$$Q_2 = \sigma_{\neg(Teacher=Peter)}(Teach)$$

gives the following result when evaluated in the second relation *Teach* of Section 2.1:

John	Mathematics
Paul	$-$

It is important to notice that the result is also a table with null values. This means that in this formalism we can have incomplete information and incomplete answers as well. Indeed, the only standard answer to q_2; i.e., the only

---

[3]To avoid excessive notation, we denote by *exp*(*Rep*(*T*)) the *intersection* of the evaluation of *exp* on each relation in *Rep*(*T*).

tuple $< a, b >$ such that $DB_2 \vdash q_2(a, b)$, is $< John, Mathematics >$. The second tuple in the table is an incomplete answer in the sense that

$$DB_2 \vdash \exists y \ (q_2(Paul, y))$$

Relational Databases with Marked Null Values

The relational algebra was also extended to tables with marked null values [15]. The only extended operator whose definition differs from the standard is the selection. To define this extension, a valuation v of the set of marked null values ω_i is defined as an assignment of an element of the domain to each marked null value. Then, extended selection is defined by

$$\sigma_{sel}(T) = \{t \mid t \in T \wedge sel_*(t) = true\}$$

where $sel_*(t) = true$, if $sel(v(t)) = true$ for every valuation v, and $sel_*(t) = false$ otherwise.

It was shown in [15] that queries formed with projection, positive selection, union and Cartesian product, can be "correctly" evaluated. For example, the query

$$q_3(x) = Teach(x, Logic) \wedge Teach(x, Programming)$$

whose translation to RA is

$$Q_3 = \pi_1(\sigma_{2=Logic \wedge 4=Programming}(Teach \times Teach))$$

gives this result, when evaluated in the third relation $Teach$ of Section 2.1:

$$\boxed{\omega_2}$$

The standard answer is empty, because there is no constant a such that $DB_3 \vdash q_3(a)$. However, here again, the marked null value ω_2 in the result can be interpreted as an incomplete answer, since we have

$$DB_3 \vdash \exists x \ q_3(x).$$

Reiter showed in [28] that, in the context of marked null values, standard relational algebra is sound but not complete, in general, for the operators projections and union. Indeed, if we denote by $\|q(x)\|$ the answer to $q(x)$, defined by

$$\|q(x)\| = \{a \mid DB \vdash q(a)\}$$

then we have

$$\pi_x \|P(x,y)\| \subseteq \|\exists y \ P(x,y)\|$$
$$\|P(x,y)\| \cup \|Q(x,y)\| \subseteq \|P(x,y) \vee Q(x,y)\|$$

The equality of these expressions is not guaranteed.

Relational Databases with Conditional Tuples

The RA has also been extended in [15] to tables with conditional tuples. The extended projection is slightly different from the standard one. The difference comes from the fact that when tuples are projected on a set of attributes X, we have to keep trace of the conditions associated with these tuples:

$$\pi_X(T) = \{t[X \cup \{con\}] \mid t \in T\}$$

where $t[X \cup \{con\}]$ denotes the projection of the tuple t on the attributes $X \cup \{con\}$.

The selection is also different from the standard one. The idea is to preserve all the tuples in the result of the selection, and to add, for each tuple, the selection condition to the previous condition. More formally, a selection is defined by

$$\sigma_{sel}(T) = \{\sigma_{sel}(t) \mid t \in T\}$$

where $\sigma_{sel}(t)$ is defined by $\sigma_{sel}(t)[X] = t[X]$, where X is the set of attributes in T except con, and $\sigma_{sel}(t)[con] = t[con] \wedge sel(t)$.

The extended Cartesian product is modified in a similar way. For each tuple in the result the condition is the conjunction of the conditions in the operands:

$$T \times U = \{t[X - \{con\}] \times u[Y - \{con'\}] \times con \wedge con' \mid t \in T \wedge u \in U\}$$

where X (respectively, Y) is the set ot attributes in T (respectively, U), and con (respectively, con') is the attribute of T (respectively, U) that contains the conditions.

The union too must be slightly modified to remove duplicated tuples.

With these RA extensions it is possible to "correctly" evaluate queries formed with projection, selection, union, and Cartesian product. For example, the query

$$q_4(x,y) = Teach(x,y) \wedge x = Paul$$

whose translation to RA is

$$Q_4 = \sigma_{Teacher=Paul}(Teach)$$

gives the following result when evaluated in the fourth table *Teach* of Section 2.1:

John	Mathematics	$true \wedge (John = Paul)$
Paul	ω_1	$\neg(\omega_1 = Mathematics) \wedge (Paul = Paul)$
ω_2	Logic	$(\omega_2 = Peter) \vee \omega_2 = Paul) \wedge (\omega_2 = Paul)$

The condition in the first line, due to the unique name axiom $\neg(John = Paul)$, is equivalent to *false*. The condition in the second line is equivalent to $\neg(\omega_1 = Mathematics)$, and the condition in the third line is equivalent to $\omega_2 = Paul$, because, due to the UNA, $(\omega_2 = Peter) \wedge (\omega_2 = Paul)$ is equivalent to *false*. Hence, a simplified representation of the result is

Paul	ω_1	$\neg(\omega_1 = Mathematics)$
ω_2	Logic	$\omega_2 = Paul$

The meaning of the second line in the result is that when ω_2 is interpreted as *Paul*, then *Teach(Paul, Logic)* is true. In other words, it is possible that Paul teaches Logic. The logical interpretation of the two lines in this incomplete answer is

$$DB_4 \vdash \exists y \, (\neg(y = Mathematics) \to q_4(Paul, y))$$
$$DB_4 \vdash \exists x \, (x = Paul \to q_4(x, Logic))$$

First-Order Deductive Databases

Techniques to compute answers efficiently have been defined for deductive databases on the basis of the definition of *Least Fixpoint (LFP)* operators. These operators compute all the ground clauses that can be inferred in one step from a set of rules and a set of ground clauses. The inference rule is a sort of hyper-resolution that allows one to infer a ground clause from a rule instance and a set of ground clauses.

Minker and Rajasekar have defined in [21] a LFP operator that computes sets of positive ground clauses. Consider the disjunctive deductive database DB_5

at the end of Section 2.1. In the first step, from

$$Teach(John, Mathematics) \wedge Permanent(John) \rightarrow$$
$$Professor(John) \vee Assistant(John)$$
$$Teach(John, Mathematics)$$
$$Permanent(John)$$

we infer

$$Professor(John) \vee Assistant(John)$$

In the second step, from

$$Professor(John) \rightarrow PhD(John)$$
$$Assistant(John) \rightarrow PhD(John)$$
$$Professor(John) \vee Assistant(John)$$

we infer

$$PhD(John) \vee Assistant(John)$$
$$PhD(John) \vee Professor(John)$$

And, in the third step, from

$$Professor(John) \rightarrow PhD(John)$$
$$PhD(John) \vee Professor(John)$$

we infer

$$PhD(John)$$

Hence, this LFP operator can be used to compute, for example, the answer to the query

$$q_5(x) = PhD(x).$$

Indeed, the only answer is

$$DB_5 \vdash PhD(John),$$

and it corresponds to what is computed by the LFP operator.

This LFP operator was then improved to concentrate on the derivation of consequences that are relevant to the query. Demolombe [5] defined a LFP operator that simulates the combination of backward chaining and forward chaining techniques for DDDBs.

In this context of disjunctive deductive databases, incomplete answers were defined in [6], where they are called *conditional answers*. The conditional answer to a query $q(x)$ is a set of ground formulas of the form $cond(a, b) \rightarrow q(a)$, where $cond(a, b)$ represents the *additional* information necessary to derive the answer $q(a)$. A general definition of conditional answers is

$$\{cond(a, b) \rightarrow q(a) \mid DB \vdash cond(a, b) \rightarrow q(a)\}.$$

To remove trivial conditional answers like $q(a) \rightarrow q(a)$, or inconsistent conditional answers where $cond(a, b)$ is inconsistent with DB, two additional conditions are imposed on conditional answers:

1. $cond(a, b) \rightarrow q(a)$ is not a tautology.

2. There is no DB consequence that strictly subsumes $cond(a, b) \rightarrow q(a)$.

For example, $Permanent(Peter) \rightarrow PhD(Peter)$ is a conditional answer to the query $q_5(x)$. Indeed, we have

$$DB_5 \vdash Permanent(Peter) \rightarrow PhD(Peter)$$
$$DB_5 \nvdash PhD(Peter)$$
$$DB_5 \nvdash \neg Permanent(Peter)$$

If we present the query

$$q_6(x) = Professor(x)$$

to the database DB_5, we get the conditional answer

$$DB_5 \vdash \neg Assistant(John) \rightarrow q_6(John)$$
$$DB_5 \vdash Permanent(Peter) \wedge \neg Assistant(Peter) \rightarrow q_6(Peter)$$

It is worth noting that in the derivation of conditional answers, negation has its standard meaning, and is not interpreted by default. No assumption is made during the derivation of answers. The idea of conditional answers is to allow the user to assume that, for example, John is not an assistant, or that Peter has a permanent position but is not an assistant. The role of the derivation technique is only to determine the weakest assumption the user has to make to guarantee that a given object is in the standard answer.

The technique for computing conditional answers is based on a specific inference rule described in [11]. The general idea is to represent the information in clausal form, and to infer consequences, with a variant of the resolution principle, that preserve $q(x)$ or instances of $q(x)$. So, if we start from the clauses in the database that contain $q(x)$ or instances of $q(x)$, of the form $q(x) \lor c(x)$, we resolve these clauses with literals in the part $c(x)$, in order to find the resolvents such that the part $c(x)$ is minimal with regard to subsumption. These last clauses contain the least incomplete information we can derive about $q(x)$ or instances of $q(x)$.

2.3   Sources of Incompleteness

One source of incompleteness is total lack of information. For example, we might have no information about the fact *Teach(Paul, Logic)*.

Another source of incompleteness is having only partial information. In most cases, this partial information is a consequence of observed atomic facts, and has the form of existentially quantified variables, or of disjunctions. For example, we may know the fact *Professor(John)*, and the rule $\forall x$ (*Professor*$(x) \rightarrow \exists y$ *Teach*(x, y)), and thereby infer the partial information $\exists y$ *Teach(John, y)*. This rule might not be represented in the database, and a user might add $\exists y$ *Teach(John, y)* manually to the database.

Disjunctive partial information too might be a consequence of direct observations and rules. For example, from the observed facts *Teach(Peter, Logic)* and *Permanent(Peter)*, and the rule $\forall x \forall y$ (*Teach*$(x, y) \land$ *Permanent*$(x) \rightarrow$ *Professor*$(x) \lor$ *Assistant*(x)), we infer *Professor(Peter)* $\lor$ *Assistant(Peter)*.

In the case of quantitative information, like the weight of a person, the measured value might be obtained from scales that are known to have accuracy within 1%. Hence, when the weight indicated is 73kg, we infer that the true value is between 72 and 74. As another example, a measured radar signal, after complex numerical treatment, may lead us to conclude that the aircraft is either F16 or Mirage2000.

Partial information may be richer than a simple disjunction. In the previous example, we may know that the possibility that the aircraft is F16 is 0.9, and the possibility that it is Mirage2000 is 0.85.

2.4   Uncertainty Constraints

When incompleteness is judged not to be acceptable for particular types of information, a formalism is needed to express constraints that exclude it from the database.

For example, if salaries are represented in the database DB_5, one may want to require that for each teacher in the database, a salary is included in the database as well. A rule of the form

$$\forall x \forall y \ (Teach(x, y) \rightarrow \exists z \ Salary(x, z))$$

is not the correct expression of this constraint. This rule denotes that for each teacher a salary value exists (in the world), but it does not indicate that this value is included in DB. We need to express that for each x that DB knows to be a teacher, DB knows the corresponding salary z, as well.

Reiter [30] introduced an epistemic modality to express this very kind of constraint. This modality is called B because, in general, a database is a collection of beliefs, not necessarily of facts. Using this modality, the constraint in the example becomes

$$\forall x \forall y \ (B(Teach(x, y)) \rightarrow \exists z \ B(Salary(x, z)))$$

This epistemic modality distinguishes between $B(\exists x \ Salary(John, x))$ that asserts that it is believed (by the database) that John has (in the world) a salary, and $\exists x \ B(Salary(John, x))$, that asserts that there exists a value x that is believed (by the database) to be John's salary.

This modality can also be used to express the constraint that for each teacher known by the database to have a permanent position, the database knows whether he is a professor or an assistant:

$$\forall x \ (B(Teacher(x, y) \wedge Permanent(x)) \rightarrow B(Professor(x)) \vee B(Assistant(x)))$$

A constraint of this form is satisfied if in each model of DB, in the logic of this modality, the constraint is true.[4]

---

[4]The epistemic logic KFOPCE used by Reiter for B, and defined by Levesque, is not described here.

3 VALIDITY

3.1 Representation of Uncertainty

The information in the database *DB* is not necessarily a correct description of the world. Yet, we may have meta-information that tells us which parts of *DB* are guaranteed to be valid descriptions.

Using Metarelations to Store Validity Views

A first method to represent this meta-information was designed by Motro [23].[5] In this method, the valid information is characterized in terms of relational database *view definitions*, that are first-order formulas, and in terms of sets of tuples that satisfy certain conditions.

These conditions are expressed with tuples in *metarelations*, which mirror the relations of the database. For each database relation R, the corresponding metarelation will be denoted $M.R$. The tuples in $M.R$ may contain variables or constants, and, roughly speaking, all the tuples in R that are instances of tuples in $M.R$ are guaranteed to be valid.

As an example, consider a database with relations *Nationality(Citizen, Country)*, and *Born(Person, Place, Date)*, and assume that the valid parts of this database are characterized in these four views:

1. $V_1(x, x_1) = \exists v \ (Nationality(x, x_1) \wedge Born(x, x_1, v) \wedge x_1 = China))$

2. $V_2(y, x_2) = Nationality(y, x_2) \wedge x_2 = France$

3. $V_3(u, x_3) = Nationality(u, x_3) \wedge x_3 = USA$

4. $V_4(z, x_4, t) = Born(z, x_4, t) \wedge x_4 = France$

V_1 expresses that for people born in China and whose nationality is also Chinese, the name and the nationality (and the place of birth) are guaranteed to be valid. Note that, for the same individuals, the date of birth is not guaranteed to be valid. V_2 and V_3 express that the names and nationalities are valid for persons

---

[5]This method was designed by Motro for representing meta-information about both completeness and validity. Due to space limitations, we only cover here its application to validity. We note that Motro now prefers the term *soundness* for validity; see Chapter 2.

of French or American nationality. V_4 expresses that for people born in France, the name, place of birth, and date of birth are valid.

In general, views are conjunctive formulas, possibly with existential quantifiers, without negation except for selection predicates. Selection predicates are conjunctions of comparisons, such as equality, greater than, and so on. It is the values of the free variables (the subject of a view) that are guaranteed to be valid.

These view definitions are stored as *metatuples* in the metarelations. First, we assure that the variables used in the entire set of views are named differently. Then, each atomic formula of every view definition (other than comparison predicates) is stored as a metarelation tuple. In these tuples, free variables are suffixed by a $*$. For example, x, in view V_1, is starred, while v is not. Intuitively, a starred variable indicates a valid value. Finally, atomic formulas formed with the equality predicate, i.e., $x = a$ or $x = y$, are stored by substituting x by a or by y throughout the metadatabase. Atomic formulas formed with comparison predicates other than equality (e.g., $x > a$) are stored in an *ad hoc* metarelation called *Comparison*. For simplicity, we assume only equality predicates, and therefore ignore this metarelation.

The metadatabase for this example is

M.Nationality	
Citizen	Country
$x*$	China$*$
$y*$	France$*$
$u*$	USA$*$

M.Born		
Person	Place	Date
$x*$	China$*$	v
$z*$	France$*$	$t*$

A possible instance of this database is

Nationality	
Citizen	Country
Lee	China
Yang	China
Pierre	France

Born		
Person	Place	Date
Paul	USA	1955
Yang	China	1920
Pierre	France	1968

According to the metadatabase, Pierre's date of birth is valid, whereas Yang's date of birth is not guaranteed to be valid. Yang's nationality is guaranteed to be valid, whereas Lee's nationality is not, because while the database includes a *Nationality* tuple for Lee it does not include a *Born* tuple for him, which is necessary to express the validity of his nationality. This latter example shows that to determine if a value is valid, it is not enough to consider the corresponding metarelation; the entire metadatabase may need to be considered.

Using Epsitemic Logic to Define Reliable Information

In another approach, presented by Demolombe and Jones [9], information validity depends on the type of information, and on the agent who stored the information in the database. The word agent should be understood in its broad sense: it may refer to a particular user, or a category of users, or, in the context of distributed databases, a particular database.

The formalization of information validity takes inspiration from signaling act theory. It is expressed in the framework of epistemic logic and logic of actions, and it covers databases that are sets of propositional calculus sentences.

A database is considered a communicative tool between agents that store information in the database, and agents that read information from it. The formalization presented in [9] allows complex situations in which the representation is not necessarily explicit sentences but possibly any kind of encoded messages. The agents who interpret messages can also be represented explicitly. These agents are not necessarily reliable but are assumed to be sincere.

The meta-information about validity defines the agents who are reliable when they assert; i.e., when they store sentences in the database. An informal example of such meta-information is "Agent Shu is reliable when he stores the fact *Nationality(Yang, China)*." The fact *Nationality(Yang, China)* is not necessarily present in the database, but, if present, is guaranteed to be valid. In a simplified version of the formalism presented in [9] this meta-information is expressed thusly

$$In.DB(Shu, Nationality(Yang, China)) \rightarrow Nationality(Yang, China)$$

meaning that if the message *Nationality(Yang, China)* is inserted by Shu, then *Nationality(Yang, China)* is valid. This formula is abbreviated

$$In.MDB(Shu, Nationality(Yang, China))$$

An extension of this formalism to First-Order Logic (FOL) allows meta-information like

$$\forall x \ (In.DB(Shu, Nationality(x, China)) \rightarrow Nationality(x, China))$$

abbreviated in

$$In.MDB(Shu, Nationality(x, China))$$

And, in general,

$$In.MDB(agt, View(x)) \overset{def}{=} \forall x (In.DB(agt, View(x)) \rightarrow View(x))$$

where $View(x)$ is any first-order formula. For a particular $View(a)$, the meaning of $In.DB(agt, View(a))$ is that $View(a)$ was stored by agent agt; i.e., all the facts of $View(a)$ were inserted in one transaction activated by agent agt.

3.2   Reasoning with Uncertain Information

Deriving Valid Answers Algebraically

Motro defined a method for reasoning about the views that define the valid information. This method extends the relational algebra in a relatively simple and elegant way, to compute the metatuples that define the tuples in an answer that are guaranteed to be valid.

Assume a RA query (involving projection, selection and Cartesian product) is expressed by the RA expression exp, and let $exp(DB)$ denote its answer. Denote exp' the corresponding expression in the extended RA. Let $meta$ denote a mapping that assigns each relation R its metarelation counterpart $M.R$. Then $meta(exp(DB))$ denotes the metatuples that characterize the valid tuples in the answer $exp(DB)$. The latter metarelation can be computed by evaluating exp' in the metadatabase $meta(DB)$; i.e., $exp'(meta(DB))$. In formal terms, $meta$ is a morphism for the above-mentioned operators:

$$meta(exp(DB)) = exp'(meta(DB))$$

The three RA operators are extended as follows:[6]

1. $M.R \times M.S = \{< r, s >| (r \in M.R) \wedge s(\in M.S)\}$

2. $\pi_{X-A} = \{t[X-A] \mid (t \in M.R) \wedge ((t[A] = v*) \vee (t[A] = v)) \wedge (v \text{ unconstrained})\}$
   where X is the set of attributes of $M.R$, A is the attribute of $M.R$ being removed, v is a variable symbol, and "v unconstrained" means that v does not occur elsewhere in the metadatabase.

---

[6]These definitions are slightly different of the definitions given by Motro, but they are compatible if we consider only the equality comparison predicate.

3. $\sigma_{A=a}(M.R) = \{t.s \mid (t \in M.R) \wedge (t[A]$ is starred$) \wedge (t[A]$ is unifiable with $a)\}$
   where s is the unifier of $t[A]$ and a.
   $\sigma_{A=B}(M.R) = \{t.s \mid (t \in M.R) \wedge (t[A]$ is starred $) \wedge (t[B]$ is starred$)$
   $\qquad\qquad\qquad \wedge (t[A]$ is unifiable with $t[B])\}$
   where s is the unifier of $t[A]$ and $t[B]$.

As an example, consider the RA query $Q_7 = \sigma_{Place=China}(Born)$. Its FOL representation is

$$q_7(x, y, z) = Born(x, y, z) \wedge (y = China)$$

When evaluated in the metadatabase described earlier its meta-answer is

$x*$	$China*$	v

This single tuple meta-answer characterizes the tuples in the answer that are guaranteed to be valid. The metatuple indicates that the name and place of birth (in this case, China) are guaranteed to be valid; note that the date of birth is not guaranteed to be valid. It is worth noting that this characterization is independent of the content of the database.

As another example, consider the RA query $Q_8 = \sigma_{Date=1920}(Born)$. Its FOL representation is

$$q_8(x, y, z) = Born(x, y, z) \wedge z = 1920$$

Its meta-answer is

$z*$	$France*$	$t*$

The tuple $< x*, China*, v >$ is not in the meta-answer, because the date of birth is not guaranteed to be valid for people born in China. Thus, the tuple $< Yang, China, 1920 >$ is in the answer, yet without any guarantee of its validity.

As a third example, consider the RA query $Q_9 = \pi_{Country}(Nationality)$. Its FOL representation is

$$q_9(x, y) = \exists x\ Nationality(x, y)$$

Its meta-answer is

France*
USA*

The tuple $< China* >$ is not in the result, because the variable x is constrained by conditions in $M.Born$. If $< China* >$ were in the result, it would imply that if the value $China$ appears in an answer then this value is valid. We can see that this is not necessarily the case, because, for example, for Lee, the value of the attribute $Country$ is not guaranteed to be valid.

Consider now the RA query $Q_{10} = \pi_{Citizen,Country,Person,Place}(\sigma_{Citizen=Person}((\sigma_{Country=USA}(Nationality)) \times Born))$. Its FOL representation is

$$q_{10}(x, y, z) = \exists u \, (Nationality(x, y) \land y = USA \land Born(z, t, u))$$

The result of $\sigma_{Nation=USA}(Nationality)$ is

u*	USA*

The result of $\sigma_{Country=USA}(Nationality)) \times Born)$ is:

u*	USA*	x*	China*	v
u*	USA*	z*	France*	t*

The result of $Q_{10} = \sigma_{Citizen=Person}((\sigma_{Nation=USA}(Nationality)) \times Born)$ is

u*	USA*	u*	China*	v
u*	USA*	u*	France*	t*

And the final result is

u*	USA*	u*	China*
u*	USA*	u*	France*

Notice that if the projection: $\pi_{Citizen,Country,Place}(M.R)$ is now applied to this final result, the result will be empty. Because both variables in the column $Person$ are constrained, neither tuples survives the projection.

It is interesting to notice that the method designed by Motro cannot work for queries with the union operator. Indeed, *meta* is not a morphism for the union. Consider, for example, the RA query $Q_{11} = Nationality \cup (\pi_{Person,Place}(Born))$. Evaluating the union in the metadatabase as usual yields

$x*$	$China*$
$y*$	$France*$
$u*$	$USA*$

Whereas the answer obtained from the database itself is

Lee	China
Yang	China
Pierre	France
Paul	USA

According to this answer, and the metatuple $< u*, USA* >$, we should be *guaranteed* that Paul has American nationality or was born in the USA, which is not the case. The only information about Paul in the database is that he was born in the USA, but no tuple in the metarelation *Born* guarantees that this information is indeed valid. Later we shall explain why this method does not work for the union.

Deriving Safe Answers Logically

In the method defined by Demolombe and Jones the meta-information is represented by sentences of the form $In.MDB(agt,f)$, whose meaning is[7]

$$In.MDB(agt,f) \stackrel{def}{=} In.DB(agt,f) \rightarrow f$$

The information stored in the database, represented by sentences of the form $In.DB(agt,f)$, is considered a set of database beliefs. This interpretation is expressed formally in the axiom schema

$$In.DB(agt,f) \rightarrow B(f)$$

where the epistemic modality is assigned the standard semantics defined in the logic KD.

---

[7]In the definition given in [9], the sentence $In.DB(agt,f) \rightarrow f$ is in the scope of a modal operator. This prevents paradoxes due to material implication.

If we denote mdb and db the set of sentences of the form $In.MDB(agt, f)$, and $In.DB(agt, f)$, respectively, then the answer to a standard query $q(x)$ is

$$\{a \mid db \vdash B(q(a))\}$$

whereas the answer to a safety query $q(x)$ is

$$\{a \mid mdb \cup db \vdash q(a)\}$$

A *safety query* retrieves the values a in the standard answer that are guaranteed to be valid. Notice that the answer to the safety query is an explicit set of elements, not formulas (views), as in Motro's approach.[8]

Consider, for example, the metadatabase mdb

$$In.MDB(agt_1, \forall x\ (Professor(x) \to PhD(x)))$$
$$In.MDB(agt_2, Professor(x))$$

and the database db

$$In.DB(agt_1, \forall x\ (Professor(x) \to PhD(x)))$$
$$In.DB(agt_1, \forall x\ (Assistant(x) \to PhD(x)))$$
$$In.DB(agt_2, Professor(John))$$
$$In.DB(agt_2, Assistant(Peter))$$

From the mdb we can infer

$$\forall x; (Professor(x) \to PhD(x))$$
$$Professor(John)$$

and from the db content we can infer

$$\forall x(Professor(x) \to PhD(x))$$
$$B(\forall x\ (Professor(x) \to PhD(x)))$$
$$B(\forall x\ (Assistant(x) \to PhD(x)))$$
$$B(Professor(John))$$
$$B(Assistant(Peter))$$

Hence, the answer to the standard query $PhD(x)$, represented by $B(PhD(x))$, is $\{John, Peter\}$, and the answer to the safety query $PhD(x)$ is $\{John\}$.

This example shows that there may be several possibilities to derive a fact of a predicate. Some derivations are based on reliable axioms and lead to valid

---

[8]Though, by *evaluating* the views described in Motro's meta-answer in the standard answer, a similar result is obtained.

conclusions, while other derivations involve nonreliable axioms and only lead to beliefs. In the case of $PhD(x)$, it is not possible to guarantee that every fact of this form is valid. When the database concludes that someone has a PhD because he is a professor, then this conclusion is valid, but if it because he is an assistant, then this conclusion is not necessarily valid.

Comparison

To compare the method developed by Motro with the method developed by Demolombe and Jones, we reformulate both in a common logical framework.

For simplicity, we ignore the agents who store the information, and we only distinguish between information that has been explicitly stored, which is considered a set of *explicit beliefs*, and the overall information, consisting of explicit beliefs and derived beliefs, which is considered a set of *beliefs*. The meta-information characterizes beliefs that are *guaranteed* to be true in the world.

Consider first the method developed by Demolombe and Jones. Let $EB(f)$ denote that f is an explicit belief. As we are ignoring the agent who stored f in the database (i.e., f is valid independently of who stored it), we have the definition

$$In.MDB(f(x)) \stackrel{def}{=} \forall x\ (EB(f(x)) \rightarrow f(x))$$

where $f(x)$ is any first-order formula.

Moreover, we assume that the form of sentences that are explicitly stored is irrelevant. That is, if we have $f \leftrightarrow g$, then we have $EB(f) \leftrightarrow EB(g)$.

The link between explicit and implicit beliefs is defined by the axiom schema:

$$EB(f) \rightarrow B(f).$$

Standard and safety queries are still represented by $B(q(x))$ and $q(x)$, respectively.

In Motro's method, a validity view $f(x)$ defines a part of the database that is guaranteed to be valid. Hence, for any x, if $f(x)$ is either explicitly or implicitly believed by the database, then $f(x)$ is true in the world. Denoting with $M.DB(f(x))$ that the view $f(x)$ is valid, we have

$$M.DB(f(x)) \stackrel{def}{=} \forall x\ (B(f(x)) \rightarrow f(x)).$$

Of course, the link between explicit beliefs and implicit beliefs, is expressed by the same axiom schema.

Using these definitions we can easily rediscover the property that the mapping *meta* is a morphism for the extended RA operators projection, selection, and Cartesian product.

In FOL projection is represented by existential quantification, and we have

$$M.DB(f(x,y)) \rightarrow M.DB(\exists y\ (f(x,y)).$$

In FOL selection is represented by Boolean expressions, denoted $sel(x)$, formed only with comparison predicates, and we have

$$M.DB(f(x,y)) \rightarrow M.DB(f(x,y) \wedge sel(x)).$$

In FOL Cartesian product is represented by conjunctions, where the operands have no common free variable, and we have

$$M.DB(f(x,y)) \wedge M.DB(g(z,t)) \rightarrow M.DB(f(x,y) \wedge g(z,t)).$$

However, we can easily verify that *meta* is not a morphism for the union, because the following property *does not* hold:

$$M.DB(f(x,y)) \rightarrow M.DB(f(x,y) \vee g(x,y))$$

Intuitively, consider a tuple $< a,b >$, and assume $B(f(a,b) \vee g(a,b))$ holds, because $B(g(a,b))$ holds but $B(f(a,b))$ does not hold. The meta-information $M.DB(f(a,b))$, whose meaning is $B(f(a,b)) \rightarrow f(a,b)$, does not allow to infer $f(a,b) \vee g(a,b)$ when $B(f(a,b))$ does not hold, or we might have $B(f(a,b) \vee g(a,b))$ true, and $f(a,b) \vee g(a,b)$ false; that is, $M.DB(f(a,b) \vee g(a,b))$ is false when $M.DB(f(a,b))$ is true.

3.3 Sources of Validity Problems

The primary reason behind database information that is not valid are changes in the real world that go unrecognized and therefore are not followed up by corresponding updates in the database. Thus, as time goes by, database information tends to lose its validity, which means that unless the information is updated, meta-information regarding validity must be retracted.

Other causes of invalid information are nonreliable sources of information. That is, when the agent who stores information in the database does not correctly transmit the messages he receives.

Another important cause of uncertainty is the systematic methods intended to reduce the incompleteness of the information stored in the database. These methods are called *Plausible Reasoning*. The idea is to define *a priori* the type of missing facts that can be assumed true. Such assumptions may be wrong and result in information whose validity is uncertain.

We briefly present here two kinds of plausible reasoning that are used in the context of intelligent databases: *default reasoning* [29, 3] and *inductive reasoning*.

Default Reasoning

An intuitive assumption accepted by many in the context of relational databases, is that there exists no true information that is not explicitly stored in the database (or is derivable from information stored in the database). This means that every sentence is either derivable from the database, or its *negation* is assumed, by default, to be derivable. This intuitive assumption was formalized by Reiter [27] with axioms called the *Closure World Assumption (CWA)*.

The CWA includes the UNA (see Section 2.1), *Domain Closure Axioms* that restrict the set of possible elements in a model to the set of elements that are actually present in the database, and *Completion Axioms* that restrict the set of possible true atomic facts in a model to the facts that are actually represented by tuples in the tables.

Consider, for example, the first database presented in Section 2.1. The DCA is expressed as follows:

$$\forall x \, ((x = John) \lor (x = Peter) \lor (x = Mathematics) \lor (x = Logic)).$$

Such axioms allow to derive sentences with universal quantifiers. For example, with the DCA we can derive that every teacher teaches either Mathematics or Logic:

$$\forall x \forall y \, (Teach(x, y) \to Teach(x, Mathematics) \lor Teach(x, Logic)).$$

In a sense, we have induced that a sentence is valid for every possible element, from the fact that it is true for the database elements.

For the same database, completion axioms express that the set of tuples that satisfy the predicate *Teach* is restricted to the tuples present in the table *Teach*:

$$\forall x \forall y \ (Teach(x,y) \rightarrow \quad (x = John) \wedge (y = Mathematics) \vee$$
$$(x = Peter) \wedge (y = Logic)).$$

From this axiom, the UNA, and general properties of equality, we can formally infer

$$\neg Teach(Peter, Mathematics).$$

A relational database completed with the CWA has only one model, up to an isomorphism, or, in other terms, has only one Herbrand model, namely the minimal Herbrand model. In the same example, the database represented by the theory DB_1 and CWA axioms, has the unique model M_1 from Section 2.1. Clearly, assuming the CWA is equivalent to selecting one of the possible models. Since this selection is based on formal criteria only, and ignores the semantics of the data, it is a source of errors. A more flexible assumption would be to assume completion axioms only for some of the predicates.

The CWA was extended by Reiter [27] to relational databases with marked null values. From a formal point of view the CWA is represented by the same type of axioms. The only change is that there are no unique name axioms for Skolem constants. For example, for the database represented by the theory DB_3, the completion axiom of *Teacher* is

$$\forall x \forall y \ (Teach(x,y) \rightarrow \quad (x = John) \wedge (y = Mathematics) \vee$$
$$(x = Paul) \wedge (y = \omega_1) \vee$$
$$(x = \omega_2) \wedge (y = Logic) \vee$$
$$(x = \omega_2) \wedge (y = Programming))$$

From the completed theory it is not possible to infer $\neg Teach(Paul, Mathematics)$, because we cannot infer $\neg(\omega_1 = Logic)$. In this case no choice is made about the course ω_1 taught by Paul.

The CWA was also extended by Reiter to disjunctive databases, that is, databases that contain ground positive clauses. Consider, for example, the disjunctive database

$$Professor(John), Professor(Peter) \vee Assistant(Peter).$$

This theory has models in which $Assistant(Peter)$ is false, and then, at least in these models $Professor(Peter)$ is true, and $Peter$ is an element of the extension of *Professor*. The completion axiom for *Professor* is

$$\forall x \ (Professor(x) \rightarrow (x = John) \vee (x = Peter)).$$

In general, the set of tuples that appear in completion axioms is the set of tuples that appear in some atom of some positive clause. The intuitive justification is that, if we have in the database a positive clause of the form $P(a) \vee c$, since the theory contains no negative literals, there exists a model in which c is false and $P(a)$ is true.

Minker defined [19] the *Generalized Closed World Assumption (GCWA)*, whose proof theoretic definition is

$$DB \vdash_{GCWA} \neg A \text{ if for every positive clause } A \vee c :$$
$$DB \vdash A \vee c \text{ implies } DB \vdash c$$

where c is a ground positive clause. This means that if there is no DB consequence of the form $A \vee c$, which is minimal with respect for subsumption, then we can infer $\neg A$.

The model theoretic definition of the GCWA is that an atom A in the Herbrand universe is false, if it is false in all the minimal Herbrand models of the database. More technically, if DB' is the database DB after the elimination of all subsumed clauses, and if $atom(DB')$ represents all the atoms that appear in a ground positive clause in DB', then A is assumed to be false if it is not in $atom(DB')$.

This definition has been extended by Lobo, Rajasekar, and Minker [18] to disjunctive deductive databases. The definition is similar: we only have to replace DB' by the set of ground positive clauses in the LFP defined in [21] (see Section 2.2).

Inductive Reasoning

Another source of uncertainty are techniques that extract rules from databases. The motivation is to have a synthetic representation of the information, which enables quick processing of certain queries, without scanning large sets of facts. The downside is that answers are not guaranteed to be valid. However, in most cases a quantitative estimation of the deviation is provided with the answer. Such rules and answers may be useful in applications such as decision support systems. For example, in financial applications, large sets of data about stocks and bonds can be efficiently summarized with such rules. In many cases, such summaries are sufficient for decision making.

Induction techniques have been studied extensively in artificial intelligence, in particular machine learning. In the context of intelligent databases, they have been applied toward knowledge discovery and data mining [26] (see also Chapter 6).

A basic goal is to *control* rule discovery. For example, a user defines the pattern of rules he is interested in, and a factor denoting the validity of the rule is computed on the basis of the database content. Another method for controlling the process of induction is to define an abstraction hierarchy on the constants or on the concepts [14, 12]. For example, in the relation *Born*, the details of the place of birth can be abstracted by the country of birth, and the details of the date of birth can be abstracted by the year of birth.

With these techniques, the fact $Born(Yang, Canton, 02-09-1920)$ can be abstracted with $Born(Yang, China, 02-09-1920)$, then $Born(Yang, China, 09-1920)$, and then $Born(Yang, China, 1920)$. It is then possible to induce empirical rules such as

$$\forall x \forall y \ (Born(x, China, y) \rightarrow 1910 < y < 1930) \ [0.70, 0.85]$$

whose meaning is that of all the people born in China, between 70% and 85% were born between 1910 and 1930. An inference method for logic programs with such rules in the case of monadic predicates was defined in [24].

Given the fact $Born(Shu, Beijin, \omega_3)$, the abstraction process and the inference process may be combined to infer that $1910 < \omega_3 < 1930$. Hence, inductive reasoning is reduce incompleteness.

3.4   Uncertainty Constraints

Initially, databases were used mainly in business applications, and validity was an important concern. This may explain the emphasis on integrity constraints in the relational model. Now the role of integrity constraints can be revisited in the context of intelligent databases. In [8] we considered the overall information in a database as a theory, and the issue was to define the role of integrity constraints in this general approach.

In our opinion, an important characteristic of the integrity constraints *IC* (within a database *DB*) is that their validity should be guaranteed. Initially, relational integrity constraints were characterized by syntactical form of the sentences that represent them [25]. For example, non-Horn clauses were claimed to be, *a priori*, ICs, because they cannot be used to derive information in a standard deductive database. In is now clear, however, that this syntactical characterization is no longer valid. For example, in a disjunctive deductive database, non-Horn clauses can be used as well to derive information or to check validity.

We consider IC a subset of the database DB. Although it is not certain that the world W is a model of DB, our assumption that the integrity constraints are valid implies that W is a model of IC. Formally, this important property of IC is stated as follows

$$IC \subseteq DB \text{ and } W \in M(IC).$$

For this reason, the IC part of a database should not change when new information is acquired by the database, and it is known that the world has not changed. If we know that the world has changed, and it is assumed that IC are still valid, then, if some update UP leads to the new inconsistent database $DB \cup UP$, there are two possible attitudes.

It is possible to reject the update UP because it may considered uncertain. This implies an implicit ordering on our confidence in the different kinds of information: at the top level are integrity constraints, then the non-IC part of DB, and then the update UP. This may be denoted

$$UP < DB - IC < IC.$$

Alternatively, we may enforce the update, and modify $DB - IC$ to restore consistency. This attitude corresponds to the ordering

$$DB - IC < UP < IC.$$

Consider this simple example:

$$DB =$$
$$\{\forall x \ (Male(x) \land Female(x) \ \rightarrow),$$
$$\forall x \ (Professor(x) \rightarrow Male(x)),$$
$$Professor(John)\}$$
$$IC =$$
$$\{\forall x \ (Male(x) \land Female(x) \ \rightarrow)\}$$

and assume the update $UP = \{Female(John)\}$. Since $DB \cup UP$ is inconsistent, we could either reject this update or modify it to restore consistency. Obviously, there are many possible ways to restore consistency; for example, we could re-move either the fact *Professor(John)* or the rule $(Male(x) \rightarrow Professor(x))\ \forall x$. Usually, one would prefer to restore consistency without removing rules.

The meta-information on information validity (Section 3.1) may be viewed as constraints about validity. For example, a sentence of the form

$$\forall x\ (EB(Professor(x)) \rightarrow Professor(x))$$

may be viewed as a description of a given state of the world and of the database content, and can be reformulated as "it is guaranteed that if the database believes that x is a professor, then x is indeed a professor."

It can also be viewed as an obligation imposed to users who store information in the database with respect to the world, and it can be reformulated as "it should be guaranteed that whenever the database believes that x is a profes-sor, then x is indeed a professor." Nevertheless, it is important to notice that this constraint is different from the integrity constraints presented above. In-deed, integrity constraints IC are used to check the internal consistency of DB, whereas this meta-information, if it is considered as an obligation, can only be checked by a user, for example the database administrator. Consequently, we propose calling the two kinds *internal integrity constraints* and *external in-tegrity constraints*. These two kinds could coexist. For example, we may have in a single database

$$DB =$$
$$\{\forall x\ (Male(x) \wedge Female(x)\ \rightarrow),$$
$$\forall x\ (EB(Professor(x)) \rightarrow Professor(x)),$$
$$EB(\forall x\ (Professor(x) \rightarrow Male(x))),$$
$$EB(Professor(John))\}$$

where the first sentence is an internal integrity constraint, the second is an external integrity constraint, and the third and fourth are explicit beliefs. When processing the update *Female(John)*, since *Professor(John)* is guaranteed to be valid, this fact should not be removed to restore consistency.

4 CONCLUSION

In this chapter we surveyed two kinds of uncertainty: incompleteness and validity.

For incompleteness, the representations covered were traditional relational databases from the point of view of OWA, null values that represent existentially quantified variables, conditional tuples, and positive disjunctive facts. We described reasoning techniques that were based on relational algebra extensions for null values or conditional tuples, or on specific inference techniques supported by specific least fixpoint operators. We noted that the sources of uncertainty are either lack of information, or availability of partial information. Constraints to limit the incompleteness can be defined in terms of epistemic logic.

For validity, the representations covered were meta-information in the form of metatuples in metarelations, or within a logical framework based on epistemic logic and logic of actions. The reasoning techniques were based on extensions to relational algebra for metarelations, or on general inference techniques for nonclassical logics. We noted that the origins of uncertainty include changes in the real world, as well as nonclassical inference that involve plausible reasoning (default reasoning or inductive reasoning). Constraints to express limited validity are sentences that play a specific role with regard to database updates.

The overall attitude in the field of intelligent databases is to formulate and attack restricted problems, rather than broad, general problems (as is the tendency in the field of artificial intelligence). This leads to solutions that are usually more efficient. For example, extensions of the relational algebra are often preferred over general inference methods. A drawback of this attitude is that it is hard to form a global view of the different techniques, and individual implementations might be difficult to integrate.

There is still much work to be done in the area of constraints. The distinction between descriptive sentences and normative sentences is not always clear for many researchers. That could be helped by using deontic logic [2].

In this chapter we considered only *qualitative* representation of uncertainty; a similar framework could be used to analyze the *quantitative* aspects of uncertainty, as well as the other two kinds of uncertainty that we mentioned in the introduction: inconsistency and vagueness.

Acknowledgments

I am very grateful to Ami Motro, who substantially helped me improve the quality of this chapter.

REFERENCES

[1] J. Biskup. A foundation of Codd's relational maybe-operations. *ACM Transactions on Database Systems*, 8(4), 1979.

[2] J. Carmo and A. J. I. Jones. Deontic database constraints and the characterisation of recovery. In A. J. I. Jones and M. Sergot, editors, *2nd International Workshop on Deontic Logic in Computer Science*, pages 56–85. Tano A. S., 1994.

[3] M. R. B. Clarke, C. Froidevaux, E. Grégoire, and P. Smets. Uncertainty conditionals and non-monotonicity. *Journal of Applied Non-Classical Logics*, 1(2), March 1991.

[4] E. F. Codd. Extending the data base relational model to capture more meaning. *ACM Transactions on Database Systems*, 4(4): 397–434, December 1979.

[5] R. Demolombe. An efficient evaluation strategy for non-Horn deductive data bases. In *IFIP Congress*. Elsevier, 1989. Extended version appeared in *Journal of Theoretical Computer Science*, No. 78.

[6] R. Demolombe. A strategy for the computation of conditional answers. In *10th European Conference on Artificial Intelligence*, 1992.

[7] R. Demolombe. Syntactical characterization of a subset of domain independent formulas. *Journal of the ACM*, 39(1), 1992.

[8] R. Demolombe and A. Jones. Integrity constraints revisited. In A. Olive, editor, *4th International Workshop on the Deductive Approach to Information Systems and Databases*. Universitat Politecnica de Barcelona, 1993.

[9] R. Demolombe and A. Jones. Deriving answers to safety queries. In R. Demolombe and T. Imielinski, editors, *Nonstandard queries and nonstandard answers*. Oxford University Press, 1994.

[10] R. Demolombe and L. Fariñas del Cerro. An algebraic evaluation method for deduction in incomplete data bases. *Journal of Logic Programming*, 5: 183–205, 1988.

[11] R. Demolombe and L. Fariñas del Cerro. An inference rule for hypothesis generation. In *Proceedings of International Joint Conference on Artificial Intelligence*, 1991.

[12] V. Dhar and A. Tuzhilin. Abstract-driven pattern discovery in databases. Submitted for publication, 1992.

[13] H. Gallaire and J. Minker. *Logic and Data Bases*. Plenum Press, 1978.

[14] J. Han, Y. Cai, and N. Cercone. Knowledge discovery in databases: an attribute-oriented approach. Submitted for publication, 1992.

[15] T. Imielinski and W. Lipski. Incomplete information in relational databases. *Journal of the ACM*, 31(4), 1984.

[16] K. C. Liu and R. Sunderaman. Indefinite and maybe information in relational databases. *ACM Transactions on Database Systems*, 15(1): 1–39, March 1990.

[17] J. Lobo, J. Minker, and A. Rajasekar. *Foundations of Disjunctive Logic Programming*. MIT Press, 1992.

[18] J. Lobo, A. Rajasekar, and J. Minker. Weak completion theory for non-Horn programs. In R. A. Kowalski and K. A. Bowen, editors, *Proceedings of 5th International Conference on Logic Programming*. MIT Press, 1988.

[19] J. Minker. On indefinite databases and the closed world assumption. In *Lecture Notes in Computer Science, No. 138*. Springer-Verlag, 1982.

[20] J. Minker. Overview of disjunctive logic programming. *Annals of Mathematics and Artificial Intelligence*, 1993.

[21] J. Minker and A. Rajasekar. Procedural interpretation of non-Horn logic programs. In *Proceedings of the Conference on Automated Deduction*, 1988.

[22] A. Motro. Completeness information and its application to query processing. In *Proceedings of 12th International Conference on Very Large Data Bases*, pages 170–178, 1986.

[23] A. Motro. Integrity = validity + completeness. *ACM Transactions on Database Systems*, 14(4): 480–502, 1989.

[24] R. Ng and V. S. Subrahmanian. Empirical probabilities in monadic deductive databases. Submitted for publication, 1992.

[25] J.-M. Nicolas and K. Yazdanian. Integrity checking in deductive databases. In H. Gallaire and J. Minker, editors, *Logic and Databases*. Plenum Press, 1982.

[26] G. Piatetsky-Shapiro and W. J. Frawley. *Knowledge Discovery in Databases*. MIT Press, 1991.

[27] R. Reiter. Towards a logical reconstruction of relational database theory. In *On Conceptual Modelling: Perspectives from Artificial Intelligence, Databases and Programming Languages*, pages 191–233. Springer-Verlag, 1984.

[28] R. Reiter. A sound and sometimes complete query evaluation algorithm for relational databases with null values. *Journal of the ACM*, 33(2), 1986.

[29] R. Reiter. Nonmonotonic reasoning. In *Annual Reviews of Computer Science, 2*, 1987.

[30] R. Reiter. What should a database know? *Journal of Logic Programming*, 14(2/3), 1992.

[31] Y. Vassiliou. Null values in data base management, a denotational semantics approach. In *Proceedings of ACM SIGMOD International Conference*, 1979.

[32] K. B. Yue. A more general model for handling missing information in relational data bases using a 3-valued logic. *SIGMOD Record*, 20(3), 1991.

5

UNCERTAIN, INCOMPLETE, AND INCONSISTENT DATA IN SCIENTIFIC AND STATISTICAL DATABASES

Stephen Kwan*
Frank Olken**
Doron Rotem* **

* *Management Information Systems Department*
School of Business
San Jose State University
San Jose, CA 95192, USA

** *Information and Computing Sciences Division*
Lawrence Berkeley Laboratory
1 Cyclotron Road
Berkeley, CA 94720, USA

1   INTRODUCTION

This chapter is a survey of several issues and applications in uncertain, inconsistent, and incomplete data in scientific and statistical databases (SSDBs).

It is our view that uncertainty in data is an intrinsic feature of scientific and statistical databases. Fundamental sources of uncertainty include quantum effects, Heisenberg uncertainty, etc. SSDBs are typically samples of some larger population (finite or infinite) or continuum (space-time). Measurement uncertainties are also ubiquitous.

One of the issues we are particularly concerned with is the interaction of uncertain data items with consistency constraints that must be satisfied by the the database. Fundamental consistency constraints are commonly dictated by physics and thermodynamics, e.g., conservation of mass, momentum, and energy. Typically, these constraints refer to aggregations across all or part of the database. Thus, uncertain data items can lead to inconsistent aggregate (derived) data.

It is often uneconomic to insist on certain data. In many cases, however, uncertain data are sufficient to decide among alternative actions (hypotheses). In such cases, knowledge of the extent of uncertainty in queries and data is generally necessary.

The chapter is divided into two parts. The first part (Section 2) describes generic sources of uncertainty for scientific and statistical databases (SSDBs). In the second part (Sections 3–7) we describe several examples of SSDBs and discuss the particular problems with uncertainty. We conclude with a research agenda.

2   SOURCES OF UNCERTAINTY

Data are raw facts captured as measurements of some real-world phenomena. They need to be recorded, retrieved, and processed within a decision-making context before they can become useful information. The functionalities to support these operations in a statistical or scientific database environment are depicted in Figure 1.

The environment described in Figure 1 is similar to that found in a conventional database system. Conventionally, one of the explicit purposes of a database system is to provide information that will reduce the decision maker's uncertainty about the environment. Realistically, the information provided to the decision maker will usually contain some elements of uncertainty. The challenge for the designer of a database system is, then, to identify the causes and sources of the uncertainty and provide remedies for avoiding or eliminating them as part of the overall design. Some recent treatments of this area are found in [43] and [46].

Five sources of uncertainty in an SSDB are identified in Figure 2. They are introduced in this section and are discussed further in later sections.

In certain situations the database is not used to record actual data but some probabilistic representation of them, and the uncertainty is considered an attribute rather than a problem associated with the data (e.g., see the work on probabilistic databases in [6] and [10]). In another situation, uncertainty

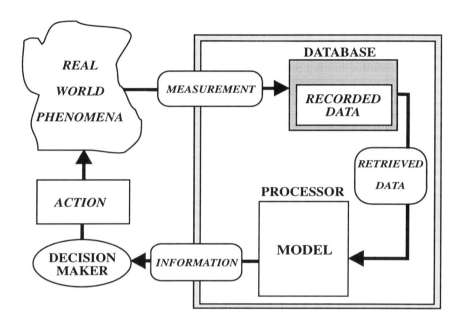

Figure 1 Schematic of an information system.

might be deliberately introduced into the data for security reasons (e.g., see the research on statistical perturbation for hiding actual data from unauthorized users in [33]). More commonly, the data that are of concern in statistical and scientific databases are inherently uncertain because of the real-world phenomena being observed and measured (1 in Figure 2). For example, this type of *phenomenal uncertainty* could be caused by quantum mechanical considerations, turbulence, etc. Examples from databases used to record data collected from physics and chemistry experiments are discussed in the second part of this chapter. Some recent research has also focused on fuzzy and imprecise values of data [50, 32].

Real-world events or phenomena of interest are observed, imperfectly measured, captured, and then recorded as some values in the database (2 and 3 in Figure 2). The deviation between the real values representing the phenomena and the recorded values in the database are depicted in Figure 3. The ideal situation is that in which there is a 1:1 mapping between the recorded and real values of the data.

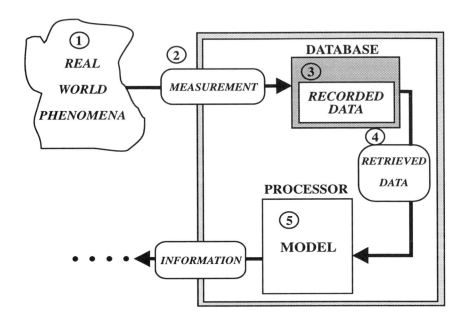

Figure 2   Sources of uncertainty.

In reality, there are probably some data values that are not recorded in the database because the observation and recording instruments are not perfect and omnipresent. This less-than-ideal but more realistic scenario is represented in Figure 4. It shows that the recorded data in the database only maps into a subset of the real data. It further shows that there are recorded data in the database that do not map at all into the real data. These discrepancies between the real data and the recorded data will result in uncertainty.

Some of the causes of the discrepancies indicated in Figure 4 are the following:

1. Incomplete processing of data

2. Incomplete recording of data

3. Sampling errors

4. Noise and measurement errors

5. Obsolete data

6. Corrupt data

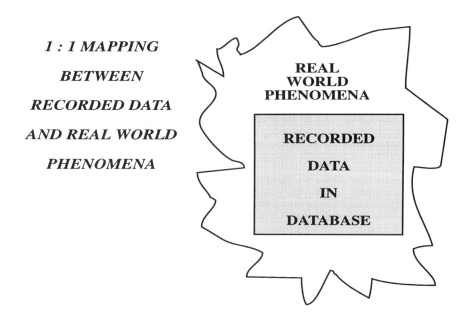

Figure 3 The relationship between real and recorded data.

2.1 Incomplete Processing of Data

Incomplete processing of data occurs when the observation or collection instrument cannot perform its functions on time. For example, a transaction processing system might not be able to process all the transactions as they arrive. Transactions that are yet to be processed are held in a queue. These unprocessed transactions could well contain real data, which will not be recorded in the database until the transactions are processed. This situation results in uncertainty because retrieved data might not reflect the changes the transactions represent. Research in this area has dealt with the incorporation of a database performance model of the processing system with various data accuracy models (e.g., see [28], which is based on premises developed in [54] and [55]). Similar difficulties could also be caused by synchronization problems in a multidatabase environment. For example, in a system that maintains mirror or shadow database [31], transactions that update the master database (or other database copies) might be delayed. Another approach to assessing data reliability could be found in [1].

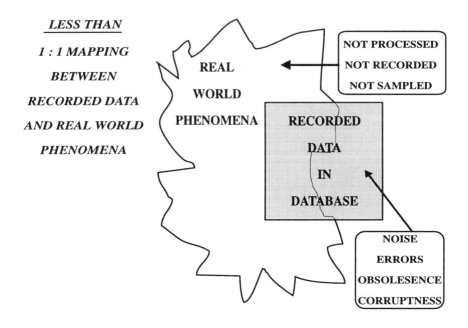

Figure 4   A realistic relationship with causes of discrepancies.

2.2   Incomplete Recording of Data

Incomplete recording of data can be caused by an information system designer or a human operator. For example, due to an oversight by an inventory clerk, certain dispensations from the warehouse during peak activity hours might go unrecorded. Another example is when, due to incomplete analysis of the system, the designer of the information system neglects to incorporate an alternative source of transaction generation. Also, real data might go uncaptured if it requires some extraordinary steps to be taken by the originator. For example, during census taking, a certain percentage of census questionnaires are never returned by the recipients. Examples of how incomplete or missing data in databases are treated can be found in [40] and [62]. More extensive discussions of this topic can be found in Section 6.

2.3 Sampling Errors

When the volume of events is large, it is impractical to record every single event. In this case, a database is used to record random samples from the actual population of events. Usually, the sampling is not exhaustive, and thus some of the real data are not recorded in the database.

Another kind of sampling, *discretization*, concerns sampling the state of continuous domains, such as space or time. It is clearly impossible to record the state of continuously varying parameters (e.g., the weather) at every point in space and time. In such cases, the continuous domain is sampled at discrete points, and the values of the parameters are recorded at these points only.

2.4 Noise and Measurement Errors

Noise and measurement errors can be caused by humans or by instruments. The resolution of the observation and measurement instrument might not be fine enough to make a precise recording of the values associated with the real data. This may result in imprecision in the data. This type of "measurement uncertainty" can be further broken down into uncertainty attributed to calibration, instrumentation, and signal processing. Nonetheless, human data-entry or processing operators are most often the culprit in introducing errors into the database (e.g., see [4]). Quite often, the errors introduced are simple transcription errors (see examples and remedies suggested in [19]). Other errors can be caused by classification and nomenclature problems. For example, objects in the database were mislabeled, misnamed, or misidentified, thus resulting in the object being misclassified.

2.5 Obsolete Data

When data are first recorded, they usually represent the most recent observations of the corresponding real data. But as time goes on, the recorded data may lose part of its value due to obsolescence. In this case, the recorded data no longer reflect reality. This is particularly prevalent in data that are sensitive to periodic or seasonal variations. Associated with this subject is the need to consider the temporal dimension of data (e.g., versioning, pedigree). In some situations experimental data are so dynamic in nature that uncertainty is introduced as soon as an observation has been made and recorded in the database.

2.6   Corrupt Data

When data are corrupted due to insufficient (or nonexistent) integrity controls, the data are no longer dependable and thus cause uncertainty in the retrieved results (3 in Figure 2; see [45]). Integrity controls might range from those dealing with essential domain and referential integrity to those dealing with application-specific consistency. Uncertainty may also result from the integration of multiple disparate databases, when perfect consolidation might not be achieved and data is lost in the process. Certain scientific databases require more stringent integrity constraints as compared to commercial or business applications. These constraints are needed to maintain unique consistency requirements, which are essential for preserving the reliability of the data.

2.7   Imperfect Retrieval

Uncertainty in data can also result from the discrepancies between the values retrieved from the database and the values recorded in the database (4 in Figure 2; see [18] for some theoretical concepts on the structure of recorded data in statistical databases). Clearly, all retrieved values are derived from the recorded values (see Figure 5). The correspondence between the retrieved and recorded values depends on the interface between the retriever (human operator) and the database [60]. Most often, this interface is based on a retrieval language, such as SQL. Hence, the correspondence between the retrieved and recorded values depends largely on the features and capabilities of the language. For example, [23] discussed the issues associated with the granularity of retrieved data based on aggregate queries. A further consideration is the difference between the retriever's concepts and the actual semantics of the database [44, 51, 7]. See also the discussion of approximate string matching in the context of genomic databases (Section 3.1).

2.8   Model Uncertainties

One further major source of uncertainty can be found in the manipulation of the data once they are retrieved (5 in Figure 2). Usually, the desired retrieval criteria, which are presented to the database, are based on a specific model (for excellent theoretical discussion and examples see [41]).

For example, one might retrieve data samples for use in estimating some statistical parameter via a maximum likelihood estimation procedure. Such procedures

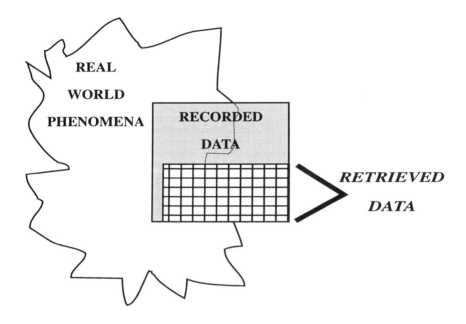

Figure 5 Recorded vs. retrieved data.

depend on the probability distribution, which is assumed to hold. Misspecification of the distribution will lead to misestimation of the aggregate parameters. Similar types of misspecification errors can affect econometric (or inventory) forecasting models. Well-known examples include uncertainties with regard to the appropriate statistical models for predicting carcinogenicity and toxicity from low-level chemical or radiation exposure.

2.9   Decision-Making Needs

It is often the case that decision makers do not need exact answers to queries in order to choose between alternative actions. Thus, the decision maker can accept some degree of uncertainty. He needs, however, to know the extent of the uncertainty with which he is confronted. Often, it will be uneconomic to attempt to answer queries exactly. See the discussion in Section 5.

Much research was performed in the area dealing with the decision maker [37], teams of decision makers [38], information analysis [13], cost-benefits of information [25, 48], decision models [11], measurement of decisions [39], application of statistical decisions [12], and so on (see Figure 1).

3 EXAMPLE DATABASES

3.1 Genomic Databases

We briefly discuss DNA sequencing as an illustration of sources of uncertainties in scientific data and some of the difficulties of representing and reasoning about these uncertainties.

Recent years have seen an explosion of DNA sequencing activity and the initiation of the Human Genome Project [56], whose goal is to determine the entire DNA sequence for a human being.

Below, we identify several steps in the process of generating a DNA sequence database. For a more extensive description see [24].

1. An organism provides the original DNA.
2. Clonal cell lines are established.
3. The DNA is subcloned.
4. Individual subclones are sequenced. This involves both chemical reactions, electrophoresis, and detection.
5. The raw signals (pixels) are processed and peaks are identified.
6. Peak intensities are compared and sequence fragments are generated.
7. Sequence fragments are assembled in large contiguous sequences.
8. Sequences are transmitted to a central database, where curators merge overlapping sequences from different investigators.

Each of these steps may introduce uncertainties and inconsistencies:

1. Different organisms of the same species have different DNA, yet we sequence the DNA from a single organism. This constitutes a sampling error.

2. Not all cells of an organism have the same DNA (notably, immune system cells or cancerous cells are different). Again, we have a sampling error. The process of immortalizing cell lines alters their DNA somewhat.

3. Subcloning DNA introduces opportunities for alteration (deletion or recombination) of DNA in the cloning system. In some cases, chimeric clones, which contain two pieces of DNA that were not originally contiguous, will be generated. In addition to these biological errors, we again have a sampling process—hence, the possibility of sampling errors (in this case incomplete data).

4. Sequencing reactions involve the use of polymerases which do not provide perfect replication. Electrophoretic mobility may be affected by the secondary structure generated by the DNA sequence. Diffusion of larger fragments is increasingly difficult to resolve. All of these lead to errors in the observed DNA sequences (see [29]).

5. Signal processing and peak picking software introduces additional uncertainties into the observed DNA sequences.

6. Comparison of peak intensities, with suitable calibration adjustments for varying dye visibilities, introduces another source of error and uncertainty in the observed DNA sequences.

7. Sequence assembly offers several possibilities of error: random errors in detecting overlaps. Confusion occasioned by repetitive DNA sequences, which are often difficult to resolve. Sequence assembly errors are typically not only single base errors but rather block rearrangements of fragments of the sequence.

8. Merging sequences at the central database offers many of the same possibilities for error as sequence assembly.

Once we begin to assemble the sequence, opportunities exist to identify inconsistencies in the data, which can help to resolve uncertainties. For human DNA, we know that the chromosomes are linear, so that circular or branching structures can be recognized as inconsistent. While identification of branches localized the source of error within a few clones, detection of cycles is intrinsically ambiguous in terms of diagnosis and error correction.

How then are we to represent the uncertainties and how are we to deal with inconsistent data? Finished sequences are simply that, sequences over a four-letter alphabet. Unfinished sequences may be much more confusing, i.e., each may be a collection of possible reconstructions.

Because of the uncertainties in determining a DNA sequence, and because of population variability and evolutionary changes (mutations) among organisms, a typical DNA sequence retrieval query is an approximate string matching query. An elaborate body of algorithms and statistics have been developed (see, for example, [53, 30, 14, 3, 59, 61, 36]). However, little work has been done to include these facilities in a general purpose DBMS.

3.2   Thermodynamic Databases

Thermodynamic reaction rate databases [15, 16, 9] are used in reactive transport codes for modeling subsurface flows of toxic and radioactive fluids (water). Such codes are important in the design, analysis, and remediation of groundwater pollution, radioactive waste disposal repositories, and geothermal reservoirs.

It is well known that chemical reactions neither create nor destroy energy. Suppose that we have a cycle of chemical reactions that brings us back to our starting reactants. Then the reaction rates for this cycle of reactions must be such that there is no net energy gain or loss. To assure that this is the case, the reaction rates are adjusted via a large-scale, least-squares calculation to assure global consistency. If modifications or additions to the database are to be made, they are accumulated for a period, and then the least-squares adjustment code is rerun, and a new consistent version of the database is released. It may be necessary to retain old versions of the database, so that reactive transport codes can be run with reaction rates consistent with earlier runs of the transport codes. It is generally not appropriate for end-users of the database to see inconsistent data.

3.3   Particle Data

The Particle Data Group at Lawrence Berkeley Laboratory produces the 650-page *Review of Particle Properties* [21] biannually. This handbook records the currently recommended values for a wide variety of parameters of high-energy particles and high energy physics particle collision and decay reactions.

The Particle Data Group maintains a database of experimental estimates of particle parameters. This database records experimentally determined values of the particle attributes along with error estimates.

The error estimates are comprised of two components: a systematic error estimate and a random error estimate. The random error estimate arises from two sources: random measurement errors, and (more important) the underlying quantum mechanical stochastic processes; e.g., radioactive decay.

The systematic error estimate reflects the impact of errors in proportionality constants used in the computation of the parameter estimate, i.e., when the proportionality constants are themselves experimentally determined.

Both the systematic and random errors are recorded as confidence intervals (e.g., one standard deviation), which may be asymmetric.

For unconstrained parameters, the consensus value is typically determined by weighted averaging of the different experimental values, with the weights determined by the error estimates.

Some parameters are constrained. Thus branching ratios for alternative reactions may be constrained to sum to 1. Reaction rates for decay reactions are constrained to sum to the aggregate decay rate for the parent particle. In such cases, constrained least squares estimation is used to estimate the individual parameters.

A more extensive discussion of the details of more complex cases can be found in the introduction to [21].

What is interesting to observe about this application is the systematic recording of data uncertainties and their propagation. Also of note is the existence (as with thermodynamic data) of integrity constraints on subsets of the data.

3.4   Demographic Statistical Databases

The most important demographic statistical database in the United States is the U.S. decennial census, which attempts to be a complete enumeration of the population. All respondents are asked basic questions about age, race, housing, education, income, etc. A sample of 5% is asked more detailed questions. For an introduction to the topic, see [35].

Among the most important sources of uncertainty in the census data are missing people. It is well known that the census undercounts poor minorities (e.g., blacks and Hispanics), illegal aliens (e.g., Hispanics, Haitians, etc.), and homeless people. There have been extensive studies of the problem by the Census Bureau as well as considerable litigation.

Some of these people are undercounted because they do not want to be found, others because census workers do not know where to look, or because the census workers are reluctant to enter dangerous areas. Homeless people may not be recognizable as such, except late at night, when they may be hidden from view.

A related problem is missing data from enumerated people. Even if found, homeless people, illegal aliens, etc. may be reluctant to cooperate with census workers. In some cases linguistic problems cause data not to be provided.

Outright deception is also a problem. Runaway teenagers may lie about their age. Welfare mothers may lie about the presence of adult males in the household (whose discovery would jeopardize their welfare payments). People receiving welfare or engaged in tax evasion may lie about their income. Affluent people may be reluctant to disclose their true income.

Another source of uncertainty has to do with classification errors. The census bureau has changed the definition of Hispanics between decennial censuses. Furthermore, since the census generally relies on self-identification for race, respondents may alter their racial classification depending on their own self-perceptions. Furthermore, racial classification is ambiguous for many Americans of mixed racial backgrounds.

3.5   Epidemiological Databases

Epidemiological databases are used to study the incidence, causation, and effectiveness of treatment of various diseases. In addition to the aforementioned demographic databases (used for the denominators in disease incidence rate calculations), major epidemiological databases include death and tumor registries. Death registries record deaths of people, their names, ages, and cause of death. Tumor registries record tumors, a person's name, etc.

A common type of epidemiological study will investigate a cohort, for example a group of workers at a particular plant. Since cancers typically take 20 years to manifest themselves, it is often impractical to track the members of the cohort over this time period. Instead, state and national death and tumor registries will be searched to determine whether there is any record of the members of the cohort dying or contracting cancer.

Because of errors in transcribing identifying information on individuals, intervening name changes, and possible coincidences, such record matching is imperfect and introduces uncertainties and errors concerning the fate of individual members of the cohort. This process of approximate record matching is known as *record linkage* and is described in [47, 2, 26]. This is an important example of approximate retrieval capability, which one would like to include in general purpose DBMSs. At present record linkage is performed by specialized file-based software. Chatterjee and Segev have proposed the inclusion of record-linkage techniques in database management systems [7, 8].

There are other sources of uncertainty concerning death and cancer records. If no autopsy is performed, then the cause of death may be misidentified. In cases of diseases to which social stigma is attached, AIDS, syphilis, etc., physicians may falsify the cause of death.

For cancer tumor registries a more subtle problem exists. There is much interest in assessing whether changes in cancer therapies have improved survival rates. Such studies are typically performed by examining five-year survival rates after cancer diagnosis. Unfortunately, improvements in cancer diagnostic techniques may mean that improved survival statistics merely signify earlier detection, not any improvement in treatment.

Another problem has to do with changing, or differing (e.g., geographically or among doctors) definitions of illness or diagnostic criteria. A recent major example has been AIDS, where diagnostic criteria have changed as the disease has become better understood. Such changes may make historical time series incommensurate with each other.

3.6 Spatial Databases

Like other engineering or scientific databases, spatial databases typically have two types of data: measurements and derived data. In surveying applications, the measurements consist of lengths, heights, and angles, while the derived data are (mostly) coordinates and areas of polygons. In estimating coordinates from survey measurement data, various geometric constraints must be satisfied, e.g., if we take survey measurements around the boundaries of a parcel we should arrive back at our starting point. It is customary to use various constrained least squares estimation algorithms to estimate coordinates from survey measurements, using estimates of the variance of each measurement.

Furthermore, geographic information systems permit us to combine derived geographic data from multiple sources—often with quite disparate error characteristics. Considerable efforts in GIS have been focused on the recording and the propagation of errors during GIS processing. See, in particular, the discussion by Maffini [34], in the proceedings of a conference that was devoted to this topic [20]. Buyong [5], explicitly addresses data modeling issues for cadastral (surveying and mapping) databases, which include both the original measurement data and the estimated coordinates.

3.7   Econometric Databases

Another important class of statistical databases are econometric databases, i.e., those containing economic statistics. The classic reference on errors and uncertainties in economic data is Morgenstern [42]. He was concerned largely with national income and trade statistics. More recent monographs include [17, 17, 35].

Morgenstern made several enduring points about sources of errors in economic data:

- Evasion and lies by respondents

- Falsification by governments

- Index number problems

- Definitional and classification problems

Morgenstern was quite concerned with evasion and lies by respondents concerning attempts to gather economic statistics. The motivation for the lies and evasions are twofold: disclosure of the information may give advantage to competitors, and disclosure of the information may result in additional taxes, or criminal penalties (e.g., for drug trafficking, prostitution, or employment of illegal aliens).

Falsification by governments is a somewhat different matter. Often, governments consider information on gold and hard currency reserves (sometimes also grain, oil, and other reserves) to be of importance for national security. Information on crop failures may induce price increases in international grain markets before the government concerned can purchase replacement stocks.

Also, governments sometimes engage in the secret sale of weapons to various parties (countries, guerilla movements), who may be under international embargo. In some cases embargo violations concern the sale of oil. Secret trading arrangements have become so common that the European Union Statistics Office prepares trade statistics with categories for both secret commodities and secret trading partners.

Index number problems concern such issues as the impact of quality changes on the validity of consumer price indices.

The classic example of definitional problems with economic statistics are unemployment statistics [35]. People who are so discouraged that they have abandoned actively searching for employment are not consider part of the workforce and are excluded from unemployment statistics. Hence, one can observe such bizarre phenomena as an increase in unemployment at the end of a recession as discouraged workers rejoin the workforce.

International comparison of unemployment rates is hampered by inconsistent definitions of the workforce and who is unemployed.

3.8   Taxonomy of Uncertainty Sources

Table 1 summarizes our examples of uncertainty in scientific and statistical databases. We tabulate both the major sources of uncertainty and the type of integrity constraints.

We see these types of integrity constraints:

- Topological; for example, chromosomes known to have linear structures

- Geometric; for example, in surveying, alternative routes to same point must generate the same final coordinates

- Conservation laws; for example, conservation of energy, mass, or momentum

- Arithmetic; for example, the sum of the parts must equal the whole, or Kirchoff-type laws

DB Application	Sources of Uncertainty	Integrity Constraints
Genomic	Random Measurement Error	Topological
Thermodynamic	Random Measurement Error	Conservation of Energy
Demographic	Finite Population Sampling Misclassification	Arithmetic
Particle Data	Stochastic Physical Process Random Measurement Error Systematic Error—Calibration	Conservation Laws Arithmetic
Epidemiological	Finite Population Sampling Misclassification	Arithmetic
Spatial	Random Measurement Error	Geometric
Econometric	Fraud, Evasion Finite Population Sampling	Arithmetic

Table 1   Sources of uncertainty.

4   DATABASE ERROR CONTROLS

4.1   Control Mechanism

By reviewing Figure 2 and the sources of uncertainty that were discussed in the previous section, it can be seen that many uncertainty problems are caused by inadequate error control mechanisms. Kuong [27] and Perry [49] offer some very good suggestions for controls that can be applied to any type of computer operations including those that employ scientific or statistical databases. The controls discussed, if implemented and employed, could reduce some of the errors and problems discussed in [4].

4.2   Source Data Automation

As part of the data-entry control mechanism, to assist in error detection and correction, automation has been often employed successfully; this includes technologies associated with automatic identification, such as barcoding, radio-frequency interrogators or identifiers, various types of magnetic and optical identification badges, and so on. The Department of Defense reported great success in its application of barcoding to many of its activities. The DOD LOGMARS project cited examples of a single error in many billions of barcode reads. More and more medical and laboratory facilities are employing such technologies in inventory, samples-tracking, patient and filing applications. The integration of automatic identification technology with recent advances in automated testing and experimental control machines is one way in which the industry is trying to reduce data-entry and tracking errors. Recent advances in miniaturization of computers and associated technologies have also improved error controls by allowing data collection in the field, using hand-held devices, thus avoiding a transcription process altogether. The collected data is subsequently uploaded into bigger computers for storage in databases.

5 DATA ACCURACY AND DATABASE PERFORMANCE

One area of research, which deals explicitly with the issue of uncertainty in data, is in the modeling of data accuracy in databases [55]. The research was motivated by the need to understand the relationship between the required degree of accuracy and the transaction activity rate. This problem was treated in [55] under several simplifying assumptions: only a single class of data with a single degree of accuracy and the same activity rate for the whole database.

Recent work in this area [28] improved upon the groundwork done in [55]. It involved the development of models that allow the estimation of the degree of accuracy of data residing in an existing database system, as well as planning resource allocation strategies to meet user requirements. The models also allowed the performance of tradeoffs between user accuracy requirements and system performance in formulating resource allocation strategies. The models took into account the following factors:

- A multi-user computer system that operates with a priority system, which is based on resource allocations modeled as a queueing network model.

- A database management system operating with multiple processing threads.

- The database contains different classes of data items. Each class could have its own accuracy requirements and activity rate.

- Each transaction generates a query and optionally an update.

- The magnitudes of the transaction amounts are allowed to follow certain distributions rather than being fixed as in [55]. Discretely valued, normally distributed and uniformly distributed transaction amounts were considered. Plainly put, the uncertainty in the data increases with the number of unprocessed transactions there are in the queue.

A major contribution of this research was in the development of a measure called *operational reliability*, which incorporates both the accuracy requirements and the operational performance of the database system. Briefly, operational reliability measures within a particular operating environment (given resource allocations) how likely it is that the system can satisfy the accuracy requirements. Ideally, the accuracy requirements can often be satisfied by devoting more resources to process the transactions. Realistically, many classes of transactions are contending for the same amount of resource allocations. Thus in most cases, a tradeoff between accuracy and resource allocation has to be made.

An interactive system implementing the model just described has been developed and used to demonstrate the applicability of the model in many varied scenarios. The system has proved to be a very powerful tool in predicting the level of accuracy achieved for various classes of items and helping to allocate the available computing resources to meet the accuracy requirements of users.

Continued research in this area by the authors include the determination of policies for allocating the computing resources among the classes of data when the total requirements exceed the capacity of the system. Considerations are given to the tradeoff between fairness of allocation and efficient operation of the system.

6 MISSING CATEGORICAL DATA

One source of uncertainty in socioeconomic databases is due to incomplete categorical data. The main difference between missing information in this context and the usual one is that in many cases correlations of the missing data with other attributes can be utilized to complete the data. The process of replacing missing information with appropriate values is called *imputation*. The main thrust of this effort is to find the most consistent imputations based on the present values in the database. The example in Table 2 shows data that illustrate this concept.

Sample No	Age	Income	House-Size	Car-Year-Model
1	Young	Low	Small	Old
2	Young	Low	Small	*a*
3	Middle	Low	Small	New
4	Middle	High	Large	New
5	Middle	Middle	Small	New
6	Middle	Low	Small	New
7	Old	*b*	Small	Old
8	Old	Middle	Small	*c*
9	Old	High	*d*	New
10	Old	High	Large	New

Table 2 Example of missing data.

A reasonable imputation procedure may replace the missing values *a*, *b*, *c*, and *d* with Old, Low, Old, and Large respectively. Of course, in more complicated situations many possible replacement values may need to be evaluated and some consistency measurement of the completed data needs to be optimized. Much research along these lines has been recently reported by [58, 57]. They use a quantity called correlation ratio [22] for measuring consistency. A program called MISTRESS has been written by the above authors and used successfully on several datasets. See also the monograph by Rubin on the statistical treatment of missing data [52].

7 CONCLUSIONS

Present commercial databases lack almost entirely any means of coping with uncertainty in data. At best, they may permit users to specify operators for string matching. Clearly, much work needs to be done to extend database technology to address the issues raised in this chapter.

In general, we need both a means to record the uncertainty of data items, and some method to propagate the uncertainty through query processing operations. We observe that many scientific databases have derived data that is estimated from measurement data, often via constrained least-squares estimations. It is our view that the data dependencies of such derived data need to be recorded. Furthermore, we believe that the estimation constraints (geometric, arithmetic, etc.) also need to be explicitly recorded. These constraints are strikingly different from those traditionally addressed in the database community.

We end with a brief enumeration of other open research topics concerning uncertainty in databases. In several cases we have examples of specialized systems that provide individual operators (e.g., approximate record matching), but typically these features have not been integrated into general purpose database systems. It is our contention that they should be.

- Inclusion of random sampling operators against database queries.

- For random samples, a scheme for representing the type of sampling used, and inclusion of this information in answers to aggregate queries.

- A data model that can manage continuous data domains and deal with interpolation.

- Incorporation of approximate string matching and approximate record matching (record linkage) [7, 8].

- Inclusion of facilities for dealing with missing data (imputation).

- Query languages extensions to permit user specification of the accuracy needed in the query result.

Acknowledgments

This work was partially supported by the Director, Office of Energy Research, Office of Basic Energy Sciences, Applied Mathematical Sciences Division and partially supported by the Director, Office of Health and Environmental Research both of the U.S. Department of Energy under Contract DE-AC03-76SF00098. The authors would also like to thank the referees for their comments.

REFERENCES

[1] N. Agmon and N. Ahituv. Assessing data reliability in an IS. *Journal of Management Information Systems*, 4(2): 34–44, Fall 1987.

[2] J. A. Baldwin, E. D. Acheson, and W. J. Graham. *Textbook of Medical Record Linkage*. Oxford University Press, 1987.

[3] M. J. Bishop and C. J. Rawlings, editors. *Nucleic Acid and Protein Sequence Analysis: A Practical Approach*. IRL Press (Oxford University Press), 1987.

[4] W. M. Bulkeley. Databases are plagued by reign of error. *Information Age column, The Wall Street Journal*, 26 May 1992.

[5] T. B. Buyong, W. Kuhn, and A. U. Frank. A conceptual model of measurement-based multipurpose cadastral systems. *URISA Journal*, 3(2): 35–49, Fall 1991.

[6] R. Cavallo and M. Pittarelli. The theory of probabilistic databases. In *Proceedings of the 13th VLDB Conference*, pages 71–81, 1987.

[7] A. Chatterjee and A. Segev. Resolving data heterogeneity in scientific and statistical databases. In H. Hinterberger and J. C. French, editors, *Proceedings of the Sixth International Working Conference on Scientific and Statistical Database Management*, pages 145–159, June 1992.

[8] A. Chatterjee and A. Segev. Approximate matchings in scientific databases. In J. F. Nunamaker Jr. and R. H. Sprague Jr., editors, *Proceedings of the Twenty-Seventh Hawaii International Conference on System Sciences. Vol. III: Information Systems: Decision Support and Knowledge-Based Systems*, pages 448–457. IEEE Computer Society Press, January 1994.

[9] J. E. Cross and F. T. Ewart. HATCHES—a thermodynamic database and management system. *Radiochemica Acta*, 52–53: 421–422, 1991.

[10] D. Barbara, H. Garcia-Molina, and D. Porter. A probabilistic relational data model. In *Proceedings of the 1990 EDBT Conference* (Venice, Italy), pages 60–74, March 1990.

[11] G. B. Davis and M. H. Olson. *Management Information Systems: Conceptual Foundations, Structure, and Development. Second Edition*. McGraw-Hill, 1985.

[12] M. H. DeGroot. *Optimal Statistical Decisions*. McGraw-Hill, 1970.

[13] J. S. Demski. *Information Analysis, Second Edition.* Addison-Wesley, 1980.

[14] R. F. Doolittle, editor. *Molecular Evolution: Computer Analysis of Protein and Nucleic Acid Sequences*, volume 183 of *Methods in Ensymology.* Academic Press, 1990.

[15] J. R. Duffield, F. Marsican, and D. R. Williams. Chemical speciation modelling and thermodynamic database compilation—I. data uncertainties. *Polyhedron*, 10(10): 1105–1111, 1991.

[16] J. R. Duffield, F. Marsican, and D. R. Williams. Chemical speciation modelling and thermodynamic database compilation—II. database compilation and sensitivity analyses. *Polyhedron*, 10(10): 1113–1120, 1991.

[17] N. Frumkin. *Tracking America's Economy.* M.E. Sharpe, 1987.

[18] S. P. Ghosh. Statistical relational databases: Normal forms. *IEEE Transactions on Knowledge and Data Engineering*, 3(1): 55–64, March 1991.

[19] T. Glib and G. M. Weinberg. *Humanized Input: Techniques for Reliable Keyed Input.* QED Information Sciences, 1977.

[20] M. Goodchild and S. Gopal, editors. *Accuracy of Spatial Databases.* Taylor and Francis, 1989.

[21] Particle Data Group. Review of particle properties. *Physical Review D*, Third Series, Vol. 50(3), 1 August 1994.

[22] L. Guttman. The quantification of a class of attributes: A theory and method of scale construction. In P. Horst, editor, *The Prediction of Personal Adjustment.* SSRC, 1941.

[23] W. Hou and G. Ozsoyoglu. Statistical estimators for aggregate relational algebra queries. *ACM Transactions on Database Systems*, 16(4): 600–654, December 1991.

[24] T. Hunkapiller, R. J. Kaiser, B. F. Koop, and L. Hood. Large-scale and automated DNA sequence determination. *Science*, 254(5028): 59–67, 4 October 1991.

[25] J. P. C. Kleijnen. *Computers and Profits: Quantifying Financial Benefits of Information.* Addison-Wesley, 1980.

[26] B. Kliss and W. Alvey, editors. *Record Link Techniques—1985, Proceedings of the Workshop on Exact Matching Methodologies.* Department of the Treasury, Internal Revenue Service, Statistics of Income Division, May 1985.

[27] J.F. Kuong. *Computer Auditing, Security, and Internal Control Manual.* Prentice Hall, 1987.

[28] S. K. Kwan and D. Rotem. Analysis and tradeoff between data accuracy and performance of databases. In *Proceedings of the Sixth International Working Conference on Scientific and Statistical Database Management* (Ascona, Switzerland), 1992.

[29] C. B. Lawrence and V. V. Solovyev. Assignment of position-specific error probability to primary DNA sequence data. *Nucleic Acids Research*, 22(7): 1272–1280, 11 April 1994.

[30] A. Lesk, editor. *Computational Molecular Biology.* Oxford University Press, 1988.

[31] B. Lindsay, L. Haas, C. Mohan, H. Pirahesh and P. Wilms. A snapshot differential refresh algorithm. In *Proceedings of the ACM-SIGMOD International Conference on Management of Data* (Washington, DC), pages 53–71, May 1986.

[32] K. Liu and R. Sunderraman. Indefinite and maybe information in relational databases. *ACM Transactions on Database Systems*, 15(1): 1–39, March 1990.

[33] H. Luchian and D. Stamate. Statistical protection for statistical databases. In *Proceedings of the Sixth International Working Conference Scientific and Statistical Database Management* (Ascona, Switzerland), 1992.

[34] G. Maffini, M. Arno, and W. Bitterlich. Observations and comments on the generation and treatment of error in digital GIS data. In M. Goodchild and S. Gopal, editors, *Accuracy of Spatial Databases*, chapter 5, pages 55–67. Taylor and Francis, 1989.

[35] M. H. Maier. *The Data Game.* M.E. Sharpe, 1991.

[36] U. Manber, editor. *Proceedings of the Third Annual Symposium on Combinatorial Pattern Matching.* Springer-Verlag, April 1992.

[37] J. G. March and H. A. Simon. *Organizations.* Wiley, 1958.

[38] J. Marschak and R. Radner. *Economic Theory of Teams*. Cowles Foundation Monograph, Yale, 1972.

[39] R. O. Mason and E. B. Swanson. *Measurement for Management Decision*. Addison-Wesley, 1981.

[40] H. Mendelson and A. N. Saharia. Incomplete information costs and database design. *ACM Transactions on Database Systems*, 11(2): 159–185, June 1986.

[41] J. C. Moore, W. B. Richmond, and A. B. Whinston. A decision-theoretic approach to information retrieval. *ACM Transactions on Database Systems*, 15(3): 311–340, September 1990.

[42] O. Morgenstern. *On the Accuracy of Economic Statistics*. Princeton, 1950.

[43] J.M. Morrissey. Imprecise information and uncertainty in information systems. *ACM Transactions on Information Systems*, 8(2): 159–180, April 1990.

[44] A. Motro. VAGUE: A user interface to relational databases that permits vague queries. *ACM Transactions on Database Systems*, 6(3): 187–214, July 1988.

[45] A. Motro. Integrity = validity + completeness. *ACM Transactions on Database Systems*, 14(4): 480–502, December 1989.

[46] A. Motro. Accommodating imprecision in database systems: Issues and solutions. *ACM SIGMOD Record*, 19(4): 69–74, December 1990.

[47] H. B. Necombe. *Handbook of Record Linkage*. Oxford University Press, 1988.

[48] M. M. Parker and R. J. Benson. *Information Economics: Linking Business Performance to Information Technology*. Prentice Hall, 1988.

[49] W. E. Perry. *Ensuring Database Integrity*. John Wiley & Sons, 1983.

[50] K. V. S. V. N. Raju and A. K. Majumdar. Fuzzy functional dependencies and lostless join decomposition of fuzzy relational database systems. *ACM Transactions on Database Systems*, 13(2): 129–166, June 1988.

[51] B. J. Read and M. A. Hapgood. Approximate joins in scientific databases in practice. In *Proceedings of the Sixth International Working Conference Scientific and Statistical Database Management* (Ascona, Switzerland), 1992.

[52] D. B. Rubin. *Multiple Imputation for Nonresponse in Surveys.* Wiley, 1987.

[53] D. Sankoff and J. B. Kruskal. *Time Warps, String Edits, and Macromolecules: The Theory and Practice of Sequence Comparison.* Addison-Wesley, 1983.

[54] J. Srivastava and D. Rotem. Analytical modeling of materialized view maintenance. In *Proceedings of the 7th Symposium on Principles of Database Systems*, pages 126–134, March 1988.

[55] J. Srivastava, J. Wang, and D. Rotem. Dynamic maintenance of approximate aggregate views. In Z. Michalewicz, editor, *Statistical and Scientific Databases.* Ellis Horwood, 1991.

[56] Office of Technology Assessment U.S. Congress. *Mapping Our Genes—The Genome Projects: How Big, How Fast?* U.S. Government Printing Office, 1988.

[57] S. Van Buuren and J. L. A. Van Rijckevorsel. Data augmentation and optimal scaling. Technical Report 03, Nederlands Instituut voor preventieve Gezondheidszorg, 1992.

[58] S. Van Buuren and J. L. A. Van Rijckevorsel. Imputation of missing categorical data by maximizing internal consistency. Technical Report 01, Nederlands Instituut voor preventieve Gezondheidszorg, 1992.

[59] G. von Heijne. *Sequence Analysis in Moecluar Biology.* Academic Press, 1987.

[60] J. A. Wald and P. G. Sorenson. Explaining ambiguity in a formal query language. *ACM Transactions on Database Systems*, 15(2): 125–161, June 1990.

[61] M. S. Waterman, editor. *Mathematical Methods for DNA Sequences.* CRC Press, 1989.

[62] M. Winslett. A model-based approach to updating databases with incomplete information. *ACM Transactions on Database Systems*, 13(2): 167–196, June 1988.

6

KNOWLEDGE DISCOVERY AND ACQUISITION FROM IMPERFECT INFORMATION

Gregory Piatetsky-Shapiro

GTE Laboratories Incorporated
40 Sylvan Road
Waltham, Massachusetts 02154, USA

1 INTRODUCTION

This chapter discusses the issues of imperfect information in the fields of knowledge discovery in databases (KDD) and knowledge acquisition for expert systems (KA) . My perspective on these issues is more of a practitioner motivated by pressing application needs and less of the researcher motivated by the desire to push the frontiers of science.

Following Smets (Chapter 8), I use imperfection as the most general label, which includes uncertainty, imprecision, and inconsistency. Given a statement S "John Smith is older than 30," uncertainty of S refers to whether S is true or not. Imprecision refers to the content of the statement. We may be able to make a more precise statement S "John Smith is 31 years old," but be less certain about it. In general, there is a tradeoff between uncertainty and imprecision. These issues are discussed at length elsewhere in this book. Despite adopting *imperfection* as a general label, I may use *uncertainty* as a general term in cases where it was used so historically, as in uncertainty management methods.

The KA field deals with methods and tools for acquiring symbolic knowledge for expert or knowledge-based systems. The steady proliferation of expert systems has significantly increased the research interest in KA. While in 1987 Knowledge Acquisition did not merit a separate entry in the *Encyclopedia of Artificial Intelligence* [68], the situation has changed since then, as indicated by numerous KA workshops in North America, Europe, and Japan (e.g., [7]). The focus of much of this effort was on developing methodologies and interactive tools to help the knowledge acquisition process. On the practical side, a number of KA tools are available commercially and a new organization, the

International Association of Knowledge Engineers (IAKE) has been formed to support activities of expert system developers.

At the same time, the rapid growth of data and information created both a need and an opportunity for extracting knowledge from databases. Scientific projects such as earth observation satellites or human genome decoding are already producing gigabytes (and soon tetrabytes) of data. Increasing computerization of all aspects of business creates very large databases that can be mined for important business knowledge.

The notion of knowledge discovery in databases has been given various names, including knowledge extraction, data mining, pattern processing, information harvesting, siftware, and even (when done poorly) data dredging. Whatever the name, the essence of KDD is the nontrivial extraction of implicit, previously unknown, and potentially useful information from data [22]. A typical KDD system (see [22, 39]), guided by domain knowledge and user preferences, searches the relevant data for patterns, evaluates their potential for arousing interest using a combination of objective (statistical, etc.) and subjective (knowledge-based) measures, and presents findings in a human-oriented way.

The research aspects of KDD are of growing interest to researchers in machine learning, statistics, intelligent databases, and knowledge acquisition, as evidenced by the number of recent special journal issues on KDD [52, 11, 54] and meetings [51, 53, 19], which culminated in the first conference on Knowledge Discovery and Data Mining [20]. The application side of KDD is of interest to any business or organization with large databases. KDD applications have been reported in many areas of business, government, and science [56, 32, 47, 18]. There are also a number of commercially available tools for discovery in data, both for generic discovery and for domain-specific applications such as marketing.

KA and KDD fields are similar in their focus on extracting interesting, useful, and reliable knowledge. They also share interest in inductive algorithms that infer rules from examples. Their different sources of knowledge—the human expert for KA and large databases for KDD—lead to differences in emphasis. KA is centrally concerned with human factors issues and deals with relatively small amounts of information chunks. Each chunk, however, can be very complex. Although databases are becoming more complex, with the addition of object-oriented, CAD/CAM, multimedia, and other nonrelational data, most of the large databases existing today are still based on the conceptually simple relational or hierarchical models. Thus, KDD systems typically deal with large

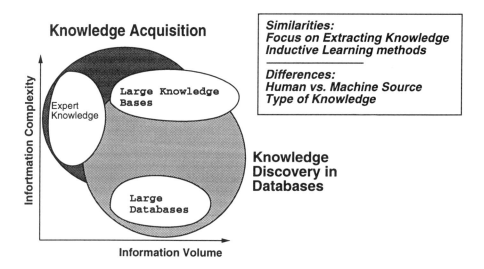

Figure 1 Comparison of KDD and KA focuses.

volumes of relatively simple data. The differences and similarities between KA and KDD are summarized in Figure 1.

At the intersection of KA and KDD we find a small but growing number of large knowledge bases. The prime example here is CYC [37], which was recently reported to contain over a million knowledge units. The goal of CYC is to serve as a repository of common-sense knowledge. Although currently knowledge is entered manually, it is expected that at some point CYC will be able to acquire knowledge automatically, e.g., by reading encyclopedia entries. Shen [69] developed an algorithm to search the CYC knowledge base for regularities of the form $(\forall xyz)[P(x,y) \wedge R(y,z) \Rightarrow Q(x,z)]$. The algorithm found a number of regularities that were both interesting and new to CYC, for example:

$$acquaintedWith(x,y) \wedge languageSpoken(y,z) \rightarrow languageSpoken(x,z).$$

KA and KDD also share a concern for intelligent, user-oriented presentation of their findings. This includes explanation of findings [70], natural language generation [65], and graphical presentation of results [34].

1.1   Enterprise Data Versus Scientific Data

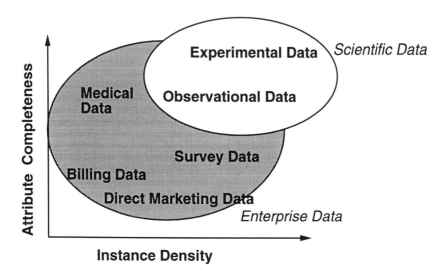

Figure 2   Enterprise data versus scientific data.

It is useful to contrast discovery in enterprise (business, social, etc.) data with the discovery in scientific data. While in both cases the goal is the discovery of patterns, there are a number of fundamental differences arising from the different nature of data.

Scientific data usually contains accurately measured numerical values, collected as a result of a well-designed experiment intended to minimize the number of observed phenomena. The control over the data collection, higher in experimental sciences, such as physics, lower in observational sciences, such as astronomy, means that usually most of the relevant attributes are measured (high attribute completeness), and the control over setting of independent variables means that most of the points in the potential instance space can be reached (high instance density). Scientific laws are usually precise, quantitative, and concise.

Discovery in enterprise data usually deals with both numerical and categorical data. The parts of business data that are collected or entered by humans typically have many errors. The data reflects the chaotic nature of the real world and is usually influenced by many different phenomena. The data is customarily collected for some other business purpose such as billing, and rarely has all the relevant fields (low attribute completeness). The data has only a few interesting extreme cases and most combinations of data values are not present (low instance density). The discovered patterns are typically imprecise, qualitative, and rarely concise. Finally, business data frequently contains sensitive personal information. Discovery in such data may lead to an invasion of privacy or other ethical or legal problems.

Figure 2 illustrates the differences among various discovery domains with respect to attribute completeness and instance density.

In the rest of this chapter I briefly review uncertainty management techniques. I then examine KDD and KA fields in more detail, highlighting their specific requirements. Finally, I examine the different problems in dealing with imperfect information in KA and KDD, and outline possible solutions.

2   UNCERTAINTY MANAGEMENT

An approximate measure of the right thing
is better than the exact measure of the wrong thing

This section gives a brief overview of uncertainty management methods, focusing on their applicability to KA and KDD. More complete surveys are given elsewhere in this book and in [5, 67]. The methods can be divided into two major classes: symbolic and numeric. The numeric methods can be subdivided into probabilistic and possibilistic approaches.

Symbolic methods: The symbolic or qualitative methods, which include various logical approaches and truth-maintenance systems, are usually designed to handle uncertainty caused by incompleteness of information, when conclusions depend on making assumptions that may or may not be retracted in the future. Symbolic methods are generally not adequate for handling uncertainty resulting from stochastic processes. They are also not appropriate for handling imprecision.

Probabilistic: These methods are best for handling processes with random components. The traditional techniques include the classical methods of probability theory and statistics, such as the Bayes rule and its variations.

One problem with these techniques is that they estimate the probability as a single value, making inferences potentially brittle: a very small change in some rule certainty (which itself may be a user's guess) might cause a big change in the conclusion. The single-point estimate of the conclusion certainty may also be misleading to a user. These problems are alleviated by interval-valued approaches, which provide the lower and upper bounds for the probability. The most popular of interval-valued techniques is the Dempster-Shafer theory [66]. The Dempster-Shafer theory also handles the proper aggregation of multiple and potentially contradictory beliefs.

Possibilistic: The possibilistic or fuzzy methods [74, 75] are best suited for handling imprecision inherent in natural language statements such as "Most tall people are not overweight." This problem is much more important for KA than for KDD. We note that fuzziness is different from randomness, since randomness deals with the probability of belonging to a well-defined set (e.g., people), while fuzziness deals with the uncertainty of belonging to a fuzzily defined set (such as tall or overweight).

Hybrid: Finally, there are various hybrid methods that combine symbolic and numeric reasoning. If symbolic methods specify the structure of inference and numeric methods quantify the certainty of inference, the hybrid methods try to perform structured and quantitative reasoning. Some convergence of structured and quantitative reasoning can be observed in numeric methods like Bayesian belief networks [48], which provide structure to reasoning about probability.

3   KNOWLEDGE DISCOVERY IN DATABASES

> *In the beginning, there was chaos. Then God said*
> *"Let chaos be measured" and there became databases.*

The first wave of computerization, which began in the 1960s, was the automation of routine tasks, such as payroll systems, accounts receivable, etc. This was the beginning step in the creation of the massive business databases we see today. The second wave of computerization, dating from the mid-1970s, was transaction processing, which allowed computers to interactively perform much more complex activities, such as airline reservations or manufacturing control. This need for managing complex transactions and easy data retrieval led to the creation of database management systems. These systems are well suited to extracting information from databases. The massive growth of data, which began in the 1980s, is leading to a corresponding explosion in information, which threatens to overwhelm the human abilities to understand it. This

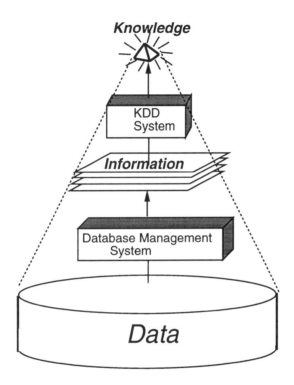

Figure 3 Knowledge discovery in databases pyramid.

set the stage for the third wave, which began in the 1990s, and has been called discovery in databases or pattern processing. According to Inmon and Oster-felt [32], the third wave has the potential to eclipse the importance of the first two waves. The importance lies in the competitive advantage from the greatly increased market responsiveness and awareness that results from rapid discovery of patterns in data. Outside of the business world, intelligent, automated data analysis is essential in many scientific fields such as astronomy, where the amounts of data vastly exceed the human capabilities to examine it. The relationship between data, information, and knowledge is shown in Figure 3.

We define *knowledge discovery in databases* [22] as a nontrivial and efficient extraction of interesting high-level patterns from data. Given a set of facts (data) F, a language L, and some measure of certainty C, we define a *pattern* as a statement S in L that describes relationships among a subset F_S of F with certainty c, such that S is simpler (in some sense) than the enumeration of all facts in F_S. A pattern that is interesting (according to a user-imposed interest measure) and certain enough (again according to the user's criteria) is called *knowledge*. The output of a program that monitors the set of facts in a database and produces patterns in this sense is *discovered knowledge*.

This definition is intentionally vague to cover a wide variety of approaches. In the following paragraphs, we examine the meaning of these terms in more detail.

Patterns and languages: Although many different types of information can be discovered in data, KDD focuses on patterns that can be expressed in a high-level language, such as

if DIAGNOSIS = PREGNANCY & PATIENT-AGE > 35
   and PREVIOUS-CHILDREN = no
then DELIVERY-TYPE = "Caesarean section"
   with   probability = 0.3

Such patterns can be understood and used directly by people, or serve as input to an expert system or another program. We do not consider low-level patterns, such as those generated by neural networks, unless they have been converted to a higher-level language [24].

Certainty: Representing and conveying the degree of certainty is essential to determining how much faith the system or user should put in the discovered pattern. Determining certainty involves many factors including the completeness and correctness of data; the size of the sample on which the discovery was performed; and, possibly, the degree of support from available domain knowledge. There are many ways to specify the certainty of a pattern (see Section 2). The quantitative uncertainty methods are generally more suitable for KDD since they best utilize the typically data-rich and knowledge-poor environment. Among them, standard statistical and Bayesian methods have been the most popular, although Dempster-Shafer [41] and fuzzy methods [73] have also been used.

Interestingness: The usual problem in KDD is not the scarcity, but the overabundance of patterns found. Filtering those patterns to separate the interesting from the obvious or irrelevant is at the heart of discovery. Patterns are interesting when they are novel, useful, and nontrivial to compute. Whether a pattern is novel depends on the assumed frame of reference, which can be either the scope of the system's knowledge or the scope of the user's knowledge. For example, a system might discover that: **if** DIAGNOSIS = PREGNANCY

then `PATIENT-SEX = FEMALE`. To the system, this pattern might be new and potentially useful; to a user this pattern would be obvious and uninteresting. A common approach to reducing the number of such obvious "discoveries" is to focus on changes, since obvious patterns do not change. The more difficult task of separating the important patterns from the useless requires domain knowledge. A general heuristic here is that rules and patterns are important to the degree they can lead to a useful action. This suggests a decision-theoretic framing of the problem of evaluating the usefulness of discovered patterns. The *utility* of a particular pattern should not be measured in isolation but instead evaluated in the context of a set of possible actions.

Nontriviality: Novelty and utility alone, however, are not enough to qualify a pattern as discovered knowledge. Numerous novel and useful patterns, such as the total number of hospital admissions for a particular group in 1993, or the the average length of stay can be computed from health-care data. These types of patterns would typically not be considered discovered knowledge because they are trivial to compute. A discovery system must be capable of deciding which calculations to perform and whether the results are interesting enough to constitute knowledge in the current context. Another way of viewing this notion of nontriviality is that a discovery system must possess some degree of autonomy in processing the data and evaluating its results.

Efficiency: Finally, we are interested in discovery processes that can be efficiently implemented on a computer. An algorithm is considered efficient if the run time and space used are a polynomial function of the low degree of the input length. In practice, efficient methods are those in which time complexity is on the order of $N \log N$ or less, to process N items. The problem of discovery of interesting concepts (patterns) that satisfy given facts is inherently hard. Recent advances in computational learning theory [26] have shown that it is not possible to always efficiently learn an arbitrary Boolean concept; the problem is NP-hard. However, these results are generally related to the worst-case performance of algorithms and do not eliminate the possibility that, on the average, we can find complex concepts fast. Efficient algorithms do exist for restricted concept classes, such as purely conjunctive concepts (for example, $A \wedge B \wedge C$), or the conjunction of clauses made up of disjunctions of no more than k literals (for example, $(A \vee B) \wedge (C \vee D) \wedge (E \vee F)$, for $k = 2$). Another possibility for efficiently finding concepts is to abandon the demands of optimality and use heuristic or approximate algorithms.

Although discovery systems vary considerably in their design, it is possible to describe a model discovery system. Figure 4 depicts the basic components of our prototypical system for knowledge discovery in databases (see [22, 39]).

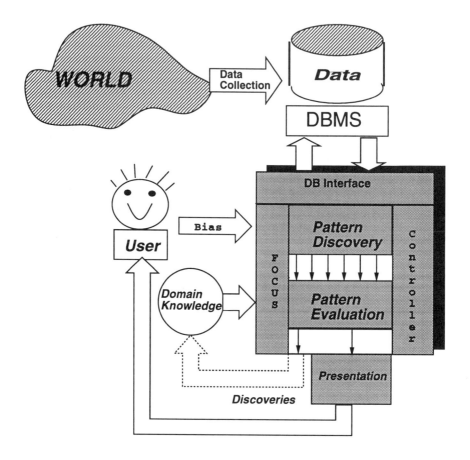

Figure 4   A model system for knowledge discovery in databases.

- **Controller** has the overall control of the application over all other components.

- **Database Interface** sends data requests to the DBMS and returns data to the KDD system.

- **Focus** module combines knowledge about the data, domain, and user biases to determine what data needs to be searched, the ordering of the search, the type of patterns to be analyzed, and the evaluation bias.

- **Pattern Discovery** methods search for patterns of potential interest. A KDD system may have one or many discovery methods.

- **Pattern Evaluation** module evaluates the discovered patterns using a combination of objectives (statistical, etc.) and subjective (knowledge-based) measures.

- **Presentation** module presents the findings to the user in a human-oriented way, with natural language and graphics. The discovered knowledge may also be fed directly into the system, potentially leading to the incremental growth of knowledge.

The pattern discovery methods are at the core of KDD systems. We examine them in more detail in the next section.

3.1 Discovery Methods

Many different discovery and learning methods have been developed. Space limitations allow only a brief overview (but see [56, 39]). In the following discussion we assume a fixed set of data items (the universe), and use *concept* to refer to a logical condition over the data, and *class* to refer to a subset of data items. Thus each concept has a corresponding class and vice versa.

There are several main categories of discovery methods:

- **Clustering:** these methods cluster together items or data records, maximizing similarity within classes and minimizing similarity between classes. The result is a set of classes. Clustering may be applied recursively to the generated classes, producing eventually the complete taxonomy of data. Traditional mathematical methods of clustering [17] mostly rely on similarity measures based on Euclidean distance between numeric attributes and work well only on numeric data. More recent conceptual clustering methods, such as Cobweb [21] can work also with nominal and structured data and determine clusters not only by attribute similarity but also by conceptual cohesiveness, as defined by background information. Auto-Class [13], a Bayesian clustering method, can determine the most likely number of classes in data.

- **Class Description:** Given a class of records or an equivalent logical description (whether generated automatically or manually) it is often useful to find additional characteristic descriptions of those records. A wide variety of approaches have been tried for this task. Given a database and a set of rules, Imielinski [30] showed how to answer a query, i.e., summarize the records retrieved, partially with facts and partially with other rules. Cai *et al.* [10] and Piatetsky-Shapiro [50] used attribute-oriented induction to extract characteristic rules from data. A fuzzy set approach to data summarization was proposed by Yager [73].

- **Class Discrimination:** Given a set of items divided into several classes, these methods find the classification rules that discriminate between the classes and can assign a new item to the proper class. The optimal solution of this problem is NP-hard, but a number of heuristic solutions have been quite successful. One of them is a top-down generation of a decision tree [58, 9]. At each level of the tree, all possible fields are examined for potential splits, and the one that produces the best split, as determined by entropy gain or other measures, is selected. The splitting is continued until either all the nodes in a subtree belong to the same class, or the size of the subtree is too small. The resulting tree can also be used to generate rules.

  Another popular approach to class discrimination is using neural networks [63].

- **Dependency Analysis:** While the class discrimination methods aim to predict one target class, dependency analysis looks at how useful each data field is in predicting other fields. The dependency $A \to B$ may be exact (functional) or probabilistic. Functional dependencies (FD) have been well studied by database researchers and a number of algorithms exist for finding the minimal set of FDs in a database [38]. Recently, major advances were made in analysis of probabilistic dependencies and combining related dependencies into a causal graph, also called a belief network [48]. These methods uncover dependencies between field pairs by analyzing their covariance with respect to subsets of other variables and are able, in some cases, to determine the direction of the dependence. A Bayesian approach was taken by Cooper and Herskovits [15]. Their method, applicable to discrete data, considers many possible graphs and selects one with the highest a posteriori probability given the existing data.

- **Deviation Detection:** There is a wide variety of these methods, including detection of changes over time, subclasses that differ from their sibling or parent classes, and anomalous instances. The common approach of these methods is that they all look for significant differences between an actual and the expected value of some function of data fields. The function is usually aggregated across a group of records. The expected value may be either a value from a previous period, a value from a similar group in another dataset, a normative value for this function, etc. The great appeal of the deviation detection is that it automatically filters most of the uninteresting patterns by focusing only on deviations or changes.

A great variety of standard statistical techniques exist for comparing means, standard deviations, and other measurements in two or more groups. The difficulty in automated deviation detection lies in automatic selection of interesting subgroups and in relating the discovered deviations to each other and to user's knowledge. Lee *et al.* [36] augmented statistical trend analysis with knowledge-based expectations. Systems like Spotlight [2] and KEFIR [40] analyze changes in data and present findings using natural language and graphics.

4   KNOWLEDGE ACQUISITION

Whereas KDD deals with extracting knowledge from large volumes of data, KA's task is extracting knowledge from a human expert. The expert is both the greatest strength of KA methods, providing all the necessary expertise, and their greatest weakness. Since the human mind cannot be directly copied to a computer, we have to rely on very imperfect means of eliciting expertise.

Here we are confronted by the so-called *paradox of expertise* [45]. The acquisition of human cognitive expertise goes through three generally distinct stages [35]. Although different terms are used for each stage, there is a general agreement on qualitative changes in the way people seem to retrieve information during problem solving.

1. At the first, novice or cognitive, stage the person performs explicit, often verbal, reasoning about actions.

2. During the second, intermediate or associative reasoning, stage the relationships noted in the first stage are used and the explicit reasoning begins to disappear.

3. In the final, expert or compiled reasoning, stage the problem-solving rules are compiled and are not consciously accessed.

The knowledge that experts acquired as novices may be retrievable in a declarative form, yet studies show that the skills are actually practiced procedurally and subconsciously [3]. In addition, studies have shown that expert's introspection about the internal processes is unreliable [45]. Thus, the *paradox of expertise*: the knowledge that we would most like to incorporate into the system is the knowledge that the expert is least capable of describing.

KA systems deal with this problem in two ways. The first way is to increase the reliability of acquired knowledge by relying more on examples of expert behavior, in which they show real expertise, and less on experts' reconstruction of their reasoning. This approach is closely related to the field of inductive learning (e.g., [42]).

The second way is to pay greater attention to human factors in order to better elicit the human expertise. A notable advance in this area is the development of the repertory grid approach [6]. This method first asks the expert to compare the objects in triples and to describe dimensions that separate those objects. After all objects are rated on all dimensions, the result is the repertory grid of objects and dimensions. Now, given the target class of objects, one can analyze the features of these objects to infer the rules for predicting the target class [23]. Many interactive tools for KA are described in [7].

4.1   KA Requirements for Uncertainty Managements

> *Probability is not about numbers. It is about structure.*
> —G. Shafer

Dealing with uncertainty has not been a main issue for the knowledge acquisition community. The main reason is that uncertainty in expert systems is frequently attributed to lack of information. Consider, for example, an expert system for telephone network management that was given a rule "On Sunday, the volume of long-distance calls is *usually* low." This rule is generally true, except for some holidays like Mother's Day,[1] or Sundays with exceptional external events, such as earthquakes or wars.

One way for the system to handle the uncertainty of this rule is to solicit more knowledge, e.g., check whether the Sunday in question is a Mother's Day and

---

[1] This USA holiday, which falls on the second Sunday in May, is typically the busiest calling day of the year.

ask the user whether some external calamity has happened recently. Some exceptions, like Mother's Day, may be encoded explicitly to refine the rule.

In domains such as design or configuration, in which uncertainty is mostly due to incomplete information, expert systems have been successfully developed and deployed without any uncertainty representation. In other domains, such as diagnostics, there may be an uncertainty in conclusions but no uncertainty in actions. For example, assume that the expert concludes that in situation X, there is something broken, and it is either A (probability = 0.75), B (probability = 0.2), or C (probability = 0.05). The rule would be *if X, try to fix A; if that fails, try to fix B; if still fails, fix C*. In such domains specific numbers do not matter as much as the ordering of possible actions.

Other systems, like KARDIO [8] deal with uncertainty of specific rules by focusing on qualitative models. For some applications, it may be sufficient to know that an increase in A causes an increase in B, and unnecessary to know exactly how much.

Still other systems handle uncertainty explicitly. One reason is that some processes, like weather or a lottery, have an inherent random component that has to be modeled in expert systems for that domain. The second reason is that a rule may have so many exceptions that they cannot all be enumerated. Then, as Pearl pointed out [67, p. 257], assigning a numeric confidence level to a rule offers a way to summarize the exceptions numerically.

The early expert system developers considered using probability theory but abandoned it because of inaccuracies that resulted from making an assumption of conditional independence, and practical inability to estimate and maintain large numbers of conditional probabilities when not making this assumption.

As a result, early expert systems used various ad-hoc approaches for handling uncertainty, such as the confidence factors of MYCIN [16]. To solve various problems of *ad hoc* approaches and to provide theoretical foundation for system conclusions, KA researchers have tried to use normative methods, such as Dempster-Shafer [25].

The last few years saw an increased interest in probability theory as a representation of uncertainty in expert systems, stimulated by the development of influence diagrams [29] and belief networks , well summarized in [48]. Belief networks, also known as Bayesian belief networks, causal probabilistic networks, and probabilistic influence diagrams, are directed acyclic graphs in which nodes represent stochastic variables and arcs represent probabilistic dependencies. Belief network representation eliminated one of the major hurdles to using probability: it was no longer necessary to represent all the pairwise dependencies and conditional probabilities.[2]

Although exact inference in general belief networks is NP-hard [14], there are several practically useful inference algorithms that either restrict networks to important special cases or use sampling [28].

Pathfinder [27] was the first major expert system that used a probabilistic model for uncertainty management. It has shown the potential to provide better decision support than traditional expert systems. Heckerman also developed similarity networks, which permit incremental construction of large belief networks from humanly manageable subproblems, involving a comparison of two variables at a time.

Finally, normative expert systems based on belief networks are also suitable for generation of theoretically justified explanations [70], a very important aspect of expert system development.

5   SOURCES OF IMPERFECTION IN DISCOVERED PATTERNS

In this section, to unify treatment of KA and KDD issues, I will use *information* to refer both to expert system knowledge bases and data in databases.

We can examine the different sources of imperfection in KDD by looking at the KDD framework (Figure 4). World, the source of all data, has many levels of uncertainty. At the most fundamental level we have the Heisenberg uncertainty principle, which implies that one cannot simultaneously determine both the speed and the location of an elementary particle beyond a certain precision. On a larger scale there are many important processes with inherently random components (e.g., weather, people's decisions, or random sampling). Data about events affected by nondeterministic processes will necessarily lead to uncertain or imprecise patterns.

The next step is data collection. If not all the relevant data are recorded, the data will be *incomplete*. If an error creeps into the recording process, the data will be *incorrect*. The data may be recorded correctly, but with precision

---

[2]Hence Shafer's quote: "Probability is not about numbers. It is but about structure."

insufficient for the current task. Then the data are *imprecise*. Measurement errors that lead to incomplete, incorrect, and imprecise data are examined in more detail in Chapter 5. A typical large database will manifest all of these problems. Incompleteness, incorrectness, and imprecision will all increase the imperfection of data patterns, but in different ways, as discussed below.

The sources of imperfection in data patterns are in line with the main sources of imperfection in expert systems, according to Bonissone [5]: the unreliability of information, the inherent imprecision of the representation language, the incompleteness of information, and the inconsistency resulting from aggregation of information from multiple sources. Inconsistency is a significant problem but is generally handled prior to pattern discovery in data and will not be discussed here (but see Chapters 2 and 4 for a discussion on inconsistency).

The following step, data retrieval from a database, does not generally introduce any additional imperfections (except for a special class of statistical DBMS which intentionally introduce randomization into data retrieval to protect privacy).

The next step is pattern discovery. As we discussed earlier, learning an arbitrary Boolean concept with a minimum guarantee of correctness is NP-hard (see Section 3), which means that perfect learning methods will be too slow in practice. Thus, a *large volume of data* is an additional cause of imperfection, since it forces us to either look for simpler patterns (more imprecision) or use approximate algorithms or sampling, which increase uncertainty in discovered patterns.

An additional source of imperfection is change. Dealing with change is both a problem and an opportunity. Understanding the changes in massive volumes of data, such as supermarket sales for an entire month, is very time consuming. Automated analysis of changes is an excellent opportunity for KDD, and several systems for this very task have already been created [65, 2, 40]. On the other hand, change constantly calls into question the validity of discovered patterns. Incremental discovery methods may be needed.

Pattern evaluation uses a combination of pattern certainty and domain knowledge to discard those patterns that are judged not interesting to the user. Incorrect domain knowledge may lead to discarding of potentially interesting patterns.

Proper presentation [71] of findings to the user is critical for the success of interactive discovery systems. One issue is presentation of uncertainty: single-valued, interval-valued, linguistic, visual, etc. Alternatively, the system may reduce the uncertainty by increasing imprecision. One way of doing it is by presenting not only what the user explicitly asked for, but also similar items [43].

In the following sections we examine in more detail these sources of imperfection, discussing randomness, incompleteness, incorrectness, imprecision, large volume, and change, and possible approaches to dealing with these problems.

5.1   Randomness

Several causes may introduce randomness and noise into patterns. The real-world source of data may have inherently random components, as discussed above. Even when the measured process is deterministic, noise can be introduced by measurement and recording errors, especially when a human is involved in data collection or entry. If the desired pattern uses an aggregate function such as AVERAGE, random noise balances itself out (by the law of large numbers) and single-item errors become less important. Since the standard deviation grows proportionally to the square root of the number of values, having more values decreases the relative error of aggregate measures.

Dealing with noisy data has also been studied in the context of a decision-tree induction [9, 61]. A decision tree is usually built using one data subset (called training data) and tested on another subset (testing data). If the data is randomly noisy, then the tree that classifies the training data perfectly will generally have a higher error on the test data than some trees that have an imperfect classification of the training data. This phenomenon is known as *overfitting* the training data.

A classical method for dealing with overfitting is by pruning the decision tree [61]. After the decision tree is built, it is reexamined bottom-up, starting from the leaves. The nodes judged not sufficiently reliable by statistical and complexity measures are discarded, leading to a simplified tree. The pruned tree is not only simpler but generally is also more accurate on the test data. Quinlan [59] also proposed pruning a decision tree by converting it to rules. His method examines each branch of the decision tree (from the root to the leaves) and considers whether removing each component condition will improve the rule. The best rules are selected from all the candidates. The final rule set is generally simpler and more accurate than the original tree.

Sampling

Sampling is often used to extract a manageable subset of data, if the database is so large that the complete and timely analysis is infeasible. The patterns discovered on a sample are inherently uncertain. In addition, patterns valid for only a small number of records in the original data are likely to be missed. There are, however, well-understood statistical techniques to measure the degree of uncertainty of sample-derived patterns and also to determine how much sampling is required to achieve a desired level of confidence in the results.

Previously [50], I have analyzed an important special case of estimating the accuracy on the entire dataset of exact rules discovered from a random sample. Assume a random sample of size S from a file of size N. Let A, B be two Boolean conditions and let $|A_S|$ be the number of records satisfying A in the sample. If $A \rightarrow B$ (exactly) in the sample, then assuming that all apriori values of accuracy for $A \rightarrow B$ are *equally likely*, we have

$$\text{ExpectedAccuracy}(A \rightarrow B) \simeq 1 - \frac{1 - S/N}{|A_S| + 2}$$

I have conducted an experiment by extracting a random 500-record sample from a 2000-record database of telephone customers and finding all exact rules in the sample using the Kid3 [50] algorithm. These rules were then tested on all 2000 records, and the actual accuracy was compared to the expected accuracy from the above equation.

While some of the rules behaved as predicted, with their actual accuracy closely matching the formula, others remain exact on the entire file, implying incorrectness of the assumption of *all apriori accuracies of $A \rightarrow B$ being equally likely*. Below we examine how domain knowledge can be used to explain and predict this behavior.

Reducing Apparent Randomness with Domain Knowledge

One can categorize data fields according to how frequently they change. At one extreme are *static* fields such as a person's date of birth, which never changes. In telephone data, CUSTOMER-TYPE and SERVICE-CLASS are static fields because they never change for a given customer entry.

Relationships between two static fields represent structural dependencies or domain knowledge. So, if (CUSTOMER-TYPE = A) → (SERVICE-CLASS = 10) holds even on a small sample, it will likely hold on the entire database.

At the other extreme are *dynamic fields*, which represent the current state of events. Most numeric fields in business databases (e.g., charges, payments, etc.) are dynamic. They have a random component, which is why statistical techniques can predict the accuracy of patterns on dynamic fields from a sample. Some nominal fields, for example, credit rating or subscriber interexchange carrier, are also dynamic since these fields can change at any time.

So, if a rule (ZIP = 02254) → (CREDIT-RATING = bad) holds on a sample, it is likely to be only approximately correct in the full file.

Domain knowledge of whether fields are static or dynamic can significantly improve the estimation accuracy. In my experiment, all the sample rules that did not remain 100-percent correct on the full file had dynamic fields in the rule.

Functional dependencies are another source of domain knowledge. Dependencies among database fields are usually an indication that one or both fields in the dependency are static.

5.2   Incomplete Information

It is 10 o'clock. Do you know where your data are?

We can distinguish two types of incompleteness:

- *Missing fields (Incomplete data)*: relevant parameters have not been measured and are not available. It may even be unknown what are all the relevant parameters.

- *Missing values*: a relevant parameter is known and has been measured. However, its value may be missing for some data items.

Incomplete data situation is the norm in business data analysis, which typically uses existing operation or billing databases, not designed with discovery in mind. For example, a telephone company wants to sell mobile phones but does not have any information about a critical parameter: the potential customer's car. So, a strong rule like

(CAR-PRICE = expensive) → (MOBIL-PHONE = yes) [probability = 0.9]

will be reflected in data with weaker rules that use other variables correlated with having an expensive car.

A promising method to deal with the structure of missing data was recently developed by Spirtes and Scheines [64]. Their method, based on a statistical concept called vanishing tetrad differences, finds situations when observed variables vary together in such a way as to imply the presence of an unobserved common cause, called a latent variable. Other researchers have used a Bayesian approach for unsupervised classification of data to determine the most probable number of values of the hidden class variable [13].

Uthurusamy *et al.* [62] have examined the problem of a decision-tree induction from an incomplete data set (which they called *inconclusive*). For data known to have little noise, they suggest that a sure sign of incompleteness is that the decision-tree program always produces a perfect classification of the training set that has a high error rate when used to classify new (test) data. The usual way to deal with such problems is by pruning. However, the assumption made by many pruning methods is that there is a single correct classification for each data item and the decision-tree can be pruned by removing preconditions of rules based on their statistical relevance to the single (usually most probable) outcome [59]. The assumption of a single correct outcome may be valid for a noisy data set, but it is not valid for an incomplete data set, which makes inappropriate the pruning methods based on the single correct class assumption, especially when the number of possible classes is three or more.

To solve this problem, Uthurusamy *et al.* proposed the INFERULE algorithm. INFERULE deals with incomplete data in two ways. First, it generates strictly binary trees by splitting on the best attribute-value pair instead of splitting on all values of an attribute. This helps in avoiding unnecessary tests and in dealing with missing field values. INFERULE also uses a splitting measure that considers subset class distribution instead of entropy. This measure is more sensitive to nodes with several possible classes than the entropy-based measures. Tests on a variety of real and artificial data showed that INFERULE performed significantly better than ID3 [58] on incomplete data sets.

Missing Values

Missing or unknown values (also called null values) are ubiquitous in real databases. Here we can distinguish between a truly missing value, which exists but is not known, and a not-applicable value, which does not exist in reality but must be entered into a database due to its inflexible design. For example, an insurance claim form usually has entries for person's marital status and spouse insurance. A missing value for marital status is a true unknown, since each person has some marital status. A missing value for spouse insurance could be either an unknown or a not-applicable value if the person is unmarried.

If the value is believed to be a true unknown, its value can be estimated by several means, e.g., asking a user; assigning a default value, such as the average; or estimating from other values in the same field. The method to be used is determined by domain knowledge.

Chapter 3 has a more detailed analysis of null values, including multiple-valued logics to reason with the unknown and not-applicable values.

5.3   Determining the Source of Uncertainty: Incompleteness vs. Randomness

If the discovered pattern is less than certain, we generally do not know whether the uncertainty is caused by the incompleteness of information or by the inherent randomness in the pattern.

For example, consider the task of predicting whether a baby will inherit a feature X. Assume that the baby will have X only if both the mother and the father have X, otherwise the baby will have O. For simplicity, assume a medical database of 100 cases, with all four situations of mother and father having or not having X occurring with equal frequency. The data can be summarized in the following table:

Mother	Father	Baby	Frequency
X	X	X	25
X	O	O	25
O	X	O	25
O	O	O	25

from which one can infer a simple and correct rule:

A: MOTHER = X, FATHER = X → BABY = X [p = 1]

Now, assume that the information on babies' fathers is not available. The data becomes

Mother	Father	Baby	Frequency
X	?	X	25
X	?	O	25
O	?	O	50

which implies two rules:

B1: MOTHER = X → BABY = X [p = 0.5]
                  BABY = O [p = 0.5]
B2: MOTHER = O → BABY = O [p = 1]

Here the first rule is uncertain, due to the missing information about the father.

We want to compare these rules with ones that arise from noisy data. We note that the noise (or error) can always be represented as a missing variable. A true noise will be uniform, with probability of error being the same everywhere. A noise variable that is very nonuniform implies that there is a missing relevant variable. The previous section talks about methods for detecting some types of hidden variables. Here we compare the different effects of noise (uniform, by definition) and a hidden variable, akin to a nonuniform noise.

Let us examine a simple case in which each parent feature could be randomly changed (X to O, O to X) with probability α. Consider the situation of Mother and Father both having X. Addition of noise can lead to four different cases: XX, $X*O$, $*OX$, and $*O*O$, (starred entries indicate a changed value), with probabilities shown in the following table where for concreteness the formulas were instantiated with $\alpha = 0.1$. A similar analysis of other situations, yields a table of 16 cases, a few of which are shown here:

Mother	Father	Baby	Expected Frequency
X	X	X	$25(1-\alpha)^2 = 20.25$
X	*O	X	$25(1-\alpha)\alpha = 2.25$
*O	X	X	$25(1-\alpha)\alpha = 2.25$
*O	*O	X	$25\alpha^2 = 0.25$
$\vdots$	$\vdots$	$\vdots$	$\vdots$
O	O	O	$25(1-\alpha)^2 = 20.25$

This table can be summarized with four rules:

C1: MOTHER = X, FATHER = X $\rightarrow$ BABY = X [p = $(1-\alpha)^2 = 0.81$]

C2: MOTHER = O, FATHER = X $\rightarrow$ BABY = O [p = $1-\alpha+\alpha^2 = 0.91$]

C3: MOTHER = X, FATHER = O $\rightarrow$ BABY = O [p = $1-\alpha+\alpha^2 = 0.91$]

C4: MOTHER = O, FATHER = O $\rightarrow$ BABY = O [p = $1-\alpha^2 = 0.99$]

Comparing this set of rules with rules $B1$ and $B2$, we notice that every C rule predicts both classes with some probability, while only one B rule predicted both classes. Also, the spread in rule certainty is smaller for noisy data than for incomplete data. I conjecture that these observations are true in general, i.e., uniformly noisy data will produce rules with a wider spread of target classes and a smaller spread of rule certainties than data with missing relevant fields.

Thus if the uncertainty in rules is localized, it may be an indication of a missing variable, while a uniformly spread uncertainty is an argument for noisy data.

5.4   Incorrect Information

We can distinguish two types of incorrect information: data errors and knowledge errors.

Data errors: These errors result from wrong data measurement or entry (especially if entry is performed manually), and can be treated as a source of random noise (see section 5.1). We can reduce sensitivity to individual errors by looking for patterns over aggregate functions, such as *sum* or *average*. Using domain knowledge, such as integrity rules or data models, may catch other data errors. Suspicious points may be found by looking at outliers.

Knowledge Errors: Incorrect domain knowledge will misdirect the system. Very large domains like logistics planning need constraints, such as "Trucks don't drive over water." Proposed knowledge has to be validated against the data before using it. Use of domain constraints narrows the search, enabling us to tackle larger problems and solve them faster. The danger is that the constraints will prevent the discovery of some unexpected solutions, such as those in which trucks drive over frozen lakes in winter [51]. Depending on our objectives, we should be able to play both sides of this knowledge trade-off.

5.5 Imprecise Information

Imprecision can be caused by aggregation, discretization, or fuzzy specification.

Aggregation: One cause of imprecision in data is aggregation. If data are aggregated or summarized, then field values, e.g., AGE = 32.5, will describe not the age of an individual, but the aggregated age of a group. Patterns found on aggregated data tend to be heuristic. Their uncertainty can be better estimated if besides average, other statistics are available, such as minimum, maximum, and standard deviation.

Discretization: The other main cause of data imprecision is discretization, when the domain of a numeric value is split into intervals and only the interval is recorded in the database. Some discretization is inevitable in recording numeric measurements: e.g., an insurance database records a child's age as 15 years, even though she is 15 years, 3 months, and 7 days old. Additional discretization is frequently done for the purpose of subsequent aggregation. For example, in another database age is discretized into ranges 0–20, 21–34, 35–49, 50–64, and over 65, to facilitate the computation of statistics on each age group.

Discretization of numeric values is also needed for applying symbolic learning and discovery algorithms to continuous data. Poor discretization will reduce pattern certainty and increase pattern imprecision.

There are many different discretization techniques, suitable for different tasks. Pednault [49] has applied the minimum description length principle to recover a smooth shape from noisy data. Chan and Wong [12] have used the entropy minimization approach to discretize continuous data for subsequent rule discovery. Kerber [33] used a bottom-up merging of intervals in such a way as to maximize the χ^2 test. He used discretization as a preliminary step before using symbolic learning techniques. Piatetsky-Shapiro and Connell [55] and later Muralikrishna and DeWitt [44] have used equi-depth histograms to develop discretization schemes that minimize error in estimating how many records satisfy a query condition. Such estimation is useful in query optimization and in speeding up learning algorithms that require frequent size estimates.

Imprecise Knowledge: Another type of imprecision is the fuzziness inherent in specifying knowledge in a natural language, e.g., John is "young." Fuzziness is more of a problem for KA, when operationalizing expert-specified rules, which frequently contain fuzzy terms. Starting with the seminal work of Zadeh [74], a number of approaches have been proposed to deal with fuzziness, including the necessity and possibility theory [75] and triangular norms [5]. These approaches are described in more detail elsewhere in this book.

5.6 Dealing with Large Volumes of Data

> *Data expand to fill the space available for storage.*
> —Parkinson's Law of Data

Databases that are measured in gigabytes and tetrabytes are quite common nowadays. The database size has two important dimensions: the number of records and the number of fields. Dealing with a large number of records is in some sense easier, since the complexity of many discovery methods is $O(NlogN)$ or better, where N is the number of records. Faster hardware and parallel processing continuously increase the number of records that can be handled in a given time. When that is still not sufficient, sampling can be used, as discussed above in Section 5.1.

Dealing with a large number of fields is more difficult, since many discovery methods need to examine combinations of two or more fields. Thus, their run-time is at least quadratic and in some cases exponential in the number of fields.

Typically, business databases collect many unrelated fields to support different applications. Any particular analysis can be limited, without much loss, to the subset of potentially interesting fields. One approach, taken in the Knowledge Discovery Workbench [57] is to use domain knowledge to explicitly define a *focus* of discovery, which generalizes the idea of a database view [72] by specifying not only what fields to analyze, but also their relative importance in pattern evaluation, the expected relationships between fields, and other parameters directing the discovery.

Another approach is to preanalyze the data to determine the field dependencies. A number of algorithms for this task have been developed recently [46, 48, 15]. One can then use the field dependencies to focus the discovery only on the fields that are relevant to the target concept. The data-driven approach of focusing discovery reduces the chance of ignoring an unexpected pattern, compared to using only the expert knowledge for focusing discovery (see Section 5.4).

The advantages of focusing were confirmed experimentally by Almuallim and Dietterich [1], who showed on a number of datasets that the accuracy of the generated tree increases significantly if the irrelevant attributes are removed before constructing a decision-tree.

5.7 Changing Information

Most large, real-world databases are being constantly updated. Thus, unless one is studying only historical data, one needs to constantly reexamine the previously derived patterns to see whether they were affected by changes. The methods for dealing with change depend on the frequency of change, relative to the timeframe of analysis. Monthly weather updates may be too frequent for global warming analysis, while second-by-second data is not frequent enough for a real-time engine control.

Some data items, such as a person's date of birth, can be considered unchangeable. Here, batch algorithms applied to snapshots of data are sufficient. Most of the pattern discovery methods fall into this category.

Some items change sufficiently rapidly to make complete reanalysis inefficient. Here, one needs to use incremental discovery algorithms, such as incremental decision trees [60].

Some data items, such as a person's pulse or the latest stock price, change so fast as to require real-time processing (e.g., [31]). Pattern discovery on such data is generally done off-line.

Other items, such as flu infections and retail sales, have known variations. Domain knowledge of such variations can be used to adjust the patterns found in data [36].

Expert systems also need to deal with change. A desirable way of accomplishing this would be to have the expert system learn [4] and improve in the course of its operation. Learning expert systems is an active area of research.

Change can also be treated as an opportunity rather than a problem. Some business databases have become so large, and are being updated so frequently, that it becomes almost impossible to understand the changes using only manual analysis. Such is the situation with supermarket sales data, collected using bar-code scanners. Two commercial systems: CoverStory [65] and Spotlight [2], were recently developed to automatically identify and describe the important changes in this data.

6 SUMMARY

I presented the perspectives of fields of knowledge discovery in databases and knowledge acquisition for expert systems on dealing with imperfect information. I examined the problems stemming from randomness, incompleteness, incorrectness, imprecision, large data volume, and change, and outlined possible solutions.

I also described some important open issues, such as determining the source of uncertainty: incompleteness vs. randomness, and reducing apparent randomness with domain knowledge.

I expect the move towards normative treatment of uncertainty and imprecision to continue, with increased applications to KDD and KA. At the same time, emergence of more complex databases and larger knowledge bases will require additional development of knowledge-based treatments of uncertainty and imprecision.

Acknowledgments

I am indebted to Chris Matheus and Bud Frawley for interesting discussions that helped shape these ideas and for many excellent suggestions. I am grateful to all UMIS workshop participants for numerous helpful comments, and especially to Philippe Bernard, Pierro Bonissone, and Alex Borgida who reviewed various drafts of this paper. I thank Brian Gaines and David Prerau for their insights on knowledge acquisition. I thank Shri Goyal for his encouragement and support.

REFERENCES

[1] H. Almuallim and T. G. Dietterich. Learning with many irrelevant features. In *Proceedings of AAAI 91*, pages 547–552, 1991.

[2] T. Anand and G. Kahn. SPOTLIGHT: A data explanation system. In *Proceedings of the Eighth IEEE Conference on Applications of AI*, 1992.

[3] J. R. Anderson. Skill acquisition: Compilation of weak-method problem solutions. *Psychological Review*, 94: 192–210, 1987.

[4] W. J. Frawley, B. Silver, G. Iba, J. Vittal, and K. Bradford. ILS: A framework for multi-paradigmatic learning. In *Proceedings of the Seventh International Conference on Machine Learning*, pages 348–356. Morgan Kaufmann, San Mateo, CA, 1990.

[5] P. Bonissone. Plausible reasoning: Coping with uncertainty in expert systems. In S. Shapiro, editor, *Encyclopedia of Artificial Intelligence*, pages 854–863. John Wiley, New York, 1987.

[6] J. Boose. Personal construct theory and the transfer of human expertise. In *Proceedings of the Fourth National Conference on Artificial Intelligence*, pages 27–33. AAAI, Menlo Park, CA, 1984.

[7] J. Boose and B. Gaines, editors. *Proceedings of the Knowledge Acquisition for Knowledge-Based Systems Workshop (KAW91)*. University of Calgary, Alberta, 1991.

[8] I. Bratko, I. Mozetic, and N. Lavrac. *KARDIO: A Study in Deep and Qualitative Knowledge for Expert Systems*. MIT Press, Cambridge, MA, 1989.

[9] L. Breiman, J. Friedman, R. Olshen, and C. Stone. *Classification and Regression Trees*. Wadsworth, Belmont, CA, 1984.

[10] Y. Cai, N. Cercone, and J. Han. Attribute-oriented induction in relational databases. In G. Piatetsky-Shapiro and W. Frawley, editors, *Knowledge Discovery in Databases*, pages 213–228. AAAI/MIT Press, Cambridge, MA, 1991.

[11] N. Cercone, editor. Special issue, Learning and discovery in databases. *IEEE Transactions on Knowledge and Data Engineering*, 5(6), 1993.

[12] K. C. C. Chan and A. K. C. Wong. A statistical technique for extracting classificatory knowledge from databases. In G. Piatetsky-Shapiro and W. Frawley, editors, *Knowledge Discovery in Databases*, pages 107–124. AAAI/MIT Press, Cambridge, MA, 1991.

[13] P. Cheeseman, J. Kelly, M. Self, J. Stutz, W. Taylor, and D. Freeman. Autoclass: A Bayesian classification system. In J. Laird, editor, *Proceedings of the Fifth International Machine Learning Conference*, pages 54–64. Morgan Kaufmann, San Mateo, CA, June 1988.

[14] G. Cooper. The computational complexity of probabilistic inference using Bayesian belief networks. *Artificial Intelligence*, 42: 393–405, 1990.

[15] G. Cooper and E. Herskovits. A Bayesian method for the induction of probabilistic networks from data. *Machine Learning*, 9(4): 309–348, 1992.

[16] R. Davis, B. Buchanan, and E. Shortliffe. Production rules as a representation for a knowledge-based consultation program. *Artificial Intelligence*, 8: 15–45, 1977.

[17] G. Dunn and B. S. Everitt. *An Introduction to Mathematical Taxonomy.* Cambridge University Press, Cambridge, MA, 1982.

[18] U. Fayyad, G. Piatetsky-Shapiro, P. Smyth, and R. Uthurusamy, editors. *Advances in Knowledge Discovery and Data Mining.* AAAI/MIT Press, Cambridge, MA, 1995.

[19] U. Fayyad and R. Uthurusamy, editors. *Proceedings of KDD-94.* AAAI, Menlo Park, CA, 1994.

[20] U. Fayyad and R. Uthurusamy, editors. *Proceedings of KDD-95.* AAAI, Menlo Park, CA, 1995.

[21] D. H. Fisher. Knowledge acquisition via incremental conceptual clustering. *Machine Learning*, 2(2): 139–172, 1987.

[22] W. J. Frawley, G. Piatetsky-Shapiro, and C. J. Matheus. Knowledge discovery in databases: An overview. In *Knowledge Discovery in Databases*, pages 1–27. AAAI/MIT Press, Cambridge, MA, 1991. Reprinted in *AI Magazine*, 13(3), 1992.

[23] B. R. Gaines and M. L. G. Shaw. Induction of inference rules for expert systems. *Fuzzy Sets and Systems*, 18: 315–328, 1986.

[24] S. Gallant. Connectionist expert systems. *Communications of ACM*, 31(2): 153–168, 1988.

[25] J. Gordon and E. Shortliffe. A method for managing evidential reasoning in hierarchical hypothesis space. *Artificial Intelligence*, 26(3): 323–358, 1985.

[26] D. Haussler. Quantifying inductive bias: AI learning algorithms and Valiant's learning framework. *Artificial Intelligence*, 36(2): 177–221, 1988.

[27] D. Heckerman. *Probabilistic Similarity Networks*. MIT Press, Cambridge, MA, 1991.

[28] M. Henrion. An introduction to algorithms for inference in belief nets. In M. Henrion and R. Shachter, editors, *Uncertainty in Artificial Intelligence 5*, pages 129–138. North-Holland, Amsterdam, The Netherlands, 1990.

[29] R. Howard and J. Matheson. Influence diagrams. In R. Howard and J. Matheson, editors, *Readings on the Principles and Applications of Decision Analysis, Vol. II*, pages 721–762. Strategic Decisions Group, Menlo Park, CA, 1981.

[30] T. Imielinski. Intelligent query answering in rule-based systems. *Journal of Logic Programming*, 4: 229–257, 1987.

[31] F. Ingrand, M. Georgeff, and A. Rao. An architecture for real-time reasoning and system control. *IEEE Expert*, 7(6): 34–44, 1992.

[32] W. H. Inmon and S. Osterfelt. *Understanding Data Pattern Processing: the Key to Competitive Advantage*. QED Technical Publishing Group, Wellesley, MA, 1991.

[33] R. Kerber. ChiMerge: Discretization of numeric attributes. In *Proceedings of the Fourth National Conference on Artificial Intelligence*, pages 123–128. AAAI, Menlo Park, CA, 1992.

[34] W. Kloesgen. Problems for knowledge discovery in databases and their treatment in the statistics interpreter EXPLORA. *International Journal of Intelligent Systems*, 7(7): 649–674, 1992.

[35] D. Laberge and S. Samuels. Towards a theory of automatic information processing in reading. *Cognitive Psychology*, 6: 293–323, 1974.

[36] J. K. Lee, S. B. Oh, and J. C. Shin. UNIK-FCST: Knowledge-assisted adjustment of statistical forecasts. *Expert Systems with Applications*, 1(1): 39–49, 1990.

[37] D. Lenat and R. Guha. *Building Large Knowledge-Based Systems*. Addison-Wesley, Reading, MA, 1991.

[38] H. Mannila and K.-J. Raiha. Dependency inference. In *Proceedings of the Thirteenth International Conference on Very Large Data Bases*, pages 155–158, 1987.

[39] C. J. Matheus, P. K. Chan, and G. Piatetsky-Shapiro. Systems for knowledge discovery in databases. *IEEE Transactions on Knowledge and Data Engineering*, 5(6): 903–913, December 1993.

[40] C. J. Matheus, G. Piatetsky-Shapiro, and D. McNeill. An application of KEFIR to the analysis of healthcare information. In *Proceedings of AAAI-94 KDD workshop*, July 1994.

[41] M. McLeish, P. Yao, M. Garg, and T. Stirtzinger. Discovery of medical diagnostic information: An overview of methods and results. In *Knowledge Discovery in Databases*, pages 477–490. AAAI/MIT Press, Cambridge, MA, 1991. Reprinted in *AI Magazine*, 13(3), 1992.

[42] R. S. Michalski, J. G. Carbonell, and T. M. Mitchell. *Machine Learning, An Artificial Intelligence Approach, Vol. II.* Morgan Kaufmann, San Mateo, CA, 1986.

[43] A. Motro. VAGUE: A user interface to relational databases that permits vague queries. *ACM Transactions on Office Information Systems*, 6(3): 187–214, July 1988.

[44] M. Muralikrishna and D. DeWitt. Equi-depth histograms for estimating selectivity factors for multi-dimensional queries. In *Proceedings of SIGMOD-88*, pages 28–36. ACM, New York, 1988.

[45] M. Musen. Building and extending models. *Machine Learning*, 4(3,4): 347–376, 1989.

[46] R. Scheines P. Spirtes, C. Glymour. *Causation, Prediction, and Search.* Lecture Notes in Statistics. Springer-Verlag, New York, 1993.

[47] K. Parsaye and M. Chignell. *Intelligent Database Tools and Applications.* John Wiley, New York, 1993.

[48] J. Pearl. *Probabilistic Reasoning in Intelligent Systems: Networks of Plausible Inference, 2nd Edition.* Morgan Kaufmann, San Mateo, CA, 1992.

[49] E. P. D. Pednault. Inferring probabilistic theories from data. In *Proceedings of AAAI-88*, pages 624–628. Morgan Kaufman, Menlo Park, CA, 1988.

[50] G. Piatetsky-Shapiro. Discovery, analysis, and presentation of strong rules. In G. Piatetsky-Shapiro and W. J. Frawley, editors, *Knowledge Discovery in Databases*, pages 229–248. AAAI/MIT Press, Cambridge, MA, 1991.

[51] G. Piatetsky-Shapiro. Knowledge discovery in real databases: A workshop report. *AI Magazine*, 11(5), 1991.

[52] G. Piatetsky-Shapiro, editor. Special issue, Knowledge discovery in data and knowledge Bases. *International Journal of Intelligent Systems*, 7(7), 1992.

[53] G. Piatetsky-Shapiro, editor. *Proceedings of KDD-93.* AAAI, Menlo Park, CA, July 1993.

[54] G. Piatetsky-Shapiro, editor. Special issue, Knowledge discovery in databases. *Journal of Intelligent Information Systems*, 4(1), 1995.

[55] G. Piatetsky-Shapiro and C. Connell. Accurate estimation of the number of tuples satisfying a condition. In *Proceedings of SIGMOD-84*, pages 220–226. ACM, New York, 1984.

[56] G. Piatetsky-Shapiro and W. J. Frawley, editors. *Knowledge Discovery in Databases.* AAAI/MIT Press, Cambridge, MA, 1991.

[57] G. Piatetsky-Shapiro and C. J. Matheus. Knowledge discovery workbench for exploring business databases. *International Journal of Intelligent Systems*, 7(7): 675–686, 1992.

[58] J. R. Quinlan. Induction of decision trees. *Machine Learning*, 1(1): 81–106, 1986.

[59] J. R. Quinlan. Generating production rules from decision trees. In *Proceedings of IJCAI-87*, pages 304–307. Morgan Kaufmann, San Mateo, CA, 1987.

[60] J. R. Quinlan. Incremental induction of decision trees. *Machine Learning*, 2(4): 161–186, 1989.

[61] J. R. Quinlan. *C4.5—Programs for Machine Learning.* Morgan Kaufmann, San Mateo, CA, 1993.

[62] S. Spangler R. Uthurusamy, U. Fayyad. Learning useful rules from inconclusive data. In G. Piatetsky-Shapiro and W. J. Frawley, editors, *Knowledge Discovery in Databases*, pages 141–158. AAAI/MIT Press, Cambridge, MA, 1991.

[63] D. E. Rummelhart and J. L. McClelland. *Parallel Distributed Processing, Vol. 1.* MIT Press, Cambridge, MA, 1986.

[64] R. Scheines and P. Spirtes. Finding latent variable models in large data bases. *International Journal of Intelligent Systems*, 7(7): 609–622, 1992.

[65] J. Schmitz, G. Armstrong, and J. D. C. Little. CoverStory—automated news finding in marketing. In *DSS Transactions*, pages 46–54. Institute of Management Sciences, Providence, RI, 1990.

[66] G. Shafer. *A Mathematical Theory of Evidence*. Princeton University Press, Princeton, NJ, 1976.

[67] G. Shafer and J. Pearl, editors. *Readings in Uncertain Reasoning*. Morgan Kaufmann, San Mateo, CA, 1990.

[68] S. Shapiro, editor. *Encyclopedia of Artificial Intelligence*. John Wiley, New York, 1987.

[69] W. Shen. Discovering regularities from knowledge bases. *International Journal of Intelligent Systems*, 7(7): 623–636, 1992.

[70] H. Suermondt. *Explanation in Bayesian Belief Networks*. Ph.D. Dissertation, Stanford University Deptartment of Computer Science, 1992. CS-92-1417.

[71] E. R. Tufte. *Envisioning Information*. Graphics Press, Cheshire, CT, 1991.

[72] J. D. Ullman. *Principles of Database Systems*. Computer Science Press, Rockville, MD, 1982.

[73] R. Yager. On linguistic summaries of data. In G. Piatetsky-Shapiro and W. J. Frawley, editors, *Knowledge Discovery in Databases*, pages 347–366. AAAI/MIT Press, Cambridge, MA, 1991.

[74] L. Zadeh. Fuzzy sets. *Information Control*, 8: 338–353, 1965.

[75] L. Zadeh. Fuzzy sets as a basis for a theory of possibility. *Fuzzy Sets and Systems*, 1: 3–28, 1978.

7

UNCERTAINTY IN INFORMATION RETRIEVAL SYSTEMS

Howard R. Turtle*
W. Bruce Croft**

*West Publishing Company
Eagan, MN 55123*

**Computer Science Department
University of Massachusetts
Amherst, MA 01002*

1 INTRODUCTION

Information retrieval (IR) is concerned with identifying documents in a collection that a user in need of information will judge to be useful or relevant. We are generally provided with a description of the user's information need, or query. We then select documents likely to be relevant by comparing the query with prestored document representations, and may, optionally, revise the query representation for subsequent retrieval. The retrieval process, then, involves query acquisition, document selection, and query revision. A document collection may include normal text documents (e.g., journal articles), but it may also include nontext materials (photographs, museum pieces, software modules, and so on). Information storage and retrieval is a central element of systems that support such functions as office automation, library automation, legal research, or software engineering. Research in IR spans many subdisciplines of computer and information science.

Any effective retrieval system includes three major components: the identification and representation of document content, the acquisition and representation of the information need, and the specification of a matching function that selects relevant documents based on these representations. Uncertainty must be dealt with in each of these components.

- **Document representation**. Given the text of a document, even humans cannot agree on the set of concepts that should be used to represent its content. The use of automated techniques for generating descriptions introduces additional uncertainty, and the situation is further complicated if we attempt to represent the degree to which each concept is a correct description of document content.

- **Representing information needs**. The same representation problems arise when representing the information need, but additional uncertainty is introduced, because the information need is generally not clearly articulated, and because it will change during the search process as the user sees what kind of documents are available.

- **Matching function**. The matching process must deal with the uncertainty inherent in the document and information need representations, but even if we had precise representations, the matching process would still be uncertain: the same concept can be represented in many ways, the same representation can be used for different concepts, and the concepts that occur in a single representation are not independent.

In addition to these three components, most current retrieval systems include a fourth,

- **Relevance feedback**. Users may be asked to select relevant documents or portions of documents from a retrieved set. This set of relevant documents can then be used to modify the representation of the information need or the matching function to improve subsequent retrieval. In some cases, a history of relevance judgments can be used to alter the document representation.

When we fix the details of the document representation, the query representation, and the matching function we have specified what is generally called a retrieval model.

Work that attempts to model the uncertainty inherent in the retrieval process can be traced back at least to the late 1950s and early 1960s in the work of Luhn [39] and of Maron and Kuhn [41]. Since the 1960s a number of retrieval models that deal with at least some aspect of uncertainty have been proposed. They have evolved from *ad hoc* models intended for use with small, highly structured document surrogates (e.g., bibliographic records containing title, author, and subject codes) to current generation models that have strong theoretical bases, are intended to accommodate a variety of full text document types, and that explicitly model uncertainty. Current models handle documents with complex internal structure, and most incorporate a learning or relevance feedback component.

Three main classes of retrieval models are in current use: exact-match models, which form the basis of most commercial retrieval systems; vector-space models, which view documents and queries as vectors in a high-dimension vector space and use distance as a measure of similarity; and probabilistic models, which view retrieval as a problem of estimating the probability that a document representation matches or satisfies a query. The vector space and probabilistic models have been shown experimentally to offer significant improvements in retrieval performance over exact-match models but have only recently been used in commercial products. The exact-match and vector-space models can be cast as probabilistic models, which use a particular set of estimates for the component probabilities [76]. For this reason, and because the probabilistic models tend to have clearer representations of uncertainty, we will focus on probabilistic retrieval models and will discuss other model forms only when the distinction is important.

A fourth class of retrieval model, logic-based models, have been receiving recent attention [80, 6]. These models view documents and queries as sets of propositions and assess similarity based on the degree to which a query can be inferred from a document, possibly using additional domain knowledge.

In what follows we first provide background information on information retrieval and how IR systems are evaluated (Section 2). We then describe a set of historically important retrieval models (Section 3) and discuss current approaches to modeling uncertainty in IR (Section 4). Finally, we conclude with a review of open problems in IR that must be addressed if we are to develop a comprehensive framework for dealing with uncertainty in information systems in general and IR systems in particular (Section 5).

2 BACKGROUND

In this section we review a few aspects of IR research that are important to an understanding of the approaches to representing uncertainty that have been proposed. We begin with a more detailed discussion of retrieval models (Section 2.1). We then discuss the Probability Ranking Principle (Section 2.2), and describe the events of interest in most probabilistic retrieval models (Section 2.3). We close this section with a brief review of the main techniques used to compare retrieval system performance (Section 2.4).

What is the liability of the United States under the Federal
Tort Claims Act for injuries sustained by employees of an
independent contractor working under contract with an agency
of the United States Government?

"united states" u.s. government (federal /2 government)
/P tort /2 claim /P injur! /P employee worker crewman
/P independent /2 contractor

(liabil,unite,state,federal,tort,claim,act,injur,sustain,employee,
independ,contractor,work,contract,agenc,government)

#sum(liabil
        #phrase(unite state)
        #phrase(federal tort claim act)
        injur
        sustain
        #syn(employee worker)
        #phrase(independ contractor)
        work
        contract
        #phrase(agenc unite state)
        government)

Figure 1 Query representation examples.

2.1 Retrieval Models

Every information system has, either explicitly or implicitly, an associated theory of information access and a set of assumptions that underlie that theory.
We use the term *theory* here in the mathematical or logical sense, in which a
theory refers to a set of axioms and inference rules that allow derivation of new
theorems. A *model* is an embodiment of the theory, in which we define the set
of objects about which assertions can be made and restrict the ways in which
classes of objects can interact. Models allow us to compare different approaches
to information access and make predictions about system performance that can
be evaluated.

In the case of IR, a *retrieval model* specifies the representations used for documents and information needs,[1] and how they are compared. For example, many retrieval models assume representations based on binary or weighted features,[2] and comparison based on a similarity measure. Early retrieval models placed less emphasis on specifying how representations should be extracted from document and query texts and which representations produce the best performance. Research on retrieval models incorporating probabilistic indexing [21, 73] and machine learning [35] explicitly address this issue. Figure 1 presents four query representation examples. The first example is a natural language description of a user's information need; this query could be used directly by several current-generation retrieval systems. The second example is an "equivalent" Boolean query that a user might provide to a more traditional exact-match retrieval system. The third representation is simply a list of terms extracted from the natural language version, in which terms have been reduced to a morphological root. This kind of representation is common with simple probabilistic and vector-space models. The final representation is also extracted from the natural language query, but it attempts to capture structural information from the query (e.g., phrases) or from some external knowledge base (e.g., synonym classes).

The vector-space model and the probabilistic model have been studied and used for some time and are quite well understood. Even so, only certain aspects of the underlying theories are clearly defined, whereas others, especially those dealing with the user, remain vague. For example, the various forms of these models usually state what independence assumptions are being made but are less clear when it comes to defining relevance. The vector-space model [60] does not attempt to define anything to do with the external realities of users and information needs, and instead can be regarded as a mathematical description of one component of an IR system, rather than the IR process as a whole [2]. The models of Robertson *et al.* [53], Fuhr [21], and Turtle and Croft [73] are somewhat more comprehensive, but they still leave a number of questions unanswered, such as how different types of information needs and goals are represented in a retrieval theory.

---

[1] An information need is the user's perceived but unstated definition of what documents will be judged useful or satisfactory. A query is a representation of this information need either in natural language or in some formal query language. Unless the distinction is important, we will use the two terms interchangeably.

[2] Attributes that can be assigned to documents or queries will generally be referred to as features or as indexing features. Example features include terms extracted from documents; manually assigned subject codes; information such as author or title; special purpose features, such as geographic names or monetary amount; and so on. Historically, the most important features were terms and we will generally use term and feature interchangeably unless the distinction is important.

Some common assumptions made in retrieval models are

- The objects being retrieved are primarily textual.

- The user's understanding of the information need will be refined during the search process.

- Retrieval is based on representations of textual content and information needs.

- Both text and information need representations are uncertain.

These assumptions have led to retrieval techniques that emphasize ranked retrieval, iterative query formulation, relevance feedback, and analysis of simple natural language queries.

Other types of information systems have different theories and assumptions associated with them. The area of database systems is particularly important, and includes theories associated with relational database systems, deductive database systems, and object-oriented systems [85]. Typical database systems represent more types of objects than typical IR systems, but the objects usually have very well-defined content. Issues involving uncertainty in query specification or object representation have largely been ignored in the database field (with a few exceptions such as [44, 27]). Ignoring these issues can be justified, since doing so has allowed significant progress in the development of database theory and in implementation areas such as query optimization. The same justification cannot be made for many commercial IR systems that also ignore retrieval models based on uncertainty. In this case, the unrealistic assumptions underlying these systems result in poor retrieval performance.

2.2   Probability Ranking Principle

The common characteristic of the probabilistic retrieval models that will be discussed here is adherence to the Probability Ranking Principle ([52]), which asserts that optimal retrieval performance is achieved when documents are ranked according to the probability that they will be judged relevant to a query. Given a query representation q_j and a document representation d_k, and if we let R denote the event that document d_k is judged relevant to q_j, then we wish to rank documents by $P(R|q_j, d_k)$ or by $P(R|q_j, d_k, K)$, where K is some body of domain knowledge that bears upon our decisions about relevance.

The application of the Probability Ranking Principle generally involves some questionable assumptions:

- Decisions about the relevance of a document to a query are assumed to be independent of other documents in the collection, that is, documents can be considered in isolation. In practice, the order in which documents are presented to a user can influence relevance judgments, but dependence between documents is generally ignored (but see [28, 66, 4]).

- More troublesome is the assumption that we can estimate these probabilities accurately enough to order documents in a way that will approximate user judgments about relevance, often in the absence of any samples of relevant documents.

Despite these problems, models based on the PRP offer the most rigorously developed theories of information retrieval. These models form the basis of retrieval systems that offer the highest levels of retrieval performance currently available.

2.3 Event Spaces and Relevance

Given sets of possible queries Q and possible documents D, most probabilistic models have as their event space the set $Q \times D$. Models differ in the structure of the query and document representations. In the simpler models, queries and documents are represented as binary valued vectors, in which each element corresponds to a feature that can be assigned to a document or query. In a simple system in which n documents contain m unique terms, there are 2^m possible document representations, of which at most n are defined. Query terms that do not occur in the document collection are generally ignored, so there are 2^m possible query representations.

More complex models modify the sets of document and query representations in any of several ways:

1. Most allow real-valued vectors in which elements represent the degree to which the feature represents the document or query, or the probability that the feature is a correct descriptor of the document or query.

2. The original feature set may be replaced with a smaller set. Some form of factor analysis is used to collapse feature sets with poor discrimination.

3. Separate feature sets (vocabularies) may be allowed for documents and queries.

4. Structured queries (e.g., using Boolean operators) may be supported in place of flat query vectors.

5. Internal document structure may be represented, so that, for example, retrieval can make use of the fact that a feature occurs in an abstract or title rather than as an author or in a footnote.

6. Relationships between documents may be represented so that retrieval can make use of semantic links between documents (e.g., citations, co-citation structure, hypertext links).

7. More complex feature sets may be supported to allow representation of features that may or may not be present in the underlying indexing set (e.g., phrases or synonym classes).

With the exception of item 2, these extensions have the effect of expanding the set of query or document representations.

The notion of relevance is difficult to define precisely and has been the subject of a great deal of debate (see [61] for a review). Ideally, relevance is a relation mapping $Q \times D$ onto a set of relevance categories, say $\{r_0, r_1\}$ if all documents are to be judged relevant or nonrelevant. Some models allow several degrees of relevance, in which case the range of the relevance relation is expanded. These multivalued relevance scales have not proven useful, and we will restrict attention to binary valued scales. Conceptually, the relevance relation is specified by the user and is defined for all query/document pairs. In practice, this relation is defined only for a small portion of the document collection for each query because the user can evaluate only a relatively small number of documents.

Because the relevance relation is unknowable prior to retrieval in operational systems, each retrieval model contains an implicit definition of relevance. For exact-match retrieval models, relevance is generally defined in terms of satisfying a first-order logic expression. For probabilistic models, relevance is defined in terms of probability of relevance, conditioned on a set of evidence that includes document and query representations. For vector-space models, relevance is defined in terms of distance between the document and query. For evaluation purposes we will assemble as complete a definition of the relevance relation as possible, and measure the degree to which the definition of relevance embodied in the retrieval model matches this standard.

2.4   Evaluation in Information Retrieval

The development of methods for evaluating retrieval systems and retrieval models remains an active area of research. See [63, 77, 56] for reviews of evaluation in information retrieval.

Evaluations are conducted in many contexts (e.g., evaluation of an operational retrieval system, a laboratory prototype, or a paper model) with widely varying objectives (e.g., quantify retrieval effectiveness, cost effectiveness, collection quality, or user satisfaction). The most common measures of retrieval performance or effectiveness are *precision* and *recall*. Precision is the proportion of a retrieved set of documents that are relevant to a query. Recall is the proportion of all documents in the collection that are relevant to a query that are actually retrieved. If we assume that the set of documents relevant to a query (*relevant*) and the set of documents retrieved by the query (*retrieved*) are known, then

$$\text{Precision} \;=\; \frac{|relevant \cap retrieved|}{|retrieved|} = P(\text{relevant}|\text{retrieved})$$

$$\text{Recall} \;=\; \frac{|relevant \cap retrieved|}{|relevant|} = P(\text{retrieved}|\text{relevant})$$

For ranked retrieval, where there is no retrieved set, we generally compute a precision/recall pair for each relevant document in the ranking and then interpolate to find precision at standard recall points (i.e., recall $= 0.1, 0.2, \ldots, 1.0$). Several other measures of retrieval effectiveness have been developed but are not widely used.

To compare the effectiveness of two retrieval models, we make use of standard test collections [64]. A test collection consists of

- **A set of documents.** Test collections may contain information extracted from the original document, such as title, author, date, and an abstract, or they may contain the full text of the documents. The collection may include additional information, such as controlled vocabulary terms, author-assigned descriptors, and citation information. Until recently, test collections were small, generally containing from a few hundred to a few thousand records. In the last few years more realistic test collections have emerged that range in size from a few hundred megabytes to a few gigabytes.

- **A set of queries.** These are often actual queries submitted by users either in natural language form or in some formal query language, although artificially constructed queries are occasionally used (e.g., queries built to retrieve known documents or the text of a sample document).

- **A set of relevance judgments.** For each query the set of documents relevant to the query is identified. For small collections, the relevance judgments may be obtained by reviewing all documents in the collection, but for large collections relevance judgments are generally obtained by reviewing the combined results from a number of different representations of the query constructed by different searchers. Relevance judgments may be made by the query submitter or by independent domain experts. Relevance judgments are inherently subjective. Different experts will judge documents differently, and a single expert may give different judgments if the same documents are presented twice. In most cases we prefer user-supplied queries and relevance judgments.

Test collections are expensive to create, primarily because developing relevance judgments for a significant number of queries is labor intensive.

When using a test collection to compare two retrieval techniques, we first evaluate each query to produce a document ranking, use the relevance judgments to compute precision at standard recall points, then average the precision values over the set of queries and compare the results.

Most data gathered during retrieval experiments do not lend themselves well to standard statistical tests both because the quantities we wish to measure are difficult to define, and because the measurements we collect do not exhibit the properties that we have come to expect in data associated with physical systems (e.g., normally distributed). As a result, conservative nonparametric tests are generally used in IR. [51] reviews many of the definitional problems that affect experiment design. [67, 77] review problems with statistical tests applied to retrieval data.

In addition to retrieval effectiveness, IR models can be evaluated with respect to their computational costs. General-purpose retrieval models must be applicable to large collections (hundreds of thousands of documents and several gigabytes of text) if they are to find widespread use. Hybrid schemes, in which an efficient model is used to identify potentially relevant documents that are then further processed using a more effective but costlier model, have been considered [18], but retrieval models that cannot be used with real collections are generally of limited interest.

3   PRINCIPAL RETRIEVAL MODELS

In this section we describe a set of retrieval models that illustrate the major uncertainty issues that have been addressed. Exact-match models (Section 3.1) do not explicitly represent uncertainty but are historically and commercially important. These exact-match models form the baseline upon which other models must improve. The Binary Independence Model (Section 3.2) is one of the most widely known probabilistic models and illustrates the features present in most such models. The 2-Poisson Model (Section 3.3) is important because it attempts to develop a detailed model of term distribution and importance in a collection.

The final two topics dealt with in this section, long-term learning (Section 3.4) and relevance feedback (Section 3.5) are not, themselves, retrieval models but are important techniques that can be adapted to many retrieval models. The set of topics dealt with here is necessarily limited. Many important areas of IR research (e.g., cluster-based retrieval[3]) have been ignored in an attempt to focus on uncertainty management issues.

3.1   Exact-Match Models

Exact-match retrieval models use matching functions that, given a query, partition the document collection into two sets, those that match the query and those that do not. Documents in the matching set are generally not ranked, although they may be ordered by date, alphabetically, or some other criterion. Exact-match models are generally simple and efficient, and form the basis of most commercial retrieval packages.

By far the most common exact-match model is the Boolean model in which a query is an expression using *and, or,* and *not* as operators and document features as terms. It is important to distinguish here between the use of these logic operators in queries (which does not imply an exact-match model) and the use of classical logic as the interpretation of those operators. A Boolean query can be interpreted using classical logic under an exact-match model, in which case the query is a simple rule that a document must satisfy in order to be retrieved, but it can also be interpreted in a probabilistic model using

---

[3]In cluster-based retrieval we assume that documents that are judged similar to each other using some standard similarity measure will be judged relevant to the same queries. When one member of a cluster is retrieved, other members of the same cluster are also considered for retrieval.

the normal interpretation of *and, or,* and *not* as the intersection, union, and complement of sets of events, or in the vector space model using special distance functions.

Exact-match models do not deal with uncertainty. All documents either match or fail to match a query. The binary nature of the retrieval decision in Boolean systems is frequently cited as a drawback [12, 60, 58, 37]. Intuitively, when given a query containing n terms combined using an *and* operator, we would like a document containing all but one term to be judged nearly as likely to match the query as a document containing all n terms, and substantially more likely to match than a document containing none of the terms.

Since uncertainty can only be dealt with outside of these exact-match models, users are forced to deal with uncertainty as part of the query formulation process. An expert searcher must anticipate the various ways in which a concept can be expressed and must assemble these variations in a complex Boolean query.

The effectiveness of simple Boolean systems decreases as the collection size and average document length increases. With large collections it is difficult to formulate a query that will produce a result set that is small enough to be useful without excluding potentially relevant documents. Further, some linguistic structures that searchers find natural are represented awkwardly in the Boolean model (e.g., morphological variants) or cannot be represented at all (e.g., phrases). As a result, most commercial retrieval packages provide proximity operators and techniques for combining related word forms. Both of these extensions are handled naturally in the more advanced probabilistic models.

Proximity operators are used most often to represent phrases and occasionally to represent higher-order structure (e.g., two phrases in the same paragraph). As an example, requiring that the terms *information* and *retrieval* occur within two words of each other is likely to find a better (smaller) set of documents dealing with information retrieval, than would be obtained with the Boolean query "*information* and *retrieval*," which simply requires that the two terms occur in the same document. The two principal techniques for handling morphological variants are stemming, in which variant forms are algorithmically mapped to a single form, and the use of wildcards, which allow users to specify query terms as simple regular expressions that will match several different document terms.

Fuzzy logic. A number of retrieval models have been proposed that attempt to provide ranked output in response to a Boolean query. The most successful of these are extensions to existing probabilistic and vector-space models, but the use of fuzzy logic has also been proposed [68, 48].

Fuzzy logic based models define a membership function $F(d_k, t_j)$ for the set of documents that are described by an indexing feature. Documents can then be ranked with respect to a query by combining membership values for individual terms using

$$
\begin{aligned}
F(d_k, t_1 \text{ and } t_2) && \min(F(d_k, t_1), F(d_k, t_2)) \\
F(d_k, t_1 \text{ or } t_2) && \max(F(d_k, t_1), F(d_k, t_2)) \\
F(d_k, \text{not } t_1) && 1 - F(d_k, t_1).
\end{aligned}
$$

When the value of the membership function is restricted to $\{0, 1\}$, the fuzzy logic model is equivalent to the conventional Boolean model. If the membership function takes on values in the range $[0, 1]$, then a natural ranking is defined. Pure fuzzy logic models have been criticized because

1. The models handle document-term weighting well, but do not directly model the use of query term weights.

2. Documents are generally ranked based on the value of only a small number of terms from the query. For example, given a query t_1 or t_2 or ...or t_n, a document containing a single term with $F(d_k, t_i) = 1$ and all $F(d_k, t_j) = 0, i \neq j$, would be ranked as highly as a document in which all terms had the maximum value.

3. Different results can be produced for logically equivalent queries.

Several models have been proposed that address these problems [3, 82], but no fuzzy logic based models have been implemented and evaluated using realistic test collections. Relatively little work has been published on fuzzy logic retrieval models since the early 1980s, in part because Boolean query models have fallen out of favor, despite their dominance in the commercial retrieval market.

3.2 Binary Independence Model

One of the simplest and most widely known probabilistic retrieval models is the binary independence model [77]. The basic idea behind this model is that query terms are distributed differently in relevant and nonrelevant documents, and we can compute the probability that a document will be judged relevant using an odds ratio and an estimate for $P(d_k|R, q_j)$.

A document collection is represented by a set of features $F = \{f_1, \ldots, f_m\}$, and each document d is represented by a binary valued feature vector $x = (x_1, \ldots, x_m)$, where $x_i = 1$ if f_i is assigned to d and $x_i = 0$ otherwise. A query q_k is a set of features contained in F. The odds that d will be judged relevant to q_k is then

$$O(R|q_k, x) = \frac{P(R|q_k, x)}{P(\bar{R}|q_k, x)} = \frac{P(R|q_k)}{P(\bar{R}|q_k)} \cdot \frac{P(x|R, q_k)}{P(x|\bar{R}, q_k)}. \tag{7.1}$$

Independence assumptions are required to compute $P(x|R, q_k)$ and $P(x|\bar{R}, q_k)$. Some formulations of the model assume that terms are distributed independently in the collection, some that terms are distributed independently in the relevant and nonrelevant subset, but most often, that the distribution of document vectors in the relevant and nonrelevant sets is given by the product of the distribution of individual terms between the relevant and nonrelevant sets, that is

$$\frac{P(x|R, q_k)}{P(x|\bar{R}, q_k)} = \prod_{i=1}^{n} \frac{P(x_i|R, q_k)}{P(x_i|\bar{R}, q_k)}. \tag{7.2}$$

Given this independence assumption, we have

$$O(R|q_k, x) = O(R|q_k) \prod_{i=1}^{n} \frac{P(x_i|R, q_k)}{P(x_i|\bar{R}, q_k)}. \tag{7.3}$$

We can split this product in two, one product for terms that are assigned to the document and one for terms that are not assigned to the document, to get

$$O(R|q_k, x) = O(R|q_k) \prod_{x_i=1} \frac{P(x_i = 1|R, q_k)}{P(x_i = 1|\bar{R}, q_k)} \prod_{x_i=0} \frac{P(x_i = 0|R, q_k)}{P(x_i = 0|\bar{R}, q_k)}. \tag{7.4}$$

If we let $p_{ik} = P(x_i = 1|R, q_k)$ and $q_{ik} = P(x_i = 1|\bar{R}, q_k)$, and further assume that terms that are not contained in the query have the same distribution in the relevant and nonrelevant sets ($p_{ik} = q_{ik}$), then

$$O(R|q_k, x) = O(R|q_k) \prod_{x_i=1 \wedge f_i \in q} \frac{p_{ik}}{q_{ik}} \prod_{x_i=0 \wedge f_i \in q} \frac{1 - p_{ik}}{1 - q_{ik}} \tag{7.5}$$

$$= O(R|q_k) \prod_{x_i=1 \wedge f_i \in q} \frac{p_{ik}(1 - q_{ik})}{q_{ik}(1 - p_{ik})} \prod_{f_i \in q} \frac{1 - p_{ik}}{1 - q_{ik}}. \tag{7.6}$$

At this point we still have an expression that will allow us to recover the probability that document d would be judged relevant, but it is customary to observe now that $O(R|q_k)$ and the second product in equation 7.6 can be dropped because they are constants for a given query. This leaves us with a function that will rank documents by the probability of relevance without giving us any information about the actual probabilities.

All that remains now is to estimate p_{ik} and q_{ik} for each query term. If we have a sample of documents that have been judged relevant (as a result of relevance feedback), then we can estimate these probabilities from this sample. Unfortunately, for the initial retrieval, and in cases where the relevance feedback sample is too small to permit reliable estimation, we must use some other estimate. A number of estimates have been used, including setting p_{ik} and q_{ik} based on the characteristics of the individual terms [15] or setting them to an average obtained from a history of past queries and relevance judgments [21].

The binary independence model has been widely studied and has been extended to incorporate nonbinary indexing weights [53, 84, 83] and term dependencies [77].

3.3 2-Poisson Model

One of the problems with the binary independence model is the estimation of the probability that a query term will be assigned to documents in the relevant and nonrelevant sets. The 2-Poisson model [5] represents an attempt to develop a model that will allow estimation of the probability that a term is an accurate characterization of document content in the absence of relevance information. While not identical, these two probabilities are closely related. If a query term t_i was a complete and unambiguous description of an information need ($q_j = \{t_i\}$), then any document that was "about" the term would be relevant to the information need and $P(t_i|d)$ would be the same as $P(R|\{t_i\}, d)$.

The 2-Poisson model assumes that a term is distributed differently in documents for which the term is an accurate description than it is in documents for which it is not an accurate description. The model further assumes that terms exhibit a Poisson distribution in each of these classes. For term t_j we have classes C_{j1} (about) and C_{j0} (not about) and a parameter λ_{jk} which is the expected frequency of t_j in class C_{jk}. The probability that a document d_m

containing l occurrences of t_j belongs to class C_{jk} is then

$$P(f_m(t_j) = l|d_m \in C_{jk}) = e^{-\lambda_{jk}} \frac{\lambda_{jk}^l}{l!}.$$

If the probability that a randomly selected document is a member of class C_{jk} is π_{jk}, then

$$P(f_m(t_j) = l) = \sum_{k=0,1} \pi_{jk} e^{-\lambda_{jk}} \frac{\lambda_{jk}^l}{l!}$$

and $\pi_{j0} + \pi_{j1} = 1$, so we can derive $P(d_m \in C_{jk}|f_m(t_j))$. The π and λ parameters can be estimated from the document collection.

The 2-Poisson model has not proven useful as a description of term distribution in a collection. Studies suggest that most terms do not fit the Poisson model well [30, 31] and studies with larger numbers of classes (n-Poisson) are inconclusive [65, 40]. Further, no attempt has been made to determine if the separation induced for terms that do fit the model corresponds to user perceptions about the usefulness of a term as an indexing feature.

While the 2- and n-Poisson models have not, as yet, proven to be useful, the importance of a model that would permit prediction of term importance in a collection is widely recognized. It is possible that refinements to the model (e.g., different distribution assumptions, normalizations for document length or term frequency) could improve accuracy enough to be useful.

3.4   Long-Term Learning

One potential objection to the 2-Poisson model, and indeed, to any model that attempts to estimate the probability that a term correctly describes a document based solely on the distribution of terms in a collection, is that the model necessarily ignores the meaning associated with the terms; terms with very similar distributions may differ substantially in the degree to which they characterize a document or a user's information need. Another way to estimate this probability is to use a history of queries and relevance judgments in an attempt to develop term-specific estimates based on the use of terms in the learning sample.

The best known of the learning based models is the Darmstadt Indexing Approach (DIA) [21, 23], which attempts to learn to estimate $P(R|\{t_i\}, d_k)$ from a sample of relevance judgments for term-document pairs. Rather than learning the probability associated with a term directly, a set of heuristically selected attributes is associated with each term-document pair (e.g., the frequency of the term in a given document, the frequency of the term in the collection, whether the term occurs in a specific document component). Any of several machine learning techniques can then be applied to develop a discriminant function that estimates $P(R|\{t_i\}, d_k)$ given the set of attributes for a term. The use of the attribute set reduces the amount of training data required and allows the learning to incorporate attributes that may be important in specific collections or with different types of terms (e.g., manually versus automatically assigned). However, the use of simple linear discriminant functions, which operate on these attribute sets, also means that the degree to which the resulting estimates are term specific depends critically on the attributes used.

Experimental results show that estimates based on the kind of long-term learning used in the DIA model can significantly improve performance. The main problem associated with using this approach is the collection of adequate training data. The approach holds real promise for commercial application where relevance feedback can be used to capture the required relevance information.

3.5 Relevance Feedback

Relevance feedback is the name given to a process where, based on user feedback about documents retrieved in an initial ranking, the description of the information need is modified to produce a new document ranking. The feedback mechanism may be fully automatic or it may propose query changes to the user. User feedback usually takes the form of simple yes/no judgments on the relevance of documents, although more detailed feedback about concepts in those documents is also possible [29, 14]. Relevance feedback is a well-established and effective technique in IR.

Much of the original work on feedback was done in the context of the vector-space model [60, 59]. The general method for producing a new query given an old query and relevance judgments is as follows:

$$Q_{new} = Q_{old} + \beta \sum_{rel} \frac{D_i}{|D_i|} - \gamma \sum_{nonrel} \frac{D_i}{|D_i|} \qquad (7.7)$$

where the summation is taken over the known relevant and nonrelevant documents, the D_i represent document vectors, and $|D_i|$ is a normalization based on document length. A particularly common form of this query modification is

known as *dec hi*, where weighted terms are added directly to the queries, and
only one nonrelevant document is used, i.e.,

$$Q_{new} = Q_{old} + \sum_{rel} D_i - D_{topnonrel} \qquad (7.8)$$

In the vector-space model, then, relevance feedback involves changing weights
associated with query terms and adding new terms to the original query.

In the probabilistic model described by Robertson and Sparck Jones [54] and
Van Rijsbergen [77], relevance feedback is described in different terms. In this
model, documents are ranked using a (generally) linear discriminant function
in which each term corresponds to a representation concept in the collection.
Typically, only the representation concepts found in the query have nonzero
values, and the coefficients of these terms are estimated using some model-
specific function. A representative function is

$$g(d) = \sum_i (\log \frac{p_i}{1 - p_i} + \log \frac{1 - q_i}{q_i}) \qquad (7.9)$$

where p_i is the probability that term i occurs in a relevant document, and q_i
is the probability that term i occurs in a nonrelevant document. The second
term in the summation is typically estimated using each term's *idf*, and the
first term is based on the characteristics of the set of known relevant documents.

In relevance feedback, we are given a sample of documents that have been
judged relevant, and must reestimate our linear discriminant function based on
this sample. This involves computing a new set of p_i values for equation 7.9
based on the relevant sample, and adding the top n relevant document terms
(according to some measure) to the original query terms. Comparisons of the effectiveness of relevance feedback using the vector-space and probabilistic models
are difficult to make due to the large number of parameters involved, although
Salton and Buckley [59] suggest that the best vector space approaches have an
advantage.

A number of models have been proposed for using relevance feedback with
Boolean retrieval systems [58, 55, 50, 49]. While some of these models have been
shown to significantly improve performance when compared to conventional
Boolean retrieval, they are not widely used. These models generally adapt
probabilistic relevance feedback techniques to estimate weights for terms in very
restricted Boolean query forms (e.g., disjunctive normal form with no negation
and *and* terms containing at most three representation concepts). These models
do not make use of any linguistic or domain knowledge.

The development of an effective relevance feedback mechanism for Boolean and structured queries [16, 80] is a potentially important area for further research. Encoding feedback information in a structured query could improve performance more than a simple query, since it is possible to encode information in the structured query that is not represented in a simple list of terms.

4 CURRENT TRENDS IN INFORMATION RETRIEVAL

One of the problems associated with all the probabilistic models discussed so far is the absence of a visible semantic component that can make use of knowledge about the structure of language or of knowledge about relationships between concepts in a domain. A great deal of work has gone into developing models that can represent and infer relationships between documents and queries using this kind of knowledge. Three principal approaches have been pursued: the use of rule-based techniques (Section 4.1), the development of probabilistic logics (Section 4.2), and the use of inference or causal networks (Section 4.3).

4.1 Rule-based Retrieval

RUBRIC [71, 70] and the related Topic and CONSTRUE systems are examples of rule-based IR systems. These systems rely upon a body of knowledge that defines the structure of a given domain and provides rules for recognizing query concepts in documents. The knowledge base is created by users and represents hierarchical relationships between concepts in the domain. Concepts may have attributes associated with them (e.g., actor, event, or location), as well as a set of rules that specify the set of text strings and proximity relationships between strings that should trigger the recognition of the concept (e.g., the concept "U.S. President" requires that the strings "President" and "Clinton" appear in the same sentence). Rules can have degrees of certainty associated with them. Links in the concept hierarchy can also have degrees of certainty that control the propagation of belief through the hierarchy.

Given a query represented as a set of concepts connected by Boolean operators, a belief is computed for each concept in a document using the recognition rules and beliefs propagated from related concepts in the hierarchy. A belief for each document is then computed using operator specific combining functions (e.g., interpreting the Boolean operators as fuzzy set operators).

Small-scale experiments with these systems have yielded promising results, and the Topic system is enjoying some commercial success, but it is not clear how well the techniques will scale up to large multidomain collections. The two main problems with rule-based approaches are the difficulty of creating the knowledge base and the ad hoc nature of the belief rules. More recent work has reported some success in automatically inducing useful knowledge bases directly from the document collection and with using probability networks in place of ad hoc rules [25].

4.2 Uncertain Logics

By the mid-1980s, researchers had begun to suspect that "simple" probabilistic models had been developed fully and that significant improvements in retrieval performance could be achieved using hybrid approaches that married symbolic logic and probability [78, 79]. Models based on these logics are similar to deductive database models in the sense that relevance is defined in terms of the degree to which a query can be proved, given a document as evidence together with a body of domain knowledge. These uncertain logic models differ from deductive databases in that the representation of documents, queries, and domain knowledge are all uncertain and the inference process must use this information to produce a ranking based on the strength of the inference chain(s) linking documents with the query.

The most fully developed models [7, 38, 46] are based on extensions to modal logic in which we rank documents by the probability that a query can be inferred from a document in the context of a body of domain knowledge, $P(d_i, K \rightarrow q_j)$. Implication here is not interpreted as material implication or conditional probability, rather a document implies a query if some sequence of substitutions based on rules in the knowledge base gives a representation that includes the query. The probability is defined based on the amount of change to the original document required to derive the query. In this model, a document is a set of uncertain propositions, a query is a logic expression, and a knowledge base is a set of rules that can be applied to documents in order to derive queries.

The development of retrieval models based on uncertain logics is relatively new. While no large-scale retrieval experiments have been conducted using these models, preliminary results are encouraging [7, 38, 46]. If problems associated with acquiring and building knowledge bases and with the cost of evaluation can be solved, these models could find widespread use.

4.3   Inference Networks

Inference network based retrieval models [72, 73] represent an extension of classical probabilistic models in which retrieval is viewed as an inference or evidential reasoning process in which multiple sources of evidence about document and query content are combined to estimate the probability that a given document matches a query. This model is intended to

- **Support the use of multiple document representations**. Research has shown that a given query will retrieve different documents when applied to different representations, even when the average retrieval performance achieved with each representation is the same [32, 15, 20].

- **Allow results from multiple queries to be combined**. Given a single natural language description of an information need, different searchers will formulate different queries to represent that need and will retrieve different documents, even when average performance is the same for each searcher [42, 32]. Documents retrieved by multiple searchers are more likely to be relevant and different search strategies are known to retrieve different documents for the same underlying information need [13].

- **Allow the use of domain knowledge when matching queries with documents**. The poor match between the vocabularies used to represent queries and documents appears to be a major cause of poor recall [26].

The network model can be used to simulate earlier probabilistic, Boolean, vector-space, and cluster-based models [76, 72]. Moreover, retrieval results produced by these disparate models can be combined to form an overall assessment of relevance.

Inference network models are based on Bayesian or causal networks [50, 45] that have been suitably restricted to allow many of the relevant probabilities to be precomputed. The inference network shown in Figure 2 consists of two component networks: a document network and a query network. The document network represents the document collection and may incorporate multiple document representation schemes. The document network is built once for a given collection, and its structure does not change during query processing. The query network consists of a single node, which represents the user's information need, and one or more query representations, which express that information need. A query network is built for each information need and attached to the static document network. Query networks may be modified during query pro-

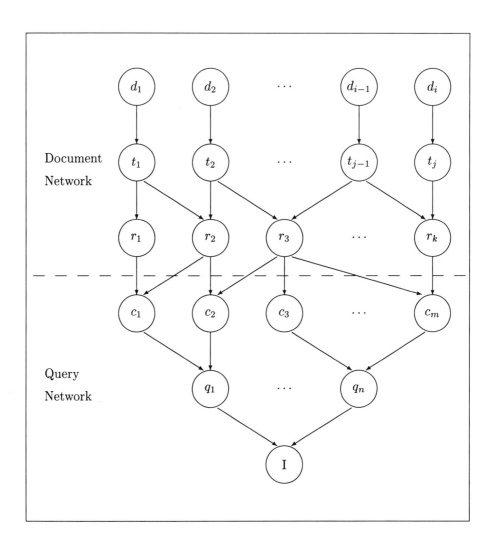

Figure 2   Basic document inference network.

cessing, as existing queries are refined or new queries are added in an attempt
to better characterize the information need.

The document network consists of document (d_i) and concept (r_k) representation nodes.[4] Each document node represents a document in the collection. Concept-representation nodes, or representation nodes, correspond to terms or indexing features that have been assigned to documents. The assignment of a representation concept to a document is represented by a directed arc to the representation node from each document to which the concept has been assigned.

Each representation node contains a specification of the conditional probability associated with the node given its set of parent nodes. Essentially, this is the probability that the representation concept is a correct descriptor of the set of parent documents. While, in principle, this would require $O(2^n)$ space for a node with n parents, in practice canonical representations are used that require $O(1)$ or $O(n)$ space. These canonical schemes use subjective probability estimates that can be justified on information theoretic grounds and which have been shown to work well in previous IR research.

The query network has a single leaf that corresponds to the information need, and multiple roots that correspond to the concepts that express the information need. As shown in Figure 2, a set of intermediate query nodes may also be used in cases where multiple query representations are used to express the information need. Links between the representation concept and query concept nodes define the mapping between the concepts used to represent the document collection and the concepts that make up the queries. These nodes represent the probability that a user query term is a correct description of a set of documents, given only information about the representation concepts assigned to that set of documents. In the simplest case, the query concepts are constrained to be the same as the representation concepts, and each query concept has exactly one parent representation node. In general, however, this mapping embodies thesaurus information and any domain knowledge about how to recognize query concepts in documents.

A query node represents a distinct query representation and contains a specification of the dependence of the query on the query concepts it contains. In most cases a single query node in Figure 2 will be replaced by a query tree in which each node corresponds to a single query operator (e.g., *and*, *or*, or *not* for Boolean queries, *phrase*, *synonym*, or *related term* for natural language queries). The conditional probability estimates at these nodes are fixed by the

---

[4]The full model includes an additional set of nodes between the document and representation concept layers. These nodes are not needed if we restrict attention to the text of a document.

operator type. Since the operators are simply different estimates for the conditional probabilities, different query types can be included in a single network.

When the query network is attached to the document network, evidence is attached to the network asserting $d_i = true$ with all remaining document nodes set to *false* (referred to as *instantiating* d_i). After propagation this gives the probability that the information need is met given d_i as evidence. This evidence is now removed and some d_j, $i \neq j$ is instantiated. This process can be repeated to compute the probability that the information need is met given each document in the collection and to rank the documents accordingly.

The inference network model has been shown to allow significant improvements in retrieval performance at computational costs that are comparable to those of many commercial Boolean retrieval systems [74, 75].

5   OPEN PROBLEMS

The current generation retrieval models discussed here all represent uncertainty and can significantly out perform simple exact match models. At the same time, their absolute performance is often disappointing and considerable room for improvement remains. Areas in which a better model of uncertainty are particularly important include improved estimation techniques (Section 5.1), improved representations of documents and queries (Section 5.2), more effective techniques for incorporating domain knowledge (Section 5.3), and improved query acquisition and feedback techniques (Section 5.4).

5.1   Parameter Estimation

All of the probabilistic models we have discussed require estimation of a set of parameters (see [24] for a review of estimation techniques). Some of these estimates are straightforward (e.g., the probability that a common term will occur in a document of a given length), but we are inevitably faced with making estimates based on unreliably small samples or, in many cases, based on no sample at all.

The small sample problem is probably unavoidable in IR. In a typical collection, most indexing features will occur in only one document and a very high percentage of the terms will occur in only a few documents. Techniques for grouping these low-frequency terms have been suggested [60], but it is hard to do this in a principled way, especially for terms that users expect to be highly selective (e.g., personal or corporate names). These kinds of estimation problems get worse when we introduce composite features like phrases or term pairs (bigrams). Some work has addressed these small sample estimation problems [19, 8, 36, 24], but current retrieval models do not generally address estimation problems or attempt to predict the effect of estimation errors on retrieval performance.

The no-sample estimation problem arises because most retrieval models are attempting to predict assignment of a feature, relevance, about which we have almost no prior knowledge. While long-term learning may provide some help here, in the vast majority of cases we will never have seen a user query before; even if the same query is submitted by two users, it is unlikely that they will judge the same documents as relevant.

The hidden nature of relevance is a fundamental problem in all IR research. A retrieval model provides an operational definition of relevance. In the absence of any relevance feedback information, this definition must be based on subjective or heuristic estimates rather than on representative samples. The effectiveness of a retrieval model will be measured in terms of the degree to which its operational definition matches the definition applied by the user. Improved retrieval models, then, will require subjective probability estimates that more closely predict user judgments.

Some recent retrieval models attempt to avoid this problem by replacing the notion of relevance with a more visible model of the inference process used to judge the degree to which queries and documents match [46, 72]. If the model of inference could be shown to be an accurate model of relevance, then these models would have, in some sense, an objective measure that could replace relevance. Models that make the inference process visible are probably to be preferred, but moving relevance outside the retrieval model is not a fundamental improvement. Ultimately, the retrieval model will be judged by how well it produces document rankings that match user judgments.

To reduce the number of parameters that must be estimated, most probabilistic models discard factors that are hard to estimate and that are constant or nearly constant for all documents. These models produce ranking information but no estimate of the actual probability that a document matches a query. An estimate of the actual probability would be useful as an indication of the overall quality of the retrieved documents. Some recent models do attempt to estimate the actual probabilities [22, 72, 10].

5.2   Representation of Queries and Documents

Despite extensive efforts in both the artificial intelligence (AI) and information-retrieval communities, we still have a relatively poor understanding of what makes a good representation of text, let alone what makes a good representation for complex documents that have a rich internal structure and may contain figures, photographs, tables, and other nontext information. Leaving the problem of nontext information aside, no current text representation completely captures the meaning of a document or information need, and there is little reason to believe that truly adequate representations are close at hand. Indeed, the notion of a single representation of meaning may not be practical since the meaning of a body of text is so heavily dependent upon the context in which it is to be interpreted.

There are, however, many representation techniques that capture at least some aspects of meaning in text. The AI community, particularly that portion interested in natural language processing (NLP), has developed a number of techniques for representing the meaning of a text [1]. The most successful representations make fairly specific assumptions about the way in which the text should be interpreted (e.g., as a story about one of a small number of topics) and about the kinds of questions that might be asked about the text (e.g., questions about actor's intentions). Some work has been done to adapt the natural language understanding techniques to an information-retrieval setting, but there is little near-term hope that these techniques could be used to represent large document collections and arbitrary queries [57].

Within the information-retrieval community, a number of techniques have been developed to represent the content of documents and information needs. These representations have a much different flavor than NLP representations. They are generally based on simple, very general, features of documents (e.g., words, citations) and represent simple relationships between features (e.g., phrases) and between documents (e.g., two documents cite the same document). The focus here is on simple, but general, representations that can be applied to most texts rather than on specialized techniques, which capture more information but are applicable only in narrow contexts. IR representations explicitly represent uncertainty and make extensive use of the statistical properties of representation features. Most IR text representations attempt to make use of information produced by human analysis (e.g., manual indexing) when available.

The text representation techniques used in IR range from simple keyword extraction to complex indexing schemes that rely on human analysis. None of these representations has been shown to work consistently better than others even though the different representations retrieve different documents. This "equal effectiveness paradox" [35] underscores the need for a theory of text representation.

We have, as yet, only very general models of term distribution in text. Some work has been done to describe the desirable qualities of an indexing feature, but we have only a limited ability to predict the importance of individual terms in the descriptions of documents and queries and how this importance is dependent upon context.

Finally, we need to develop representation techniques that can be used in multiple applications. Many sources of uncertainty that arise when dealing with text are common to NLP, IR, and other text handling systems (e.g., synonymy, ambiguity, anaphora, and so on). Techniques for representing and managing these kinds of uncertainty would be generally useful even if additional representation tools were required in specific domains.

5.3   Use of Domain Knowledge

Closely related to the issue of text representation is the representation and use of uncertain, incomplete, and contradictory knowledge about the use of language or about concepts in a given domain. The principal sources of this kind of knowledge are

1. **Phrase identification**. Phrase structure in text can be identified using ordinary NLP techniques, using a stochastic tagger [9], or using general-purpose or domain-specific dictionaries. Phrases represent more precise indexing features than the terms that make up the phrase, but it is only recently that techniques have been developed that can use phrases to improve performance [16].

   Our understanding of how to represent phrases is still rudimentary. The handling of documents that contain some or all of the terms in a phrase, but not the actual phrase, is important. Phrase quality also appears to be important (e.g., a phrase identified by NLP techniques alone is less likely to be a correct descriptor of a query or document that a phrase identified using a domain-specific dictionary).

2. **Thesauri**. A number of thesauri are available, ranging from untyped general-purpose thesauri (e.g., Roget's or Wordnet [43]) to typed general-purpose thesauri (where links are typed as broader, narrower, or related terms) to typed domain-specific thesauri (e.g., "note" is a kind-of financial instrument but only in the finance domain). These sources of domain knowledge are widely believed to be useful for improving retrieval performance and some work has been done [62, 81], but results thus far are inconclusive.

3. **Sense disambiguation**. A variety of techniques have been developed for selecting (or at least guessing) the correct sense for ambiguous terms [33, 34]. This information should be useful in reducing the uncertainty associated with the assignment of indexing features to queries, but it is, as yet, unclear how this information can be incorporated in a retrieval model.

4. **Domain specific knowledge bases**. For some domains, knowledge bases have been developed that specify how concepts should be recognized in text. These range from ad hoc collections of rules developed within a given domain (e.g., medical searchers have a predefined script that specifies all common forms that might be used to describe a concept like cancer) to more formal schemes where a domain expert develops a description of the relationships between concepts in a domain (as in the RUBRIC or Topic systems [70, 25] or in [7]). These knowledge bases are similar to thesauri but generally exhibit richer structure. Some work has been done to represent uncertainty in these knowledge bases [70, 25], but much work remains.

Unlike most AI systems, where the acquisition of large amounts of domain knowledge is a major problem, in IR we have many sources of domain knowledge available. Our problem is how to represent the knowledge they contain and to use the knowledge to improve retrieval performance.

5.4   Query Acquisition and Relevance Feedback

Through most of the discussion so far we have ignored the process of query acquisition and simply assumed that queries are provided by users. Most retrieval models do not attempt to model the acquisition process even though improvements in the initial query formulation can have a major impact on retrieval performance [17, 11]. Some work has been done with retrieval models that incorporate information about user experience and intentions [69], but these models are relatively weak and do not represent uncertainty. It is also likely that information about the collection or about the domain could be used to focus the query acquisition process by suggesting features that could be useful in refining the query.

The relevance feedback techniques discussed earlier can be used to improve the initial query formulation given a set of relevance judgments, but the effectiveness of feedback techniques is heavily dependent upon the quality of the initial query: more relevant documents found by the initial query means a larger learning sample.

Most of the work with relevance feedback has been conducted with small test collections and more recent work suggests that the same techniques are not nearly as effective with large collections, in part because the feature selection problem is much more difficult with long documents. Improved feedback techniques will probably require better models of term importance in text collections.

Acknowledgments

The authors would like to thank Keith van Rijsbergen for his helpful comments on an earlier draft of this paper.

REFERENCES

[1] J. Allen. *Natural Language Understanding.* Benjamin/Cummings, Menlo Park, CA, 1987.

[2] P. Bollmann and V. Raghavan. The axiomatic approach for theory development in IR. In *NSF Workshop on Future Directions in Text Analysis, Retrieval and Understanding,* pages 16–22, 1991.

[3] A. Bookstein. Fuzzy requests: An approach to weighted Boolean searches. *Journal of the American Society for Information Science,* 30(4): 240–247, July 1980.

[4] A. Bookstein. Set-oriented retrieval. *Information Processing and Management,* 25(5): 465–475, 1989.

[5] A. Bookstein and D. R. Swanson. Probabilistic models for automatic indexing. *Journal of the American Society for Information Science*, 25: 312–318, 1974.

[6] Y. Chiaramella and J. P. Chevallet. About retrieval models and logic. *Computer Journal*, 35(3): 233–242, June 1992.

[7] Y. Chiaramella and J. Nie. A retrieval model based on an extended modal logic and its application to the RIME experimental approach. In J.-L. Vidick, editor, *Proceedings of the 13th International Conference on Research and Development in Information Retrieval*, pages 25–43. ACM, September 1990.

[8] K. W. Church and W. A. Gale. A comparison of the enhanced Good-Turing and deleted estimation methods for estimating probabilities of English bigrams. *Computer Speech and Language*, 5: 19–54, 1991.

[9] K. W. Church. A stochastic parts program and noun phrase parser for unrestricted text. In *Proceedings of the Second Conference on Applied Natural Language Processing*, pages 136–143, February 1988.

[10] W. S. Cooper, F. C. Gey, and D. P. Dabney. Probabilistic retrieval based on staged logistic regression. In Nicholas Belkin, Peter Ingwersen, and Annelise Mark Pejtersen, editors, *Proceedings of the Fifteenth Annual ACM SIGIR Conference on Research and Development in Information Retrieval*, pages 198–210. ACM, June 1992.

[11] W. B. Croft. The role of context and adaptation in user interfaces. *International Journal of Man-Machine Studies*, 21: 283–292, 1984.

[12] W. B. Croft. Boolean queries and term dependencies in probabilistic retrieval models. *Journal of the American Society for Information Science*, 37(2): 71–77, 1986.

[13] W. B. Croft. Approaches to intelligent information retrieval. *Information Processing and Management*, 23(4): 249–254, 1987.

[14] W. B. Croft and R. Das. Experiments with query acquisition and use in document retrieval systems. In Jean-Luc Vidick, editor, *Proceedings of the 13th International Conference on Research and Development in Information Retrieval*, pages 349–368. ACM, September 1990.

[15] W. B. Croft and D. J. Harper. Using probabilistic models of document retrieval without relevance information. *Journal of Documentation*, 35: 285–295, 1979.

[16] W. B. Croft, H. R. Turtle, and D. D. Lewis. The use of phrases and structured queries in information retrieval. In *Proceedings of the Fourteenth International Conference on Research and Development in Information Retrieval*, pages 32–45. ACM, October 1991.

[17] P. J. Daniels. Cognitive models in information retrieval—an evaluative overview. Technical report, Department of Information Science, The City University, London, May 1986. Final report of British Library Research and Development Department Project number SI/S/753.

[18] DARPA. Tipster information package. Information package related to Defense Advanced Research Project Agency BAA 90-16, July 1990.

[19] T. Dunning. Accurate methods for the statistics of surprise and coincidence. *Computational Linguistics*, 19(1): 61–74, March 1993.

[20] E. A. Fox, G. L. Nunn, and W. C. Lee. Coefficients for combining concept classes in a collection. In *Proceedings of the Eleventh Annual International ACM SIGIR Conference on Research and Development in Information Retrieval*, pages 291–308. ACM, 1988.

[21] N. Fuhr. Models for retrieval with probabilistic indexing. *Information Processing and Management*, 25(1): 55–72, 1989.

[22] N. Fuhr. Optimum polynomial retrieval functions based on the probability ranking principle. *ACM Transactions on Information Systems*, 7(3): 183–204, July 1989.

[23] N. Fuhr and C. Buckley. Probabilistic document indexing from relevance feedback data. In J.-L. Vidick, editor, *Proceedings of the 13th International Conference on Research and Development in Information Retrieval*, pages 45–61. ACM, September 1990.

[24] N. Fuhr and H. Hüther. Optimum probability estimations from empirical distributions. *Information Processing and Management*, 25(5): 493–507, 1989.

[25] R. M. Fung, S L. Crawford, L. A. Applebaum, and R. M. Tong. An architecture for probabilistic concept-based information retrieval. In J.-L. Vidick, editor, *Proceedings of the 13th International Conference on Research and Development in Information Retrieval*, pages 455–467. ACM, September 1990.

[26] G. W. Furnas, T. K. Landauer, L. M. Gomez, and S. T. Dumais. The vocabulary problem in human-system communication. *Communications of the ACM*, 30(11): 964–971, November 1987.

[27] H. Garcia-Molina and D. Porter. Supporting probabilistic data in a relational system. In *Proceedings of EDBT*, pages 60–74, 1990.

[28] W. Goffman. A searching procedure for information retrieval. *Information Storage and Retrieval*, 2: 73–78, 1964.

[29] D. Harman. Towards interactive query expansion. In Y. Chiaramella, editor, *Proceedings of the 11th International Conference on Research and Development in Information Retrieval*, pages 321–332. ACM, June 1988.

[30] S. P. Harter. A probabilistic approach to automatic keyword indexing—part I. On the distribution of specialty words in a technical literature. *Journal of the American Society for Information Science*, 26(4): 197–206, 1975.

[31] S. P. Harter. A probabilistic approach to automatic keyword indexing—part II. An algorithm for probabilistic indexing. *Journal of the American Society for Information Science*, 26(5): 280–289, 1975.

[32] J. Katzer, M. J. McGill, J. A. Tessier, W. Frakes, and P. DasGupta. A study of the overlap among document representations. *Information Technology: Research and Development*, 1: 261–274, 1982.

[33] R. Krovetz and W. B. Croft. Word sense disambiguation using a machine readable dictionary. In N. J. Belkin and C. J. van Rijsbergen, editors, *Proceedings of the 12th International Conference on Research and Development in Information Retrieval*, pages 127–136, June 1989.

[34] M. Lesk. Automatic sense disambiguation using machine readable dictionaries: How to tell a pine cone from an ice cream cone. In *SIGDOC Proceedings*, pages 24–26, 1986.

[35] D. D. Lewis. *Representation and Learning in Information Retrieval*. Ph.D. Dissertation, Computer Science Department, University of Massachusetts, Amherst, MA 01003, February 1992.

[36] R. M. Losee. Parameter estimation for probabilistic document-retrieval models. *Journal of the American Society for Information Science*, 39(1): 8–16, 1988.

[37] R. M. Losee and A. Bookstein. Integrating Boolean queries in conjunctive normal form with probabilistic retrieval models. *Journal of the American Society for Information Science*, 39(3): 315–321, 1988.

[38] X. Lu. Document retrieval: A structural approach. *Information Processing and Management*, 26(2): 209–218, 1990.

[39] H. P. Luhn. A statistical approach to mechanised encoding and searching in library automation. *IBM Journal of Research and Development*, 1: 309–317, 1957.

[40] Eugene L. Margulis. N-Poisson document modelling. In N. Belkin, P. Ingwersen, and A. M. Pejtersen, editors, *Proceedings of the Fifteenth Annual ACM SIGIR Conference on Research and Development in Information Retrieval*, pages 177–189. ACM, June 1992.

[41] M. E. Maron and J. L. Kuhns. On relevance, probabilistic indexing and information retrieval. *Journal of the ACM*, 7: 216–244, 1960.

[42] M. McGill, M. Koll, and T. Noreault. An evaluation of factors affecting document ranking by information retrieval systems. Technical report, Syracuse University, School of Information Studies, 1979.

[43] G. A. Miller, R. Beckwith, C. Fellbaum, D. Gross, and K. J. Miller. Introduction to WordNet: An online lexical database. *International Journal of Lexicography*, 3(4): 235–244, 1990.

[44] A. Motro. VAGUE: A user interface to relational databases that permits vague queries. *ACM Transactions of Office Information Systems*, 6(3): 187–214, July 1988.

[45] R. E. Neapolitan. *Probabilistic Reasoning in Expert Systems*. John Wiley & Sons, 1990.

[46] J.-Y. Nie. Towards a probabilistic modal logic for semantic-based information retrieval. In Nicholas Belkin, Peter Ingwersen, and Annelise Mark Pejtersen, editors, *Proceedings of the Fifteenth Annual ACM SIGIR Conference on Research and Development in Information Retrieval*, pages 140–151. ACM, June 1992.

[47] J. Pearl. *Probabilistic Reasoning in Intelligent Systems: Networks of Plausible Inference*. Morgan Kaufmann Publishers, 1988.

[48] T. Radecki. Fuzzy set theoretical approach to document retrieval. *Information Processing and Management*, 15: 247–259, 1979.

[49] T. Radecki. Incorporation of relevance feedback into Boolean retrieval systems. In G. Salton and H. J. Schneider, editors, *Research and Development in Information Retrieval*, pages 133–150, 1983.

[50] T. Radecki. Probabilistic methods for ranking output documents in conventional Boolean retrieval systems. *Information Processing and Management*, 24(3): 281–302, 1988.

[51] S. E. Roberston. The methodology of information retrieval experiment. In K. Sparck Jones, editor, *Information Retrieval Experiment*, chapter 1, pages 9–31. Butterworth, 1981.

[52] S. E. Robertson. The probability ranking principle in IR. *Journal of Documentation*, 33(4): 294–304, December 1977.

[53] S. E. Robertson, M. E. Maron, and W. S. Cooper. Probability of relevance: A unification of two competing models for document retrieval. *Information Technology: Research and Development*, 1(1): 1–21, January 1982.

[54] S. E. Robertson and K. Sparck Jones. Relevance weighting of search terms. *Journal of the American Society for Information Science*, 27: 129–146, May-June 1976.

[55] G. Salton, E. Voorhees, and E. A. Fox. A comparison of two methods for Boolean query relevancy feedback. *Information Processing and Management*, 20(5/6): 637–651, 1984.

[56] G. Salton, editor. *The SMART Retrieval System—Experiments in Automatic Document Processing*. Prentice-Hall, 1971.

[57] G. Salton. On the use of knowledge-based processing in automatic text retrieval. In *Proceedings of the 1986 ASIS Annual Conference*, pages 277–287, 1986.

[58] G. Salton. A simple blueprint for automatic Boolean query processing. *Information Processing and Management*, 24(3): 269–280, 1988.

[59] G. Salton and C. Buckley. Improving retrieval performance by relevance feedback. *Journal of the American Society for Information Science*, 41(4): 288–297, June 1990.

[60] G. Salton and M. J. McGill. *Introduction to Modern Information Retrieval*. McGraw-Hill, 1983.

[61] T. Saracevic. Relevance: A review of and a framework for thinking on the notion in information science. *Journal of the American Society for Information Science*, 26(6): 321–343, 1975.

[62] P. Shoval. Principles, procedures and rules in an expert system for information retrieval. *Information Processing and Management*, 21(6): 475–487, 1985.

[63] K. Sparck Jones. Retrieval system tests 1958-1978. In K. Sparck Jones, editor, *Information Retrieval Experiment*, chapter 12, pages 213–255. Butterworth, 1981.

[64] K. Sparck Jones and C. J. van Rijsbergen. Information retrieval test collections. *Journal of Documentation*, 32(1): 59–75, 1976.

[65] P. Srinivasan. A comparison of two-Poisson, inverse document frequency and discrimination value models of document representation. *Information Processing and Management*, 26(2): 269–278, 1990.

[66] K. H. Stirling. The effect of document ranking on retrieval system performance: A search for an optimal ranking rule. *Proceedings of the American Society for Information Science*, 12: 105–106, 1975.

[67] J. M. Tague. The pragmatics of information retrieval experimentation. In K. Sparck Jones, editor, *Information Retrieval Experiment*, chapter 5, pages 59–102. Butterworths, 1981.

[68] V. Tahani. A fuzzy model of document retrieval systems. *Information Processing and Management*, 12(3): 177–188, 1976.

[69] R. H. Thompson and W. B. Croft. Support for browsing in an intelligent text retrieval system. *International Journal of Man-Machine Studies*, 30: 639–668, 1989.

[70] R. M. Tong and D. Shapiro. Experimental investigations of uncertainty in a rule-based system for information retrieval. *International Journal of Man-Machine Studies*, 22: 265–282, 1985.

[71] R. M. Tong, D. G. Shapiro, B. P. McCune, and J. S. Dean. A rule-based approach to information retrieval: Some results and comments. In *Proceedings of the National Conference on Artificial Intelligence*, pages 411–415, 1983.

[72] H. R. Turtle. *Inference Networks for Document Retrieval*. Ph.D. Dissertation, Computer Science Department, University of Massachusetts, Amherst, MA 01003, February 1991. Available as COINS Technical Report 90-92.

[73] H. R. Turtle and W. B. Croft. Inference networks for document retrieval. In J.-L. Vidick, editor, *Proceedings of the 13th International Conference on Research and Development in Information Retrieval*, pages 1–24. ACM, September 1990.

[74] H. R. Turtle and W. B. Croft. Efficient probabilistic inference for text retrieval. In *RIAO91 Conference Proceedings*, pages 644–661, April 1991.

[75] H. R. Turtle and W. B. Croft. Evaluation of an inference network-based retrieval model. *ACM Transactions on Information Systems*, 9(3): 187–222, July 1991.

[76] H. R. Turtle and W. B. Croft. A comparison of text retrieval models. *Computer Journal*, 35(3): 279–290, June 1992.

[77] C. J. van Rijsbergen. *Information Retrieval*. Butterworths, 1979.

[78] C. J. van Rijsbergen. A non-classical logic for information retrieval. *Computer Journal*, 29(6): 481–485, 1986.

[79] C. J. van Rijsbergen. Towards an information logic. In N. J. Belkin and C. J. van Rijsbergen, editors, *Proceedings of the Twelfth Annual International ACM SIGIR Conference on Research and Development in Information Retrieval*, pages 77–86. ACM, 1989.

[80] C. J. van Rijsbergen. Probabilistic retrieval revisited. *Computer Journal*, 35(3): 291–298, June 1992.

[81] E. M. Voorhees. Using wordnet to disambiguate word senses for text retrieval. In R. Korfhage, E. Rasmussen, and P. Willett, editors, *Proceedings of the Sixteenth Annual ACM SIGIR Conference on Research and Development in Information Retrieval*, pages 171–180. ACM, June 1993.

[82] W. G. Waller and D. H. Kraft. A mathematical model for weighted Boolean retrieval systems. *Information Processing and Management*, 15(5): 235–245, 1979.

[83] C. T. Yu, W. Meng, and S. Park. A framework for effective retrieval. *ACM Transactions on Database Systems*, 14(2): 147–167, June 1989.

[84] C. T. Yu and H. Mizuno. Two learning schemes for information retrieval. In Y. Chiaramella, editor, *Proceedings of the 11th International Conference on Research and Development in Information Retrieval*, pages 201–218, 1988.

[85] S. B. Zdonik and D. Maier. *Readings in Object-Oriented Database Systems*. Morgan Kaufmann, San Mateo, CA, 1990.

8

IMPERFECT INFORMATION: IMPRECISION AND UNCERTAINTY

Philippe Smets

IRIDIA
Université Libre de Bruxelles
Brussels, Belgium

IS can do practically everything.	T	What IS can do today is highly limited.
What IS cannot do is useless anyway.	R	*Useless* confused with *cannot be done.*
So why worry about uncertainty?	U	No future without using uncertainty.
	T	
The Information Systems Radical	H	*The Uncertainty Zealot*

1 IMPERFECT INFORMATION

Imperfection, be it imprecision or uncertainty, pervades real-world scenarios and must therefore be incorporated into every information system that attempts to provide a complete and accurate model of the real world. Yet, this is hardly achieved in today's information systems. A major reason might be the inherent difficulty of understanding the various aspects of imprecision and uncertainty.

Is the world itself imprecise or uncertain? This remains an open question. Whatever the answer, there is no doubt that our *image* of the world is never perfect. The information that is available about the real world, which is the information that can be stored in an information system, is almost always imperfect.

Until recently, almost all aspects of imperfect information have been modeled by the theory of probability. In the last 20 years, however, several new models for representing imperfect information have been developed. The relatively large number of such models may reflect the sentiment that imperfection has many different aspects, and probability theory, as good as it may be, might not be able to cope with all of them.

Why should we worry about all these new models, when we want to introduce uncertainty into information systems? The use of inappropriate, unjustified, or purely *ad hoc* models can lead to results that might be misunderstood by end users.[1]

Newcomers to the area of uncertainty modeling are often overwhelmed by the multitude of models. One frequent reaction is to adopt one of the models, and use it in every context. Another reaction is to accept all the models and to apply them more or less randomly. Both attitudes are inappropriate.

In this chapter we consider the major aspects of imperfection, noting that an exhaustive consideration of all aspects is not practically possible. We propose a classification in which imprecision, inconsistency, and uncertainty are the major classes. We then present the various approaches that have been proposed to model imprecision and uncertainty. These models are grouped into two large categories: the symbolic models and the quantitative models. This general introduction considers only the ideas underlying the models. Further details, as well as applications for information systems, may be found in other chapters of this book. A detailed analysis of imperfect information may be found in [44]. [4] presents a survey of the probability-oriented linguistic terms. A recent review on the representation of uncertainty in artificial intelligence may be found in [25].

2   VARIETIES OF IMPERFECT INFORMATION

Appendix A contains a structured thesaurus on the different aspects of imperfection that can exist in an item of information. Appendix B provides dictionary-style definitions for each of these aspects.

We use imperfection as the most general concept. The major types of imperfection are imprecision, inconsistency, and uncertainty. Hence, information is perfect when it it precise, certain, and free of inconsistencies.

---

[1]Such was the case with models that were based on *certainty factors*, where the true meaning of the numbers was not well-defined, eventually leading to the demise of those models.

Imprecision and inconsistency are properties related to the *content* of the item or statement. In the former case more than one world is compatible with the available information; in the latter case no world is compatible with it. On the other hand, uncertainty is a property that results from lack of information about the world for deciding if a statement is true or false. Hence, imprecision and inconsistency are essentially properties of the information itself, whereas uncertainty is a property of the relationship between the information and our knowledge of the world.

To illustrate the difference between imprecision and uncertainty, consider these two situations:

1. John has at least two children, and I am sure of it.

2. John has three children, but I am not sure of it.

In the former case, the number of children is imprecise but certain. In the latter case, the number of children is precise but uncertain. Both aspects can coexist but are distinct. Often, less precise information can be stated with more certainty, and more precise information can be stated with less certainty. There appears to be an Information Maximality Principle, which states that the "product" of precision and certainty cannot be beyond a certain critical level, and any increase in one would be balanced by a decrease in the other.

Below, we consider separately the various aspects of imprecision, inconsistency, and uncertainty.

2.1 Imprecision

Imprecision can be characterized by the presence or absence of an error component.

Imprecision Without Error

The statement "the food is hot" is *ambiguous* (synonymous with *amphibologic*), as it could mean either that the food is spicy or that its temperature is high.

The statement "age in the 30s" is *approximate*. The statement "age close to 30" is *fuzzy*. In the former case, given an individual age, the statement is *either correct or incorrect*; for example, it is correct for someone who is 36 and incorrect for someone who is 28. In the latter case, given an individual age, the statement is *more correct or less correct*; for example, it is more correct for 28 than for 36. Once fuzziness is introduced, correctness is no longer a matter of all-or-nothing, but it admits degrees.

Information can also be *missing* or *incomplete*. Deficiency is a property that results from incompleteness of what concerns the user. Indeed, even incomplete information can sometimes be sufficient from the user's point of view. Consider the statement "the name of John's wife is Joan or Jill." If one wants to determine whether John is a bachelor or not, this information, although incomplete, is sufficient. But if one wants to address John's wife by her name, this incomplete information is insufficient.

Imprecision Combined with Error

The information discussed so far was not erroneous, as the true value was compatible with the available information. In the presence of errors, additional kinds of imprecision are encountered. Information is *incorrect*, when it is simply wrong, as in "age is 37" when the actual age is 25. Information is *inaccurate* when it is wrong but the error is small; for example, "age is 37" when it is 36.

Information is *invalid* when it is not only erroneous but also might potentially lead to unacceptable conclusions. The information "John is a widower," when in reality John is a bachelor, is erroneous but also invalid, as it could imply the unjustified payment of a widower's pension.

Distortion is analogous to inaccuracy combined with invalidity. Information is *biased* if it has been subjected to a systematic error. For example, when all ages collected are two years less than the true age. This might happen as a result of a single error, for example, when ages are computed as the difference between the birth date and the present date, and the present date is wrong by two years.

Nonsensical and *meaningless* information are extreme cases of erroneous information. Such errors are often discovered instantaneously: "age is 245 years," "marital status is apple," and so on. Meaningless is less pernicious, as it has a flavor of irrelevancy.

2.2   Inconsistency

When several statements are combined, new kinds of imperfection can appear. Two statements may *conflict*; for example, "John is a bachelor," and "John's wife is Joan." This conflict may lead to *incoherent* conclusions. Indeed, a conclusion that can be drawn from these two statements is that John is a married bachelor.

Logicians use inconsistency to define the incoherence that results from conflicting information. Inconsistency also characterizes the fact that an agent might react differently when put in identical situations. Conclusions will be confused when there is some incoherence that can be resolved by small corrections to the data. Consider, for example, these three statements: "John will arrive in Brussels by train at 3:05 PM," "the train is scheduled to arrive in Brussels at 3:15 PM," and "there are no trains scheduled to arrive in Brussels in the afternoon." The incoherence resulting from the first two statements is considerably smaller than the incoherence resulting from the first and third statements.

2.3   Uncertainty

The third major kind of information imperfection, uncertainty, concerns the state of knowledge (of an agent) about the relationship between the world and the statement about the world. A statement is either true or false, but the agent's knowledge about the world might not allow him to state confidently if that statement is true or false. Certainty is complete knowledge of the true value of the data. Uncertainty is partial knowledge of the true value of the data. Uncertainty leads to *ignorance*. It is essentially, if not always, an epistemic property caused by lack of information. A major cause of uncertainty is imprecision. Whether uncertainty is an objective or a subjective property is a still-debated philosophical question.

Objective Uncertainty

Some specialists have argued that uncertainty related to *randomness* is an objective property, and the term *likely* qualifies an event that will probably occur. They contend that the fact that "an event is likely" is independent of one's opinion about the occurrence of the event, and that likelihood (as well as randomness) is an objective property of the experiment that generates the event. The concept of *propensity* of an event is covered by such objective randomness.

Before discussing the propensity of an event, its *dispositionality* might be considered. Only possible events can be probable. *Possibility* concerns the ability of the event to occur, its "happen-ability," if you wish (whereas probability concerns its tendency to occur). Similarly, possibility concerns the ability of a proposition to be true. *Necessity* is the dual of possibility: it is the impossibility of the contrary.

Subjective Uncertainty

Objective properties of uncertainty are supposedly linked to the world and to the information. Subjective properties of uncertainty are linked to the agent's opinion about the true value of the information, as derived from the available information.

Information is *believable* or *probable* for the agent, if the agent accepts it, even if temporarily. Information is *doubtful* if it is not believable and will be accepted by the agent only with strong reluctance.

The relationship between probability (equated to belief in the subjective context) and possibility, as discussed in objective uncertainty, can also be discussed in the subjective context. *Possibility* and *necessity* are the epistemic properties that reflect the agent's opinion about the truth of a statement. In particular, only possible statements can be believed.

Unreliability reflects the agent's opinion about the source of the information; an opinion that is transferred secondarily to the information. *Irrelevance* concerns the opinion about the information, and *decidability* concerns the ability to decide if the information is true or false.

A major source of uncertainty is *imprecision*. Consider the example that concerned ambiguity (which is an instance of imprecision). When one is told that the food is hot, one is in a state of uncertainty, not knowing whether it is spicy or has high temperature. Nevertheless, that state of uncertainty can be corrected. In a Thai restaurant, *hot* will probably mean "spicy," whereas in an English restaurant, *hot* will probably mean "of high temperature."

Uncertainty usually admits some kind of ordering, and therefore it suggests quantitative modeling. The model based on probability may be the most famous but is hardly the only one. Imprecision induces uncertainty, but the nature of this uncertainty and its quantification will depend on the type of imprecision.

3 MODELING

Models for imperfect information can be separated into symbolic (qualitative) and numeric (quantitative) models. Most quantitative models concern uncertainty. An exception is fuzzy set theory, which concerns imprecision. In contrast, symbolic models focus more on deduction based on soft knowledge, than on choosing a specific representation of imperfection.

3.1 The Symbolic Approach: Nonmonotonic Logics

Traditionally, logicians have focused on deduction schemes that permit the deduction of true conclusions from true premises. However, when these methods are applied to commonsensical problems, they often collapse.

In classical logic, if you know that Tweety is a bird, you cannot deduce that Tweety flies, because the rule "all birds fly" is false (because it has exceptions).

Nevertheless, it is a common-sense attitude to conclude that Tweety flies, unless there are reasons to believe otherwise, and even to go on deducing other facts that are deducible from the fact that Tweety flies. Of course, the new deductions could be defeated by a new piece of evidence. Thus, that Tweety flies is a temporary defeasible deduction, which can nevertheless be assumed as a working hypothesis. Consequently, new deduction operators had to be defined that could model this defeasible reasoning; deduction operators are nonmonotonic in that the set of deductions they allow does not have to increase monotonically by the adjunction of new pieces of information, and could possibly decrease (when a new piece of information justifies the retraction of previously deduced facts). As an example, the information "Tweety is a penguin" coupled with the information "penguins do not fly" justifies the retraction of the previously deduced fact that Tweety flies, and a new deduction that Tweety does not fly.

Since the late 1970s, many nonmonotonic logics have been introduced [2, 17, 27, 31]. The properties of nonmonotonic deduction operators have been defined, and special techniques like default logic, hypothetical reasoning, and defeasible reasoning have been proposed. Their aim is to reason from rules with nonexplicit exceptions within classical logic. Such logics try to deduce as much as possible from these rules, in that they apply them, except when the data can be proved to belong to the set of exceptions, or when inconsistency would be deduced.

Nonmonotonic reasoning is conceptually satisfactory, but its cost might become prohibitively expensive. In classical logic, any fact, once deduced, will remain true. Obviously, in nonmonotonic reasoning, this is no longer true. All assumptions that were used in deducing a fact must be recorded. So whenever an assumption previously accepted turns out to be false, the deduced facts must be reconsidered. When this occurs, a fact will have to be retracted, unless another chain of reasoning can be applied that will lead to its deduction. Clearly, the storage of all underlying assumptions used to deduce the fact may cause considerable overhead.

3.2   The Quantification of Imprecision: Fuzzy Sets

In essence, imprecision is represented by disjunctive information that characterizes a set of possible values to which the actual value is known to belong. Recently, the classical concept of set has been extended to fuzzy sets that can be used to characterize ordered disjunctive information.

Classically, sets are crisp in the sense that an element either belongs to a set or is excluded from it. [50] introduces the idea of noncrisp sets, called *fuzzy sets*. The idea is that belonging to a set admits a *degree*, which is not necessarily 0 or 1, as in classical set theory. For some elements of the universe of discourse, one may not be able to conclude whether or not they belong to the set; at most one may assess a degree of membership $\mu_A(x)$ of the element x in the fuzzy set A. In other words, Zadeh generalizes the classical characteristic function $I_A(x)$ of a set, which maps the elements of the universe to the set $\{0,1\}$

$$I_A(x) = \begin{cases} 1 & \text{if } x \in A \\ 0 & \text{if } x \notin A \end{cases}$$

to a function that maps the universe to the *interval* $[0,1]$.

New concepts like fuzzy quantities (e.g., several, few), fuzzy probability (likely), fuzzy quantifiers (most), fuzzy predicates (tall), and the impact of linguistic hedges (very) have then been formalized [11]. Fuzziness can be used to formalize vague predicates such as "John is tall." Such predicates are vague because the words used to define them are vague [1].

Classical set operators, such as union, intersection, and negation, have been generalized. The most classical solution is based on the min-max operators:

$$\mu_{\overline{A}}(x) = 1 - \mu_A(x)$$
$$\mu_{A \cup B}(x) = max(\mu_A(x), \mu_B(x))$$
$$\mu_{A \cap B}(x) = min(\mu_A(x), \mu_B(x))$$

Other operators have been proposed that belong to the family of triangular norms and co-norms [12, 49]. The generalization of the implication operator turns out to be less obvious, especially when it is considered in the context of the *modus ponens* as encountered in approximate reasoning [39].

The law of excluded middle does not apply to fuzzy sets. Indeed, $\mu_{A \cap \overline{A}}(x) = min(\mu_A(x), \mu_{\overline{A}}(x))$ can be larger than 0. While this may look odd at first, it simply admits the possibility that one can be considered tall and not tall simultaneously, a perfectly valid possibility.

Mathematically, fuzzy set theory generalizes the classical set theory. The model can be used wherever sets can be used, and therefore is not restricted to any particular form of imperfect information. Its simplest domain of application is the modeling of imprecision and vagueness. Fuzziness creates an order among the possible values to which the actual value is known to belong.

Several authors have tried to dismiss fuzzy set theory, by claiming that it is subsumed by probability. This Procrustean attitude[2] misfires completely. Fuzzy set theory concerns the belonging of a well-defined individual to an ill-defined set, whereas probability concerns the belonging of a yet undefined individual to a well-defined set (introducing random sets does not change this conceptual picture). Of course, there are mathematical relationships between the two theories, but the main difference is in the problems that they try to model. Fuzziness deals with imprecision, whereas probability deals with uncertainty (of course, imprecision induces uncertainty). One could claim that when John is known to be tall, it is possible to construct a probability measure on John's height. This does not mean, however, that a grade of membership is a probability [35].

---

[2]Procrustes was a mythical Greek giant , who wanted captives to sleep in his beds. But he wanted them to fit the beds perfectly, so when they were smaller than the beds, he stretched them, and when they were longer, he chopped off the excess.

3.3   The Quantification of Uncertainty: Sugeno's Fuzzy Measures

Sugeno [45] studied functions that express uncertainty associated with the statement "x belongs to S," where S is a crisp set[3] in a universe X, and x is an arbitrary element of X, which is not *a priori* located in any of the subset of X. The Sugeno measure g satisfies

$$G1: \quad g(\emptyset) = 0 \text{ and } g(X) = 1$$
$$G2: \quad \forall A, B \subseteq X : A \subseteq B \Rightarrow g(A) \leq g(B)$$
$$G3: \quad \forall A_i \subseteq X, i \in N : A_1 \subseteq A_2 \subseteq \ldots \text{ or } A_1 \supseteq A_2 \supseteq \ldots \Rightarrow$$
$$\lim_{i \to \infty} g(A_i) = g(\lim_{i \to \infty} A_i)$$

The Sugeno measure for finite X is just a normalized measure, monotonous for inclusion. It fits with probability measures, possibility measures, necessity measures, belief functions, possibility measures, and so on. It has been called a fuzzy measure but should not be confused with fuzzy sets.

3.4   Possibility and Necessity Measures

Possibility Measure

Incomplete information, such as "John's height is above 170," implies that any height h above 170 is possible and any height equal to or below 170 is impossible. This can be represented by a *possibility* measure defined on the domain of heights, whose value is 0 if $h < 170$ and 1 if $h \geq 170$ (with 0 indicating impossible and 1 indicating possible).

When a predicate is vague, like in "John is tall," possibility can admit degrees, and the larger the degree, the larger the possibility. Although possibility is often associated with fuzziness, nonfuzzy (crisp) events can admit different degrees of possibility as well, as shown in the following example. Suppose you try to squeeze soft balls into a box. One can state: it is possible to put 20 balls in the box, impossible to put 30 balls, quite possible to put 24 balls, not so possible to put 26 balls, and so on. These are degrees of realizability and are unrelated to any supposedly underlying random process. Similarly, a salesman might forecast next year's sales in this way: it is possible to sell about 50,000, impossible to sell more than 100,000, quite possible to sell 70,000,

---

[3]Generalization to fuzzy sets S is possible but not important here.

hardly possible to sell more than 90,000, and so on. These statements express the possible values for next year's sales. In addition, the salesman could also express his belief about what he will actually sell next year, but this concerns another task for which the theories of probability and belief functions are more adequate.

For a space Ω of possible worlds, let $\Pi : 2^\Omega \to [0,1]$ be the possibility measure that associates each subset $A \subseteq \Omega$ with its possibility $\Pi(A)$, where A denotes both a subset of Ω and the proposition represented by this subset. The fundamental axiom is that the possibility of the disjunction of two propositions A and B is the maximum of the possibility of the individual propositions A and B [52, 13]:

$$\Pi(A \vee B) = max(\Pi(A), \Pi(B)) \tag{8.1}$$

Usually one requires also $\Pi(\Omega) = 1$.

As in modal logic, where the necessity of a proposition is the negation of the possibility of its negation, the *necessity* measure $N(A)$ of a proposition A is defined as

$$N(A) = 1 - \Pi(\neg A).$$

It follows that

$$N(A \wedge B) = \min(N(A), N(B)).$$

Note that one has only

$$\Pi(A \wedge B) \leq \min(\Pi(A), \Pi(B))$$
$$N(A \vee B) \geq \max(N(A), N(B))$$

Related to the possibility measure $\Pi : 2^\Omega \to [0,1]$, one can define a possibility distribution $\pi : \Omega \to [0,1]$,

$$\forall x \in \Omega : \pi(x) = \Pi(\{x\}).$$

From Equation 8.1 it follows that

$$\forall A \subseteq \Omega : \Pi(A) = \max_{x \in A} \pi(x).$$

An important point in possibility theory (or in fuzzy set theory), when only the max and min operators are used, is that the actual *values* of the possibility measure (or the grades of membership) do not matter; what matters is the *order* that they impose on the elements of the domain. Any strictly monotonous transformation of the values (such as a change of scale) would not affect conclusions. This property explains why authors insist on the fact that possibility theory is essentially an ordinal theory, an attractive property in general. Yet, this robustness property does not apply once addition and multiplication are introduced, as is the case with probability and belief functions.

As an example of a possibility measure versus a probability measure, consider the number of eggs X that Hans will eat tomorrow morning [52]. Let $\pi(u)$ be the degree of ease with which Hans can eat u eggs. Let $p(u)$ be the probability that Hans will eat u eggs tomorrow morning. Assume the values of $\pi(u)$ and $p(u)$, as known to us, are as follows:

u	1	2	3	4	5	6	7	8
$\pi(u)$	1	1	1	1	.8	.6	.4	.2
$p(u)$	.1	.8	.1	0	0	0	0	0

We observe that, whereas the possibility that Hans may eat three eggs for breakfast is 1, the probability that he may do so might be quite small, 0.1. Thus, a high degree of possibility does not imply a high degree of probability, and a low degree of probability does not imply a low degree of possibility. However, if an event is impossible, it is bound to be improbable. This heuristic connection between possibilities and probabilities may be stated in the form of what might be called the possibility-probability consistency principle [52].

Physical and Epistemic Possibility

Two forms of (continuous-valued) possibility have been described: physical and epistemic. These two forms can be recognized by their different linguistic uses: "it is possible that" and "it is possible for" [21]. When one says that it is possible that Paul's height is 170, it means that for all one knows, Paul's height may be 170. When one says that it is possible for Paul's height to be 170, it means that physically, Paul's height can be 170. The form "possible that" is related to our state of knowledge and is called *epistemic*. The form "possible for" deals with actual realizability, which is independent of our knowledge. The distinction is not unrelated to the one between the epistemic concept of probability (the credibility) and the aleatory one (the chance). These forms of possibilities are evidently not independent concepts, but the exact structure of their interrelations has yet to be established clearly.

3.5 Relationship Between Fuzziness and Possibility

Zadeh introduced both the concept of fuzzy set [50] and the concept of possibility measure [52]. The former allows one to describe the grade of membership of a well-known individual in an ill-defined set. The latter allows one to describe the individuals that satisfy ill-defined constraints or that belong to ill-defined sets.

For instance, $\mu_{Tall}(h)$ quantifies the membership of a person with height h in the set of *Tall* men, and $\pi_{Tall}(h)$ quantifies the possibility that the height of a person is h given that this person belongs to the set of *Tall* men. Zadeh's *possibilistic principle* postulates that

$$\forall h \in H : \pi_{Tall}(h) = \mu_{Tall}(h),$$

where H is the set of heights: $H = [0, \infty)$.

This notation is often confusing and is better written as

$$\forall h \in H : \pi(h|Tall) = \mu(Tall|h),$$

or better yet

$$\forall h \in H : \mu(Tall|h) = x \Rightarrow \pi(h|Tall) = x.$$

This last expression avoids the confusion between the two concepts. It shows that they share the same scale without implying that a possibility is a membership and vice versa. The preceding expression clearly indicates the domain of the measure (sets for the grade of membership μ, and height for the possibility distribution π) and the background knowledge (the height for μ, and the set for π). The difference is analogous to the difference between a probability distribution $p(x|\theta)$ (the probability of the observation x given the hypothesis θ) and a likelihood function $l(\theta|x)$ (the likelihood of the hypothesis θ given the observation x) in which case the equivalent of Zadeh's possibilistic principle is the *likelihood principle*:

$$l(\theta|x) = p(x|\theta).$$

The likelihood of a hypothesis θ given an observation x is equal to the probability of the observation x given the hypothesis θ. The original form of Zadeh's possibilistic principle is the one most frequently encountered, but its meaning should be interpreted with care. It states that the possibility that a tall man has height h is equal numerically to the grade of membership of a man with height h to the set of tall men.

The possibility measure Π is related to the possibility distribution π by

$$\Pi_A(X) = \max_{x \in X} \pi_A(x),$$

where X is a crisp set. It generalizes to

$$\Pi_A(X) = \max_{x \in \Omega} \min(\pi_A(x), \mu_X(x)),$$

where Ω is the domain of x and X is a fuzzy subset of Ω. One can thus express the possibility that the height of a person is about 180 given that the person is tall.

In general, the following holds

$$\Pi_A(X \cup Y) = \max(\Pi_A(X), \Pi_A(Y))$$
$$\Pi_{A \cup B}(X) = \max(\Pi_A(X), \Pi_B(X))$$

The same relationships do not hold for the intersection. Indeed,

$$\mu_{A \cap B}(X) = \min(\mu_A(X), \mu_B(X)),$$

but one should not conclude that

$$\Pi_{A \cap B}(X) = \min(\Pi_A(X), \Pi_B(X))$$

as sometimes assumed erroneously. Nor do we have

$$\Pi_A(X \cap Y) = \min(\Pi_A(X), \Pi_A(Y)).$$

By duality, the following relationships hold for the necessity measure

$$N_A(X \cap Y) = \min(N_A(X), N_A(Y))$$
$$N_{A \cap B}(X) = \min(N_A(X), N_B(X))$$

but now the similar relationships for the union do not hold.

The link between fuzzy set and possibility measure is established through Zadeh's possibilistic principle. A similar principle could also be used to link both fuzzy sets and possibility measures with partial truths. Let $\nu(A)$ denote the degree of truth of the proposition A. We assume

$$\nu(\text{John is Tall}|\text{height}(\text{John}) = h) = \mu_{Tall}(h) = \pi_{Tall}(h).$$

That is, the degree of truth (if such a thing exists) of a proposition "John is tall" knowing that "John's height is h" is equated with the grade of membership of a person with height h in the set of *Tall* men, and therefore with the possibility that the height of a *Tall* person is h.

3.6 Probability Theory

Since its inception as a model for uncertainty in the seventeenth century, probability has been given at least four different meanings.

A probability measure quantifies the degree of probability $P(A)$ (whatever probability means) that an arbitrary element $x \in \Omega$ belongs to a well-defined subset $A \subseteq \Omega$. It satisfies the following properties:

$P1:$ $P(\emptyset) = 0$ and $P(\Omega) = 1$
$P2:$ $\forall A, B \subseteq \Omega : A \cap B = \emptyset \Rightarrow P(A \cup B) = P(A) + P(B)$
$P3:$ $\forall A, B \subseteq \Omega : P(B) > 0 \Rightarrow P(A|B) = P(A \cap B)/P(B)$

where $P(A|B)$ is the probability that $x \in A$ given that $x \in B$. This definition can be extended to fuzzy events [51, 34], which further enhances, if still necessary, the difference between probability and fuzziness.

As an example consider the probability that the next person who enters the room is tall. Could we say that this probability is .7, or is that probability itself a fuzzy probability? This is still unresolved and might explain the lack of interest in the concept at the present.

Related to the probability measure $P : 2^\Omega \to [0, 1]$, a probability distribution is defined $p : \Omega \to [0, 1]$,

$$\forall x \in \Omega : \ p(x) = P(\{x\}).$$

By property P2,

$$\forall A \subseteq \Omega : \ P(A) = \sum_{x \in A} p(x).$$

Notice that the relationship between P and p is the same as the relationship between Π and π (but not as the one between *bel* and m, as *bel* and m are both defined on 2^Ω; see Chapter 12 on belief functions).

The Classical Theory

The original definition of probability, as argued by Laplace, assumed the existence of a fundamental set of equipossible events. The probability of an event is then the ratio of the number of favorable cases to the number of all equipossible cases. Of course, the concept of equipossible cases is hardly defined in general. It works with applications in which symmetry can be assumed, as is the case in most games of chance (dice, cards, and so on). When symmetry cannot be assumed, the Principle of Insufficient Reason is invoked (also called the Principle of Indifference [24]). Its essence is that alternatives are considered equiprobable if there is no reason to expect or prefer any one over the others. As innocent as it might seem, the Principle of Insufficient Reason is a dangerous tool, whose application has led to many errors. It is hardly defended today.

To demonstrate the danger inherent in its application, suppose that all that is known about John's wife is that her name is either Joan or Jill or Joey. It is then acceptable that none of the three names is to be considered as more likely than the others. But is there any reason for the fact "the name is Joan" to be less likely than the fact "the name is either Jill or Joey"? Probability theory would require a yes answer, as the Principle of Insufficient Reason and Axiom P2 allocate a probability 1/3 to the first event and 2/3 to the second. Common sense does not require such a clear yes.

Relative Frequency Theory

Probability is essentially the convergence limit of relative frequencies under repeated independent trials [30, 28]. It is not concerned with capturing commonsensical notions, as it is a purely prescriptive definition. The definition tries to comply with the operationalist version of scientific positivism: theoretical concepts must be reducible to concrete operational terms. It is strongly related to the concept of proportion, and to its direct generalization, measurability (limited to its objective form).

It is by far the most widely accepted definition, even though it has been shown not to be immune to criticism. Consider these flaws: convergence limits cannot be observed; it postulates that past observed propensities for events to occur will continue on into the future; it does not apply to single events; it suffers from the difficulty of specifying the appropriate reference class; it never explains how long a run should be so that it will converge to its limit. Nevertheless, it works and this pragmatic argument explains its popularity.

Subjective (Bayesian, Personal) Probability

For the Bayesian school of probability, the probability measure quantifies an agent's credibility that an event will occur or that a proposition is true. It is a subjective, personal measure.

The additivity of the credibility measure (Axiom P2) is essentially based on betting behavior arguments. Bayesians define $P(A)$ as the fair price p, the agent proposes that a player should pay to play a game against a banker, where the player receives \$1 if A occurs and \$0 if A does not occur. The concept of fairness is related to the fact that after determining p the agent is willing to be either the player or the banker. To avoid Dutch books (a set of simultaneous bets that would lead to a sure loss), the agent must assess the probability of the subset of Ω according to Axioms P1 and P2. The justification of Axiom P3 by diachronic[4] Dutch books [23, 46, 47] is less convincing, as it is based on a Temporal (Diachronic) Coherence postulate [23, 14], which is debatable. It claims that hypothetical bets (bets on the hypothesis that A occurs) should be the same as factual bets (bets after A has occurred) [25, 16].

Another algebraic justification for the use of probability measures to quantify credibility is based on Cox's axiom [6]. In essence, it states that the credibility of $\overline{A}$ should be a function of the credibility of A, and the credibility of A and B should be a function of the credibility of A given B and the credibility of B. Adding a strict monotonic requirement leads to the conclusion that the probability measure is the only measure that satisfies both requirements [10].

As compelling as Cox's justification appears to be, it can nevertheless be criticized. Strict monotony kills possibility measures, and possibility theory or belief functions theory advocates reject, of course, the first requirement as not obvious [5].

Logical Probabilities

Attempts have been proposed to avoid the subjective component of the Bayesian probability. These attempts endorse the objectivity of scientific rationalism.

[24] defined probability as a logical relationship between a proposition and a corpus of evidence. While propositions are ultimately either true or false (no fuzzy propositions are involved here), we express them as being probable in relationship to our current knowledge. A proposition is probable with respect to a given body of evidence regardless of whether anyone thinks so.

Bayesians consider the same kind of relationship between knowledge and a proposition but admit it is subjective and therefore that the probability of a proposition is not an objective property that exists regardless of whether anyone thinks so.

---

[4] Involving time, where there might be some bets before and after some event.

The concept of *corroboration* introduced by [29] and the concept of *confirmation* introduced by [3] both fit well with the overall schema of defining a logical measure of probability.

This approach, as intellectually attracting as it seems, unfortunately fails to explain how to define the probability weight to be assigned to these relationships. On that point Bayesians are strongest, as they can use their betting behavior for a guideline. The existence of such operational method to assess a measure of probability is important as it provides a meaning to the .7 stated in the proposition "the probability of A is .7." The lack of such well-established and widely accepted operational meaning in fuzzy set theory and possibility theory, in upper and lower probabilities theory, and in belief functions theory has been the source of serious criticisms (but see [41] for fuzzy set theory and [42] for the transferable belief model).

3.7   Upper and Lower Probability Models

[43, 43, 18, 19, 48] suggested that personal degrees of belief cannot be expressed by single numbers, and that one can only assess intervals that bound them. The bounds of such intervals are referred to as upper and lower probabilities. Such intervals are easily obtained in two-person situations when one person, Y_1, communicates the probability of some events in Ω to a second person, Y_2, saying only that, for all $A \subseteq \Omega$, the probabilities $P(A)$ belong to an interval. Suppose Y_2 has no other information about the probability on Ω. In that case, Y_2 can only build a set $\mathcal{P}$ of probability measures on Ω compatible with the boundaries provided by Y_1. All that is known to Y_2 is that there exists a probability measure P and that $P \in \mathcal{P}$. Later, should Y_2 learn that an event $A \subseteq \Omega$ has occurred, $\mathcal{P}$ should be updated to $\mathcal{P}_A$, where $\mathcal{P}_A$ is this set of conditional probability measures obtained by conditioning the probability measures $P \in \mathcal{P}$ on A [36, 15, 22].

One obtains a similar model by assuming that one's belief is not described by a single probability measure, as Bayesians do, but by a family of probability measures (usually the family is assumed to be convex). Conditioning on some event $A \subseteq \Omega$ is obtained as in the previous case.

A special case of upper and lower probabilities has been described by Dempster [1, 9]. Dempster assumes the existence of a probability measure on a space X and a one-to-many mapping M from X to another space Y. The lower probability of A in Y is the probability of the largest subset of X, such that its image under M is included in A. The upper probability of A in Y is the probability of the largest subset of X, such that the images under M of all its elements have a nonempty intersection with A. In the artificial intelligence community, this theory is often called the Dempster-Shafer theory.

A generalization of an upper and lower probability model to second-order probability model is quite straightforward. Instead of acknowledging that $P \in \mathcal{P}$, one can accept a probability measure P^* on $\mathcal{P}_\Omega$, the set of probability measures on Ω. So for all $\mathcal{A} \subseteq \mathcal{P}_\Omega$, one can define the probability $P^*(\mathcal{A})$ that the actual probability P on Ω belongs to the subset $\mathcal{A}$ of probability measures on Ω. In that case, the information $P \in \mathcal{P}$ induces a conditioning of P^* into

$$P^*(\mathcal{A}|\mathcal{P}) = \frac{P^*(\mathcal{A} \cap \mathcal{P})}{P^*(\mathcal{P})}.$$

Second-order probabilities, i.e., probabilities over probabilities, do not enjoy the same support as subjective probabilities. Indeed, there seems to be no compelling reason to conceive a second-order probability in terms of betting and avoiding Dutch books. So the major justification for the subjective probability modeling is lost. Further, introducing second-order probabilities directly leads to a proposal for third-order probabilities that quantifies our uncertainty about the value of the second-order probabilities, and so forth. Such iteration leads to an infinite regress of metaprobabilities that cannot be easily avoided.

3.8 Credibility: The Transferable Belief Model

Information can induce subjective, personal credibility (hereafter called *belief*) that a proposition is true. At times, its origin can be found either in the random nature of the underlying event or in the partial reliability that we give to the source of information.

In the first case, one ends up with a probability measure if one accepts the frequency principle, which states that, given the chance that a random event X might occur is p, our degree of belief that it will occur is also p [20]. That is,

$$\text{chance}(X) = p \Rightarrow \text{belief}(X) = p.$$

This is one of the fundamental requirements for the classical Bayesian model, as it relates chance and belief.

When randomness is not involved, there is no necessity for beliefs at the credal states (the psychological level where beliefs are entertained) to be quantified by probability measures [26]. The coherence principle advanced by the Bayesians to justify probability measures is adequate in a context of decision [7], but it cannot be used when all one wants to describe is a cognitive process, and beliefs *can* be entertained outside any decision context. In the Transferable Belief Model [31] it is assumed that beliefs at the credal level are quantified by belief functions [26]. When decisions must be made, the belief held at the credal level induces a probability measure held at the pignistic level (the level at which decisions are made). This probability measure is used to make decisions using expected utilities theory. Relationships between belief functions held at the credal level and probabilities held at the pignistic level are given in [33].

4   COMBINING MODELS OF IGNORANCE

The various forms of ignorance can be encountered simultaneously and it is necessary to be able to integrate them. In common-sense reasoning, two forms of ignorance, sometime three, are often encountered in the same statement. As an example, consider the following example of generalized *modus ponens*.

(1) I strongly believe that "When company sales are large, salaries are good". (2) It is quite possible and I somewhat believe that "The sales of Company X are large." Now what can I say about the salary of the employees of Company X? This example may be too complex to be encountered in practice, but it includes most forms of ignorance.

Consider now this more realistic example that links possibility, belief, and surprise. Consider these two statements: "It is *quite* possible that John will come *but* I do not believe that he will" and "It is *hardly* possible that John will come *and* I do not believe that he will." Now suppose that one is told, "John came." Given the former statement, one's reaction would likely be, "Well, so he came!" Given the latter statement, the reaction will be of considerable surprise "Really!? Are you sure!?" Therefore, any model of the concept of *surprise* would have to consider both the degrees of possibility and of beliefs.

To deal with problems like this, beliefs, possibilities, and fuzziness will need to be combined, and a set of metalanguages will have to be constructed. Care must be given, however, to the domains of each operator. For instance, probability deals with two domains, the set of propositions and the truth domain (usually disregarded as it contains only two elements, but it must be considered once fuzzy propositions are accepted).

The first problem is to investigate the connections between the probability theory in its frequency approach and the physical possibility theory. The next problem is to investigate the connections between subjective probability measures, belief functions, and epistemic possibility measures. Finally, one must establish the connections between the physical properties and the epistemic properties. Additionally, there is the problem of extending these theories to the case of fuzzy propositions.

Almost no work has been done in this area. Yet, its importance for information fusion is obvious. When several sensors provide information, how do we recognize the nature of the ignorance involved and select the appropriate model? How do we collapse them into more compact forms? How do we combine them? How do we manage the redundancies, the correlations, and the contradictions? All these problems must be studied and the implementation of potential solutions must be tested.

Understanding the meaning of statements and their translation into appropriate models is delicate, if not hazardous. For example, should "usually bald men are old" be translated to a large $P(bald|old)$ or to a large $P(old|bald)$? Given "when x shaves, usually x does not die," which conditioning is appropriate: $P(dead|shaving)$ or $P(shaving|dead)$? Is this a case of plausibility or possibility? These examples are just illustrative of the kind of problems that must be addressed.

5   CONCLUSION

Clearly, there is need for cooperation between the scientific communities of information systems and uncertainty. An outright rejection of the problem of uncertainty by the information systems community is unrealistic (even the "simple" problem of null values has yet to receive satisfactory treatment). On the other hand, highly sophisticated solutions might be unacceptable when implemented. As indicated in the introductory remark, truth lies halfway between the attitudes of the information systems radical and the uncertainty zealot.

We have shown that imprecision and uncertainty have multiple forms, and that none of the models available today can manage satisfactorily all these forms. It is important to maintain an open mind and to avoid dogmatic attitudes that lead to claims like "my theory can deal with every problem" or "the problems not addressed by their models are unimportant." Each model is best at managing certain forms of imperfection; the models are complementary, not competing.

When confronted with imperfect information, users should first try to classify the form of imperfection, and then adopt the model that is most appropriate. The real challenge is in recognizing the nature of the imperfection that emerges in a given problem. This chapter tried to provide some assistance to meet this challenge. Other chapters in this book present in-depth studies of the major uncertainty models: those based on logic, on probability functions, on possibility functions, and on belief functions. Later chapters discuss synthesis and integration.

APPENDIX A

A Structured Thesaurus of Imperfection

I. Imprecision: Related to the content of the statement.
Informational property, External world.
Several worlds satisfy the statement.

I.1. Data Without Error
Vagueness:

Ambiguous	Has several meanings.
Amphibologic	Has several meanings.
Approximate	Close to reality and well-defined.
Vague	Not well-defined.

Missing:

Incomplete	Something missing.
Deficient	Missing, applies when needed.

I.2. Data Tainted with Error

Erroneous	Simply wrong.
Incorrect	Simply wrong.

Inaccurate	Essentially imprecise, but not completely erroneous.
Invalid	Would lead to unacceptable conclusions.
Distorted	Wrong but not far from correct.
Biased	Tainted by a systematic error.
Nonsensical	Cannot be fitted to reality.
Meaningless	Cannot be fitted to reality.

II. Inconsistency: No world satisfies the statement.

Conflicting	Disagreement among the data.
Incoherent	A property of the conclusions drawn from the data.
Inconsistent	Incoherent with a temporal connotation.
Confused	A milder form of incoherence.

III. Uncertainty: Caused by lack of information, by some imprecision. Imposes ordering on the several worlds that satisfy the statement.

Property of the information: Objective. External uncertainty.
Propensity.

| Random | Subject to change. |
| Likely | Will probably occur. |

Disposition.

| Possible | Ability to occur, to be true. |
| Necessary | Negation is impossible, not possible. |

Property of the observer: Subjective. Internal uncertainty.
Ignorance, Epistemic property, Internal state of knowledge.

Believable	Observer accepts the data but is ready to reconsider it.
Probable	Observer accepts the data but is ready to reconsider it.
Doubtful	Observer can hardly accept the data.
Possible	Observer considers that the data could be true.
Unreliable	Observer's opinion about the source of the data.
Irrelevant	Observer does not care about the data.
Undecidable	Inability to decide if true or false.

APPENDIX B

Thesaurus on Uncertainty and Incompleteness

Imperfect: Incomplete or flawed.

Negligent: Fails to deal with something or someone with the required amount of care or concern, or fails to do something that ought to be done. Lack of proper care or attention.

Imprecise: Not clear, not accurate, not accurately expressed.

Vague: Not clearly explained or expressed, and therefore understandable in different ways. Results in uncertain or ill-defined meaning.

Ambiguous: Unclear or confusing because it can have more than one possible meaning. Can be due to vagueness.

Amphibologic: Synonymous with *ambiguous*.

Approximate: A value is approximate if it is close (or similar) to the correct value, but it is probably slightly different from the correct value because it has been calculated quickly rather than exactly. A concept is described approximately if the description provides some indication of what the concept is like, but the description is not intended to be absolutely precise or accurate.

Fuzzy: Not clearly defined. Indistinct or vague.

Missing: Not present, although expected.

Incomplete: Does not have all the components that it should have.

Deficient: Does not have the full amount that is necessary to function properly. Incomplete or insufficient in some essential respect.

Erroneous: Incorrect or only partly correct.

Incorrect: Wrong, untrue, inaccurate.

Inaccurate: Not precise; does not conform exactly to a standard.

Invalid: Unacceptable because it is based on a mistake. Not logically sound.

Distorted: Meaning has been changed, misrepresented.

Biased: Has been subjected to a constant error.

Nonsensical: Does not make sense, absurd, untrue.

Meaningless: Without meaning but also without importance or relevance.

Conflicting: Incompatible, impossible for all to be true, or for all to be believed by the same person.

Incoherent: Unclear and difficult to understand; rambling in its reasoning.

Inconsistent: Unpredictable; behaves differently in situations that warrant the same behavior.

Confused: Does not have any order or pattern and is therefore difficult to understand.

Uncertain: Lacks complete knowledge about the value of interest.

Random: Happens or is chosen without a definite plan, pattern, or purpose. Made or done without method or conscious choice.

Likely: Is probably the case or will probably happen (in a particular situation).

Believable: Thought to be likely.

Doubtful: Unlikely or uncertain.

Unreliable: Cannot be trusted or relied upon.

Irrelevant: Not related to the issue at hand, and therefore unimportant.

Ignorance: Lack of knowledge.

Undecidable: Validity or truth cannot be decided; questionable.

APPENDIX C

Models for Uncertainty on Finite Frames

The major axioms of each model (not complete). Note that possibility, probability, and belief are special cases of Sugeno measures.

Sugeno Measures: $g : 2^\Omega \to [0, 1]$

$$g(\emptyset) = 0 \text{ and } g(X) = 1$$
$$\forall A, B \subseteq X : \ A \subseteq B \ \Rightarrow g(A) \ \leq g(B)$$

Possibility Measure: $\Pi : 2^\Omega \to [0, 1]$

$$\forall A, B \subseteq \Omega : \ \Pi(A \vee B) = \max(\Pi(A), \Pi(B))$$

Probability Measure: $P : 2^\Omega \to [0, 1]$

$$\forall A, B \subseteq \Omega : \ P(A \cup B) = P(A) + P(B) - P(A \cap B)$$

Belief Measures: $bel : 2^\Omega \to [0, 1]$

$$\forall A, B \subseteq \Omega : \ bel(A \cup B) \geq bel(A) + bel(B) - bel(A \cap B)$$

Acknowledgments

This work was supported in part by the CE-ESPRIT III Basic Research Project 6156 (DRUMS II), and the Communauté Française de Belgique, ARC 92/97-160 (BELON). The author is indebted to Hector Garcia-Molina, Joerg Gebhardt, Frank Klawonn, Rudolf Kruse, Henri Prade, and the UMIS participants for many suggestions about this presentation.

REFERENCES

[1] M. Black. Vagueness: an exercise in logical analysis. *Philosophy of Science*, 4: 427–455, 1937.

[2] D. G. Bobrow. Special issue on non-monotonic logics. *Artificial Intelligence*, 13, 1980.

[3] R. Carnap. *Logical Foundations of Probability*. Chicago University Press, 1950.

[4] D. A. Clark. Verbal uncertainty expressions: a review of two decades of research. *Current Psychology: Research and Reviews*, 9: 203–235, 1990.

[5] M. R. B. Clarke, C. Froidevaux, E. Gregoire, and Ph. Smets. Uncertainty, conditional and non-monotonicity: Positions and debates in non-standard logics. *Journal of Applied Non-Classical Logics*, 1: 103–310, 1991.

[6] R. T. Cox. Probability, frequency and reasonable expectation. *Amer. J. Phys.*, 14: 1–13, 1946.

[7] M. Degroot. *Optimal Statistical Decisions*. McGraw Hill, New York, 1970.

[8] A. P. Dempster. Upper and lower probabilities induced by a multivalued mapping. *Ann. Math. Statistics.*, 38: 325–339, 1967.

[9] A. P. Dempster. A generalization of Bayesian inference. *Journal Royal Statistical Society*, B.30: 205–247, 1968.

[10] D. Dubois, P. Garbolino, H. E. Kyburg, H. Prade, and Ph. Smets. Quantified uncertainty. *Journal of Applied Non-Classical Logics*, 1: 105–197, 1991.

[11] D. Dubois and H. Prade. *Fuzzy Sets and Systems: Theory and Applications*. Academic Press, New York, 1980.

[12] D. Dubois and H. Prade. A review of fuzzy sets aggregation connectives. *Information Sciences*, 36: 85–121, 1985.

[13] D. Dubois and H. Prade. *Theory of Possibility*. Plenum, London, 1988.

[14] J. Earman. *Bayes or Bust? A Critical Examination of Bayesian Confirmation Theory*. MIT Press, Cambridge, MA, 1992.

[15] R. Fagin and J. Halpern. A new approach to updating beliefs. In L. N. Kanal P. P. Bonissone, M. Henrion and J. F. Lemmer, editors, *Uncertainty in Artificial Intelligence 6*, pages 347–374. North Holland, Amsterdam, 1991.

[16] B. De Finetti. *Theory of Probability Vol. 1 and Vol. 2.* Wiley, London, 1974.

[17] M. L. Ginsberg. *Readings in Nonmonotonic Reasoning.* Morgan Kaufmann, San Mateo, CA, 1988.

[18] I. J. Good. *Probability and the Weighting of Evidence.* Hafner, 1950.

[19] I. J. Good. *Good Thinking: the Foundations of Probability and Its Applications.* University of Minnesota Press, Minneapolis, 1983.

[20] I. Hacking. *Logic of Statistical Inference.* Cambridge University Press, 1965.

[21] I. Hacking. *The Emergence of Probability.* Cambridge University Press, 1975.

[22] J. Y. Jaffray. Bayesian updating and belief functions. *IEEE Trans. SMC,* 22: 1144–1152, 1992.

[23] R. Jeffrey. Conditioning, kinematics and exchangeability. In B. Skyrms and W. L. Harper, editors, *Causation, Chance and Credence Vol. 1,* pages 221–255. Reidel, Dordrecht, 1988.

[24] J. M. Keynes. *A Treatise on Probability.* Harper and Row, New York, 1962.

[25] P. Krause and D. Clark. *Representing Uncertain Knowledge. An AI Approach.* Intellect, Oxford, 1993.

[26] I. Levi. *Decisions and Revisions: Philosophical Essays on Knowledge and Value.* Cambridge University Press, Cambridge, 1984.

[27] W. Lukaszewicz. *Nonmonotonic Reasoning.* Ellis Horwood, Chichester, 1990.

[28] R. Von Mises. *Probability, Statistics and Truth (2nd Edition).* Allen and Unwin, London, 1957.

[29] K. R. Popper. *The Logic of Scientific Discovery.* Basic Books, New York, 1959.

[30] H. Reichenbach. *The Theory of Probability.* University of California Press, Berkeley, 1949.

[31] R. Reiter. Nonmonotonic reasoning. *Annual Review of Computer Science,* pages 147–186, 1987.

[32] L. J. Savage. *Foundations of Statistics*. Wiley, New York, 1954.

[33] G. Shafer. *A Mathematical Theory of Evidence*. Princeton University Press, Princeton, 1976.

[34] Ph. Smets. Probability of a fuzzy event: an axiomatic approach. *International Journal of Fuzzy Sets and Systems*, 7: 153–164, 1982.

[35] Ph. Smets. Probability of a fuzzy event. In M. G. Singh, editor, *Systems and Control Encyclopedia*, pages 1802–1805. Pergamon, Oxford, 1985.

[36] Ph. Smets. Upper and lower probability functions versus belief functions. In *Proceedings of ISFK International Symposium on Fuzzy Systems and Knowledge Engineering* (Guangzhou, China, July 10–July 16), pages 17–21. ISFK, 1987.

[37] Ph. Smets. Belief functions. In D. Dubois Ph. Smets, A. Mamdani and H. Prade, editors, *Nonstandard Logics for Automated Reasoning*, pages 253–286. Academic Press, London, 1988.

[38] Ph. Smets. Constructing the pignistic probability function in a context of uncertainty. In L. N. Kanal M. Henrion, R. D. Shachter and J. F. Lemmer, editors, *Uncertainty in Artificial Intelligence 5*, pages 29–40. North Holland, Amsterdam, 1990.

[39] Ph. Smets. Implication and modus ponens in fuzzy logic. In H. T. Nguyen I. R. Goodman, M. M. Gupta and G. S. Rogers, editors, *Conditional Logic in Expert Systems*, pages 235–268. Elsevier, Amsterdam, 1991.

[40] Ph. Smets and R. Kennes. The transferable belief model. *Artificial Intelligence*, 66: 191–234, 1994.

[41] Ph. Smets and P. Magrez. The measure of the degree of truth and of the grade of membership. *International Journal of Fuzzy Sets and Systems*, 25: 67–72, 1988.

[42] C. A. B. Smith. Consistency in statistical inference and decision. *Journal of the Royal Statistical Society*, B23: 1–37, 1961.

[43] C. A. B. Smith. Personal probability and statistical analysis. *Journal of the Royal Statistical Society*, A128: 469–499, 1965.

[44] M. Smithson. *Ignorance and Uncertainty: Emerging Paradigms*. Springer-Verlag, New York, 1989.

[45] M. Sugeno. Fuzzy measures and fuzzy integrals: a survey. In G. N. Saridis M. M. Gupta and B. R. Gaines, editors, *Fuzzy Automata and Decision Processes*, pages 89–102. North Holland, Amsterdam, 1977.

[46] P. Teller. Conditionalization and observation. *Synthesis*, 26: 218–258, 1973.

[47] P. Teller. Conditionalization, observation and change of preference. In W. Harper and C. A. Hooker, editors, *Foundations of Probability Theory, Statistical Inference and Statistical Theory of Science*, pages 205–259. Reidel, Doordrecht, 1976.

[48] P. Walley. *Statistical Reasoning with Imprecise Probabilities*. Chapman and Hall, London, 1991.

[49] R. Yager. Connectives and quantifiers in fuzzy sets. *International Journal Fuzzy Sets and Systems*, 40: 39–76, 1991.

[50] L. Zadeh. Fuzzy sets. *Information and Control*, 8: 338–353, 1965.

[51] L. Zadeh. Probability measures of fuzzy events. *J. Math. Anal. Appl.*, 23: 421–427, 1968.

[52] L. Zadeh. Fuzzy sets as a basis for a theory of possibility. *International Journal Fuzzy Sets and Systems*, 1: 3–28, 1978.

9

PROBABILISTIC AND BAYESIAN REPRESENTATIONS OF UNCERTAINTY IN INFORMATION SYSTEMS: A PRAGMATIC INTRODUCTION

Max Henrion
Henri J. Suermondt*
David E. Heckerman**

Institute for Decision Systems Research
Los Altos, California, USA

* Hewlett-Packard Laboratories
Palo Alto, CA, USA

** Microsoft Research Laboratories
Redmond, Washington, USA

1 INTRODUCTION AND OVERVIEW

A great deal has been written about the underlying principles of alternative methods of representing uncertainty—not the least about probability and Bayesian methods. While we cannot entirely resist discussing basic principles, we will focus on the pragmatic issues, which too often get lost under the mass of philosophy and mathematics. We will address such questions as: How can we use probability to represent the various types of uncertainty? How can we quantify these uncertainties? How much effort is necessary to do so? How can we obtain the greatest benefits from representing uncertainty while minimizing the effort? There are a variety of reasons to represent uncertainty and a variety of probabilistic and Bayesian ways to do so, requiring varying amounts of effort. We discuss an approach to resolve these issues, so that the costs will be commensurate with the benefits.

We start, in Section 2, with a review of selected key ideas in Bayesian probability. In Section 3, we discuss whether and how the Bayesian approach can address five different types of uncertainty. In Section 4, we illustrate these issues with three example problems and a detailed discussion to illustrate how each can be addressed in a Bayesian framework. In Section 5, we go on to discuss the issue of representing uncertainty in large databases. We will argue that simply adding an uncertainty field to qualify each qualitative or numerical field is generally not very useful. It would be simultaneously oversimplified and far too complicated. We propose a much easier approach in which uncertainty is represented at an aggregate level rather than at the level of each data point. We will outline ways to check samples of data in a database, and hence quantify the uncertainties statistically based on empirical findings. In Section 6, we conclude with a brief summary.

2   BASIC ISSUES IN BAYESIAN PROBABILITY

Since there already exist numerous excellent introductions to probabilistic and Bayesian representations of uncertainty, we will not attempt to replicate them here [19, 9]. However, we will emphasize a few frequently misunderstood points that we believe are essential to an adequate understanding. This discussion is drawn from Morgan & Henrion [17].

A *probability* is simply a number expressing the chance or degree of belief that a proposition is true or that some event occurred, with a value in the range from 0 (certainly false) to 1 (certainly true). In the *propensity view*, probability is a physical property of a device, for example, the tendency of a particular coin to come up heads. In the *frequency view*, probability is a property of a population of similar events, for example, the fraction of heads in a long sequence of coin tosses. A *subjective probability* is a number expressing a person's degree of belief in the proposition or occurrence of an event based on the person's current information. This emphasis on probability as a personal belief depending on available information contrasts with the propensity and frequency views of probability as something existing outside any observer.

A subjectivist might start with some prior belief about the fairness of the coin, perhaps based on experience with other coins, and then update this belief using Bayes' rule as data become available from experimental tosses. After many coin tosses, the belief of the subjectivist will, in general, converge to the observed frequency as the data overwhelm the prior belief. Thus, in the long run, the subjectivist and the frequentist will tend to agree about a probability. The key distinction is that the subjectivist is willing to assign probabilities to events that are not members of any obvious repeatable sequence, for example, the discovery of room-temperature superconductivity before the year 2000, but the frequentist is not. Almost all real-world information systems represent at least some uncertain events or quantities for which empirical data are unavailable or too expensive to collect; so, they must resort to the use of expert opinion. The appeal of subjective probability is that it is applicable whether there is little or much data available.

Many people find the subjectivist (also known as Bayesian or personalist) view of probability natural. However, a few find the use of probability a stumbling block, often because the distinction between subjective and classical views is not made clear, as it rarely is in introductory courses on probability and statistics. An indication of this confusion is the common misapprehension that probabilistic methods are applicable only when large amounts of data are available. Subjective probabilities are used often to encode expert knowledge in domains where little or no direct empirical data are available. However, if and when data do become available, Bayesian statistics provides a consistent framework to combine data with judgment to update beliefs and refine knowledge.

If a probability depends on who is assessing it, then it does not make sense to talk about "the" probability. Therefore, the subjectivist talks about "your" probability or "expert A's" probability. To draw attention to the fact that the probability is based or conditioned on the information available to the assessor, it is often explicitly specified. $P(X \mid s)$ is used to notate the probability of a proposition or event X conditioned on s, the assessor's prior state of information or background knowledge. If the assessor gets a new piece of evidence E, the revised probability of X is written $P(X \mid E, s)$, where the comma denotes the conjunction of evidence E and prior knowledge s. We often call $P(X \mid s)$ the *prior probability* (that is, prior to observing E) and $P(X \mid E, s)$ the *posterior probability*.

Although the Bayesian view of uncertainty emphasizes its roots in subjective opinion (the prior), Bayesian statistics also provides a powerful and highly developed armamentarium of tools for obtaining and incorporating whatever empirical data are available. Ultimately we will be most confident in a database that has been checked against empirical reality, and most comfortable with measures of uncertainty that are based on empirical tests of the reliability. These statistical methods for using empirical data and combining it with expert opinion are unavailable to nonprobabilistic formalisms.

3 PROBABILISTIC REPRESENTATIONS OF ALTERNATIVE TYPES OF UNCERTAINTY

In the following, we will describe how to handle five important different types of "imperfect information" or uncertainty using a Bayesian probabilistic approach. The types we will address are

- Simple uncertainty

- Imprecision

- Ignorance (or missing data)

- Linguistic vagueness

- Linguistic ambiguity

We hope that we will dispel any misunderstanding that probability is intrinsically unable to represent any of these types of imperfect information. We will leave it to the reader to judge the relative merits of alternative approaches in each case in terms of naturalness, clarity, convenience, and generality.

3.1 Uncertainty and Imprecision

Elsewhere in this book, for example, in Chapters 2, 8, and 10, a useful distinction between uncertainty and imprecision is pointed out. The statement "John may be 35 years and 20 days old" is precise but expresses uncertainty (through the "may be" phrase); the statement "John is definitely in his thirties" is imprecise but expresses no uncertainty. We are puzzled by the claim that probability can represent uncertainty but not imprecision, since we find the concepts practically inseparable. Smets (Chapter 8) points out that there is often a tradeoff between precision and certainty: "Often the more imprecise you are, the more certain you are; and the more precise, the less certain." He conjectures that there may be some Information Maximality Principle that places a limit on the product of the precision[1] and the certainty.

---

[1]Here we follow Smets and Prade's terminology for imprecision and precision, rather than the standard statistical terminology, which uses precision as the reciprocal of variance.

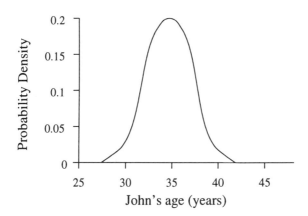

Figure 1 Your probability density function on John's age.

The representation of the uncertainty about a quantity as a probability distribution makes the relationship between imprecision and uncertainty very clear. Suppose John's age is a continuous variable, and your opinion about its value is represented by the density function depicted in Figure 1. Figure 2 illustrates that your probability that John's age is within an interval increases monotonically with the size of the interval (imprecision).

In Figure 3, we interpret certainty to be the probability, and precision to be the reciprocal of imprecision (the range). In this case, the Principle of Information Maximality seems to hold: The product certainty × precision has a maximum. It is the maximum of the probability density function. More generally, we can show that the maximum of the product of the probability and precision is the maximum of the probability density function in the interval. This follows immediately from the definition of probability density.

If there is finite probability mass in the probability distribution, the density function will have a delta function at that point, and the proposed measure of information will be unbounded. Therefore, this Principle of Information Maximality does not hold in all cases.

While uncertainty and imprecision are distinct concepts, the example makes clear that when using a probabilistic representation, it is more natural and convenient to represent them together. We clearly disagree with the suggestion that probability is suitable for representing uncertainty but not imprecision.

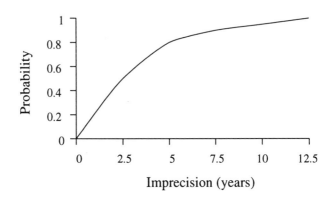

Figure 2   Your probability that John's age is in the interval of specified imprecision (width) centered on 35. Your probability increases monotonically with
imprecision.

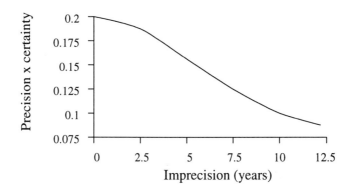

Figure 3   The product of "precision" ($= 1/$imprecision) and "certainty" ($=$
probability). The maximum is equal to 0.2, which is equal to the density at
the mode of the probability distribution, not by coincidence.

3.2   Ignorance or Missing Information

In most current databases, the only type of uncertainty that is represented explicitly is missing data or null values. One can view missing information as an extreme kind of imprecision. The missing value could be anywhere in the entire range available for it. A missing gender in a personnel database allows that the person could be male or female. A missing age allows that the person may be any age between 0 and 120 (or 1024, depending on how many bits have been allocated for the representation). In practice, we may have a lot of relevant information that can reduce our uncertainty. For example, if the person is a senior engineer and the company reflects common gender distributions, we may conclude with a high probability that the person is male. The trick is to see how to establish the relevance of available information and apply it. We illustrate a Bayesian approach in Section 4, where we focus on missing information in Problem A.

3.3   Linguistic Vagueness

Probabilists generally try to avoid linguistic vagueness by requiring that variables and propositions be crisply defined. However, it is clear that people use vague terms widely and find them useful, and it seems desirable that information systems should be able to handle vague language at least in user inputs, and perhaps also in internal representations. There have been a few attempts by Bayesians to show how linguistic vagueness can be handled within a Bayesian framework [3, 6].

The general approach is to look at a vague statement, S, as a communication act from a speaker A to a hearer B. B expresses his opinion about what A means by S as a probability distribution. For example, suppose Susan tells Mary, "John is middle-aged." Mary can represent her opinion about what Susan means by middle-aged as the probability that Susan would make this statement as a function of her knowledge of John's age. Mary can use this uncertain information to update her own prior probability about John's age. We illustrate this approach in more detail in our discussion of Problem C in Section 4.

Recently, there has been a rapid escalation in the use of Bayesian techniques for information retrieval, both in research and commercial development. For example, Turtle has developed belief-network models for information retrieval with remarkable success [24]. Their work has led to a belief-network implementation of information retrieval that serves as the core search engine for West Publishing's legal database. A sampling of other Bayesian approaches can be found in [12]. All Bayesian methods address the inherent uncertainty in two fundamental relationships: (1) the relationship between the semantic content of a document and the appearance of words or phrases in the document, and (2) the relationship between the semantic content of a query and the appearance of words or phrases in the query. For example, a document on terrorism or a query about documents on terrorism may contain the words or phrases "bomb," "responsible party," "retaliation," and so on. Whether or not a document or query is about terrorism, given that it contains such words, is uncertain. The interested reader should consult Chapter 7 to understand how such relationships are modeled within a Bayesian framework.

3.4   Linguistic Ambiguity

Linguistic ambiguity arises from the fact that the meaning of natural language is highly context dependent. Does

"John went to the bank"

refer to a financial institution or a riverbank? The previous context can help clarify this:

"John needed some money. He went to the bank."

"John was tired of rowing. He went to the bank."

Conditioning is a powerful tool for expressing context dependence and making inferences about probable interpretations making use of contextual information. Charniak and Goldman [2] have demonstrated the application of Bayesian belief networks and probabilistic reasoning as a practical tool for language understanding. Without context, the interpretation of most words is uncertain. In most, but not all cases, the context will generally move the subjective probability of one interpretation to near 1 and the rest to zero, reducing the ambiguity.

4 EXAMPLE PROBLEMS AND THEIR BAYESIAN SOLUTIONS

In this section, we shall take a pragmatic look at the problem of uncertainty in information systems. We use concrete examples to illustrate how probabilistic approaches can be used to solve real-world problems of uncertainty in information systems. For each problem, we address the additional information that needs to be modeled in order to apply uncertain reasoning techniques, the method of uncertain reasoning, and the expected results.

Although uncertainty appears in almost every aspect of everyday life, in this article we limit ourselves to modeling uncertainty in areas in which we can demonstrate a clear need for such models. Although the scale of these problems is limited for demonstration purposes, the techniques we describe can be generalized easily. The problems are the following:

Problem A. Aggregation of incomplete data (null values)

> You are trying to get a better picture of the age distribution of employees in your company. Unfortunately, the "date of birth" field was left blank for a substantial number of your employees in your personnel database. This illustrates the well-known database problem of null values. Fortunately, the remainder of your database is fairly complete; for each employee, you have available (among other pieces of information) their start date and current income. You are interested in determining the average age of your employees.

Problem B. Automated classification

> You are the Chief Information Officer for a community hospital. Given the increasingly competitive nature of health-care delivery, you are requested to find ways to improve the waiting times for the hospital's emergency room (ER). Currently, nurses in the ER accumulate a set of diagnostic findings—coded in a standard manner—for each patient who enters the ER. You would like to use these findings for automated triage (severity screening), so that the most serious patients get attention more rapidly and so that physicians can perform their tasks more efficiently and effectively.

Problem C. Evaluation of poorly defined queries

> Your mail-order company has been maintaining detailed customer pro-
> files for many years. These profiles include detailed and accurate
> records of every order placed by every customer, as well as records
> on payment, and miscellaneous records such as whether the product
> was returned. You receive a memo from higher up that the company
> would like you to identify good customers so that they can send them
> a thank-you gift. The memo is rather vague; you are told only that
> you should identify customers with high-order volume and prompt
> payment.

These problems illustrate different sources and types of uncertainty. In Problem A, the value of particular fields in the database is uncertain. In this problem, there is no specific *representation* of uncertainty in the information system
itself; rather, this problem represents the category of uncertainty referred to
as ignorance or missing information, discussed in Section 3.2. In Problem B,
there are also missing, uncertain, data—the diagnoses—but the focus in this
problem is on representation of uncertainty and reasoning methods *within* the
information system in order to derive the necessary information. This type of
uncertainty was presented in Section 3.1. In Problem C, the *data* within the
information system are not uncertain;[2] the uncertainty is introduced at query
time, because the query is poorly defined. This problem corresponds to that of
linguistic vagueness, presented in Section 3.3. Our uncertainty in Problem C
is whether a particular response satisfies the query criteria.

4.1   Problem A. Aggregation of Incomplete Data (Null Values)

The problem of null values in a database is well-documented (Chapters 2, 3,
and 15)). Even popular spreadsheet programs allow users to take special actions
depending on whether a value is null or not. For example, in one widely used
spreadsheet product, when the user wants to determine a database aggregate,
such as the average age we are trying to derive, the program allows the options
of "omit records with null values" and "treat null values as zero." These two
strategies are typical reflections of the level of (or lack of) sophistication with

---

[2]For the purposes of this example, we assume that the order records in the database are
perfectly accurate.

which null values are commonly treated. Clearly, treating missing values as zero is simply incorrect in this example; we can safely assume that the employee is very unlikely to be a newborn. To omit records with null values for the age field is a more appropriate strategy, in that it introduces less of a bias into our aggregates, provided that the missing ages are distributed rather evenly across the spectrum of possibilities. Clearly, the base (i.e., the number of records from which the aggregate is derived) will decrease, but the resulting aggregates will reflect accurately what the average age is for those employees for whom information is available.

However, we can do better than that. Provided that we are willing to introduce some uncertainty into our resulting average, we can provide an estimate of aggregated ages for all employees, not just for those whose ages we know exactly. We take advantage of the fact that we have information about the employees beyond the (often missing) date of birth. Given that information, we may be able to estimate the likely age of the employee.

Problem Formulation

For employee x, let us introduce the following notation:

$a(x)$ age

$t(x)$ the number of years the employee has been in the company

$i(x)$ income

  n the total number of employees

  n' the number of employees for whom you have age information

We are trying to determine the average age:

$$A \equiv \sum_x \frac{a(x)}{n}.$$

If we took the "omit null values" strategy, this would translate into

$$A' \equiv \sum_{x:a(x)\neq null} \frac{a(x)}{n'}.$$

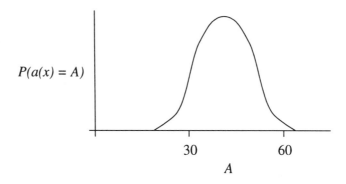

$P(a(x) = A)$

30   60

A

Figure 4 Age distribution curve. On the x-axis we show the age, A; on the y-axis, we show probability. The curve reflects the probability that the age of a particular employee x, $a(x)$, is equal to A.

Clearly, A would be equal to A' provided that either no data are missing or that the average age for the employees whose age data are missing happens to equal A. The "omit null values" strategy is functionally equivalent to the assumption that all missing values of $a(x)$ are equal to A'.

Instead of assuming that the age of employees for whom the age is unavailable corresponds to the average age A', we can estimate the age. Let us refer to the estimated age of employee x as $e[a(x)]$. Such estimation can be done either manually for each employee, or automatically, as a function of other employee properties. Clearly, if $a(x)$ is known, $e[a(x)] = a(x)$. We find that our new age estimate is

$$A'' \equiv \sum_x \frac{e(a(x))}{n}.$$

Probabilistic Approach to the Problem

How does one determine the estimate of an employee's age, $e(a(x))$? Let us first consider the base case, in which we do not use other information such as income or the number of years the employee has been in the company. We can generate a distribution that shows the probability of $a(x) = A$ for various A. We can envision something like that shown in Figure 4.

This curve can be derived from our data on the remaining employees, or by population data, such as the census, or by a combination of the two; formal

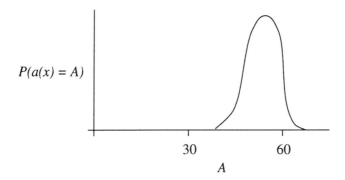

$P(a(x) = A)$

30   60

A

Figure 5 Age distribution curve, conditioned on the finding that employees have been in the company at least 20 years. On the x-axis we show the age, A; on the y-axis, we show probability. The curve reflects the probability that the age of a particular employee x, $a(x)$, is equal to A. We see that, as compared to Figure 4, the curve is shifted to the right: higher ages are more likely.

methods exist for combining data from more than one source using Bayesian updating [25].

Now, as the simplest way to determine the value of $e(a(x))$ for a particular employee, we take the expected value of the curve shown in Figure 4. In Section 4.2, we address a refinement that allows us to specify whether certain ages are more important than others, in which case we can weigh the distribution using decision-theoretic methods.

An important feature of probability theory, as discussed in Section 2, is the ability to include conditional information. Thus, we can condition our probability distribution over various ages on other information, such as income and the number of years the employee has been in the company. For example, in Figure 5, we show what the age probability distribution might look like for employees who have been in the company for more than 20 years. Again, we can estimate our probability distribution or derive it from data on the employees for whom age information is available. Thus, we can custom-tailor the level of specificity of our uncertainty representation.

A clear benefit to modeling the probability distribution, rather than simply taking the mean age for the category we are interested in, is that we can derive not just the mean age, but in addition, we can automatically combine the probability distributions for all our employees whose age information was missing, and generate a probability distribution of our mean age. The end result would be that we could make confidence-interval statements like: "The mean age of our employees is 95% certain to be between 40 and 45," rather than being restricted to a point estimate.

Discussion of Problem A

A key aspect of probabilistic modeling of missing values is that it is a generalization of intuitive operations such as averaging. As a default, we can let the probability that $a(x) = A$ simply equal the proportion of employees that have age A. Thus, it is trivial to automatically generate a default probability distribution from our available employee data.

In addition, probabilistic modeling allows us to combine statistical data with our own estimates. For example, if we know that all employees of a particular age were omitted, we could modify the probability distribution over ages so that the probability of that age is increased. Probability provides us with a well-developed calculus for such evidential reasoning.

Another attractive feature of probability is its link to formal decision theory [19]. For example, our default $e(a(x))$ is the expected value. However, we may have a reason to bias our age estimate, for example, because of penalties for over- or underestimating the average age. In that case, utility theory provides a clear methodology for making explicit our preferences. Thus, we can express the utility of assuming that x has age A_1 when his true age is A_2 for any combination of A_1 and A_2, and use this utility distribution, in combination with the probability distribution, to determine an estimate $e(a(x))$ that takes into account the cost of various possible errors in our age assumptions.

4.2   Problem B. Automated Classification

Automated classification is among the most well-known applications of reasoning under uncertainty in computer science. In virtually all application domains other than the most trivial examples, classification is an uncertain and challenging task; therefore, the problem has been of strong interest to researchers in artificial intelligence. There have been numerous systems that have applied uncertain reasoning techniques in medical diagnosis alone, several of which have found real-world, day-to-day clinical application [15].

Our goal in this example is to illustrate not only that the uncertainty can be modeled but also that the techniques for doing so scale up to real-world scope.

Problem Formulation

The data we have available are diagnostic findings. For the sake of simplicity, we shall assume that these findings have been coded in a standard manner; the problem of unifying medical vocabularies is well known but falls outside the scope of this chapter.

We are trying to derive the possible causes for the patient's symptoms. Given a set of findings $F = \{f_1, f_2, ..., f_n\}$, we are trying to determine, for a set of diseases $D = \{d_1, d_2, ...\}$, the probability that the patient has disease d_i. Given our notions of the severity and need for immediate treatment of disease d_i, we can make a triage decision as to how urgently the patient should be seen. The triage decision consists of assigning the patient to an urgency category U, where U is in $\{u_1, ..., u_m\}$.

A Decision-Theoretic Approach to the Problem

Our first step is to perform inference to derive the probabilities for various diseases, given the findings entered by the nurses. Numerous systems have been developed to date to perform such inference probabilistically [15, 13]. The complexity of probabilistic representations of classification systems can be custom-tailored, depending on the performance requirements for the system and domain-specific knowledge about the relations among findings and diseases. The medical knowledge underlying such a system can be obtained directly from statistical data, or assessed from domain experts.

A good example of a system that could be used to infer the probability of various diseases from a set of findings is the QMR-BN system, which has knowledge of almost 600 diseases and 4000 findings. In this system, probabilistic dependencies among findings and diseases are modeled in a Bayesian belief network [16]. A system like QMR-BN can be used to determine probabilities for various diseases in real time; for details on the inference methodology for such a system, see [21, 14].

The next step is to model the triage decision. Our decision consists of assigning the patient to an urgency category U. We need to explicitly model, for each disease (or combination of relevant diseases, if necessary in the domain), the utility of assigning the patient to urgency category u_i given that disease. Thus, we can express the fact that when the patient has a very serious, acute condition—for example, a myocardial infarction—it is very bad to assign the patient to a low-priority status.

Although the utility-assessment process appears to require a lot of manually assessed data, we can pragmatically make modeling assumptions that greatly facilitate the assessment task. For example, rather than manually assessing the utility of each triage category given each possible disease, we can simply pick one triage category that is "correct" for each disease, and then assign default utilities for "triage correct," "triage too high," and "triage too low." These default utilities can then be used for any disease.

Now we have our model in place, and we can determine automatically, given a set of findings, which triage category is the optimal one to call for a particular patient. The methodology for determining the optimal decision is that of expected-utility decision making [19]: we choose the triage category such that the expected utility of calling the patient in that category is maximal.

Discussion of Problem B

The triage decision is a prototypical example of a decision problem that is ideally suited to automated decision support . Such an ideal problem involves

- A decision that needs to be made many times

- A body of knowledge involving uncertainty that is relatively constant from decision to decision

- A set of utilities that is largely constant from decision to decision

- Evidence—a set of problem-specific findings—that can be used to infer the proper context of each decision

In the case of the triage decision, we need to make the same decision many times a day. For these decisions, the domain knowledge (which findings are made more likely given which diseases) is constant. The utility structure (how bad it is to not treat problem x immediately) can also be reused. The triage findings can then be used to custom-tailor the probability model, through Bayesian inference, to a patient-specific assessment that lets us make the optimal triage decision.

A feature of probabilistic systems, which is often cited, is the fact that such systems use theoretically sound, axiomatic inferencing methods. Thus, the inference results—the probabilities of various diagnoses—and the decision recommendations of the system can be proven to be consistent, given the model and the axioms of probability, which have been mathematically well accepted for over three centuries. What makes this soundness attractive in the medical setting is the fact that we can perform our quality assurance and system validation by checking the model, before it is ever used in a clinical setting. During system testing, whenever we encounter an inference result that is improper (from a domain perspective), we can guarantee that such impropriety is not due to the system's reasoning but, rather, that it implies that the model needs to be further refined.

The claim is often made that probability is too complex or that too many numbers are required to be used for real-world classification problems. There are several systems, including QMR-BN, that provide evidence against such claims. Although the construction of a large diagnostic system can involve considerable effort, especially when a high degree of diagnostic accuracy is expected for a large domain, numerous methods exist to assist in the rapid prototyping and development of such systems [11, 23]. In addition, several methodologies exist to derive probabilistic classification systems from data [4, 18, 10, 22]. This example illustrates a problem in which a probabilistic methodology can be used in a large-scale, everyday setting.

4.3   Problem C. Evaluation of Poorly Defined Queries

There are many types of and sources of uncertainty. A key distinction is whether the uncertainty is a feature of the data or of the query. In Section 4.1, we discussed an example in which the uncertainty was in the data; in this example, we focus on a case in which a poorly defined query leads to uncertainty as to how well a particular item satisfies the user's expectations given the query.

Problem Formulation

Our problem-formulation task consists primarily of determining the mapping of imprecise query terms to well-defined entities in the database. We must define what we mean by *high order volume* and *prompt payment*. Finally, we must determine how these entities should be combined to define a good customer.

Let us define the following entities for a customer x:

$s(x)$ The "true" status (good vs. bad) of customer x (for example, in the eyes of management)

$v(x)$ Order volume of x (in \$)

$n(x)$ The number of days from shipment of the bill to receipt of payment

For the sake of simplicity and without loss of generality, let us restrict ourselves to the vague concepts we are interested in ($v(x)$ is "high" and $n(x)$ is "prompt") and their complements. Additional vague terms may be defined as needed for other queries.

Let us define a good customer as a customer whose order volume is high and whose payment is prompt. If either of these criteria fails, the customer is not a good customer.

A Probabilistic Formulation of the Problem

We need to determine a probability that given a particular numerical value of $v(x)$, it will be considered high (vs. not high) and similarly, that given a numerical value of $n(x)$, it is prompt. This is clearly a subjective assessment; we can make it conditionally dependent on contextual factors (total sales in the time period; etc.), but the bottom line is that we will have to come up with a distribution like the ones shown in Figure 6. In Figure 6(a), we show the probability $P(v(x) = $ "high") as a function of $v(x)$. In Figure 6(b) we show $P(n(x) = $ "prompt") as a function of $n(x)$. Notice that both these distributions are monotonic; thus, a higher order volume implies a greater probability that the order volume will be considered high, and a faster payment implies a greater probability that the payment will be considered prompt.

Next, we must decide how to combine the two criteria: how do we decide that the customer is a good customer? The simplest case is to state that only those customers are good who have high $v(x)$ and prompt $n(x)$. If we assume that $P(n(x) = $ "prompt") and $P(v(x) = $ "high") are marginally independent, then $P(s(x) = $ "good") is equal to the product of the two. The marginal independence assumption entails, in this case, that our perception of whether

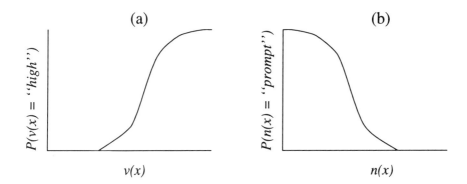

Figure 6 Probability distributions of interpretations of query terms. (a) The probability that a particular numerical value of $v(x)$, order volume, will we considered high. (b) The probability that a particular number of days between shipment and payment, $n(x)$, will be considered prompt.

a particular sales volume is high is not influenced by whether we consider a particular payment time prompt.[3]

At this point, we have a method to determine for any customer, given particular numerical values for order volume and payment promptness, the probability that we will consider that customer a good customer. The remaining task is to set a cutoff threshold for the probability that a customer is good. This can be done arbitrarily, for example, by simply taking the 100 customers who have the greatest probability of being good. Alternatively, we can approach this threshold problem in a decision-theoretic manner. The labeling of a customer as good can be viewed as a decision similar to the triage one, discussed in Section 4.2. Thus, given our utilities (for example, for calling a good customer a bad one and vice versa), and our uncertainties (what is the probability that this customer is a good one?), we can determine how to label the customer.

Discussion of Problem C

In the current version of the example, using the marginal independence assumption, we have made promptness and order volume equally important consider-

---

[3]Note that the independence assumption applies only to the mappings from numerical values to the corresponding vague terms. It does *not* imply that the underlying numerical values are independent from one another as well.

ations in the determination of whether a customer is good. If our preference model distinguished between these two (for example, if we could be more forgiving of a customer who did not pay promptly if the order volume were very high), we could introduce dependencies between the two variables. For example, we could make the probability that a particular $n(x)$ is considered prompt a function not just of $n(x)$, but also of $v(x)$. Such conditional modeling makes probability particularly flexible for many domains.

This example illustrates that vague queries can be modeled explicitly using probability theory. Clearly, what makes a good customer is a subjective consideration. The uncertainty is whether what we call good, high, and prompt truly fits these labels according to the person who evaluates the query return. Thus, the probability distributions shown in Figure 6 reflect our probability (degree of belief) that whoever looks at the query result will be satisfied by our labeling.

The subjective notion of probability—degree of belief—allows us to determine a probability of virtually anything. This counters the frequent, mistaken, assumption that probabilities are appropriate only for repetitive, artificial events such as coin flips and dice rolls. The subjective notion of probability found prominence thanks to De Finetti [7] and forms the basis for modern decision theory [20].

4.4   Discussion

We have presented three problems of uncertainty in information systems. In the first problem, we applied uncertain reasoning to estimate the value of a missing (continuously valued) field to determine an aggregate. In the second problem, we modeled the probabilities of various possible discrete values of a missing field to make a classification decision. In the third problem, we showed a probabilistic approach to vague queries; the implicit decision in this problem was whether to include a particular record in the query result.

We see several common threads among these problems in terms of the benefits of modeling the uncertainty explicitly using probability. Probabilities provide us with a common language to model different types of uncertainty. The key premise of reasoning about uncertainty is that we have to make explicit what we are uncertain about. Once we have outlined what is uncertain, we can derive a domain model that lets us determine a probability distribution for our uncertain items. These uncertain items can be discrete or continuous valued; qualitative or quantitative. We can base our distributions on statistical data, subjective assessments, or a combination of the two. We can determine distributions for items *per se*, or in a manner that is conditional on other (possibly uncertain) items.

We have illustrated in the examples how we can combine uncertain information with user preference models to arrive at a decision recommendation. This normative model of decision making—formal decision theory—provides a powerful extension of probability theory that has found application in a wide range of domains in which sound, justifiable decisions are required.

5   REPRESENTING UNCERTAINTY IN LARGE DATABASES

Let us now consider the problem of representing the uncertainty about the contents of a database explicitly in that database. One might conceptualize the representation of uncertainty inside a database simply as a matter of adding one or two extra fields to each attribute value to express its uncertainty, whether as belief, imprecision, ignorance, or vagueness. Figure 7 provides a small example of this approach: we have added uncertainty to a personnel record. We add a probability to each qualitative assertion—name, job description, marital status, city, state, and country of residence—and a standard deviation to each quantitative field—the date of birth and zip code.

We interpret each probability as the chance (our degree of belief) that the entry is correct, and the standard deviation as enclosing an interval which contains the true value with a 70% probability (assuming a normal distribution). This is a primitive but usable approach (except that treating a zip code as a quantity, and putting a standard deviation on it, is nonsense).

In fact we have a variety of choices of how to use probability to represent uncertainty about a numerical quantity, such as the age of person. These are a few of the possibilities:

- Mean and standard deviation
- Interval and corresponding probability
- Probability histogram over the entire range

Name: Thomas Bayes, $p = 0.95$

Title: Reverend, $p = 0.8$

Birthdate: 1738 ± 5

Marital status: Single $p = .3$, married $p = .7$

Address:
   City: Santa Catalina $p = 0.01$

   State: CA, $p = 0.05$

   Zip: 92001 ± 20

   Country: USA, $p = 0.15$

Figure 7   An example of how one might add uncertainty fields to a personnel record. (Not recommended!)

For a discrete-valued quantity, such as marital status, one could specify

- Most likely value, and its probability

- The complete probability mass function, with a probability for each possible value

Simpler representations may be less powerful, but they require fewer judgments or data to specify, take less memory space, and, depending on the inference method employed, necessitate less computational effort.

5.1   On the Complexity of Representing Uncertainty

The approach just described seems to imply that a database that represents uncertainty will require about twice as many data elements (linear complexity) as one that ignores uncertainty. This view is simultaneously far too simple and far too complicated.

It is too simple because it ignores the relationships among data values. These relationships often become more critical when one considers uncertainty. For example, consider the relationship between the city, state, zip, and country in

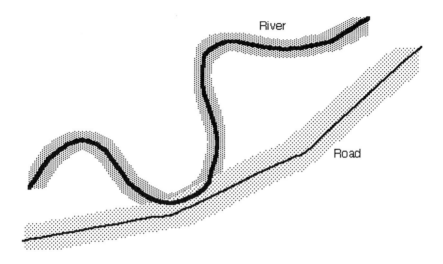

Figure 8 Uncertainty in a geographic database: The shaded lines represent the uncertainty about the location of the river and road respectively. Does the road cross the river?

an address. In most cases, there are strong relations among these. The zip code usually implies a city in the United States. A city usually implies a country. The events that each is correct cannot be considered independent, and so the probabilistic relation is quite complex.

For a still more complex example, consider a geographic database, containing information about the location of points on a river and a road, as in Figure 8. Does the road actually cross the river where they are close to each other? If we see only the certain representation (dark lines), we conclude they do not. Inspection of the shaded areas, which represent uncertainty (an 80% probability interval) for points along the paths, suggests that the road might cross the river. However, the graphic representation suggests that the probability bands are independent. Whether they are in fact independent depends on how the data was gathered. Typically in geographic information, relative locations for nearby features is much more accurate than absolute locations. If that is true in this case, we might be relatively sure that the road does not cross the river, because the relative distance between them at their closest approach may be quite accurate.

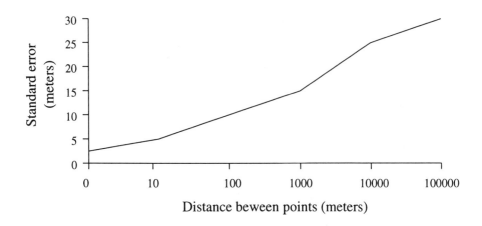

Figure 9   The uncertainty expressed as the standard deviation error in the represented distance between two features as a function of the represented distance in a geographic database.

Representing the uncertainty about the spatial relationship raises a host of complicated representational issues that do not arise in a deterministic perspective. The number of pairwise relations between elements is quadratic in the number of elements. If we do not limit ourselves to pairwise relations, the complexity may be exponential in the size of the deterministic database. This seems to imply that a full representation of probabilistic relationships is demanding indeed.

On the other hand, this approach may be vastly more complicated than necessary. Adding a separate uncertainty field to each coordinate of each data point in a digitized road may be quite unnecessary. Analysis of the reliability of the measurement and digitizing process that generated these data points will often reveal an absolute error, which is large but varies slowly with location, and a relative error, which is much smaller. These uncertainties are characteristics of the data-generating process, not of each individual data point—for example, the process of obtaining satellite photographs and extracting line data.

Therefore, a model of this uncertainty can be based on the data-generating process. For example, the uncertainty about the relative location may be expressed as a simple function of the relative distance between the two points, as shown in Figure 9. The same function may apply to any line of a given type (road or river) for the entire map database. In this case, the representation of the uncertainty is vastly simpler in terms of the number of parameters than the data points whose uncertainty it represents.

5.2 Estimating Uncertainty from Empirical Data

The best way to assess the uncertainty in a database is to audit a sample of the data against reality. In a personnel database, we can check the accuracy of a selected sample of records. If 5% of a randomly selected sample of personnel report that their addresses are incorrect, the law of large numbers lets us infer that about 5% of the unchecked individuals have incorrect addresses at that time. Sampling theory can tell us how large a sample we need to estimate the accuracy with a specified level of precision. But generally, the sample size need only be a small fraction of the number of entries in the database.

As people move and some forget to register their changed addresses, the percentage of incorrect addresses will increase. A more sophisticated approach would check samples of people with different times since last entry, and develop a model of how accuracy decays over time. Again, we have a variety of choices of how large a sample we take and how complicated a model we wish to develop. But in any case, the number of parameters of the model should be smaller than the number of entries in the database by a large factor. Even if we wanted to estimate a more complex model, we would not be able to, since the number of parameters of the model must be much fewer than the number of sample points, which is usually limited by the size of the database.

In summary, we can obtain a reasonable estimate of the reliability or uncertainty of a class of data in a database by empirical checking of a small sample. We have a variety of choices of levels of sophistication in modeling the uncertainty. But, the models will have many fewer parameters than the size of the database. Hence, representing the uncertainty need not add significantly to the size of the database. In other words, it is possible to add very useful quantification and modeling of the uncertainty in a database with an amount of effort in data gathering, modeling, and computational effort that is a small fraction of the total effort to create the deterministic database. Moreover, if we choose to use probability to represent the uncertainty, we can choose standard statistical methods to estimate the uncertainties on the basis of a small sample of empirical data.

5.3 Extracting Data Relationships from Empirical Data

So far we have assumed that the model structure is created by the user, possibly employing statistical analysis of the data to estimate uncertain values. An alternative approach is to generate the model structure automatically from data as well. There have been several centuries of research on the data-driven construction or adaptation of probabilistic models. Most of this work has addressed the problem of using data to tune model parameters for a fixed model structure [1, 8, 5]. Recently, however, several researchers have concentrated on Bayesian approaches that use data to learn the structure of a belief-network model. We can consider such approaches to be a form of knowledge discovery. These approaches have two basic components: an evaluation metric and a search procedure. Given a body of data, the search procedure identifies candidate belief networks for evaluation; the evaluation metric computes the probability of the model, given the data. The algorithms select the belief network (or belief networks) with the highest probability (or probabilities). Cooper and Herskovits identified a set of weak assumptions that allows the computation of the probability of a discrete-valued belief network given data in time $O(mn)$, where n and m are the number of variables and cases in the dataset, respectively [4]. Singh and Valtorta [22] have used a fundamental relationship between conditional independence and belief-network structure identified by Pearl and Verma [18], to guide search efficiently. Preliminary empirical studies with this method shows that it identifies model structure accurately [22].

6 CONCLUSIONS

We have tried to provide a brief introduction to Bayesian probabilistic schemes for representing uncertainty in information systems, focusing on the pragmatic issues. We have illustrated how Bayesian methods may base probabilities on pure judgment or may incorporate whatever empirical data are available. We have explained and illustrated how Bayesian methods can be used to represent imprecision, ignorance, linguistic vagueness, and ambiguity, as well as simple uncertainty. We do not see any inherent limitation in the application of probability to represent these concepts if they are clearly defined. The current state of the art of representing linguistic vagueness and ambiguity with probability is at a relatively early stage. The representation of simple uncertainty, imprecision, and ignorance is relatively straightforward using probability. Techniques are widely used. We have provided some simple examples.

We believe there are significant advantages in representing these types of uncertainty within the unified and well-developed framework provided by probability. We have touched on only a few of these in the previous discussion. Some other advantages, which we have not discussed in detail, include

- The existence of a clear, operationally based meaning for probability

- The existence of well-developed and widely used tools for eliciting expert judgment in the form of Bayesian belief networks and subjective probabilities

- The ability of probabilistic reasoning to replicate qualitatively intuitive patterns of commonsense reasoning, such as discounting correlated evidence sources, conditioning on evidence, and explaining away

- The ability to combine judgmental information with empirical observations, according to their availability

- The availability of standard statistical techniques to use empirical data to quantify uncertainties

- The use of sampling techniques to check and quantify the accuracy of the data within a database

- The direct relation of probability to decision theory, which provides a way to use probabilistic results as the basis for practical decision making

Whatever representation of uncertainty one chooses, the most challenging questions are how to apply the representation to large databases, and how to estimate the uncertainty from limited data. We have described briefly how it is possible to do this using probabilities, and how one can estimate the reliability or uncertainty in databases from small empirical samples.

We have argued that adding an "uncertainty field" to each data field is not generally a good way to quantify uncertainty in a database. It is simultaneously insufficient (because it does not represent uncertainty in key relationships) and excessive (since there is generally no need to represent the uncertainty in each data element individually). It is usually preferable to develop aggregate models of uncertainty in a database, as exemplified in the representation of standard error as a function of distance in a geographic database in Figure 9. We have outlined an approach in which empirical checking of a small sample of a database can be used to quantify the uncertainties expressed in an uncertainty model (that is, small relative to the size of the entire database). This approach may be much more attractive for builders of information systems who would like to express the uncertainty in a sound and convincing manner, yet are not able to expend resources that are a large multiple of the cost of the original deterministic database.

Acknowledgments

The research of Max Henrion was supported by the National Science Foundation under Grant Project IRI-9120330 to the Institute for Decision Systems Research, and by the Rockwell Science Center, Palo Alto Laboratory.

REFERENCES

[1] T. Bayes. An essay towards solving a problem in the doctrine of chances. *Biometrika*, 46: 293–298, 1958. Reprint of original work of 1763.

[2] E. Charniak and R. P. Goldman. A semantics for probabilistic quantifier-free first-order languages, with particular application to story understanding. In N. S. Sridharan, editor, *Proceedings of the Eleventh International Joint Conference on Artificial Intelligence,* Detroit, MI, pages 1074–1079. Morgan Kaufmann, San Mateo, CA, 1989.

[3] P. Cheeseman. Probabilistic versus fuzzy reasoning. In L. N. Kanal and J. F. Lemmer, editors, *Uncertainty in Artificial Intelligence*, pages 85–102. North-Holland, Amsterdam, The Netherlands, 1986.

[4] G. F. Cooper and E. H. Herskovits. A Bayesian method for the induction of probabilistic networks from data. *Machine Learning*, pages 9, 309–347, 1992.

[5] P. Diaconis and B. Efron. Computer-intensive methods in statistics. *Scientific American*, 248: 116–130, 1983.

[6] C. Elsaesser and M. Henrion. Verbal expressions for probability updates: How much more probable is 'much more probable'? In M. Henrion and R. Shachter, editors, *Uncertainty in Artificial Intelligence 5*, pages 319–330. North-Holland, Amsterdam, The Netherlands, 1990.

[7] B. De Finetti. *Theory of Probability*. Wiley, New York, 1970.

[8] R. A. Fisher. *The Design of Experiments*. Oliver and Boyd, Edinburgh, 1935.

[9] M. H. De Groot. *Optimal Statistical Decisions*. McGraw-Hill, New York, 1969.

[10] D. Heckerman, D. Geiger, and D. Chickering. Learning Bayesian networks: The combination of knowledge and statistical data. *Machine Learning* 20: 197–244, 1995.

[11] D. E. Heckerman. *Probabilistic Similarity Networks*. MIT Press, Cambridge, MA, 1991.

[12] D. E. Heckerman, A. Mamdani, and M. Wellman. Real-world applications of Bayesian networks. Special issue, Uncertainty in AI. *Communications of the ACM* 38(3): 24–26, 1995

[13] M. Henrion. An introduction to algorithms for inference in belief nets. In M. Henrion and R. Shachter, editors, *Uncertainty in Artificial Intelligence 5*, pages 129–138. North-Holland, Amsterdam, The Netherlands, 1990.

[14] M. Henrion. Search-based methods to bound diagnostic probabilities in very large belief nets. In B. D'Ambrosio, P. Smets, and P. P. Bonissone, editors, *Uncertainty and Artificial Intelligence: Proceedings of the Seventh Conference,* Los Angeles, CA, pages 142–150. Morgan Kaufman, San Mateo, CA, 1991.

[15] M. Henrion, J. S. Breese, and E. Horvitz. Decision analysis and expert systems. *Artificial Intelligence Magazine*, 12: 64–91, 1991.

[16] B. Middleton, M. Shwe, D. E. Heckerman, M. Henrion, E. J. Horvitz, H. Lehmann, and G. F. Cooper. Probabilistic diagnosis using a reformulation of the Internist-1/QMR knowledge base: II. evaluation of diagnostic performance. *Methods of Information in Medicine*, 30: 256–267, 1991.

[17] G. M. Morgan and M. Henrion. *Uncertainty: A Guide to Dealing with Uncertainty in Quantitative Risk and Policy Analysis*. Cambridge University Press, New York, 1990.

[18] J. Pearl and T. Verma. A theory of inferred causation. In Allen, Fikes, and Snadewall, editors, *Principles of Knowledge Representation and Reasoning: Proceedings of the Second International Conference*, pages 441–452. Morgan Kaufmann, San Mateo, CA, 1991.

[19] H. Raiffa. *Introduction to Decision Analysis*. Harvard University Press, Cambridge, MA, 1968.

[20] L. J. Savage. *The Foundations of Statistics.* Wiley, New York, 1954.

[21] M. Shwe, B. Middleton, D. E. Heckerman, M. Henrion, E. J. Horvitz, H. Lehmann, and G. F. Cooper. Probabilistic diagnosis using a reformulation of the Internist-1/QMR knowledge base: I. the probabilistic model and inference algorithms. *Methods of Information in Medicine*, 30: 241–255, 1991.

[22] M. Singh and M. Valtorta. An algorithm for the construction of Bayesian network structures from data. In D. Heckerman and A. Mamdani, editors, *Proceedings of Ninth Conference on Uncertainty in Artificial Intelligence,* Washington, DC, pages 259–265. Morgan Kaufmann, San Mateo, CA, 1993.

[23] C. S. Spetzler and C. S. Stael von Holstein. Probability encoding in decision analysis. *Management Science*, 22: 340–358, 1975.

[24] H. Turtle. *Inference Networks for Document Retrieval.* Ph.D. Dissertation, Computer Science Department, University of Massachusetts, Amherst, MA, 1991. Available as COINS Technical Report.

[25] R. L. Winkler. The consensus of subjective probability distributions. *Management Science*, 15(2): B61–B75, 1968.

10

AN INTRODUCTION TO THE FUZZY SET AND POSSIBILITY THEORY-BASED TREATMENT OF FLEXIBLE QUERIES AND UNCERTAIN OR IMPRECISE DATABASES

Patric Bosc
Henri Prade*

IRISA/ENSSAT
Université de Rennes I
6 rue de Kérampont – BP 447
22305 Lannion Cedex, France

* IRIT
Université Paul Sabatier
118 route de Narbonne
31062 Toulouse Cedex, France

1   INTRODUCTION

The information to be stored in databases is not always precise and certain, and, occasionally, some information might be missing altogether.[1] When the available information is imperfect, it is often desirable to try to represent it in the database nonetheless, so that it can be used to answer queries of interest as much as possible. A related issue is the handling of imperfect or flexible queries. For example, a natural query language may use a word or a phrase whose meaning is vague or even entirely unclear. As another example, a query may reflect a user's uncertainty about what he is looking for. In addition, one may want to use vague predicates in a query to express preferences among the admissible answers.

---

[1]This latter situation corresponds to the null value "unknown" in the database literature.

Fuzzy set and possibility theory [91, 92] offer a unified framework both for managing imperfect information, and for handling flexible queries. A fuzzy set F is an extension of a standard set, viewed in terms of membership function. It describes a subpart of a universe U whose boundaries are not strictly defined, attaching a grade of membership (whose values are from [0,1]) to each element of U. This provides a gradual transition between full membership in the set and nonmembership. It is then possible to represent gradual properties, vague classes, and approximate descriptions (like those used in natural languages).

Assume the fuzzy set F represents a concept, and let x be a value in the universe U. It is then possible to estimate the extent to which x is compatible with the concept represented by F. In other situations, when one wishes to represent an ill-known value x, the notion of possibility distribution may be used to specify the extent to which elements of U are possible as the actual value of x.

Fuzzy sets encode preference orderings, whereas possibility distributions encode plausibility orderings about what the real value of a variable or the real state of the world might be. Thus, it should be emphasized that fuzzy sets and plausibility distributions deal with two different issues. Indeed, the graph in Figure 1 may be interpreted as the membership function of a fuzzy set called *high*, and thus could be taken as a description of the concept "high"; in this case, the figure shows that a particular value a, for instance the precisely-known salary of an individual called John, is compatible at degree .8 with the concept "high." Alternatively, the graph may be interpreted as the possibility distribution of John's salary; that is, it describes the possible values of the salary of John, which is only known to be high; in this case, the figure shows that it is possible at degree .8 that a is the actual salary value. Possibility distributions restrict the possible values of variables on universes of mutually exclusive values, while fuzzy sets represent gradual properties whose satisfaction may be a matter of degree.

This chapter is a general introduction to fuzzy set and possibility theory-based approaches to the management of imprecise and uncertain information and the handling of flexible queries. It provides only an overview and refers the reader to the literature for more details. The chapter is organized as follows. Section 2 defines the basic vocabulary and introduces the fundamental concepts for characterizing the various forms of imperfect information. Section 3 examines the main kinds of fuzzy databases, and briefly considers the corresponding issues in information-retrieval systems. Section 4 is devoted to flexible queries. Section 5 deals with the management of imprecise and uncertain information in databases. Section 6 discusses integrity constraints and especially functional dependencies whose expressions involve tolerance, graduality, or uncertainty.

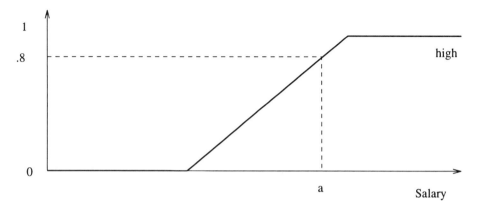

Figure 1 Fuzzy set or possibility distribution?

In the concluding remarks, other topics related to uncertainty and imprecision in database systems are briefly mentioned; in particular, the update of databases with new information, the management of fuzziness and uncertainty in object-oriented representations, and the summarization of data.

2 IMPERFECT INFORMATION: VOCABULARY

In this section we define the main terms that are used when referring to imperfect information. By information, we mean data (facts) as well as general knowledge (rules). We distinguish among four main types of defects that may pervade information, namely: uncertainty, imprecision, vagueness, and inconsistency. The distinction between imprecision and uncertainty has been pointed out in [39].

2.1 Uncertainty

Uncertainty refers to lack of sufficient information about the state of the world, for determining whether a Boolean statement (which can only be true or false) is indeed true or false. Examples of such statements are: "It will rain at 5 PM today," "Tweety flies" (knowing only that Tweety is a bird and that birds usually fly), "the number of inhabitants of Palma de Mallorca is over 500,000" (but the person who gave me this information is not fully reliable).

In such situations, the best that we can do is to try to estimate the tendency of the statement to be true (or false). Several frameworks are possible: (1) numerical methods such as probability theory, possibility theory, belief functions, and ad hoc methods based on certainty factors; (2) purely symbolic deduction methods using nonclassical mechanisms for producing plausible conclusions in spite of partial lack of information (defeasible reasoning).

2.2   Imprecision

Imprecision refers to the contents of the considered statement and depends on the "granularity" of the language used in that statement. For instance, the sentence "Paul is between 25 and 30 years old" is clearly imprecise. The sentence "Paul is 26 years old" is precise if we only expect an age value specified in years, but is imprecise if we expect a more accurate age value (for example 25 years, 9 months, and 5 days). Imprecise statements may stem from disjunctive information, such as "Paul is 25 or 26 years old," or negative information, such as "Paul is not between 25 and 30 years old." An extreme situation is when Paul's age is entirely unknown, which means that any value of the universe may equally be assigned. Imprecision is represented in terms of subsets of the relevant attribute domain, which are not singletons. These subsets constrain the possible values that can be assigned to the attribute for the considered object.

A given statement may be both uncertain and imprecise; for instance, when the information "Paul is between 25 and 30 years old" is provided by a source that is not fully reliable. Generally, a balance exists between uncertainty and imprecision: the more imprecise the statement, the more certain we are about it, and conversely, the more precise the statement, the more uncertain we are. For instance, the statement "Paul is between 30 and 50 years old" is almost certain (assuming, for example, a brief encounter with Paul), since it is very imprecise; on the other hand, the statement "Paul is between 35 and 40 years old" is more precise, but the uncertainty should be expected to increase.

Imprecision may also be due to multiple data sources that use different vocabularies for expressing attribute values, corresponding to different partitions of the same universe of discourse. In that case, there is not a one-to-one correspondence between the labels of the elements of the different partitions. Given two partitions $P_1 = (A_1, ..., A_n)$ and $P_2 = (B_1, ..., B_m)$ of a domain D, we can only define an upper approximation A_i^+ and a lower approximation A_i^- of the element A_i of P_1 in terms of those of P_2, namely $A_i^+ = \bigcup_{A_i \cap B_j \neq \emptyset} B_j$, $A_i^- = \bigcup_{B_j \subseteq A_i} B_j$, thus creating a rough set [62].

2.3 Vagueness and Gradual Properties

A vague statement contains vague or gradual predicates. It may also include vague quantifiers. For instance, "Paul is a young researcher" refers to Paul's age using the linguistic term *young*. Note that the meaning of a vague predicate depends on the context: a large butterfly is smaller than a small elephant. The context may even depend on the person making the statement, so it is not a universally accepted meaning of *young* in a given context that we try to represent in practice, but the intended meaning of a given person. Fortunately, fuzzy sets are rather easy to elicit since it is sufficient in practice to identify their support (the elements with nonzero membership) and their core (the elements with membership 1).[2]

A statement such as "Paul is young" is not necessarily true or false, and as already mentioned, it may be used in two different situations. First, when Paul's age is precisely known, for instance 30 years old, and the statement is assigned a degree of truth that estimates to what extent 30 agrees with *young* in the considered context. Second, when the only information available about Paul's age is that "Paul is young," and the statement represents a flexible constraint on the acceptable values for Paul's age. In both cases, an ordering among the values compatible with the concept *young* is defined.

Note that it is possible to encounter second-order imprecision and uncertainty if the value of a degree of truth or of a measure of uncertainty (probability, possibility, etc.) is imprecise, vague, or not known with complete certainty. For instance, we may want to express that "it is not entirely certain that John is ill-paid." This induces a possibility distribution of the type shown in Figure 2. Such a possibility distribution expresses that there is a possibility equal to $1 - \alpha$ that John is not-ill paid, and thus that "John is ill-paid" is only certain at degree α.

---

[2]See Section 4.1.

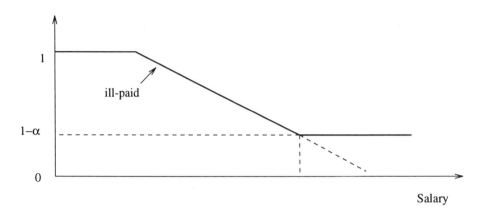

Figure 2   Representing vague and uncertain information.

2.4   Inconsistency

A statement is inconsistent if there is no possible assignment of the variables under consideration (or no model) that renders the statement true. The two items of information "Paul is 25" and "Paul is older than 27" illustrate this situation, since there is no way of assigning a value to Paul's age that agrees with both items. Inconsistency may be due to distinct sources of information with different levels of reliability. Acknowledging this fact may lead to a solution; see [25], where a set of n certainty degrees associated with the n sources under consideration is attached to each proposition in a possibilistic logic framework.

3   FUZZY DATABASES

The terms *fuzzy database* and *fuzzy database system* have been used for referring to any fuzzy set-based approach in information management. Most of the approaches assume the framework of the relational model of data, although the handling of fuzzy information in the entity-relationship model has been also explored [97, 74].

Ignoring fuzzy or flexible queries (e.g., [79, 94, 39, 10]), which are the topic of the next section, the term *fuzzy database* has at least four different meanings, depending on the way we use fuzzy sets for representing uncertain and vague data, or for modeling fuzzy concepts.

A first interpretation extends ordinary relations to fuzzy relations, where a fuzzy relation is a fuzzy subset of the Cartesian product of domains. Each tuple is therefore assigned a grade of membership, expressing the extent to which it belongs to the fuzzy relation. Such sets of weighted tuples can be used for storing information [48, 3, 51], or they may be produced when a nonfuzzy database answers a fuzzy query [79, 10]. In this latter case, the relation represents a fuzzy concept. Consider, for example, the query "employees who are middle-aged and recently-engaged." The weight attached to each tuple of the result represents the extent to which the corresponding employee is middle-aged and recently-engaged. The data are neither imprecise nor uncertain but are associated with a level of compatibility with a particular concept.

From a formal point of view, relations with weighted tuples can be seen as fuzzy relations. Yet they can be interpreted in at least two different ways, depending on the intended meaning of the weights.[3] Weights may represent (1) the compatibility of tuples with respect to a fuzzy concept (as described above), but also (2) the certainty we have in the information stored in the tuple; i.e., the information in the tuple is qualified with a certainty equal to the weight. This applies as well to relations modeling the association between values. Consider, for instance, the fuzzy relation *Likes (Person, Movie)*. The weight associated with each of its tuples can be understood either as indicating the certainty of that information or the intensity of the association. Note that if the weight models uncertainty, *Likes* is an ordinary predicate, whereas if it models intensity, it is a fuzzy predicate (the fuzzy relation is then the extension of the fuzzy predicate). Clearly, the interpretation of the weights should be taken into account when defining operations for manipulating these weights.

A second view of fuzziness in databases relies on the notion of interchangeability or tolerance relations defined on attribute domains [16, 17, 18, 63, 52, 93, 73]. Given an attribute domain D, an interchangeability relation T may be defined through its membership function μ_T from $D \times D$ to $[0,1]$, such that the closer d and d' are to each other (the more interchangeable they are), the closer to 1 is the degree of membership $\mu_T(d, d')$. When a distance function is not available and the domains are finite, the value of μ_T for each pair (d, d') could be given explicitly by an expert. For infinite domains (e.g., intervals of real numbers) μ_T may be built from a distance function. For example, given a distance function $\delta(d, d')$, we may define μ_T as $\max(0, 1 - \delta(d, d')/\lambda)$, where λ is a positive real number. The interchangeability relation attached to each attribute domain may be understood as a standard amount of fuzziness, which should be attached to each apparently precise value of this attribute stored in the database in order

---

[3]Unfortunately, sometimes this meaning remains unclear in the fuzzy set literature.

to compensate for the inherent imprecision or uncertainty of this value [68]. In this case we acknowledge that there is an approximate synonymy between close elements in attribute domains and that when a precise attribute value is stored, another value, close to the former value, might have been stored as well. For instance, this approach may be used to represent data received from measurement devices, in order to represent the error on the measure. Another use of fuzzy relations expressing proximity is when a tolerance is added to a request in order to enlarge the set of acceptable values.

A third type of fuzzy database that we shall consider in greater detail in Section 5 allows for the representation of ill-known attribute values by means of possibility distributions [92]. For instance, in a database describing houses, if the size is not perfectly known, it will be described by means of a possibility distribution (which restricts the set of possible values for the size of a particular house). This approach has been further developed in [80, 81, 82, 64, 65, 66, 94, 83]. In this approach, attribute values are allowed to be precise, imprecise, vague, pervaded with uncertainty, unknown, or inapplicable, according to the nature of the available information. In all these cases, the information is represented by means of a possibility distribution $\pi_{A(x)}$, which restricts the possible values of an attribute A for the considered object x. $\pi_{A(x)}$ takes its values in the interval [0,1]. At the two extremes, $\pi_{A(x)}(u) = 0$ means that u is impossible and thus totally excluded as a value of $A(x)$, and $\pi_{A(x)}(u) = 1$ means that u is an entirely possible value for $A(x)$. $\pi_{A(x)}$ can also represent intermediate levels of possibility, and, in this framework, possibility is no longer an all-or-nothing notion but becomes a matter of degree. Clearly, several distinct values can be entirely possible for $A(x)$ in case of imprecise information. Note that the values restricted by $\pi_{A(x)}$ are mutually exclusive as possible values of $A(x)$, and thus $\pi_{A(x)}$ is defined on D if A is a single-valued attribute, and on 2^D if it is an attribute that can have several values simultaneously.

Precise, imprecise, or vague information can be qualified in terms of its uncertainty. As already mentioned, one interpretation of a weighted tuple is to view the weight attached to the tuple as an estimate of the reliability, or the certainty, of the information in the tuple. Modeling this certainty in terms of a necessity measure in the framework of possibility theory leads to associating the level of certainty of the entire tuple with each of the elements of the tuple, and to modify each possibility distribution in the tuple into another possibility distribution reflecting this level of certainty. Figure 2 shows an example of how a possibility distribution, here representing the fuzzy set of possible values compatible with the concept "ill-paid," is modified into another possibility distribution to acknowledge the fact that the information is only certain at the degree α.

Note that in the previously mentioned representation of information by means of possibility distributions, the values that are outside the fuzzy set whose membership function is equal to the possibility distribution, are definitely excluded as possible values (since their possibility degree is 0). In other words, we are totally certain that the value of the attribute for the considered item is among the values with nonzero degree of possibility. However, we may imagine, as suggested in [32], having to store in a database a value (or a set of values) that is individually judged as possible for the considered attribute of the object under consideration without knowing the complete set of its possible values. In this case we are no longer certain that the value of the attribute is among the stored values; we only know that certain values are possible, but there may be other possible values as well. This corresponds to possibility-qualified information and may be considered as a fourth kind of fuzziness in databases. If more information of this kind becomes available, the scope of possibilities would be enlarged, whereas in the case of a possibility distribution restricting with certainty the possible values, the scope of possible values can only diminish with the arrival of new information. In case of possibility-qualified information, the intended purpose is to express that there is a "guaranteed possibility" for a given attribute value to apply to the considered item. For instance, when we have examples of possible prices for a used car, these prices do not necessarily intend to state with certainty all the possible prices.

An alternative to the relational model of databases are deductive databases, which use a logical framework to represent data and integrity constraints. In this framework, uncertainty can be handled with possibilistic logic, and flexible queries require fuzzy predicates. For brevity, this approach is not discussed here, but details may be found in [23, 24, 26]. Also [77] shows how to handle certainty degrees using fuzzy set combination operations in a logic programming style.

Flexible querying is also desirable in information-retrieval systems, since users of such systems expect results that are ordered lists of documents that match their specifications. Both queries and documents are often described with sets of keywords, and one may then attach a value to each keyword in a query to express its importance in the overall request, and to each keyword in a document, to express the appropriateness of the keyword in the overall description [57, 60, 6, 46, 47, 87, 5, 56, 53, 58, 59, 7]. Fuzzy thesauri taking into account the approximate synonymy between keywords can be also introduced [72]. Chapter 7 of this book is devoted to uncertainty in information retrieval systems.

4 FLEXIBLE QUERIES

When querying a database, one may wish not to define precise conditions of acceptance or rejection because the satisfaction of such conditions may be regarded as a matter of *degree*. This also occurs when one wishes to express *preferences* and thus distinguish between acceptable and nonacceptable answers in a more refined way than with a strictly Boolean filter. Towards this end, *vague predicates* are allowed in the requests; such predicates are represented by fuzzy sets and model gradual properties whose satisfaction is a matter of degree; we can thus express that among acceptable attribute values, some are preferred. A query looking for "hotels not too expensive close to downtown" illustrates this expression of preferences. The primary advantage of such flexible queries is to provide answers when a crisp query might produce an empty answer (which often leads to repeated reformulations of the queries by the users). In addition, this approach can order the individual elements of the answer with respect to their suitability (whereas ordinary queries are answered with a simple, at times very large, set).

4.1 The Fuzzy Set Approach

Overview

We assume that vague query conditions are represented by fuzzy sets. A query is constructed using several types of vague predicate expressions:

Atomic predicate: An atomic predicate is defined by a fuzzy set on a domain D, i.e., by a membership function from D to [0,1]; examples of such vague predicates are "tall," "young," and "important." In practice, unimodal functions with a trapezoidal shape are often used.

Modified predicate: Modifier functions, from [0,1] to [0,1], can be applied to fuzzy set membership functions to model the effect of linguistic hedges such as "very," "more or less," "rather," and so on. The most usual modifier functions are of the form $y = x^\alpha$, or are translating operations. Antonyms can also be treated in this way: the antonym ant(T) of a fuzzy label T is obtained by defining the membership function of ant(T) as the symmetrical to the membership function of T with respect to the axis passing by the middle of the domain D (on which these functions are defined). For example, if $D = [a, b]$ and $\mu_{ant(T)}(x) = \mu_T(a + b - x)$. Thus, ant(ant$(T)$) = T.

Compound predicate: A compound predicate is defined as a combination of membership functions representing atomic predicates by means of fuzzy set connectives; for instance, we may have a request for "inexpensive, low-mileage cars" (see Section 4.1).

Queries may also involve vague quantifiers, such as "most," "a few," or "about a dozen." Queries may inquire about the relative cardinalities of some subsets, such as "Is it true that most of the employees which satisfy A also satisfy B?" Queries may even look for objects that satisfy most of the prescribed conditions.

Queries that look for the maximal, minimal, or average values, or more generally for the value of any scalar function over a set of objects specified in a fuzzy way, can also be handled. An example of such a query is "What is the average salary of young employees?" See [31] for discussion of scalar and fuzzy-valued solutions.

Connectives

Compound conditions are represented with fuzzy set operations. Fuzzy set theory offers a panoply of aggregation options, which is considerably richer than that available in the classical Boolean framework. These include a variety of conjunctions and disjunctions, as well as trade-off operations. Let $A_i(x)$ be the precise value of the attribute A_i for the item x and let P_i be the subset expressing a restriction on $A_i(x)$. Conjunctive (respectively, disjunctive) aggregations of the elementary degrees of matching $\mu_{P_i}(A_i(x))$ are usually performed by applying the min (respectively, max) operation to the degrees. Using min for evaluating a conjunction of required properties means that the grading of the least-satisfied property will be used as the global level of satisfaction (this type of logical conjunction may seem as too requiring in some situations; see below for other possible candidates for modelling the $\wedge$ connective). Min-based aggregation provides a rather crude ranking, since only the least specified property is considered; it is still possible to keep an egalitarian approach in the aggregation of the degrees of satisfaction of the required properties, by refining the min-ordering into, for instance, a "leximin" ordering where the other degrees of satisfaction also influence the ranking; see [22] for different refinements of the min-ordering. Negation is modeled by $1 - \mu_{P_i}(A_i(x))$, which represents the extent to which $A_i(x)$ belongs to the complement of P_i. In some applications, we may like to express that some elementary conditions are less important than others. Conjunctive and disjunctive aggregations are respectively generalized in that case by [29, 76]

- $\min_i \max(\mu_{P_i}(A_i(x)), 1 - w_i)$

- $\max_i \min(\mu_{P_i}(A_i(x)), w_i)$

where the weight w_i indicates the importance of the condition on the attribute A_i in the overall request. The weights are supposed to satisfy the normalization condition $\max_i w_i = 1$. Clearly, when all the elementary conditions are equally important (i.e., $\forall i, w_i = 1$), the two operations above reduce, respectively, to min and max. When $w_i = 0$, no condition on the attribute A_i is taken into account. In the case of the conjunctive combination, we observe that even if $A_i(x)$ fails to satisfy the restriction P_i of importance w_i, this could not drive the global result of the combination below $1 - w_i$. Consider, for instance, a search for an apartment that is "inexpensive and large," where the second criterion is considered less important. The expression is $\min(\mu_{Inexpensive}(Price), \max(\mu_{Large}(Area), 1 - w))$. In this expression, if the price is inexpensive but the area is not large, the global rating will be $1 - w$ rather than 0. Thus, an apartment cannot be rejected only on the basis of its area.

Conjunction and disjunction operations, other than min and max, can also be used. There exist more "drastic" conjunction operations (e.g., the product $a \cdot b$, or $\max(0, a + b - 1)$) and less drastic disjunction operations (e.g., the "probabilistic sum" $a + b - a \cdot b$, or the "bounded sum" $\min(1, a + b)$). There also exist many trade-off operations between min and max (e.g., the arithmetic mean), which can model compensatory conjunction: a low degree of satisfaction for one elementary condition can be somewhat balanced by a high degree of satisfaction for another condition [96].

Overviews of fuzzy set aggregation connectives can be found in [28, 89]. See also [78] for an applied perspective based on a so-called *extended continuous logic*, analogous to the fuzzy set framework. Finally, we mention the ordered weighted average (OWA) operations, defined by $OWA(a_1, ..., a_n) = w_1 b_1 + \cdots + w_n b_n$ where b_i denotes the ith largest value among the a_i and the sum of the w_i equals 1; this aggregation performs a somewhat dynamic weighting (the weights apply after the values to be aggregated are ordered and do not depend on the places of these values in the initial list), which contrasts with the ordinary weighted mean [88].

Elicitation of Membership Functions and Connectives

An important issue is the elicitation of the fuzzy set membership functions representing the fuzzy predicates or fuzzy predicate expressions involved in queries. There are two main approaches. A first solution makes available to the user a standard vocabulary with a set of connectives (and possibly fuzzy set modifiers) for specifying requests; this requires that users be familiar with the intended meaning of the fuzzy vocabulary. A better solution, in general, involves a procedure for elicitating the intended meaning of the user's words. It is preferable to find out what the user means by *not-too-expensive*, than to find a universally valid representation of *expensive* and the modifier *not-too* (which may not exist even in a precisely defined context).

The procedure first elicitates the membership functions of the fuzzy labels referring to a specific domain, mainly by identifying when this function should be 0 and when it is equal to 1, and by providing gradual transition(s) elsewhere. Then, we have to identify the intended meaning of the connectives used in the query in case of compound predicates. Indeed, a conjunction may have a variety of different meanings ranging from a purely logical interpretation (requiring the more or less complete satisfaction of each of the conditions involved in the conjunction) to a compensatory interpretation (allowing for trade-offs between the levels of satisfaction of the conditions). A simple procedure for the elicitation of connectives is presented in [39, Chapter 3]. It requires global ratings given by the user for few prototypical objects.

When using the max or min operations and the complementation to 1 (which is an order-reversing operation), it can be shown that computation is not sensitive to slight variations of the membership grades, since these operations are concerned only with the ordering among the degrees. Thus, a precise identification of the membership functions is not necessary in practice. However, it is important to be aware that fuzzy sets require a commensurability hypothesis; i.e., the use of a common scale for grading the compatibility with respect to the different predicates.

4.2 Flexible Querying of Conventional Databases

In this section, we consider the problem of flexible querying in conventional databases, in which data are assumed to be precisely known. We begin with a review of the approaches suggested in the literature and their position with respect to fuzzy sets. Then, we describe briefly an extended SQL-like language. Finally, we discuss aspects of query processing.

Fuzzy-Set-Based Approach

The framework of an extension of the relational algebra (the relational operations selection, projection, and join, and the set operations) to fuzzy relations is shown in Figure 3. In such extensions, the result of a product-selection-projection query is a set of tuples, accompanied by their degrees of membership in the answer. Answers are then ordered.

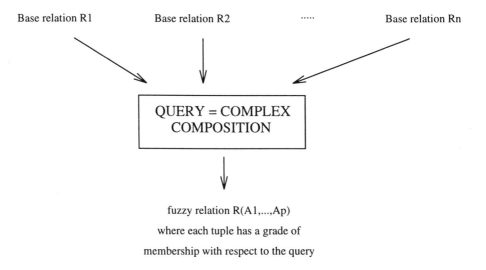

Figure 3   Framework of an extension of relational algebra to fuzzy relations.

Extensions of Relational Systems

The other approaches to flexible querying that have been proposed can be divided into three groups: (1) introduction of a complementary criterion in the query, (2) use of similarities and distances, and (3) description of explicit preferences and weighting.

Complementary Criterion

In the PREFERENCES system [49], a query is composed of a principal condition C and a preference clause P, both of which are based on Boolean expressions. The meaning of such a query is "find the tuples that satisfy C and rank them according to their satisfaction of P." This system allows for the combination of preference clauses by means of two constructors: nesting (hierarchy of conditions) and juxtaposition (conditions of equal importance). From the subset R_C of the tuples of a relation R satisfying condition C, the nesting (respectively, juxtaposition) of preference clauses $P_1, \ldots, P_n$ leads to these sets: S_1 is the subset of R_C satisfying P_1 but not P_2 (respectively, satisfying exactly one clause); S_2 is the subset of R_C satisfying P_1 and P_2 but not P_3 (respectively, satisfying exactly two clauses); and so on, until finally, S_n is the subset of R_C satisfying P_1 through P_n. The user receives as an initial response the highest nonempty set S_i. The user can go back to the earlier sets, an action that corresponds to a weakening of the preference condition.

A significant advantage of this system is the avoidance of successive formulations, which would otherwise be necessary for obtaining the desired set of tuples. The authors rightly point out that to handle an equivalent formulation in a conventional language would be tiresome. However, it must be noticed that the discrimination capacity remains limited, since it directly depends on the number of preference predicates given by the user. If n such predicates are provided (in practice, n is small, usually less than 10), every tuple belongs to one of n possible classes. Hierarchical requirements, in the sense of [49], can be handled in the framework of possibility theory in terms of *conditional* priority, where a requirement (modeled by a fuzzy F) with priority p, is represented by the modified fuzzy set $\max(\mu_F, 1 - p)$; see [35].

Another solution based on a complementary criterion was offered in the system DEDUCE2 [19]. However, it has been shown that the composition of predicates, which is based on ranks issued from sorts, is not semantically founded [14].

Similarities and Distances

A different approach to flexible querying is to include query conditions based on the notion of *similarity* (denoted here by $\approx$) instead of strict equality. Consider conditions of the type $A \approx v$, where v represents an ideal value, but where other values are nevertheless acceptable. For instance, *Salary* $\approx \$2000$ means that \$2000 is a perfect match but close values (e.g., values in the interval 1950–2050 are also satisfactory). The evaluation of such conditions on the attribute A of an element x is made using *distances*, as follows: if $A(x)$ is sufficiently similar to v, then the dissimilarity between x and the ideal value will be estimated by the distance between $A(x)$ and v (which is supposed to remain below some threshold), otherwise the dissimilarity will be considered infinite. In the presence of connectors such as conjunction and disjunction, an overall distance must then be calculated, thus allowing the elements under consideration to be ordered. These ideas have been demonstrated with several systems, including ARES [43] and VAGUE [54]. A technique that uses "nearest neighbors" without an explicit similarity operator was proposed in [40].

In ARES, elementary distances are attached to a given domain and are stored in a relation that specifies the distance between any two values. Queries may include both Boolean predicates and predicates involving similarity (these can only be conjoined). For each predicate that involves similarity, the user specifies a threshold. The global distance is defined as the sum of the elementary distances attached to the similarity predicates of the query.

VAGUE is different from ARES in three major aspects: the disjunction of predicates is allowed, similarity predicates can be explicitly weighted, and the global distance mechanism for a conjunction is based on the Euclidian distance. ARES and VAGUE share a common characteristic, namely the fact that only elements that satisfy (however weakly) every term of a conjunction are retrieved. This behavior may cause discontinuity, since an element that satisfies weakly each term will be retrieved, whereas an element that satisfies strongly all terms but one will be rejected. This drawback may be avoided in a fuzzy set framework.

In the "nearest neighbors" approach, a query involves a set of values, which characterize an ideal tuple X. Each candidate tuple is then compared with X by means of a global function that gathers the results of local distance functions applied to some attributes. One of the most used global functions is the Lp-norm defined as

$$\sqrt[p]{\sum_{i=1}^{n} dist_i(x)^p} \quad \text{where} \quad dist_i(x) = \frac{|x_i - X_i|}{\max_i - \min_i},$$

where x_i and X_i are the values of the ith attribute of the current tuple and the prototype, which can vary between $\min_i$ and $\max_i$.

Criteria with Preferences and Weighting

In the area of information retrieval, the flexible retrieval system MULTOS [70] has been described. Its principle is the replacement of a traditional selection criterion with a set of criteria to which an explicit preference level (expressed by a value between 0 and 1, or by a linguistic term) is attached. Thus, a user interested in the year of publication might write something like: {year ∈ [1978, 1982] "preferred," year ∈ [1983, 1988] "accepted"}. Furthermore, he can weight each set of criteria, e.g., the subject matter is more important (high), than the price of the document (medium), which in turn is more important than the year of publication (low). Conjunction and disjunction connectives allow the combination of several criteria. In particular, the semantics of the conjunction is expressed by the weighted sum (the aforementioned linguistic values high, medium, and low being encoded by values between 0 and 1) of the results, weighted according to the preference attached to them ("accepted," "preferred").

An analysis of these three kinds of nonfuzzy approaches [14, 12] claimed that in every case (1) each of the queries is expressible in the fuzzy sets framework, (2) the ordering mechanism is essentially a mean, (3) the allowed queries have a very special typology, and (4) each system proposes only one (or two) aggregation mechanism(s), leading the authors to conclude that fuzzy sets provide a more general framework for choosing and expressing the appropriate aggregation mechanism.

Survey of an Extended SQL-Like Language

SQL-like query languages are a popular standard for accessing databases. This motivated the extension of SQL to a language SQLf that allows processing of fuzzy queries [10, 11]. The basic statement in SQL is

select attributes **from** relations **where** condition

The basic idea is the introduction of imprecise predicates into the condition (Boolean conditions being a special case). Furthermore, to ensure the calibration of the number of responses, a number of desired responses (quantitative aspect) and the minimum degree of satisfaction required for selection (qualitative aspect) may be specified. The result of such a query is a fuzzy relation.

Elementary predicates (unary or n-ary, and including fuzzy relational comparators) allow comparisons between attributes and values, or between attributes. Modified predicates are also allowed, with modifiers such as "very," "fairly," and "relatively." With these two basic types of predicates, compound predicates can be defined using connectives. Conjunction and disjunction (binary or n-ary), defined in terms of intersection and union of fuzzy sets, generalize the Boolean *and* and *or*. It is also possible to define other aggregation operators, such as the mean (arithmetic, geometric, or weighted), which convey compensation effects. In SQL, it is possible to nest blocks using operators, such as **in** or **exists**, and it is useful to study how these constructs can be extended as well. This point is important because it poses the question of preserving the equivalences of different formulations of the same query. To illustrate, consider this database

$$\text{Emp (Emp\_no, Name, Dept\_no, Salary, Job)}$$
$$\text{Dept (Dept\_no, Budget)}$$

Listed below are four equivalent formulations of an SQL query. Notice that the corresponding forms with fuzzy conditions remain mutually equivalent.

Number and name of every employee working for a department whose budget is 100 times the employee's salary

Number and name of every employee working for a department whose budget is *about* 100 times the employee's salary

(a) **select** Emp_no, Name
from Emp, Dept
where Dept.Dept_no = Emp.Dept_no
and Dept.Budget = Emp.Salary * 100

(a′) **select** Emp_no, Name
from Emp, Dept
where Dept.Dept_no = Emp.Dept_no
and Dept.Budget $\approx$ Emp.Salary * 100

(b) **select** Emp_no, Name
from Emp
where Dept.Dept_no **in**
(**select** Dept_no
from Dept
where Budget = Emp.Salary * 100)

(b′) **select** Emp_no, Name
from Emp
where Dept.Dept_no **in**
(**select** Dept_no
from Dept
where budget $\approx$ Emp.Salary * 100)

(c) **select** Emp_no, Name
from Emp
where (Salary * 100) **in**
(**select** Budget
from Dept
where Dept_no = Emp.Dept_no)

(c′) **select** Emp_no, Name
from Emp
where (Salary * 100) **in**$_f$
(**select** Budget
from Dept
where Dept_no = Emp.Dept_no)

(d) **select** Emp_no, Name
from Emp
where exists
(**select** *
from Dept
where Dept_no = Emp.Dept_no
and Budget = Emp.Salary * 100)

(d′) **select** Emp_no, Name
from Emp
where exists
(**select** *
from Dept
where Dept_no = Emp.Dept_no
and Budget $\approx$ Emp.Salary * 100)

The comparison operator ≈ means "approximately equal to." In the right column, the operators **in**, **in**$_f$, and **exists** correspond, respectively, to the membership of an element in a fuzzy set, the fuzzy membership of an element in a fuzzy set, and the nonemptiness of a fuzzy set. It can be shown that, given appropriate definitions for the extended nesting operators, queries (a′), (b′), (c′) and (d′) give the same result, in the same way that queries (a), (b), (c) and (d) are equivalent in the nonfuzzy case.

It is also possible to introduce fuzzy operators for sets of tuples, and thus extend the partitioning constructs of SQL. Here, we find two main types of imprecise conditions: (1) a fuzzy predicate is applied to the result of a function that aggregates tuples (for example, max, sum, or mean), and (2) fuzzy quantifiers. Thus, the query "find the best 10 departments for which the average salary of the secretaries is about \$6000" will be expressed by

> **select** 10 Dept_no
> **from** Emp
> **where** job = "secretary"
> **group by** Dept_no
> **having** avg(salary) ≈ 6000

and the query "find the 10 best departments for which most of the young employees are well-paid"

> **select** 10 Dept_no
> **from** Emp
> **group by**Dept_no
> **having** most-of (young **are** well-paid)

See [13, 44] for queries that involve fuzzy quantifiers. See also [90] for the definitions of fuzzy quotient operators from fuzzy quantifiers and OWA operations. See [8, 34] for complementary points of view.

Query Processing

Presently, the evaluation of queries expressed in declarative languages of the relational type remains, in spite of many research works, an open problem. Indeed, nobody knows how to find the best plan of execution (algorithm) of an arbitrary query in reasonable time. Therefore, it is clear that we cannot hope to achieve optimal response to the evaluation of imprecise queries in as much as such queries are at least as complex as ordinary queries. The increase in complexity is due to two main causes: (1) the usual access mechanisms such as indexes are no longer usable, and (2) the operations to be carried out depend on a larger volume of data since operations, such as selections or joins, produce more tuples than in the Boolean framework. In what follows, we outline a structure of an index usable with fuzzy predicates, and an approach, called derivation, that allows the evaluation of relational queries that require only one projection, several selections, and several joins.

Fuzzy Predicates Indexing

In a conventional DBMS, an index provides direct access to the tuples that have a given value of the indexed attribute. Unfortunately, such structures are only usable with conventional predicates, where a value (or an interval) is specified. To handle imprecise predicates, we can construct an index for a given fuzzy predicate which, representing a degree of membership at each input, associates the tuples satisfying this predicate with the degree under consideration. As shown in Figure 4, this method can use existing indexes. Such structures provide efficient access to tuples whenever the degree is known.

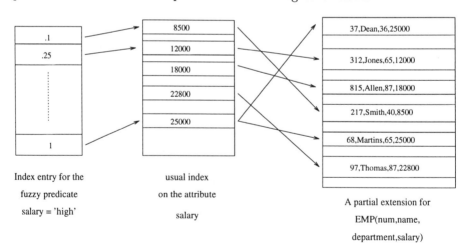

Figure 4　Index architecture for a fuzzy predicate.

Derivation Method

For simplicity, we consider here compound fuzzy predicates applied to a single relation and their λ-level cuts; i.e., the elements (tuples) satisfying these predicates at a level higher than or equal to λ. The idea is to derive one (or more) Boolean condition(s) necessary for the membership of an element in a λ-cut. Consequently, we can evaluate this condition, using a standard DBMS, and construct a subset (with cardinality much lower than that of the original relation) to which the original fuzzy predicate will then be applied. In some cases, necessary and sufficient conditions are found, which permits the direct construction of the desired λ-cut. The problem to be solved is the distribution of the λ-cut operation over a compound predicate.

If the fuzzy predicate under consideration is atomic and represented by a trapezoid (a common case in practice), the λ-cut corresponds to the membership of the variable in an interval. Thus we obtain a simple Boolean condition, which is both necessary and sufficient, in the form $x \in [v1,v2]$. If a linguistic modifier is used, it is easy to show that we are back to a condition of the same type. In the case of compound predicates, the idea is to express the λ-cut of the compound predicate in terms of λ-cuts bearing on the constituting predicates (and therefore expressible as condition of the form $x \in [v1,v2]$). Here, two situations may occur [15]: (1) it is possible to find an equivalent formula, and (2) it is only possible to find an expression whose result is a superset of the elements satisfying the initial λ-cut. A large number of connectors have been examined and necessary conditions have been provided for each of them. Once the final expression is obtained, the idea is to submit it to the standard DBMS (which should be able to process it efficiently) and get a reasonable subset of tuples against which the initial fuzzy query will be processed.

A Strategy for Processing Quantified Queries

Next, we consider queries in which a condition applies to a set of tuples and not to individual tuples, as was the case in the derivation method. We point out a strategy [13] whose goal is essentially to avoid the exhaustive scan of the elements of a set, thus likely to reduce the number of disk accesses, which are the main component in the cost of query evaluation.

The following two queries demonstrate the use of fuzzy quantification:

- Find the best 10 departments in which *at least three* employees are "middle-aged"
  select 10 Dep
  from Employee
  group by Dep
  having at least three **are** middle-aged

- Find the best 10 departments where *almost all* "low salary employees" are "recently engaged"

  select 10 Dep
  from Employee
  group by Dep
  having almost-all low-salary **are** recently-engaged

A naive algorithm would be to access all the tuples of a given partition (tuples that have the same value for the considered attribute) and to compute the value of the quantified proposition. If this value is over a given threshold (λ-cut), the partition is retained and the next partition is considered.

Another idea is to take advantage of properties of the quantifier (especially monotonicity if the quantifier is represented as an OWA aggregation) to improve the evaluation. This goal can be achieved for queries of the first example, as far as the number of tuples of any partition can be known without scanning the partition. It is then possible to get conditions for partial evaluations of the OWA aggregation, to decide after each new tuple access whether: (1) it is guaranteed that the desired degree (λ) will not be attained (failure condition), (2) it is guaranteed that this degree will be attained (success condition), or (3) none of the previous conclusions holds and a new access is needed. In case 1 or 2 it is possible to reach a conclusion about a partition before all its tuples have been accessed, and thus save data accesses [13].

5 IMPERFECT DATA IN A DATABASE

5.1 Representation

Presently, commercial database systems accept only two types of values: precise values and null values of various kinds. The representation of disjunctive information, and, more generally, of imprecise, vague, or uncertain data in databases has been investigated in logical (see Chapter 4), or in probabilistic frameworks [85, 4] (see Chapter 9). See [95] for a general overview of both logical and numerical uncertainty formalisms.

In the possibility theory-based approach [64, 65, 66, 69], the information available about the value of a single-valued attribute A in a tuple x is represented by a possibility distribution $\pi_{A(x)}$ on $D \cup \{e\}$ where e is an extra element that represents the case when the attribute A does not apply to the tuple x. The possibility distribution $\pi_{A(x)}$ can be viewed as a fuzzy restriction of the possible value of $A(x)$ and defines a mapping from $D \cup \{e\}$ to $[0,1]$. If information is consistent, there should exist a value in $D \cup \{e\}$ for $A(x)$, which suggests the normalization condition $\max_d \pi_{A(x)}(d) = 1$ (i.e., at least one value in $D \cup \{e\}$ is entirely possible). For instance, the information "Paul is young" will be represented by: $\pi_{Age(Paul)}(e) = 0$ and $\pi_{Age(Paul)}(d) = \mu_{Young}(d), \forall d \in D$. Here, μ_{Young} is a membership function that represents the vague predicate "young" in a given context. It is important to notice that the values restricted by a possibility distribution are considered as mutually exclusive. The degree $\pi_{A(x)}(d)$ rates the possibility that $d \in D$ is the correct value of the attribute A for the element x. $\pi_{A(x)}(d) = 1$ means that d is an entirely possible value for $A(x)$; it does *not* mean that it is certain that d is the value of A for x (i.e., that d is necessarily the value of A for x), unless $\forall d' \neq d, \pi_{A(x)}(d') = 0$. Moreover, the possibility distribution $\pi_{A(x)}$ is supposed to be normalized on $D \cup \{e\}$, i.e., $\exists d \in D$ such that $\pi_{A(x)}(d) = 1$ or $\pi_{A(x)}(e) = 1$, since either at least one value of the attribute domain is entirely possible, or the attribute does not apply.

This approach proposes a unified framework for representing precise, imprecise, and vague values of attributes, and the following kinds of null values; (1)' the value of A for x is entirely unknown: $\forall d \in D, \pi_{A(x)}(d) = 1, \pi_{A(x)}(e) = 0$; (2) the attribute A does not apply to x: $\forall d \in D, \pi_{A(x)}(d) = 0, \pi_{A(x)}(e) = 1$; and (3) it is not known which of the previous cases (1 or 2) holds: $\forall d \in D, \pi_{A(x)}(d) = 1$, and $\pi_{A(x)}(e) = 1$. The versatility of this approach is demonstrated in Figure 5, which shows the salary of John, assuming different degrees of knowledge.

In these examples, we considered a single-valued attribute, but multiple-valued attributes can be handled as well. Multiple-valued attributes can be handled as single-valued ones if we work with possibility distributions defined on the power set of the attribute domains (rather than on the attribute domains themselves). Indeed, in the case of multiple-valued attributes, the mutually exclusive possibilities are represented by subsets of values. As an example, consider the languages spoken by an employee, with the universe {English, German, Spanish, Italian}. Suppose the following is known: we are certain that a certain employee speaks English, it is totally possible that he also speaks German or Spanish, but Italian is unlikely and incompatible with Spanish. The resulting distribution is (the possibility degree is given after the subset):

{English}/1
{English,German}/1
{English,Spanish}/1
{English,German,Italian}/0.3
{English,German,Spanish}/1
{English,Italian}/0.3

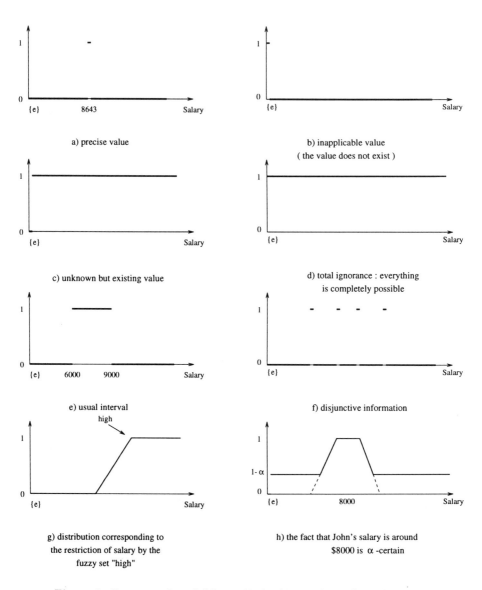

a) precise value

b) inapplicable value
(the value does not exist)

c) unknown but existing value

d) total ignorance : everything
is completely possible

e) usual interval

f) disjunctive information

g) distribution corresponding to
the restriction of salary by the
fuzzy set "high"

h) the fact that John's salary is around
$8000 is α -certain

Figure 5 Representation of different kinds of incomplete information.

See [69, 68] for details and [30] for lower and upper approximations of possibility
distributions on 2^D in terms of subsets of D. Relevant keywords for a document
is a good example of a multiple-valued attribute; see [67] for a treatment of
keywords in this spirit. Another issue that can be handled in the possibilistic

framework is interactivity constraints, e.g., "John and Paul have the same age, which is between 20 and 30."

Clearly, a similar approach can be developed in the probabilistic framework by using probability distributions instead of possibility distributions. However, because of their ordinal nature, possibility distributions may be easier to elicitate. Also, their normalization is easier when the attribute domain is not available in its entirety. Moreover, the probabilistic framework does not allow us to extend to gradual scales the modal distinction between what is just possible and what is certain or necessarily true, as explained in Section 5.2. In other words, whereas for a probability measure, $P(A) = 1 \Leftrightarrow P(\bar{A}) = 0$, we have for a possibility measure, $\Pi(A) = 0 \Longrightarrow \Pi(\bar{A}) = 1$ *but not* $\Pi(\bar{A}) = 1 \Longrightarrow \Pi(A) = 0$. This enables us to distinguish between the certainty that A is false ($\Pi(A) = 0$) and the total lack of certainty that A is true ($\Pi(\bar{A}) = 1$). Possibility theory is well-suited for modeling states of partial ignorance.

5.2 Matching

When a condition applies to imperfectly known data, the result may no longer be a single value. Since we do not know the precise values of some attributes for some items, we may be uncertain whether these items satisfy the condition. For this reason we use two degrees, attached to two points of view: the extent to which it is *possible* that the condition is satisfied, and the extent to which it is *certain* that the condition is satisfied. From the possibility distributions $\pi_{A(x)}$ and a subset P (conventional or fuzzy), we can compute the fuzzy set ΠP (respectively, NP) of the items whose value for attribute A possibly (respectively, necessarily) satisfies the condition P. The membership degree of an item x in ΠP and NP are [39, 66]:

$$\mu_{\Pi P}(x) = \Pi(P; A(x)) = sup_{d \in D} \min(\mu_P(d), \pi_{A(x)}(d))$$
$$\mu_{NP}(x) = N(P; A(x)) = inf_{d \in D \cup \{e\}} \max(\mu_P(d), 1 - \pi_{A(x)}(d))$$

$\Pi(P; A(x))$ estimates the extent to which there is a value restricted by $\pi_{A(x)}$ compatible with P, and $N(P; A(x))$ estimates to what extent all the values possible for $A(x)$ are included in P. It can be shown that ΠP and NP always satisfy $\Pi P \supseteq NP$, provided that $\pi_{A(x)}$ is normalized, i.e., $\forall x \mu_{NP}(x) \leq \mu_{\Pi P}(x)$. Thus, in the case of incomplete information, we are able to compute the set of items which (more or less) *possibly* satisfy an elementary condition, and to distinguish among them the items which (more or less) *certainly* satisfy this condition. For nonfuzzy requests (i.e., P is an ordinary subset of D), a stronger inclusion holds, since then NP is included in the core of ΠP (the set of items with possibility degree equal to 1). When the information is precise (i.e., $\pi_{A(x)} = 1$ for one element d and 0 for all other elements of $D \cup \{e\}$), it can be shown that $\mu_{\Pi P}(x) = \mu_P(A(x)) = \mu_{NP}(x)$. (See Figures 6 and 7.)

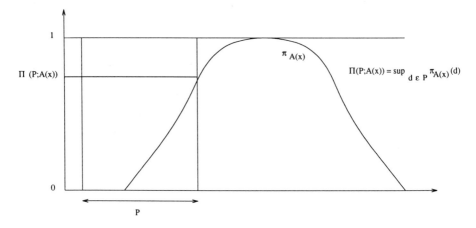

Figure 6   The possibility degree (nonfuzzy query).

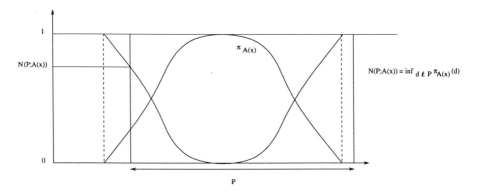

Figure 7   The necessity degree (nonfuzzy query).

Note that similar pattern matching degrees can be defined in the framework of belief functions (see Chapter 12), where P and $A(x)$ are represented in terms of basic probability assignments [37].

Selections involving disjunction, conjunction or negation of elementary conditions can be handled with the following basic relationships of possibility theory, which express decomposability properties of possibility and necessity degrees with respect to conjunctions and disjunctions, provided that the attribute values are logically independent (for every value of $A_1(x)$, all values compatible with $\pi_{A_2(x)}$ are allowed, and vice versa):

$$
\begin{aligned}
N(P; A(x)) &= 1 - \Pi(\bar{P}; A(x)) \\
N(P_1 \times P_2; A_1(x) \times A_2(x)) &= \min(N(P_1; A_1(x)), N(P_2; A_2(x))) \\
\Pi(P_1 + P_2; A_1(x) \times A_2(x)) &= \max(\Pi(P_1; A_1(x)), \Pi(P_2; A_2(x))) \\
N(P_1 + P_2; A_1(x) \times A_2(x)) &= \max(N(P_1; A_1(x)), N(P_2; A_2(x))) \\
\Pi(P_1 \times P_2; A_1(x) \times A_2(x)) &= \min(\Pi(P_1; A_1(x)), \Pi(P_2; A_2(x)))
\end{aligned}
$$

where

- the attributes A, A_1, A_2, and the subsets P, P_1, P_2, refer, respectively to the same domain

- overbar denotes set complementation (defined by $\mu_{\bar{P}}(d) = 1 - \mu_P(d)$)

- $A_1(x) \times A_2(x)$ denotes an extended Cartesian product, expressing a conjunction, given by

$$
\pi_{A_1(x) \times A_2(x)}(d_1, d_2) = \min(\pi_{A_1(x)}(d_1), \pi_{A_2(x)}(d_2))
$$

- $P_1 \times P_2$ is similarly defined

- $P_1 + P_2 = \overline{\bar{P}_1 \times \bar{P}_2}$ expresses a disjunction, given by

$$
\mu_{P_1+P_2}(d_1, d_2) = \max(\mu_{P_1}(d_1), \mu_{P_2}(d_2)).
$$

Note that the above expressions of $N(P_1 + P_2; A_1(x) \times A_2(x))$ and $\Pi(P_1 \times P_2; A_1(x) \times A_2(x))$ require logical independence of the attribute values respectively restricted by $\pi_{A_1}(x)$ and $\pi_{A_2}(x)$. See [38] for weighted conjunctions and disjunctions. These combination formulas are consistent with the fuzzy set operations (based on min and max), when the available information becomes precise, because then the measures of possibility and necessity become equal to a membership degree. Selections involving fuzzy comparators, e.g., approximate equalities or strong inequalities, can be also handled [66].

The case of other fuzzy set combining operations in compound requests (e.g., product, arithmetic mean), for which no decomposition formula exists for the possibility and necessity measures, in presence of incomplete information, can be dealt with by using a fuzzy-real-valued compatibility degree for estimating the agreement between the information and the request. Then an extended version of the considered combination operation is performed on these fuzzy real values and, finally, possibility and necessity degrees can be extracted in a standard way from the global compatibility measure, which has been thus computed. The reader is referred to [39, Chapter 3, pp. 98–99 and Chapter 4, pp. 125–126] for detailed definitions and justifications.

For simplicity, we have focused on the selection operation. Queries requiring an extended join operation on relational tables containing fuzzy information are discussed in [66].

Possibility theory offers a powerful tool for the representation and the treatment of flexible queries as well as partial information. In spite of the apparent complexity of the expressions of the possibility and necessity degrees, the approach is computationally tractable, at least when we assume possibility distributions that are defined on small-sized discrete domains, or whose shape is trapezoidal when the domain is continuous. See [27] for the use of fuzzy discrimination trees in the pattern matching procedure. Moreover, extensions of indexing techniques have been proposed [61].

The approach is robust due to the use of the operations max and min, which are not very sensitive to small variations. In practice, it is sufficient to elicitate possibility distributions in a rough way; i.e., identifying the values that are entirely impossible, and the values that are the most possible, and then remembering that it is mainly the ordering of possibility degrees that is meaningful in possibility theory (Section 4.1).

6 INTEGRITY CONSTRAINTS AND FUZZY FUNCTIONAL DEPENDENCIES

Integrity constraints have been recognized as essential in database management systems because they allow automatic handling of many data properties that should be maintained continuously. However, it has been pointed out that sometimes exceptions to these properties occur and should be accounted for. Soft integrity constraints, such as "generally, managers earn more than their subordinates," can deal naturally with exceptions. Moreover, it is clear that many data properties (not necessarily constraints) can be viewed only in terms of soft conditions. This subject has not received much attention (except functional dependencies, for which several extensions have been proposed).

Soft constraints, expressing either qualitative relationships, e.g., "the larger X is, the smaller Y must be," or tolerance, e.g., "the salaries of all employees are approximately equal," may have different applications: (1) integrity checking (clearly, the most important use), and we believe that many constraints are indeed fuzzy, (2) cooperative answers, and (3) concluding default values for missing data. This last use is investigated with a fuzzy approach in [2].

Functional dependencies have been widely studied in the conventional framework because they are helpful in the process of database design for coping with redundancy. The standard definition of functional dependencies is as follows. Let X and Y be two sets of attributes of relation scheme R. Y functionally depends on X, denoted $X \to Y$, if for every instance r of relation scheme R

$$\forall t_1, t_2 \in r : \quad t_1[X] = t_2[X] \Longrightarrow t_1[Y] = t_2[Y]$$

where $t[X]$ denotes the projection of a tuple t on the set of attributes X.

In the fuzzy framework, one can think of several different extensions: (1) replacing equalities by similarities; (2) choosing an implication operator that considers the degree of satisfaction of the (extended) equalities; (3) replacing the universal quantifier "for all" by the quantifier "for most."

Depending on the modeling of the implication in the fuzzy case, various kinds of dependencies can be expressed. A dependency might state that the more similar $t_1[X]$ and $t_2[X]$ are, the more *certain* the identity (or the similarity) of $t_1[Y]$ and $t_2[Y]$ is; or purely gradual dependencies expressing that the more similar $t_1[X]$ and $t_2[X]$ are, the more similar $t_1[Y]$ and $t_2[Y]$ are [32]. These generalized dependencies include classical functional dependencies as a particular case, if the fuzzy equality relations are such that $\mu_{EQ}(a, b) = 1$ if and only if $a = b$. Then they are stronger since they require equalities in the classical cases and approximate equalities in other cases. Otherwise, the two kinds of dependencies are not comparable. Researchers have dealt mainly with the first two kinds [1, 71, 50], paying attention to the properties of fuzzy functional dependencies (reflexivity, augmentation, transitivity, and so on). In so doing, and when appropriate choices are made for the implication, it has been shown that Armstrong's axioms still define a valid and complete system for the deduction of all dependencies from a given set.

Several approaches to the definition of extended functional dependencies have been proposed in the literature and we consider three of them. In [71], the authors advocate the definition: $X \to Y$ if $\mu_{EQ_1}(t_1[X], t_2[X]) \le \mu_{EQ_2}(t_1[Y], t_2[Y])$, where EQ_i is a similarity function such that $\mu_{EQ_i}(a, a) = 1$ (EQ_i is defined on the domain of X if $i = 1$ and on the domain of Y if $i = 2$). In [20], the authors suggest the choice of another implication (Gödel's): $X \rightarrow_\alpha Y$ if $\min_{t_1,t_2 \in r} I(\mu_{EQ_1}(t_1[X], t_2[X]), \mu_{EQ_2}(t_1[Y], t_2[Y])) \geq \alpha$, where $I(a, b) = 1$ if $a \leq b$, and $I(a, b) = b$ otherwise. However, with this definition, a dependency may fail because of the presence of a pair of tuples not very similar in X and still less similar in Y. This leads to this third definition [21]. $X \rightarrow_{\alpha,\beta} Y$ if $\forall t_1, t_2 \in r : \mu_{EQ_1}(t_1[X], t_2[X]) \geq \alpha \implies \mu_{EQ_2}(t_1[Y], t_2[Y])) \geq \beta$.

The issue of replacing a relation by two of its projections, when a fuzzy functional dependency holds, has been addressed in [71] and the only condition is that the similarity relations used are such that $\mu_{EQ_i}(a, b) = 1$ iff $a = b$. However, it should be noted that fuzzy functional dependency checking cannot reduce to uniqueness of keys inside relations. Consequently, these dependencies cannot affect the database design process, as pointed out in [9].

When data are precisely known, the semantics of fuzzy functional dependencies in the above-mentioned cases is clear. However, when data are represented by possibility distributions, the calculation of similarity between two distributions becomes crucial, and the fact that two distributions are identical does not provide any information about the similarity of the values themselves. Consequently, this notion should be used with care, and the meaning of a dependency in case of ill-known values must be clearly stated.

7 CONCLUDING REMARKS

In conclusion, we mention other uncertainty problems in databases, for which fuzzy set and possibility theory-based methods might prove useful:

- **Database updates**: This problem has been particularly investigated in logical deductive databases [84, 45]. In possibility theory, so-called possibilistic imaging [33] (closely related to the fuzzy set extension principle) has been shown to be in perfect agreement with [45]'s postulates for updates. Generally speaking, possibility theory enables us to express preferences among candidates for the new value and to express the imprecision and the uncertainty pervading the laws of evolution of the real world.

- **Fuzziness and uncertainty in object-oriented representations**: The reader is referred to [36] for a preliminary study, where an object-centered representation is presented in which both a range of allowed values and a range of typical values can be specified for the attributes describing a class. These ranges may be fuzzy. Then various kinds of (graded) inclusion relations can be defined among classes. Another approach is presented in [42]; see also [55].

- **Linguistic summaries**: [86] advocates the use of fuzzy sets and fuzzy quantifiers in linguistic summaries of the form "most A's are B." Other summaries expressing gradual relationship such as "the older a person, the bigger the salary" are also worth producing. More generally, fuzzy sets may be useful for expressing typical values of attributes or exceptions to rules.

Imprecision and uncertainty are practically unavoidable if we are to represent the available information without losing significant parts of it. Allowing flexible queries is also highly desirable. Fuzzy sets and possibility theory offer a technically sound and powerful framework both for representing imprecision and uncertainty and for handling flexible queries. Admittedly, until now only prototypes of fuzzy extensions of query languages like SQL have been developed in laboratories (this may be due to the smallness of the research community in fuzzy databases), but more applications can be expected in the future. Already the interest in fuzzy information retrieval systems has increased considerably in the recent years, especially in Japan. The handling of imprecise, uncertain, or vague information in database systems should also be of practical interest, at least to carry it a little further than the treatment of standard null values. Among application-oriented works using the fuzzy pattern matching techniques (Section 5.2) in information systems, we mention the systems CLASSIC [41] and FLORAN [75]. The implementations that already exist (especially for fuzzy querying systems) tend to show that, when clearly identified, problems can be computed in reasonable time.

Acknowledgments

This chapter benefited from many comments provided by Robert Demolombe, Guy Hulin, Ami Motro, and Philippe Smets.

REFERENCES

[1] M. Anvari and G. F. Rose. Fuzzy relational database. In J.C. Bezdek, editor, *Analysis of Fuzzy Information, volume II: Artificial Intelligence and Decision Systems*, pages 203–212. CRC Press, Boca Raton, FL, 1987.

[2] I. Arrazola, A. Plainfossé, H. Prade, and C. Testemale. Extrapolation of fuzzy values from incomplete data bases. *Information Systems*, 14(6): 487–492, 1989.

[3] J. F. Baldwin and S. Q. Zhou. A fuzzy relational inference language. *Fuzzy Sets and Systems*, 14: 155–174, 1984.

[4] D. Barbará, H. Garcia-Molina, and D. Porter. The management of probabilistic data. *IEEE Transaction on Knowledge and Data Engineering*, 4(5): 487–502, 1992.

[5] G. Biswas, J. C. Bezdek, M. Marques, and V. Subramanian. Knowledge-assisted document retrieval; Part I: The natural language interface; Part II: The retrieval process. *J. American Society for Information Science*, 38(2): Part I: 83–96; Part II: 97–110, 1987.

[6] A. Bookstein. Fuzzy requests: an approach to weighted Boolean searchers. *J. American Society for Information Science*, 31: 240–247, 1980.

[7] G. Bordogna, P. Carrara, and G. Pasi. Query term weights as constraints in fuzzy information retrieval. *Information Processing and Management*, 27(1): 15–26, 1991.

[8] P. Bosc, D. Dubois, O. Pivert, and H. Prade. Fuzzy division for regular relational databases. In *Proc. Int. Joint Conf. of 4th IEEE Int. Conf. on Fuzzy Systems (FUZZ-IEEE'95) and 2nd Int. Fuzzy Engineering Symp. (IFES'95)*, pages 729–734, Yokohama, Japan, March 20–24 1995.

[9] P. Bosc, D. Dubois, and H. Prade. Fuzzy relational dependencies: An overview and a critical discussion. In *Proc. 3rd IEEE Int. Conf. on Fuzzy Systems (FUZZ-IEEE'94)*, pages 325–330, Orlando, FL, June 26–29, 1994.

[10] P. Bosc, M. Galibourg, and G. Hamon. Fuzzy querying with SQL: extensions and implementation aspects. *Fuzzy Sets and Systems*, 28: 333–349, 1988.

[11] P. Bosc and O. Pivert. About equivalences in SQLf, a relational language supporting imprecise querying. In *Proc. Int. Fuzzy Engineering Symp. (IFES'91)*, pages 309–320, Yokohama, Japan, November 13–15, 1991.

[12] P. Bosc and O. Pivert. Discriminated answers and databases: Fuzzy sets as a unified expression means. In *Proc. 1st Int. IEEE Conf. on Fuzzy Systems (FUZZ-IEEE'92)*, pages 745–752, San Diego, CA, March 1992.

[13] P. Bosc and O. Pivert. On the evaluation of fuzzy quantified queries in a database management system. In *Proc. North American Fuzzy Logic Processing Society Conf. (NAFIPS'92)*, pages 15–17, Puerto Vallarta, Mexico, December 1992.

[14] P. Bosc and O. Pivert. Some approaches for relational databases flexible querying. *Int. J. Intelligent Information Systems*, 1: 323–354, 1992.

[15] P. Bosc and O. Pivert. Some properties of alpha-cuts of fuzzy predicates. In *Proc. 11th Meeting on Cybernetics and Systems Research*, Vienna, Austria, 1992.

[16] B. P. Buckles and F. E. Petry. A fuzzy representation of data for relational databases. *Fuzzy Sets and Systems*, 5: 213–226, 1982.

[17] B. P. Buckles and F. E. Petry. Generalized database and information systems. In J. C. Bezdek, editor, *Analysis of Fuzzy Information; Vol. II: Artificial Intelligence and Decision Systems*, pages 177–201. CRC Press, Boca Raton, FL, 1987.

[18] M. Cayrol, H. Farreny, and H. Prade. Fuzzy pattern matching. *Kybernetes*, 11: 103–116, 1982.

[19] C. L. Chang. Decision support in an imperfect world. Technical Report RJ3421 (40687), IBM Research Lab., San Jose, CA, 1982.

[20] G. Q. Chen and J. Vandenbulcke. A step towards the theory of fuzzy relational database design. In M. Roubens R. Lowen, editors, *Proc. Int. Fuzzy Systems Association Congress (IFSA'91)—Computer, Management & Systems Science*, pages 44–47, Brussels, Belgium, 1991.

[21] J. C. Cubero and M. A. Vila. A new definition of fuzzy functional dependency in fuzzy relational databases. *Int. J. Intelligent Systems*, 9(5): 441–448, May 1994.

[22] D. Dubois, H. Fargier, and H. Prade. Refinements of the maximin approach to decision-making in a fuzzy environment. *Fuzzy Sets and Systems*, 81(1): 103–112, 1996.

[23] D. Dubois, J. Lang, and H. Prade. Automated reasoning using possibilistic logic: semantics, belief revision and variable certainty weights. In *Preprints of the 5th Workshop on Uncertainty in Artificial Intelligence*, pages 81–87, Windsor, Ontario, August 18–20, 1989.

[24] D. Dubois, J. Lang, and H. Prade. Handling uncertainty, context, vague predicates, and partial inconsistency in possibilistic logic. In *Preprints of the Fuzzy Logic in Artificial Intelligence Workshop held in conjunction with IJCAI'91*, pages 13–23, Sydney, Australia, August 25, 1991.

[25] D. Dubois, J. Lang, and H. Prade. Dealing with multi-source information in possibilistic logic. In B. Neumann, editor, *Proc. 10th Europ. Conf. on Artificial Intelligence (ECAI'92)*, pages 38–42, Vienna, Austria, August 3–7, 1992.

[26] D. Dubois, J. Lang, and H. Prade. Possibilistic logic. In D.M. Gabbay et al., editors, *Handbook of Logic in Artificial Intelligence and Logic Programming*, volume 3, pages 439–513. Oxford University Press, UK, 1994.

[27] D. Dubois, X. Mo, and H. Prade. Fuzzy discrimination trees. In *Proc. Int. Fuzzy Engineering Symp. (IFES'91)*, pages 250–260, Yokohama, Japan, November 13–15, 1991.

[28] D. Dubois and H. Prade. A review of fuzzy set aggregation connectives. *Information Sciences*, 36: 85–121, 1985.

[29] D. Dubois and H. Prade. Weighted minimum and maximum operations in fuzzy set theory. *Information Sciences*, pages 205–210, 1986.

[30] D. Dubois and H. Prade. Incomplete conjunctive information. *Comput. Math. Appl.*, 15(10): 797–810, 1988.

[31] D. Dubois and H. Prade. Measuring properties of fuzzy sets: a general technique and its use in fuzzy query evaluation. *Fuzzy Sets and Systems*, 38: 137–152, 1990.

[32] D. Dubois and H. Prade. Certainty and uncertainty of (vague) knowledge and generalized dependencies in fuzzy data bases. In *Proc. Int. Fuzzy Engineering Symp. (IFES'91)*, pages 239–249, Yokohama, Japan, November 13–15 1991.

[33] D. Dubois and H. Prade. Belief revision and updates in numerical formalisms—an overview, with new results for the possibilistic framework. Technical report, IRIT, Université Paul Sabatier, Toulouse, France, 1992.

[34] D. Dubois and H. Prade. Semantics of quotient operators in fuzzy relational databases. *Fuzzy Sets and Systems*, 78: 89–93, 1996.

[35] D. Dubois and H. Prade. Using fuzzy sets in database systems: Why and how? In H. Christiansen, H. L. Larsen, and T. Andreasen, editors, *Proc. Workshop on Flexible Query-Answering Systems (FQAS'96)*, pages 89–103, Roskilde, Denmark, May 22–24, 1996.

[36] D. Dubois, H. Prade, and J. P. Rossazza. Vagueness, typicality and uncertainty in class hierarchies. *Int. J. Intelligent Systems*, 6: 167–183, 1991.

[37] D. Dubois, H. Prade, and C. Testemale. Fuzzy pattern matching with extended capabilities: proximity notions, importance assessment, random sets. In W. Bandler and A. Kandel, editors, *Proc. N. Amer. Fuzzy Information Processing Society (NAFIPS'86): Recent Developments in the Theory and Applications of Fuzzy Sets*, pages 125–139, New Orleans, LA, June 2–4, 1986.

[38] D. Dubois, H. Prade, and C. Testemale. Weighted fuzzy pattern matching. *Fuzzy Sets and Systems*, 28(3): 313–331, 1988.

[39] D. Dubois, H. Prade (with the collaboration of H. Farreny, R. Martin-Clouaire, and C. Testemale). Possibility theory: an approach to computerized processing of uncertainty. *Plenum Press, New York*, 1988.

[40] J. H. Friedman, F. Baskett, and L. J. Shustek. An algorithm for finding nearest neighbors. *IEEE Trans. on Computers*, pages 1001–1006, 1975.

[41] C. Granger. An application of possibility theory to object recognition. *Fuzzy Sets and Systems*, 28: 351–362, 1988.

[42] N. Van Gyseghem, R. De Caluwe, and R. Vandenberghe. UFO: uncertainty and fuzziness in an object-oriented model. In *Proc. 2nd Int. IEEE Conf. on Fuzzy Systems (FUZZ-IEEE'93)*, pages 773–778, San Francisco, CA, March 1993.

[43] T. Ichikawa and M. Hirakawa. Ares: a relational database with the capability of performing flexible interpretation of queries. *IEEE Trans. on Software Engineering*, 12(5): 624–634, 1986.

[44] J. Kacprzyk, S. Zadrozny, and A. Ziolkowski. Fquery III+: a "human-consistent" database querying system based on fuzzy logic with linguistic quantifiers. *Information Systems*, 14(6): 443–453, 1989.

[45] H. Katsuno and A. O. Mendelzon. On the difference between updating a knowledge base and revising it. In J. Allen, R. Fikes, and E. Sandewall, editors, *Proc. 2nd Int. Conf. on Principles of Knowledge Representation and Reasoning (KR'91)*, pages 387–394, Cambridge, MA, April 22–25, 1991.

[46] L. J. Kohout, E. Keravnou, and W. Bandler. Automatic documentary information retrieval by means of fuzzy relational products. In H. J. Zimmermann, L. A. Zadeh, and B. R. Gaines, editors, *Fuzzy Sets and Decision Analysis TIMS/Studies in the Management Sciences, Vol. 20*, pages 383–404. North-Holland, Amsterdam, 1984.

[47] D. H. Kraft and D. A. Buell. Fuzzy sets and generalized Boolean retrieval systems. *Int. J. Man-Machine Studies*, 19: 45–56, 1983.

[48] T. L. Kunii. Dataplan: an interface generator for database semantics. *Information Sciences*, 10: 279–298, 1976.

[49] M. Lacroix and P. Lavency. Preferences: putting more knowledge into queries. In *Proc. 13th Very Large Data Bases Conference*, pages 217–225, Brighton, UK, 1987.

[50] W. Y. Liu. The reduction of the fuzzy data domain and fuzzy consistent join. *Fuzzy Sets and Systems*, 50: 89–96, 1992.

[51] D. Y. Ly and D. B. Liu. *A Fuzzy PROLOG Database System*. Research Studies Press Ltd., Taunton, 1990.

[52] E. McClelland, R. Trueblood, and C. Eastman. Two approximate operators for a data base query language: sounds-like and close-to. *IEEE Trans. on Systems, Man and Cybernetics*, 18(6): 873–884, 1988.

[53] S. Miyamoto. *Fuzzy Sets in Information Retrieval and Cluster Analysis*. Kluwer, Dordrecht, 1990.

[54] A. Motro. VAGUE: a user interface to relational databases that permits vague queries. *ACM Trans. on Office Information Systems*, 6: 187–214, 1988.

[55] N. Mouaddib. Fuzzy identification in fuzzy databases: the nuanced relational division. *International journal of intelligent systems*, 9(5): 461–474, May 1994.

[56] T. Murai, M. Miyakoshi, and M. Shimbo. A fuzzy document retrieval method based on two-valued indexing. *Fuzzy Sets and Systems*, 30: 103–120, 1989.

[57] C. V. Negoita and P. Flondor. On fuzziness in information retrieval. *Int. J. Man-Machine Studies*, 8: 711–716, 1976.

[58] K. Nomoto, S. Wakayama, T. Kirimoto, Y. Ohashi, and M. Kondo. A document retrieval system based on citations using fuzzy graphs. *Fuzzy Sets and Systems*, 38: 207–222, 1990.

[59] Y. Ogawa, T. Morita, and K. Kobayashi. A fuzzy document retrieval system using the keyword connection matrix and a learning method. *Fuzzy Sets and Systems*, 39: 163–179, 1991.

[60] P. Bollmann P and E. Konrad. Fuzzy document retrieval. In *Proc. 3rd European Meeting on Cybernetics and Systems Research*, pages 355–363, Vienna, Austria, 1976.

[61] P. Bosc P and M. Galibourg. Indexing principles for a fuzzy data base. *Information Systems*, 14(6): 493–499, 1989.

[62] Z. Pawlak. *Rough Sets—Theoretical Aspects of Reasoning about Data.* Kluwer, Dordrecht, 1991.

[63] H. B. Potoczny. On similarity relations in fuzzy relational databases. *Fuzzy Sets and Systems*, 12: 231–235, 1984.

[64] H. Prade. The connection between Lipski's approach to incomplete information data bases and zadeh's possibility theory. In L. Troncale, editor, *Systems Science and Science (Proc. 16th Annual Meeting of the Soc, for General Systems Research with the Amer. Assoc. for the Advancement of Science)*, pages 402–408, Washington, DC, January 5–9, 1982.

[65] H. Prade. Lipski's approach to incomplete information data bases restated and generalized in the setting of Zadeh's possibility theory. *Information Systems*, 9(1): 27–42, 1984.

[66] H. Prade and C. Testemale. Generalizing database relational algebra for the treatment of incomplete/uncertain information and vague queries. *Information Sciences*, 34: 115–143, 1984.

[67] H. Prade and C. Testemale. Application of possibility and necessity measures to documentary information retrieval. In B. Bouchon and R. R. Yager, editors, *Uncertainty in Knowledge-Based Systems Lecture Notes in Computer Science*, volume 286, pages 265–274. Springer-Verlag, Berlin, 1987.

[68] H. Prade and C. Testemale. Fuzzy relational databases: representational issues and reduction using similarity measures. *J. American Society for Information Science*, 38(2): 118–126, 1987.

[69] H. Prade and C. Testemale. Representation of soft constraints and fuzzy attribute values by means of possibility distributions in databases. In J. C. Bezdek, editor, *Analysis of Fuzzy Information—Vol. 2: Artificial Intelligence and Decision Systems*, pages 213–229. CRC Press, Boca Raton, FL, 1987.

[70] F. Rabitti. Retrieval of multimedia documents by imprecise query specification. *Lecture Notes on Computer Science*, 416: 203–218, 1990.

[71] K. V. S. V. N. Raju and A. K. Majumdar. Fuzzy functional dependencies and lossless join decomposition of fuzzy relational database systems. *ACM Trans. on Database Systems*, 13(2): 129–166, 1988.

[72] L. Reisinger. On fuzzy thesauri. In G. Bruckman, F. Ferschl, and L. Schmetterer, editors, *Proc. Symp. on Comput. Stat. (Compstat'74)*, pages 119–127, Vienna, Austria, 1974. Physica-Verlag.

[73] E. A. Rundensteiner, L. W. Hawkes, and W. Bandler. On nearness measures in fuzzy relational data models. *Int. J. Approximate Reasoning*, 3: 267–298, 1989.

[74] E. H. Ruspini. Issues in the representation of imprecision and uncertainty in information systems. In J. C. Bezdek, editor, *Analysis of Fuzzy Information, volume II: Artificial Intelligence and Decision Systems*, pages 231–239. CRC Press, Boca Raton, FL, 1987.

[75] S. Salotti. *Filtrage flou et représentation centré objet pour raisonner par analogie: le système FLORAN*. Ph.D. Dissertation, Paris XI-Orsay, 1992.

[76] E. Sanchez. Importance in knowledge systems. *Information Systems*, pages 455–464, 1989.

[77] N. Steger, H. Schmidt, U. Guntzer, and W. Kiessling. Semantics and efficient compilation for quantitative deductive databases. In *Proc. 5th Int. Conf. on Data Engineering*, pages 660–668, Los Angeles, CA, February 6–10, 1989.

[78] S. Y. W. Su, J. Dujmovic, D. S. Batory, S. B. Navathe, and R. Elnicki. A cost-benefit decision model: Analysis, comparison, and selection of data management systems. *ACM Trans. on Database Systems*, 12(3): 472–520, 1987.

[79] V. Tahani. A conceptual framework for fuzzy query processing—a step toward very intelligent database systems. *Information Processing Management*, 13: 289–303, 1977.

[80] M. Umano. Freedom-0: a fuzzy database system. In M. M. Gupta and E. Sanchez, editors, *Fuzzy Information and Decision Processes*, pages 339–347, North-Holland, Amsterdam, 1982.

[81] M. Umano. Retrieval from fuzzy database by fuzzy relational algebra. In E. Sanchez and M. M. Gupta, editors, *Fuzzy Information, Knowledge Representation and Decision Analysis*, pages 1–6. Pergamon Press, New York, 1983.

[82] M. Umano and S. Fukami. Perspectives of fuzzy databases. *Japanese J. of Fuzzy Theory and Systems (English translation, Allerton Press, New York)*, 3: 75–91, 1991.

[83] R. Vandenberghe, A. Van Schooten, R. De Caluwe, and E. E. Kerre. Some practical aspects of fuzzy database techniques: an example. *Information Systems*, 14(6): 465–472, 1989.

[84] M. Winslett. *Updating Logical Databases*. Cambridge University Press, UK, 1990.

[85] E. A. Wong. Statistical approach to incomplete information in database systems. *ACM Trans. on Database Systems*, 7(3): 470–488, 1982.

[86] R. R. Yager. A new approach to the summarization of data. *Information Sciences*, 28: 69–86, 1982.

[87] R. R. Yager. A note on weighted queries in information retrieval systems. *J. American Society of Information Sciences*, 38: 23–24, 1987.

[88] R. R. Yager. On ordered weighted averaging aggregation operators in multicriteria decisionmaking. *IEEE Trans. on Systems, Man and Cybernetics*, 18: 183–190, 1988.

[89] R. R. Yager. Connectives and quantifiers in fuzzy sets. *Fuzzy Sets and Systems*, 40: 39–76, 1991.

[90] R. R. Yager. Fuzzy quotient operators for fuzzy relational databases. In *Proc. Int. Fuzzy Engineering Symp. (IFES'91)*, pages 289–296, Yokohama, Japan, November 13–15, 1991.

[91] L. A. Zadeh. Fuzzy sets. In *Information and Control*, volume 8, pages 338–353. Academic Press, New York, 1965.

[92] L. A. Zadeh. Fuzzy sets as a basis for a theory of possibility. *Fuzzy Sets and Systems*, 1: 3–28, 1978.

[93] M. Zemankova. FILIP: a fuzzy intelligent information system with learning capabilities. *Information Systems*, 14(6): 473–486, 1989.

[94] M. Zemankova-Leech and A. Kandel. *Fuzzy Relation Data Bases—A Key to Expert Systems*. Verlag TÜV Rheinland,Köln, 1984.

[95] E. Zimanyi. *Incomplete and uncertain information in relational databases*. Ph.D. Dissertation, Université Libre de Bruxelles, Belgium, 1992.

[96] H. J. Zimmermann and P. Zysno. Latent connectives in human decision making. *Fuzzy Sets and Systems*, 4: 37–51, 1980.

[97] A. Zvieli and P. P. Chen. Entity-relationship modeling and fuzzy databases. In *Proc. 2nd IEEE Data Engineering Conf.*, pages 320–327, Los Angeles, CA, February 5–7, 1986.

11

LOGICAL HANDLING OF INCONSISTENT AND DEFAULT INFORMATION

Philippe Besnard
Luis Fariñas del Cerro*
Dov Gabbay**
Anthony Hunter**

IRISA
Rennes, France

* IRIT
Université Paul Sabatier
Toulouse, France

** Department of Computing
Imperial College
London, UK

1   INTRODUCTION

The subjects of this chapter are two important and related kinds of uncertainty in information systems: inconsistent information and default (defeasible) information. In many information system applications, there is a need to represent and reason with inconsistent data. For example, in a tax collection agency, database records on individual taxpayers should be allowed to have inconsistent information, as such information could be used to direct enquiries by tax inspectors. Default information , such as rules that are usually true but are allowed to have exceptions, tends to reduce the size of databases significantly, yet without significant loss of utility for many applications. For example, a market research agency could use default information in its consumer profiles: for its kind of business such a level of accuracy could be deemed sufficient.

Once we allow uncertainty of either kind in an information system, we must also incorporate a reasoning component that would conclude answers from this more general information. Such a component must be based on an appropriate formal model of deduction. It would be natural to consider using classical logic for this purpose. Unfortunately, classical logic is unsatisfactory because it allows arbitrary conclusions to be drawn from inconsistent information. Similarly, default information cannot be handled adequately in classical logic because there is a dynamic need to change conclusions whenever new information is added to the system. These shortcomings force us to consider nonclassical logics for our model of reasoning. These alternative logics are referred to as *logics for practical reasoning*.

A number of logical systems have been developed for these forms of reasoning. In the following two sections we discuss some of the issues behind inconsistent information and default information, and then we present paraconsistent logic and default logic as important candidates for reasoning with these respective forms of information. Then, in Section 4, we present labeled deductive systems as a general framework for capturing these logics and tailoring them for individual applications. We conclude in Section 5 with a brief summary.

Note that in this chapter we do not review the literature on handling inconsistent information in relational databases. For this, see Chapters 3 and 4 in this book. Other references include [3, 4, 9, 17].

2   HANDLING INCONSISTENT INFORMATION

There are many situations in which information and its contrary both appear in an information system. In some situations such inconsistencies could be useful, such as in a collection database, where they could initiate profitable enquiries. In other situations they are undesirable, such as in a bank database of customer accounts, where they need to be identified and corrected (through a revision of the database).

In some situations it is not even clear that inconsistencies should be corrected. For example, the tax agency database may include an item of legislation that prohibits citizens from having more than one spouse. Now, suppose, quite unexpectedly from the point of view of the database designer, that this database includes a taxpayer who has two spouses. Although, this creates an inconsistency, revising the database might not be the most appropriate solution.

Using $\forall$ to represent "for all," $\wedge$ to represent conjunction, and $\rightarrow$ to represent implication, we can represent the previous example with these formulae

$$\forall x, y \; Spouse(x, y) \wedge Spouse(x, z) \rightarrow y = z$$
$$Spouse(MrBigamist, MsVictim)$$
$$Spouse(MrBigamist, MsMisled)$$
$$MsVictim \neq MsMisled$$

Using classical logic, it would be possible to infer any arbitrary conclusion from this information. This is because the classical logic incorporates the following proof rule, called *ex falso quodlibet*,

$$\frac{\alpha \quad \neg\alpha}{\beta}.$$

This proof rule states that from the two items α and $\neg\alpha$, any conclusion β may be inferred. Applying *ex falso quodlibet* to *MrBigamist*'s case (substituting *MsVictim* = *MsMisled* for α), we could draw irrelevant and inappropriate conclusions, such as

$$Rain\text{-}falls(mainly\text{-}on\text{-}the\text{-}plain).$$

What is required for reasoning with databases in which inconsistencies are allowed to occur is a logic that does not incorporate the rule of *ex falso quodlibet*. One such class of logics is the paraconsistent logics (for a review of paraconsistent logics see [2]). These logics use the same language as classical logic, but they use only a subset of the proof rules. This implies that for any given database we may infer fewer conclusions. Reasoning that is supported by paraconsistent logics includes *modus ponens*,

$$\frac{\alpha \quad \alpha \rightarrow \beta}{\beta}.$$

So, for example, from

$$\forall x, y \; Spouse(x, y) \rightarrow Spouse(y, x)$$
$$Spouse(MrMartin, MrsMartin)$$

we may infer

$$Spouse(MrsMartin, MrMartin).$$

Other reasoning that is supported by paraconsistent logics includes the rule of disjunctive introduction,

$$\frac{\alpha \rightarrow \gamma \quad \beta \rightarrow \gamma}{\alpha \vee \beta \rightarrow \gamma}.$$

In many ways, a paraconsistent logic is a useful substitute for classical logic. But it does lack some intuitive proof rules, such as *modus tollens,*

$$\frac{\alpha \to \beta \quad \neg\beta}{\neg\alpha}.$$

So, for example, from

$$\forall x, y \ Spouse(x, y) \to Spouse(y, x)$$
$$\neg Spouse(MrMartin, MrsJones)$$

the conclusion $\neg Spouse(MrsJones, MrMartin)$ cannot be inferred, although it is clearly a desirable inference.

Returning to the original information in the *MrBigamist* example, a paraconsistent logic allows us to infer useful conclusions from the data. Furthermore, it is very robust in the sense that regardless of the information that is introduced into the database, the reasoning process will always give sensible conclusions.

Another advantage of a paraconsistent logic is that it does not force any decision to be made on whether a particular item of information in the database is "false." Thus, we are not forced to decide which of *Spouse(MrBigamist, MsVictim)* and *Spouse(MrBigamist, MsMisled)* is false. Similarly, we do not have to decide which of *MsMisled* $\neq$ *MsVictim* or *MsMisled* = *MsVictim* holds.

In general, a paraconsistent logic can be used to give guidance on the source of the inconsistency, and indicate actions that should be taken on the database. For example, paraconsistent logics can be used as a formal basis for truth maintenance systems, which are meant to partition the database into consistent subsets of data (for example, [18]).

3   HANDLING DEFAULT INFORMATION

It is noteworthy that practical reasoning relies much more on exploiting *general* rules (i.e., rules that are not necessarily universal) than on a myriad of individual facts. General rules tend to be less than perfectly accurate and may therefore have exceptions. Nevertheless, in modeling practical reasoning it is intuitive to resort to general rules and therefore allow the inference of useful conclusions, even if it does entail making some mistakes, because not all exceptions to these rules are necessarily known. Clearly, it is more efficient to state (and deal with) a single general proposition than to state (and deal with) possibly thousands of instances of such a general proposition.

An example of an application in which general rules would be beneficial is marketing, where decisions are usually based on generalities about customers rather than on perfectly accurate information about each and every customer.

Consider the following example. In general, a person who is a customer of a telephone company has a telephone instrument. Of course, exceptions exist: deaf people, for instance, have special instruments that are not "telephones" *stricto sensu.* So, if Fernandez is a customer of the telephone company, then it makes sense to conclude that he has a telephone. The statement "a customer of a telephone company has a telephone, unless proven otherwise" is *default information.* The principle by which it is to occur in reasoning is "if x is a customer of a telephone company, then x has a telephone, unless it is proven that x counts as an exception."

Such reasoning may be represented with this notation:

$$\frac{PhoneCustomer(x) \; : \; \neg Exception(x)}{HasPhone(x)} .$$

This rule is applied as follows. Given a certain value v for x, if

$$PhoneCustomer(v)$$

is inferred and

$$Exception(v)$$

cannot be proven, then

$$HasPhone(v)$$

is concluded (and is called a *default conclusion*).

As a special case, if

$$PhoneCustomer(Fernandez)$$

is inferred and

$$Exception(Fernandez)$$

cannot be proven, then

$$HasPhone(Fernandez)$$

is concluded.

Note the flexibility of this use of default information. From the fact that Fernandez is a customer of a telephone company, and in the absence of any evidence that Fernandez counts as an exception, the general rule leads to the conclusion that Fernandez has a telephone. Importantly, there is no need *to prove* that Fernandez is not an exception (for instance, that he is not deaf). It is sufficient to establish that no proof is available according to which Fernandez may be classified as an exception; clearly, this is much less demanding.

Furthermore, there is no need to have a list of all exceptions. The default information

$$\frac{PhoneCustomer(x) \ : \ \neg Exception(x)}{HasPhone(x)}$$

need not be modified as information about exceptions evolves. For example, suppose that "deaf people have no telephones." Then, adding the formula

$$\forall x \ Deaf(x) \rightarrow Exception(x)$$

is enough to block the default conclusion $HasPhone(x)$ for x that correspond to deaf persons (while still permitting the default conclusion $HasPhone(x)$ for x that do not correspond to deaf persons). As an illustration, consider

$$PhoneCustomer(Baker)$$
$$PhoneCustomer(Cook)$$
$$Deaf(Cook)$$

Then,

$$\frac{PhoneCustomer(x) \ : \ \neg Exception(x)}{HasPhone(x)}$$

can be applied to $x = Baker$ because $PhoneCustomer(Baker)$ can be established and $Exception(Baker)$ cannot be proven, so the default conclusion

$$HasPhone(Baker)$$

is inferred. Consider now the case $x = Cook$, and try to apply the default information,

$$\frac{PhoneCustomer(x) \ : \ \neg Exception(x)}{HasPhone(x)},$$

Clearly $PhoneCustomer(Cook)$ can be inferred. However, the general rule cannot be applied because $Exception(Cook)$ can be proven (via $Deaf(Cook)$ and $\forall x \ Deaf(x) \rightarrow Exception(x)$).

Conveniently, all new exceptions discovered with time can be taken into account by simply adding them to the knowledge base; there is no need to modify the general rule. The general rule will simply cease to yield some previous conclusions (the ones corresponding to the newly introduced exceptions). Consider this example:

$$PhoneCustomer(Fernandez)$$
$$Deaf(Fernandez)$$
$$\forall x \; Deaf(x) \rightarrow Exception(x)$$

When only *PhoneCustomer(Fernandez)* was known, *HasPhone(Fernandez)* was inferred. If, in addition, *Deaf(Fernandez)* and $\forall x \; Deaf(x) \rightarrow Exception(x)$ are known, then *HasPhone(Fernandez)* is no longer inferred. Such behavior is termed *nonmonotonic reasoning* because a conclusion drawn in the presence of certain information is withdrawn upon the introduction of additional information. That is, the set of conclusions does not increase monotonically as information increases.

An interesting observation is that some exceptions just *fail to obey* the general rule, while others *explicitly oppose* it. For instance, for deaf we might want to assert both

$$\forall x \; Deaf(x) \rightarrow Exception(x)$$

and

$$\forall x \; Deaf(x) \rightarrow \neg HasPhone(x)$$

whereas for hearing-impaired people, we might want to stay agnostic about whether or not they have telephones, and assert only

$$\forall x \; HearingImpaired(x) \rightarrow Exception(x)$$

Also, there is no need to know the reason why an item is an exception to the general rule. Indeed,

$$PhoneCustomer(Baker)$$
$$Exception(Baker)$$

is sufficient to block the default conclusion, without providing a reason why Baker is a telephone company customer without a telephone.

Observe that priorities among general rules can be rendered. Consider an example of a computer club whose members use telephone lines equipped with modems to transmit data. They must count as exceptions to our general rule, unless they have more than a single telephone line:

$$\frac{MemberComputerClub(x) \; : \; SingleLine(x)}{Exception(x)}.$$

Consider an individual *Smith*, such that

$$PhoneCustomer(Smith)$$
$$MemberComputerClub(Smith)$$

Because $\neg SingleLine(Smith)$ cannot be proven,

$$Exception(Smith)$$

is inferred by this new rule, and the earlier rule is blocked; i.e., $HasPhone(Smith)$ is not inferred.

If one tries to apply the earlier rule

$$\frac{PhoneCustomer(x) \ : \ \neg Exception(x)}{HasPhone(x)}$$

first, then $HasPhone(Smith)$ is inferred on condition that $\neg Exception(Smith)$ could not be inferred. Applying, the new rule now, yields $Exception(Smith)$, violating the proviso imposed on the earlier application, and thus voiding it.

To summarize, default logic [19] aims at formalizing reasoning from default information by means of formulas of classical logic and the so-called *default rules*, namely the expressions

$$\frac{\alpha \ : \ \beta}{\gamma}$$

where α, β, and γ are formulas of classical logic. The inference rules are those of classical logic plus a special mechanism to deal with default rules: basically, if α is inferred, and $\neg\beta$ cannot be inferred, then infer γ. The above examples demonstrated the main ideas; more complete treatment may be found in [1], for instance.

4 LABELED DEDUCTIVE SYSTEMS FOR PRACTICAL REASONING

Developing logics for practical reasoning creates new demands on the apparatus for defining the language and the proof theory. We approach this problem as follows: we augment the language by labeling its formulae, and we define the proof theory to manipulate both the formulae and the labels on formulae. This approach has driven the development of a general framework, called Labeled Deductive Systems (LDS), for presenting logics that handle labeled formulae [12, 14].

The basic unit of information in LDS is a labeled formula $i : \alpha$, where i is a label, and α is an unlabeled formula. A logic can then be defined in terms of allowed operations on the labeled formulae. For example, logical consequence can be defined on labeled formulae,

$$\frac{\{i_1 : \alpha_1, \cdots, i_n : \alpha_n\}}{j : \beta}$$

where $i_1, \ldots, i_n$ are labels, j is a function of i_1, ..., i_n, and α_1, ..., α_n, β are formulae.

Different applications of LDS are made possible by different definitions for the logical manipulation of formulae α and for the algebraic manipulation of the labels i. Furthermore, many existing logics fit into the LDS framework, including temporal logics [10], modal and many-valued logics [8], resource logics [15], and nonmonotonic logics [13, 11, 16].

4.1 LDS for Default Logic

We begin by showing how default logic can be handled by LDS. We assume the usual set of logical formulae, which we denote F, and we label each item in F with the symbol 0. We assume that default rules have the form,

$$i : \frac{\alpha : \beta}{\gamma},$$

where $\alpha, \beta, \gamma \in F$, and $i \in 2^{\mathcal{N}}$ is a unique label (i.e., i is a set of integers), and we let D denote the set of default rules. Instead of using quantified default rules, we use their instantiated form, as common in default logic. However, we also introduce labeling of the default rules. As before, we regard α as a precondition, β as a justification, and γ as the consequent. A database Δ is a subset of $D \cup F$.

An example of a database is the default rules

$$\{1\} : \frac{PhoneCustomer(Baker) : \neg Exception(Baker)}{HasPhone(Baker)}$$

$$\{2\} : \frac{PhoneCustomer(Cook) : \neg Exception(Cook)}{HasPhone(Cook)}$$

and the data

$$\{0\} : \quad PhoneCustomer(Baker)$$
$$\{0\} : \quad PhoneCustomer(Cook)$$

In the following we provide the definition of an *extension*, which is a consistent set of conclusions of a database.

The notion of an extension in the LDS framework, is captured with two mechanisms. The first mechanism concerns the derivation of formulae using the proof rules of classical logic and the default rules. When we apply a proof rule or a default rule, we keep track of the data and default rules used by propagating the labels. For instance, from $i : A$ and $j : B$ we obtain $i \cup j : A \wedge B$.

The second mechanism concerns the propagated labels. They indicate which default rules have been applied to obtain a specific formula, and hence each label delineates a subset of the data. Basically, we have to test that the default rules applied to infer a formula with a given label do not have their justification contradicted by the subset of data corresponding to that label.

So, for the above example, by the first mechanism we get the following labeled formulae,

$$\begin{aligned}
&\{0\}: && PhoneCustomer(Cook) \\
&\{0\}: && PhoneCustomer(Baker) \\
&\{2,0\}: && HasPhone(Cook) \\
&\{1,0\}: && HasPhone(Baker)
\end{aligned}$$

and by the second mechanism, we have the following extension,

$$\begin{aligned}
&PhoneCustomer(Cook) \\
&PhoneCustomer(Baker) \\
&HasPhone(Cook) \\
&HasPhone(Baker)
\end{aligned}$$

4.2 LDS for Paraconsistent Logic

LDS can also be used for presenting paraconsistent logics. For this we consider the system C_ω of da Costa [7] that is formalized by the following proof method of Carnielli *et al* [5, 6]. First, da Costa introduces the notion of a well-behaved formula: $\neg(\alpha \wedge \neg\alpha)$ is not valid in general, but if it does hold for a formula α, it is a well-behaved formula, and is denoted α°. Second, each formula α is labeled with either a + symbol or a − symbol, and we call $+ : \alpha$ and $- : \alpha$ *signed formulae*. Intuitively, $+ : \alpha$ and $- : \alpha$ can be interpreted as α being true and α being false, respectively. Any set of sets of signed formulae is called a *form*.

Let α and β be two formulae. Below are a set of production rules that can be used to transform a set of formulae into either a new set of formulae, or set of sets of formulae.

$$\{\delta, + : (\alpha \wedge \beta)\} \Rightarrow \{\delta, + : \alpha, + : \beta\}$$
$$\{\delta, - : (\alpha \vee \beta)\} \Rightarrow \{\delta, - : \alpha, - : \beta\}$$
$$\{\delta, - : (\alpha \rightarrow \beta)\} \Rightarrow \{\delta, + : \alpha, - : \beta\}$$
$$\{\delta, + : (\neg\neg\alpha)\} \Rightarrow \{\delta, + : \alpha\}$$
$$\{\delta, - : (\neg\alpha)\} \Rightarrow \{\delta, + : \alpha\}$$
$$\{\delta, - : (\neg\neg\alpha)\} \Rightarrow \{\delta, - : \alpha\}$$
$$\{\delta, - : (\alpha \diamond \beta)^{\circ}\} \Rightarrow \{\delta, - : (\alpha^{\circ} \diamond \beta^{\circ})\}, \text{where } \diamond \in \{\wedge, \vee, \rightarrow\}$$
$$\{\delta, - : (\alpha \wedge \beta)\} \Rightarrow \{\{\delta, - : \alpha\}, \{\delta, - : \beta\}\}$$
$$\{\delta, + : (\alpha \vee \beta)\} \Rightarrow \{\{\delta, + : \alpha\}, \{\delta, + : \beta\}\}$$
$$\{\delta, + : (\alpha \rightarrow \beta)\} \Rightarrow \{\{\delta, - : \alpha\}, \{\delta, + : \beta\}\}$$
$$\{\delta, + : (\neg\alpha)\} \Rightarrow \{\{\delta, - : \alpha\}, \{\delta, - : \alpha^{\circ}\}\}$$

Given a form C, we denote by $R(C)$ the result of applying one of the rules to the form. A tableau is a sequence of forms $C_1, \ldots, C_n$, such that $C_{i+1} = R(C_i)$. To test if a formulae can be inferred from a set of formulae, we label it with the $-$ symbol, add it to the data, and construct a tableau. The formula can be inferred if the tableau is closed. A tableau is closed if every set of formulae of its form is closed, and a set of formulae is closed if there is a formula α for which $+ : \alpha$ and $- : \alpha$ belong to that set.

For example, consider the following market research data on voting. In this example, there is a symmetry about whether or not Dick is a Pacifist. In other words, there is an argument that Dick is a Pacifist, and an argument that Dick is not a Pacifist.

$$Dick \rightarrow (Republican \wedge Quaker)$$
$$Quaker \rightarrow Pacifist$$
$$Republican \rightarrow \neg Pacifist$$
$$Dick$$

Running the tableaux rules for this set, the resulting open tableau is the proposed solution to the problem introduced by the inconsistency. Here we consider only the two main forms, one of which is closed and the other is not. The rest of the closed forms will be omitted.

$$
\begin{aligned}
C_0 \ &= \ \{+ : (Dick \rightarrow (Republican \wedge Quaker)), \\
&\qquad + : (Quaker \rightarrow Pacifist), \\
&\qquad + : (Republican \rightarrow Pacifist), + : (Dick)\} \\
C_1 \ &= \ C_0 \cup \{+ : (Republican \wedge Quaker)\} \\
C_2 \ &= \ C_1 \cup \{+ : (Republican) + : (Quaker)\} \\
C_3 \ &= \ C_2 \cup \{+ : Pacifist, + : (\neg Pacifist)\} \\
C_4 \ &= \ \{\{C_3 \cup \{- : Pacifist\}\}, \{C_3 \cup \{- : Pacifist^\circ\}\}\}
\end{aligned}
$$

The set $\{C_3 \cup \{- : Pacifist\}$ is closed, and the set $\{C_3 \cup \{- : Pacifist^\circ\}\}$ is not closed. This means that we can restrict our considerations to the following set of signed elementary expressions of the open set $- : Pacifist^\circ$, $+ : Pacifist$, $+ : Quaker$, $+ : Republican$, $+ : Dick$. This set gives us a solution to the problem in the sense that we consider $Dick$ as a $Quaker$, $Pacifist$, and $Republican$, but his $Pacifism$ is controversial. This also shows how even though the database is inconsistent, the technique allows us to identify $Pacifist/\neg Pacifist$ as being central to this inconsistency problem.

The computational complexity of the deduction method presented is similar to classical logic. This is in contrast to the usual nonmonotonic logics, where complexity is extremely high. This is due to the fact that paraconsistent logics block certain deductions from inconsistencies, whereas many nonmonotonic logics, such as default logic, use consistency checking to ensure that each extension is free from inconsistencies.

Nevertheless, it is perhaps now evident that using default or defeasible data, and using inconsistent data are two interrelated problems. A significant part of reasoning with default rules is resolving inconsistencies. Similarly, many problems of inconsistencies in information arise from the use of default information.

Note that the above example captures an equivalence regarding the $Pacifist/ \neg Pacifist$ nature of $Dick$. On other words, there is no apparent way of determining a priority on the information. This contrasts with many examples in which some kind of priority can be identified to resolve the problem. We return to this issue later.

4.3   Skeptical and Credulous Views

In reasoning with both inconsistent information and default information, there is the question of whether to adopt a skeptical or credulous view. In a skeptical view, the logic is cautious and does not allow conflicting inferences, whereas in a credulous view, the logic is less cautious, and does allow conflicting inferences. The rationale behind a credulous view is that the user makes a selection from the conflicting inferences. For example, take the following defaults rules,

$$\{3\}: \frac{Aircraft(x) \ : \ RequireRunway(x)}{RequireRunway(x)}$$

$$\{4\}: \frac{Helicopter(x) \ : \ \neg RequireRunway(x)}{\neg RequireRunway(x)}$$

and the following facts

$$\{0\}: \quad Aircraft(Sikorsky)$$
$$\{0\}: \quad Helicopter(Sikorsky)$$

From this, there are two extensions. The first contains $RequireRunway(Sikorsky)$ and the second contains $\neg RequireRunway(Sikorsky)$. A credulous view would allow both as possible inferences, whereas a skeptical view would allow neither. Similarly, in paraconsistent logics, we may have the following data,

$$\{5\}: \quad Aircraft(x) \rightarrow RequireRunway(x)$$
$$\{6\}: \quad Helicopter(x) \rightarrow \neg RequireRunway(x)$$
$$\{0\}: \quad Aircraft(Sikorsky)$$
$$\{0\}: \quad Helicopter(Sikorsky)$$

In the same way, this paraconsistent logic gives both $RequireRunway(Sikorsky)$ and $\neg RequireRunway(Sikorsky)$ as inferences. As with default reasoning, a credulous view would allow both as acceptable inferences, whereas a skeptical view would allow neither. However, it is not clear in general whether reasoning should be skeptical or credulous.

4.4 Resolving Conflicts

One solution to these kinds of problems is to use the labels to resolve the conflict. Essentially, the labels can be used to capture extra information about the formulae in the database, and about the inferences, so that a judicious choice can be made. For a variety of applications, LDS meets the need for extra information about data. This may be further object-level information or metalevel information or semantic information. A label can represent a wide variety of notions. Take the labeled formula $k : \alpha$. The label k could capture any of the following:

- the fuzzy reliability of α

- the origin, or source, of α

- the priority of α

- the time when α holds

- a proof of α in, for example, a truth maintenance system

So, for example, with the database about aircraft, we could introduce an ordering over formulae that captures a notion of specificity. For the above database, the default,

$$\{4\} : \frac{Helicopter(x) \; : \; \neg RequireRunway(x)}{\neg RequireRunway(x)}$$

is more specific than the default,

$$\{3\} : \frac{Aircraft(x) \; : \; RequireRunway(x)}{RequireRunway(x)}$$

since helicopters are a subclass of aircraft. The ordering can then be used to allow the inference $\neg RequireRunway(Sikorsky)$ in preference to its complement.

Note that using such a selection technique with paraconsistent logic then means the system can change inferences in the light of new information. Hence the behavior is very similar to that of default logic. For example, for the following data,

$$\{5\} : \quad Aircraft(x) \to RequireRunway(x)$$
$$\{6\} : \quad Helicopter(x) \to \neg RequireRunway(x)$$
$$\{0\} : \quad Aircraft(Sikorsky)$$

The inference $RequireRunway(Sikorsky)$ is selected. However, it is then retracted when the fact $Helicopter(Sikorsky)$ is added to the this data.

As another example of how labels can be used to resolve conflict, consider a groupware system that collates office memos, and users query this system about company regulations. Suppose that information in memo $\{7\}$ includes the following statement,

$$\{7\} : ExportCustomer(x) \to ChargeCustomerInDollars(x)$$

and memo $\{8\}$ includes statements,

$$\{8\} : \quad ExportCustomer(x) \to ChargeCustomerInDeutchmarks(x)$$
$$\{8\} : \quad \neg ChargeCustomerInDollars(x) \lor$$
$$\neg ChargeCustomerInDeutchmarks(x)$$

If a user has the fact *ExportCustomer(Philips)*, then the groupware data is inconsistent using classical logic. However, if the labels correspond to the data of the memo, then there is a preference for information from the more recent memo. In this example, if {7} corresponds to 23 January 1992, and {8} corresponds to 25 February 1993, then the inconsistency can be resolved. As before, if new information is added to the system, such as new memos, then inferences might have to be retracted.

This feature of retracting inferences in the light of new data is termed nonmonotonicity. It is not a desirable concept *per se*. It means a lack of monotonicity, and hence the lack of a property that classical logic and some of its close relatives have. The term nonmonotonic logic was used because the logics being developed for reasoning with default information seemed to have nonmonotonicity as their prime characteristic.

Nonmonotonicity is required when only a partial knowledge of a situation is possible. Rarely does a system have at its disposal all the information that would be desirable. However, to wait until all required information has been assimilated would involve delay, even infinite delay. Obviously this is not satisfactory. To ameliorate, some nonmonotonic reasoning mechanism must be resorted to. In other words, we argue that some form of plausible reasoning is required. Where everything pertinent to the investigation is known, monotonicity is more appropriate.

5 CONCLUSIONS

The ubiquitous usage by organizations of information that incorporates defaults and inconsistencies contrasts sharply with the low level of computer-based handling of such information. The situation will change as the expanding role of information technology means that handling of such information will become increasingly significant. Indeed, as defaults and inconsistencies pervade virtually any real-world scenario, techniques for handling them must be incorporated into any information system that attempts to provide a substantive model of the real world.

In this chapter, we have illustrated the argument to handle default and inconsistent information with examples of situations where such information could be potentially useful. There are a variety of techniques proposed to handle such information. However, it seems that only via formal techniques, such as logics of practical reasoning, can we hope to provide a viable framework for incorporating default and inconsistent information into information systems. This includes developing logical proof systems and means for harnessing extra information about formulae, such as semantic or metalevel information. In this way, we can identify and resolve the conflicts that arise when using default or inconsistent information.

Acknowledgments

The authors wish to thank Philippe Smets, Curtis Dyerson, and Ami Motro for helpful feedback.

REFERENCES

[1] P. Besnard. *Introduction to Default Logic.* Springer-Verlag, 1989.

[2] P. Besnard. Paraconsistent logics approach to knowledge representation. In *Proceedings of World Conference on the Fundamentals of Artificial Intelligence*, pages 107–114. Angkor, 1991.

[3] A. Borgida. Language features for flexible handling of exceptions in information systems. *ACM Transactions on Database Systems*, 10(4): 565–603, December 1985.

[4] A. Borgida and K. Williamson. Accommodating exceptions in databases and refining the schema by learning from them. In *Proceedings of the Eleventh International Conference on Very Large Data Bases* (Stockholm, Sweden, August 21–23), pages 72–81, 1985.

[5] W. A. Carnielli, L. Fariñas del Cerro, and M. Lima-Marques. Contextual negation and reasoning with contradiction. In *Proceedings of the Twelfth International Joint Conference on Artificial Intelligence (*Sydney, Australia, August), pages 532–537, 1991.

[6] W. A. Carnielli and M. Lima-Marques. Reasoning under inconsistent knowledge. *Journal of Applied Non-Classical Logics*, 2: 49–79, 1992.

[7] N. da Costa. On the theory of inconsistent information. *Notre Dame Journal of Formal Logic*, 15: 497–510, 1974.

[8] M. D'Agostino and D. Gabbay. Labelled refutation systems. In *Proceedings of the Workshop on Theorem Proving with Analytic Tableaux and Related Methods* (Marseilles, France, April), pages 243–281, 1993.

[9] H. Dreizen and S. Chang. Imprecise schema: A rationale for relations with embedded subrelations. *ACM Transactions on Database Systems*, 14(4): 447–479, December 1989.

[10] M. Finger and D. Gabbay. Labelled database management system. In *Proceedings of the International Conference on Database Theory*, volume 646 of *Lecture Notes in Computer Science*, pages 188–200. Springer-Verlag, 1992.

[11] D. Gabbay. Abduction in labelled deductive systems: A conceptual abstract. In *Symbolic and Quantitative Approaches to Uncertainty*, volume 548 of *Lecture Notes in Computer Science*, pages 3–12. Springer-Verlag, 1991.

[12] D. Gabbay. Labelled deductive systems. Technical report, Centrum fur Informations und Sprachverabeitung, Universitat Munchen, 1991.

[13] D. Gabbay. Theoretical foundations for non-monotonic reasoning, part 2: Structured non-monotonic theories. In *Proceedings of Scandinavian Conference on Artificial Intelligence*, pages 19–40. IOS Press, 1991.

[14] D. Gabbay. Labelled deductive systems: A position paper. In *Logic Colloquium 90*, volume 2 of *Lecture Notes in Logic*, pages 66–88. Springer-Verlag, 1993.

[15] D. Gabbay and R. de Queiroz. Extending the Curry-Howard interpretation to linear, relevant and other resource logics. *Journal of Symbolic Logic*, 57: 1319–1366, 1992.

[16] A. Hunter. A conceptualization of preferences in non-monotonic proof theories. In *Logics in AI*, volume 633 of *Lecture Notes in Computer Science*, pages 174–188. Springer-Verlag, 1992.

[17] P. King and C. Small. Default databases and incomplete information. *Computer Journal*, 34: 239–244, 1991.

[18] J. Martins and S. Shapiro. A model of belief revision. *Artificial Intelligence*, 35: 25–79, 1988.

[19] R. Reiter. A logic for default reasoning. *Artificial Intelligence*, 13: 187–214, 1980.

12

THE TRANSFERABLE BELIEF
MODEL FOR BELIEF
REPRESENTATION

Philippe Smets
Rudolf Kruse*

IRIDIA
Université Libre de Bruxelles
Brussels, Belgium

* Faculty of Computer Science
University of Magdeburg
Magdeburg, Germany

1   INTRODUCTION

As shown in Chapter 8, there are different forms of imperfect data, be they uncertain or imprecise. Models have been proposed for each form, but modeling combined forms of imperfect data has hardly been achieved. It would nevertheless seem useful to have a single model that could represent several forms of uncertainty. Possibly, this could be achieved by simulating what might be the human approach to such problems.

Imprecision and uncertainty about the value of an attribute induce *beliefs*; that is, subjective opinions held by an agent at a given time, about what this value actually is. For example, the information that John is in his 40s induces a belief about John's age; e.g., an equiprobability over the range 40–49.

Bayesians claim that this belief is always quantified by a probability measure. At times they go so far as to disregard all other models. Even though the probability model is by far the oldest and the most popular for belief representation, we think that it has certain limitations that can be handled by some of the alternative or complementary models that have been proposed recently.

The generalization of the Bayesian model has been achieved either by nonstandard probability models or by nonprobability models [12]. The *nonstandard probability models* are those models where beliefs are still quantified by underlying probability measures.

(1) Koopman [14], Good [5], Kyburg [18], Smith [43], Walley [48], and Voorbraak [47] propose that beliefs be quantified by a family of probability measures. It is not always clear if the author claims that belief states are represented by a set of probability functions, or if there exists some underlying probability measure whose value is only known to belong to some subset of probability measures. These approaches usually result in a theory of upper and lower probabilities.

(2) Dempster [1] assumes the existence of a domain X on which there is a known probability measure P_X, of another domain Y, and of a one-to-many mapping M from X to Y. For instance, let $X = \{x_1, x_2\}$, $P_X(x_1) = .7$, $P_X(x_2) = .3$, $Y = \{y_1, y_2\}$, $M(x_1) = \{y_1\}$ and $M(x_2) = \{y_1, y_2\}$. The probability measure P_Y on Y, induced by P_X and M, is not well-defined. Indeed, $P_Y(y_1)$ is at least .7 and at most 1, and $P_Y(y_2)$ is at least 0 and at most .3. The imprecision about the value of the probability on the subsets of Y is due to the one-to-many nature of M. Indeed, we have no information about how the .3 given to x_2 is distributed among y_1 and y_2. One can at most assess the upper and lower limits of the probabilities that could be allocated to the subsets of Y. Dempster's model assumes the existence of a probability measure on the space $X \times Y$ that quantifies the beliefs over the space $X \times Y$. This joint probability measure is partially known. Its marginalization on X is the given probability measure P_X. But given the one-to-many nature of M, it is impossible to decide on the particular distribution of each probability $P_X(\{x\})$ given to the singletons $\{x\}$ of X among the elements of Y. Hence one can only assess the upper and lower probabilities for the subsets of Y. The particularity of this model is in the fact that the lower probability function happens to be a belief function. Usually, the Dempster-Shafer models described in the artificial intelligence literature correspond to Dempster's model or to some equivalent model, as it is the case with the models related to the probability of knowing [24], the probability of provability [50], and the probability of deductibility [66, 41].

(3) Other modeling, such as the hint model of Kohlas [11, 13] or Shafer's model for evidential reasoning [26, 60], are based on similar ideas of an underlying probability space and a one-to-many mapping. Their description of the induced belief on Y is very similar to Dempster's solution, except that they don't acknowledge the existence of a probability measure over the space $X \times Y$ that quantifies the agent's opinion about the subsets of $X \times Y$. That distinction becomes important when revision (conditioning) of beliefs is considered.

(4) From the semantical point of view, it is often reasonable to separate the representation of information sources from the representation of the data provided by these information sources. A uniform approach to the handling of imprecise and uncertain data is discussed in [4].

The *nonprobabilistic models* are represented, among others, by the possibilistic model (Chapter 10) and the transferable belief model to be described in this chapter. No concept of probability measure is considered. When there is nevertheless a probability measure representing some forms of uncertainty, it is treated just as any other forms of imperfect data: it just induces possibilities or beliefs. These are related, of course, to the probability measure but are not necessarily identical to it.

In this chapter we assume that (1) every form of uncertainty and imprecision induces a belief held by an agent at a given time, (2) this belief is quantified by a belief function, and (3) the relation between the various forms of imperfect data can be achieved by considering the beliefs they induce.[1] We describe the model for belief representation based on belief functions, called the transferable belief model, and some of its applications in information sciences. How to appropriately build the belief induced from imperfect data has hardly been resolved so far and will not be addressed here.

2 THE TRANSFERABLE BELIEF MODEL

The transferable belief model is a model for representing the quantified beliefs held by an agent at a given time on a given frame of discernment Ω. One of the elements of Ω, denoted $\overline{\omega}$, corresponds to the actual state of nature, to the actual world. Unfortunately, the agent is not certain about which element of Ω is $\overline{\omega}$. The agent can only express his subjective opinion about the fact that a subset of Ω might contain $\overline{\omega}$. The belief $bel(A)$ given by the agent Y at time t to a subset A of Ω expresses the strength of the agent's beliefs that $\overline{\omega}$ is an element of A, based on the information available to Y at time t. As in the Bayesian approach, this degree of belief is usually quantified by a probability measure. Hence, the transferable belief model considers the same problem considered by the Bayesian model, except that it does not rely on probabilistic quantification but on belief functions.

---

[1] Note that we are not saying that every form of uncertainty and imprecision is represented by a belief function. We only assume that they induce it.

The *transferable belief model* has two levels: the *credal level* and the *pignistic level*.[2] The credal level is the level of intellectual activity in which beliefs are entertained. It is where one expresses the strength of one's beliefs about the fact that $\overline{\omega}$ belongs to the various subsets of Ω. It is where one's knowledge is stored, revised, updated, combined, and so on.

The pignistic level is also a level of intellectual activity, but it is completely oriented toward making decisions. When a decision must be made, the beliefs held at the credal level transmit the needed information to the pignistic level, to ensure optimal decisions. The pignistic level contains only the machinery that transforms beliefs (as held at the credal level) into optimal decisions. The pignistic level is active only when decisions must be made.

We will assume that the beliefs held at the credal level are quantified by the belief functions that will be presented in this survey.

When decisions must be made, we accept the Savage axioms [25] that claim that optimal decisions can only be achieved if the decider uses additive weights to represent his uncertainty on the possible states, and utilities that describe the consequence of each decision in each state. The additive weights correspond to a probability measure on the states, but Savage does not claim that such probability measure is precisely the way the decider's beliefs are represented; only that when a decision must be made, the decider must generate a set of probabilities on the set of states and make decisions by maximizing the expected utility computed from the utilities and the probability measure.

The origin of the probability measure is not discussed in Savage's approach. That it could be generated from the belief function that represents the decider's beliefs held at the credal level is perfectly acceptable under Savage's approach. Once these two distinct levels are considered, it is necessary to describe the nature of the relationship between the beliefs held at the credal level and the probabilities needed at the pignistic level. This relationship is described in Section 3.9.

Bayesians usually argue that beliefs coexist necessarily with decisions and do not exist by themselves. We do not share this opinion. That our beliefs are necessary ingredients for our decisions does not mean that beliefs cannot be held without manifesting themselves behaviorally [44]. We claim that beliefs can indeed be held without any concept of decision, thus justifying a distinct

---

[2]The terms originate from Latin, where *credo* means "I believe" and *pignus* means "a bet."

credal state. For instance, a person may entertain beliefs about metaphysical problems even if this person is not about to make any decision related to this subject, and a person may hold beliefs about the status of the traffic light near home in Brussels even if this person is not presently in Brussels and is not about to make any decision that depends on the state of this traffic light. However, the debate about the credal level is not purely academic because it can be shown that in some situations decisions are different depending on whether one considers the credal level or not.

A full description of the model for beliefs representation based on belief functions can be found in Shafer's book [26]. A somewhat revised version appears in [31]. The transferable belief model is described in [42]. The axiomatic justification of the use of belief functions to quantify beliefs is given in [37]. Justifications of the conditioning rule can be found in [10], in [20], and in [15], where differences between various revision concepts are considered. Further results on Bayes theorem and the disjunctive rule of combination appear in [28, 38]. Measures of uncertainty related to belief functions are surveyed in [21, 22]. Many algebraic properties on belief functions can be found in [2, 3]. Polemics on the use of belief functions in artificial intelligence, essentially in the context of logical deductions, are in two special issues of the *International Journal of Approximate Reasoning* (Vol. 4, 1990, and Vol. 6, 1992). Jeffrey's rule of conditioning is presented in [39], and the avoidance of Dutch Book is explained in [40].

3   THE MATHEMATICS OF THE TBM

As a didactic tool, we shall use one example throughout this chapter. To avoid the need for contextual background, the subject of this example is a murder mystery. Of course, the example could easily be rephrased into a diagnostic problem or a prediction problem.[3]

Example: A man named Ron was murdered. You, the reader, are the policeman in charge of finding the killer(s) (the killing might have been committed by several persons jointly). There are three suspects: John, Paul, and Sarah.
□

---

[3]Comments that are not essential for the understanding of the basic model, but are potentially useful for further studies, are marked **Note**.

3.1   The Frame of Discernment

Let L be a finite *propositional language.*

Example: The three atomic propositions are "John is a murderer of Ron,", "Paul is a murderer of Ron," and "Sarah is a murderer of Ron." They are denoted by J, P, and S, respectively.   □

Let $\Omega = \{\omega_1, \omega_2, ...\omega_n\}$ be the set of worlds that correspond to the interpretations of L.

Example: The eight possible worlds are

$$\omega_1 = \neg J \wedge \neg P \wedge \neg S \text{ (None of the three suspects is a murderer of Ron.)}$$
$$\omega_2 = \neg J \wedge \neg P \wedge S \quad \text{(Sarah is the only murderer among the three suspects.)}$$
$$\omega_3 = \neg J \wedge P \wedge \neg S \quad \text{(Paul is the only murderer among the three suspects.)}$$
$$\omega_4 = \neg J \wedge P \wedge S \quad \text{(Paul and Sarah are murderers; John is not.)}$$
$$\omega_5 = J \wedge \neg P \wedge \neg S \quad \text{(John is the only murderer among the three suspects.)}$$
$$\omega_6 = J \wedge \neg P \wedge S \quad \text{(John and Sarah are murderers; Paul is not.)}$$
$$\omega_7 = J \wedge P \wedge \neg S \quad \text{(John and Paul are murderers; Sarah is not;)}$$
$$\omega_8 = J \wedge P \wedge S \quad \text{(John, Paul, and Sarah are murderers.)}$$

□

Propositions identify subsets of Ω.

Example: The proposition "Paul is a murderer of Ron" identifies the subset $\{\omega_3, \omega_4, \omega_7, \omega_8\}$ of Ω.   □

Beliefs and probabilities given to propositions can thus be identically considered as beliefs and probabilities given to subsets of Ω, and the set notation will be used hereafter. By definition, there is an actual world $\bar{\omega}$, and it is an element of Ω. For $A \subseteq \Omega$, $bel(A)$ and $P(A)$ denote, respectively, the degrees of belief and probability that the actual world $\bar{\omega}$ belongs to A. For simplicity, we assume that bel and P are defined for all subsets of Ω; so bel and P are functions from 2^{Ω} to $[0, 1]$. Ω is called the *frame of discernment.*

All the beliefs that you entertain[4] at time t, about which world is the actual world $\bar{\omega}$, are defined relative to a given *evidential corpus* (EC_t^Y); i.e., the set

---

[4]Recall that you, the reader, assume the role of the agent (in this example, the policeman) whose beliefs are being considered.

of pieces of evidence in your mind at time t. Our approach is normative: you are an ideal rational agent and EC_t^Y is deductively closed. Your credal state on a frame of discernment Ω describes your subjective, personal judgment that $\overline{\omega} \in A$ for every subset A of Ω. By a prevailing abuse of language, the actual world $\overline{\omega}$ is called the "true" world, and we say that "A is true" or "the truth is in A" to mean that $\overline{\omega} \in A$. Your credal state results from EC_t^Y, which induces in you some partial beliefs on the subsets of Ω. These partial beliefs quantify the strength of your belief that $\overline{\omega} \in A$, $\forall A \subseteq \Omega$. It is an epistemic construct as it is relative to the knowledge included in your evidential corpus EC_t^Y.

Example: To simplify the example, suppose you know that exactly one of the three suspects is the murderer of Ron. Then EC_t^Y contains the fact that Ron was murdered by a single person; i.e., the murderer is one of John, Paul, and Sarah. The available information is represented by $\overline{\omega} \in \{\omega_2, \omega_3, \omega_5\}$. □

3.2   The Basic Belief Masses

Example: A partially reliable witness testifies to you that the murderer is a male. Assume the reliability you assign to this testimony is .7. Suppose that *a priori* you have an equal belief that the murderer is either male or a female. A classical probability analysis would compute the probability $P(M)$ of M where $M =$ "the killer is a male" as follows: $P(M) = .7 + .5 \times .3 = .85$ (the probability that the witness is reliable (.7) in which case M is true, plus the probability of M given that the witness is not reliable (.5) weighted by the probability that the witness is not reliable (.3)). The .7 can be viewed as the justified component of the probability given to M, whereas the .15 can be viewed as the aleatory component of that probability.

The TBM models this situation differently. In contradistinction, the TBM deals only with the *justified* components. It gives a belief (or support) .7 to M. The .7 and .3 are parts of an initial unitary amount of belief that supports $J \vee P$ (the males) and $J \vee P \vee S$ (anybody), respectively. These parts are called the basic belief masses. They are denoted by $m(J \vee P) = .7$, $m(J \vee P \vee S) = .3$. The .7 that supports $J \vee P$ supports the fact that the murderer is either John or Paul. It is kept to the disjunction $J \vee P$ (i.e., $\{\omega_3, \omega_5\}$) without being further distributed between $\{\omega_3\}$ and $\{\omega_5\}$. That is, the .7 supports $\overline{\omega} \in \{\omega_3, \omega_5\}$ without supporting any proposition strictly more specific like $\{\omega_3\}$ and $\{\omega_5\}$. Identically, the .3 is a "specific" support given to $\overline{\omega} \in \{\omega_2, \omega_3, \omega_5\}$ that cannot be distributed any more specifically among the subsets of $\{\omega_2, \omega_3, \omega_5\}$. These basic belief masses allocation (the .7 and .3) is at the core of the assumptions underlying TBM.   □

Formally, the TBM is defined as follows.

Basic Assumption: *The TBM postulates that the impact of a piece of evidence on an agent is translated by an allocation of parts of an initial unitary amount of belief among the subsets of Ω. For $A \subseteq \Omega$, $m(A)$ is a part of the agent's belief that supports A, i.e., that the actual world $\overline{\omega}$ is in A, and that, due to lack of information, does not support any strict subset of A.*

The $m(A)$ values, $A \subseteq \Omega$, are called the *basic belief masses (bbm)* and the function m is called the *basic belief assignment (bba)*.[5] Formally, $m : 2^\Omega \to [0, 1]$ and
$$\sum_{A \subseteq \Omega} m(A) = 1.$$

Every $A \subseteq \Omega$ such that $m(A) > 0$ is called a *focal element*. The difference from probability models is that masses can be given to any subsets of Ω instead of only to the elements of Ω, as would be the case in probability theory.

3.3   Conditioning

Example: Suppose you learn that Paul was not the murderer because he was dead the day before Ron was murdered (a perfect alibi). The world ω_3 is thus impossible, and hence you know for sure that $\overline{\omega} \in \{\omega_2, \omega_5\}$. The bbm .7 that was initially allocated to $\{\omega_3, \omega_5\}$ now supports specifically that the murderer is John, i.e., $\{\omega_5\}$, and the bbm .3 initially allocated to $\{\omega_2, \omega_3, \omega_5\}$ now supports that the murderer is John or Sarah, i.e., $\overline{\omega} \in \{\omega_2, \omega_5\}$. Indeed, the reliability .7 you gave the testimony initially supported "the murderer is John or Paul"; the new information about Paul implies that the .7 now supports "the murderer is John."   □

In general terms, the additional knowledge that $\overline{\omega} \in B \subseteq \Omega$ results in a transfer, for each $A \subseteq \Omega$, of the bbm $m(A)$ initially allocated to A to $A \cap B \subseteq \Omega$. Hence the name Transferable Belief Model.

---

[5]Shafer talks about basic probability masses and assignment. To avoid confusion, we have tried to avoid the word *probability*, whenever possible.

This transfer of belief corresponds to the *unnormalized rule of conditioning.*[6] Let m be a basic belief assignment on the frame of discernment Ω, and suppose that the conditioning evidence tells you that the truth is in $B \subseteq \Omega$, then the basic belief assignment m is transformed into $m_B : 2^\Omega \to [0,1]$ with

$$
m_B(A) = \begin{cases} \sum_{X \subseteq \overline{B}} m(A \cup X) & \text{for } A \subseteq B \\ 0 & \text{otherwise} \end{cases}
$$

Note: In this presentation we have accepted that a nonnull basic belief mass could be given to $\emptyset$. In most presentations of models based on belief functions, it is assumed that $m(\emptyset) = 0$. The meaning of the basic belief mass given to $\emptyset$ is analyzed in [36]. It corresponds to the amount of contradiction present in the basic belief assignment m, as could be encountered when two sources of information give support to contradictory hypothesis.

3.4 Belief and Plausibility Functions

Given Ω, the *degree of belief* of $A \subseteq \Omega$, denoted $bel(A)$,[7] quantifies the total amount of justified specific support given to A. It is obtained by summing all the basic belief masses given to propositions $X \subseteq A$ (and $X \neq \emptyset$). Formally, $bel : 2^\Omega \to [0,1]$ and

$$
bel(A) = \sum_{\emptyset \neq X \subseteq A} m(X).
$$

We say *justified*, because we include in $bel(A)$ only the basic belief masses given to subsets of A. For instance, consider two distinct elements ω_1 and ω_2 of Ω. The basic belief mass $m(\{\omega_1, \omega_2\})$ given to $\{\omega_1, \omega_2\}$ could support ω_1 if further information indicates this. However, given the available information, the basic belief mass can only be given to $\{\omega_1, \omega_2\}$. Note: as $m(\emptyset)$ might be positive, it should not be included in $bel(A)$ (nor in $pl(A)$, see below); $m(\emptyset)$ is given to the subset $\emptyset$ that supports not only A but also $\overline{A}$. This is the origin of the specific support.

---

[6] When $m(\emptyset) = 0$ is assumed, the result is further normalized by dividing each term in m_B by $1 - m_B(\emptyset)$. The resulting conditioning rule is then called the *Dempster rule of conditioning.*

[7] We use *bel* and *pl* to denote unnormalized belief and plausibility functions, keeping *Bel* and *Pl* for the normalized form developed by Shafer.

The function *bel* is called a *belief function*. Belief functions satisfy the following inequalities [26]:

$$\forall n \geq 1, A_1, A_2, \ldots A_n \subseteq \Omega$$
$$bel(A_1 \cup A_2 \cup \ldots \cup A_n) \geq \sum_i bel(A_i) - \sum_{i>j} bel(A_i \cap A_j) \qquad (12.1)$$
$$\ldots - (-1)^n bel(A_1 \cap A_2 \cap \ldots \cap A_n)$$

The *degree of plausibility* of A, denoted $pl(A)$, quantifies the maximum amount of potential specific support that could be given to $A \subseteq \Omega$. It is obtained by adding all the basic belief masses given to propositions X that are compatible with A; i.e., to propositions X for which $X \cap \overline{A} \neq \emptyset$. Formally, $pl : 2^\Omega \to [0, 1]$ and

$$pl(A) = \sum_{X \cap A \neq \emptyset} m(X) = bel(\Omega) - bel(\overline{A}).$$

We say *potential*, because the basic belief masses included in $pl(A)$ could be transferred to nonempty subsets of A if some new information would justify such a transfer. Such would be the case if we learn that $\overline{A}$ is impossible.

The function pl is called a *plausibility function*. It is in one-to-one correspondence with the belief function induced by the same bba. It is simply another way of presenting the same information and could be avoided, except that it provides a convenient alternate representation of our beliefs.

The unnormalized rule of conditioning expressed with *bel* and *pl* is

$$bel(A|B) = bel(A \cup B) - bel(\overline{B})$$
$$pl(A|B) = pl(A \cap B)$$

The state of *total ignorance* is hard to represent in probability theory. Most Bayesians reject the existence of such a state, thus avoiding the many problems related to its representation by a probability function. In the TBM, total ignorance is represented elegantly by a vacuous belief function; i.e., a belief function such that $m(\Omega) = 1$, and hence $bel(\Omega) = 1$, and $bel(A) = 0$ for all $A \subset \Omega$. This belief function does not support any particular subset of Ω (or, alternatively, all subsets receive the same degree of support), which clearly corresponds to total ignorance. Such a representation is not possible in probability theory. For example, when $\Omega = \{\omega_1, \omega_2, \omega_3\}$, $bel(\{\omega_1\}) = bel(\{\omega_2\}) = bel(\{\omega_3\}) = bel(\{\omega_1, \omega_2\}) = bel(\{\omega_1, \omega_3\}) = bel(\{\omega_2, \omega_3\})$.

3.5   The Rules of Combination

Example: Suppose a second witness, with reliability .6, tells you that the murderer is John or Sarah. The issue now is how to combine the bba m_1 (that represents your beliefs on Ω as induced by the testimony of the first witness) and m_2 (that represents your beliefs on Ω as induced by the testimony of the second witness) into a new bba m_{12} that will represent your beliefs on Ω as induced by the joint testimony of the two witnesses. When the two witnesses are fully reliable, their joint testimony supports that the murderer is John, and the combined bbm $m_{12}(J) = .7 \times .6 = .42$ (the reason for this product is explained below). When the first witness is reliable and the second is not, their joint testimony supports that the murderer John or Paul, and $m_{12}(J \vee P) = .7 \times .4 = .28$. Similarly, $m_{12}(J \vee S) = .3 \times .6 = .18$ and $m_{12}(J \vee P \vee S) = .3 \times .4 = .12$. In fact, the proposed combination rule consists of allocating the product of two bba $m_1(A) \times m_2(B)$ to the intersection $A \cap B$ of their focal elements A and B. □

Formally, suppose two belief functions bel_1 and bel_2 are induced by two distinct pieces of evidence. The issue is to define a belief function $bel_{12} = bel_1 \oplus bel_2$ that *combines* the two belief functions. Shafer proposed to use Dempster's rule of combination to derive bel_{12}. The underlying intuitive idea is that the product of two bbm $m_1(X)$ and $m_2(Y)$ induced by the two distinct pieces of evidence on Ω supports $X \cap Y$; that is,

$$m_{12}(A) = \sum_{X \cap Y = A} m_1(X) \times m_2(Y).$$

Note: [2, 32, 9, 10, 6] provide different justifications for the origin and the unicity of this rule. These justifications are obtained without introducing any underlying probability concepts. They are based essentially on the associativity and commutativity properties of the combination operator.

Note: Dempster's rule of combination is a rule to combine conjunctive pieces of information. Let bel_1 and bel_2 be the belief functions induced by the two distinct pieces of evidence E_1 and E_2, respectively. Then bel_{12} is the belief function induced on Ω by the conjunction E_1 and E_2. In [38] we present the disjunctive rule of combination that allows us to derive the belief function induced on Ω by the disjunction of E_1 and E_2. It corresponds to a situation where you could assess your belief on Ω if E_1 were true, and your belief on Ω if E_2 were true, but you only know that the disjunction E_1 or E_2 is true.

In connection with this disjunctive rule of combination, we derive the *Generalized Bayesian Theorem* [38]. Suppose you have a vacuous *a priori* on a space Θ (i.e., you are in a state of total ignorance). Suppose that for each $\theta_i \in \Theta$, you know what would be your beliefs on another space X if θ_i happened to be true. Let $bel_X(.|\theta_i)$ and $pl_X(.|\theta_i)$ denote the conditional belief and plausibility functions on X given each $\theta_i \in \Theta$. Now suppose that you learn that $x \subseteq X$ holds. The Generalized Bayesian Theorem allows you to derive the conditional belief $bel_\Theta(.|x)$ and plausibility $pl_\Theta(.|x)$ on the frame of discernment Θ, given an observation $x \subseteq X$. One has

$$bel_\Theta(\theta|x) \quad = \quad \prod_{\theta_i \in \bar{\theta}} (bel_X(\bar{x}|\theta_i)) + m(\emptyset|\theta_i)) - \prod_{\theta_i \in \Theta} (bel_X(\bar{x}|\theta_i)) + m(\emptyset|\theta_i))$$

$$pl_\Theta(\theta|x) \quad = \quad 1 - \prod_{\theta_i \in \theta} (1 - pl_X(x|\theta_i))$$

The theorem has been further generalized to when there is some nonvacuous beliefs on Θ [38].

Note: All combinations were performed for beliefs induced by distinct pieces of evidence. The concept of *distinctness* is presented in [35]. It fits essentially and intuitively with the idea that the two pieces of evidence involved are unrelated or independent; i.e., that the knowledge of any of them does not interfere with the beliefs that would be specifically induced by the other.

Note: The problem of combining *nondistinct* pieces of evidence was first considered in [30]. [19] and [8] introduce the concept of a *cautious rule of (conjunctive) combination*. It is based on the idea that each expert provides a belief function that results from his own expertise, plus a common background. The rule permits to disentangle the underlying common background and is idempotent. [19] solved the case where the experts opinions are described by simple belief functions; i.e., belief functions with two focal elements: Ω and a nonempty strict subset of Ω. [8] presents the solution when the experts opinions are described by separable belief functions; i.e., belief functions obtained by applying Dempster's rule of combination to several simple support functions. The generalization to an arbitrary pair of belief functions is under way, and its use for pooling expertise provided by experts who share a common background will be studied in a forthcoming paper. Here, we restrict ourselves to an idealized situation where the experts are independent; i.e., they do not communicate, and they do not use common evidence.

3.6 Justifications for the Use of Belief Functions

The use of belief functions at the credal level can be justified by at least three different approaches. Initially, Shafer justified the use of belief functions by claiming that any measure of belief must satisfy the relationships of Equation 12.1. In the TBM, we prefer to start from the basic belief masses that represent a certain part of our belief allocated to a proposition and that cannot be allocated to more specific propositions. Finally, in [37] we proposes a set of axioms that should be satisfied by any measure of belief, and this set of axioms justifies the use of belief functions to represent quantified beliefs.

3.7 Discounting

Example: Let us now disregard the previous testimonies, and suppose an agent H tells you that his beliefs over Ω is such that $m_H(\{\omega_1\}) = .2$, $m_H(\{\omega_1, \omega_2\}) = .3$, $m_H(\{\omega_1, \omega_2, \omega_3\}) = .5$. Should you have no other evidence over Ω, you would adopt m_H as representing your beliefs on Ω. But suppose now that you have some doubt about H's reliability. Let .7 be your degree of belief that H is reliable, or equivalently the strength with which you believe what H is saying. Your beliefs about what H is saying are represented by the bbm $m_0(\text{reliable}) = .7$ and $m_0(\text{reliable or not reliable}) = .3$. The issue is how to combine the beliefs induced in you by H's testimony and your beliefs about H's reliability. The approach is that you should discount H's beliefs by multiplying m_H by a factor .7 ($m_0(\text{reliable})$) and transfer to Ω the part of m_H that has been lost. Let m_Y be the resulting bba. It follows:

$$m_Y(\{\omega_1\}) = .2 \times .7 = .14$$
$$m_Y(\{\omega_1, \omega_2\}) = .3 \times .7 = .21$$
$$m_Y(\{\omega_1, \omega_2, \omega_3\}) = .5 \times .7 + (1 - .7) = .65$$

□

Formally, suppose you have no beliefs whatsoever on a frame of discernment Ω, but a somewhat reliable agent communicates to you his beliefs on Ω, beliefs that are represented by the basic belief assignment m_Ω. Should the agent be fully reliable, you would accept his beliefs and would be tempted to adopt his beliefs as yours. But the agent is not fully reliable. Let m_0 represents your *a priori* beliefs about the reliability of this agent, with $m_0(\text{reliable}) = 1 - \alpha$ and $m_0(\text{reliable or not reliable}) = \alpha$. Combining your *a priori* belief m_0 with m_Ω on Ω provided by the agent leads to the discounted belief bel_Ω^α that quantifies your belief on Ω induced by both your *a priori* and the agent's beliefs. [26] introduces the concept of discounting factors, [38] explains its origins. bel^{α}_{Ω} is such that

$$\forall A \subseteq \Omega, A \neq \Omega, bel^{\alpha}_{\Omega}(A) = (1 - \alpha)bel_{\Omega}(A),$$

and

$$bel^{\alpha}_{\Omega}(\Omega) = bel_{\Omega}(\Omega).$$

3.8   Static and Dynamic Components

It is important to note that the TBM includes *two components*: a *static* component, the basic belief assignment; and a *dynamic* component, the transfer process underlying the conditioning, the combination, and the discounting processes. Many authors on the Dempster-Shafer model consider only the basic belief assignment and discover that the basic belief masses are probabilities on the power set of Ω. Often, however, they do not study the dynamic component, and their comparisons are therefore incomplete, if not misleading. The transfer of belief masses is studied, among others, in [17], using the more general concept of specialization [16].

3.9   The Pignistic Probability BetP

Example: After the first testimony, if you had to bet on who is the murderer, or, equivalently, on which of the worlds in Ω corresponds to the actual world $\bar{\omega}$, you would have to build a probability function $BetP$ on Ω. Recall that your bba was described by a bbm .7 on $J \vee P$ and .3 on $J \vee P \vee S$. The .7 could as well be given to John or to Paul. So we could distribute it equally between John and Paul. Identically, the .3 could be distributed equally among the three suspects. In that case the probability $BetP$ would be

$$\begin{aligned} BetP(John) &= .7/2 + .3/3 = .45 \\ BetP(Paul) &= .7/2 + .3/3 = .45 \\ BetP(Sarah) &= .3/3 = .10 \end{aligned}$$

That this is indeed the only adequate solution is not discussed here.   □

In [33, 42], we show how to make *decisions* when the beliefs are quantified by belief functions (see also [45, 70, 7] for other solutions). The satisfaction of some natural rationality requirements leads to the derivation of a unique transformation between the belief functions and the probability functions that must be used once decisions must be made. We call this transformation the *pignistic transformation*. Let $BetP(A)$ be the pignistic probability derived from the bba $m : 2^\Omega \to [0, 1]$. $BetP$ is a classical probability measure, but we denote it $BetP$ to avoid confusion. $BetP$ deals with betting weights, not with beliefs quantification, whereas bel deals with such beliefs quantification. We have

$$\forall A \subseteq \Omega \; BetP(A) = \sum_{B \subseteq \Omega} \frac{m(B)}{bel(\Omega)} \frac{|A \cap B|}{|B|} \tag{12.2}$$

where $|A|$ is the number of elements in A. $BetP$ is the appropriate probability function to be used to make decisions (using expected utilities theory).

$BetP$ is the only probability measure that satisfies the following *rationality requirement* [33]. Assume two source of evidence E_1 and E_2 that induce the belief functions bel_1 and bel_2 on the same frame Ω, and assume a random device that selects the source that will be available to you. If you knew the evidence that would be selected (E_1 or E_2), you would bet on Ω according to a probability function P_i induced from the corresponding bel_i ($i = 1, 2$) by the pignistic transformation. These probability functions P_i are the conditional probability functions on Ω given E_i. Prior to selecting the source, the probability measure P on Ω is then $P(A) = pP_1(A) + (1 - p)P_2(A)$ for all $A \subseteq \Omega$, where p is the probability of selecting E_1. But prior to the selection of the source, your belief on Ω is given by $bel(A) = pbel_1(A) + (1 - p)bel_2(A)$ for all $A \subseteq \Omega$. The probability function induced from that combined belief function bel should be equal to P. The only transformation that satisfies this requirement is the pignistic transformation as described in Equation 12.2. Note that Strat and Jaffray's solutions do not satisfy the rationality requirement just described.

Note: In this transformation the bbm $m(A)$ given to a focal element $A \subseteq \Omega$ is distributed equally among the elements of A. For $\omega \in \Omega$, $BetP(\omega)$ results from the addition of all these parts of masses allocated to ω. It is quite similar to the application of the Principle of Insufficient Reason at the level of each bbm, but its justification is *not* based on the assumption of an Insufficient Reason.

Note that $BetP$ is not a representation of your beliefs on Ω. It is the additive measure induced on Ω by your beliefs held at the credal level (and quantified in the transferable belief model by a belief function) when decisions must be made, and that must be used to compute the expected utility to be maximized in order to select the optimal decision.

4   APPLICATIONS TO DATABASES

In this and the following two sections we present applications related to databases, source reliability, and medical diagnosis.

In databases, uncertainty and beliefs can be encountered at two levels: the attribute level and the tuple level.

At the attribute level, it might occur that the actual value of an attribute in a given tuple is not known exactly. The crudest way to represent the available knowledge is to represent the value of the attribute as a disjunctive set of possible values, which is compatible with the available knowledge. The next level of sophistication acknowledges that some values are more suitable than others: either more possible, more probable, or more believable. One ends up with a possibility, a probability, or a belief distribution over the domain of the attribute. Conceptually, the three representations are very similar, but they diverge in their interpretations. The value of the attribute is the disjunction of several weighted subsets of the corresponding domain.

The TBM could be applied if the knowledge about the actual value of the attribute could only be described by our belief about it. In that case, the value of the attribute will be described by a basic belief assignment m (or any related functions) on the corresponding domain.

As an example, assume the attribute is the age of a person, where a person is described by a tuple in a relation. Assume that the age of John is known only by a basic belief assignment on the domain of ages $D = [0, 120]$. For instance, the available information about John's age could be described by the bbm $m([40, 49]) = .6$, $m([30, 59]) = .3$, $m([0, 120]) = .1$. This bbm could represent the information that John is in his forties (.6 given to [40, 49]), or close (.3 given to [30, 59]), but the source is not fully reliable (hence the .1 on D).

Suppose now that you wish to select those tuples in which the age is between 35 and 52. Should you select John? One answer is to create a new relation R with the tuples that satisfy the selection criteria 35–52. John's tuple would be included, with certain weights that would represent the degree of belief and plausibility that John's tuple belongs to R. So the belief that John belongs to R is bel(John belongs to R) $= .6$ and pl(John belongs to R) $= 1$. Thus, for each tuple, a pair of weights is added to quantify the degree of belief and plausibility that the tuple belongs to the relation. This illustrates how uncertainty at the tuple level would be handled.

5 APPLICATION WITH SOURCES RELIABILITY

It is possible to record the *source* of the information stored in databases and use this to *discount* data when appropriate. Consider the relation *AGE* of Table 1. For example, the semantics of the first tuple are that, according to Paul, John is 45 (this is equivalent to $m([45]) = 1$); the semantics of the second tuple are that Peter believes (at level .6) that Henri is 45, and has no other specific knowledge about Henri's age; the semantics of the third tuple are that, according to Peter, Jack is between 30 and 40.

Name	Age	Source
John	45	Paul
Henri	$m([45]) = .6$	Peter
	$m([0, 120]) = .4$	
Jack	$m([30, 40]) = 1$	Peter
Jim	$m([32]) = 1$	Peter
Phil	$m([54] = .5$	Paul
	$m([52, 55] = .3$	
	$m([40, 50]) = .2$	
Henri	$m([30, 50]) = 1$	Paul

Table 1   Relation *AGE*.

The user of this database might have his own opinions about the reliability of these sources. Such reliability information is shown in Table 2. Note that reliability can be "iterated": we can represent the reliability of the information that describes the reliability of the sources, and so on.

Source	Reliability
Paul	$m(\text{reliable}) = .7$
Peter	$m(\text{reliable}) = .8$

Table 2   The reliability of sources (per individual user).

Suppose this user wants to quantify his beliefs about Henri's age. Peter is the only source for Henri's age. We use the belief presented in Table 1, discounted by the factor .2. (obtained from Table 2). As detailed in Section 3.7, the final bbm is $m([45]) = .8 \times .6 = .48$ and $m([0, 120]) = 1 - .48 = .52$. Table 3 shows the relation AGE for this individual user after the discounting factors of Table 2 have been applied to Table 1.

Name	Age
John	$m([45] = .70$
	$m([0, 120]) = .30$
Henri	$m([45]) = .48$
	$m([0, 120]) = .52$
Jack	$m([30, 40]) = .80$
	$m([0, 120]) = .20$
Jim	$m([32]) = .80$
	$m([0, 120]) = .20$
Phil	$m([54] = .35$
	$m([52, 55] = .21$
	$m([40, 50]) = .14$
	$m([0, 120]) = .30$
Henri	$m([30, 50]) = .70$
	$m([0, 120]) = .30$

Table 3   Relation AGE after discounting sources (per individual user).

Notice that Henri's age is provided by two sources (Paul and Peter). One could combine the two bbm presented in Table 1, but because Peter and Paul are two different sources of information, discounting must be done before combination. The result of combining the two belief functions over Henri's age in Table 3 is

$$
\begin{aligned}
m([45]) &= .48 \times (.7 + .3) = .480 \\
m([30, 50]) &= .52 \times .7 = .364 \\
m([0, 120]) &= .52 \times .3 = .156
\end{aligned}
$$

The final AGE relation is the one given in Table 3, but with Henri's data combined as above. Table 4 shows belief and plausibility (for this user) for age in the range $[44, 56]$. A selection on belief larger than .5 would retrieve John and Phil.

Name	bel	pl
John	.70	1.00
Henri	.48	1.00
Jack	.00	.20
Jim	.00	.20
Phil	.56	.86

Table 4 Relation $AGE \in [44, 56]$.

6 APPLICATION FOR DIAGNOSIS

The major advantage of using the TBM model in diagnostic applications is that the Bayesian theorem can be applied in cases where there are no prior beliefs on the set of diagnoses [29]. This addresses a major criticism of the Bayesian approach in diagnosis: where do the *a priori* beliefs on the set of diagnoses come from? In addition, the TBM approach benefits from the advantage that one must provide only the available information on the set of symptoms, without the need to force probabilization. Within each diagnostic class, one must provide only the symptoms that are supported and the level of support, not a full probability function on the entire set of symptoms. One can even introduce a diagnostic class of the "still unknown diseases" in which case the belief function over the symptoms is, of course, vacuous. Furthermore, one may compute the support given to the fact that a patient belongs to the class of "still unknown diseases." This cannot be achieved in probability theory because the state of complete ignorance on the domain of symptoms (as required in the "still unknown diseases" class) cannot be represented adequately in probability theory.

To illustrate the use of the TBM for diagnosis problems, consider this example. Let $\Theta = \{\theta_1, \theta_2, \theta_\omega\}$ be a set of diseases with three mutually exclusive and exhaustive diseases. θ_1 and θ_2 are two known diseases; i.e., we have beliefs on what symptoms might occur when θ_1 occurs or when θ_2 occurs. θ_ω corresponds to the complement of $\{\theta_1, \theta_2\}$ relative to all possible diseases. It represents all the other diseases, including those not yet known. In such a context, our belief on the symptoms can only be vacuous, as we know nothing about the symptoms of a still unknown disease. The vacuous belief function characterizes a state of total ignorance perfectly.

Consider now two sets of symptoms $X = \{x_1, x_2, x_3\}$ and $Y = \{y_1, y_2\}$. Tables 5 and 6 show the beliefs over X and Y for each of the diseases. Essentially, the beliefs represent the facts that θ_1 supports x_3 and y_2, and θ_2 supports x_1 or x_2 (without preference) and y_1. When we only know that θ_1 or θ_2 holds, we have balanced support over X, and some support in favor of y_1.

X	$\{\theta_1\}$ m	bel	$\{\theta_2\}$ m	bel	$\{\theta_w\}$ m	bel
$\{x_1\}$	.0	.0	.0	.0	.0	.0
$\{x_2\}$	.0	.0	.0	.0	.0	.0
$\{x_3\}$	.5	.5	.2	.2	.0	.0
$\{x_1, x_2\}$	.2	.2	.6	.6	.0	.0
$\{x_1, x_3\}$	.0	.5	.1	.3	.0	.0
$\{x_2, x_3\}$	.0	.5	.1	.3	.0	.0
$\{x_1, x_2, x_3\}$	.3	1.0	.0	1.0	1.0	1.0

Table 5 Conditional beliefs (*bel*) and bbm (*m*) on the symptoms $x \subseteq X$ within each of the mutually exclusive and exhaustive diagnoses θ_1, θ_2, and $\theta_w \in \Theta$.

Y	$\{\theta_1\}$ m	bel	$\{\theta_2\}$ m	bel	$\{\theta_w\}$ m	bel
$\{y_1\}$	.1	.1	.6	.6	.0	.0
$\{y_2\}$	.7	.7	.0	.0	.0	.0
$\{y_1, y_2\}$	.1	.9	.4	1.0	1.0	1.0

Table 6 Conditional beliefs (*bel*) and bbm (*m*) on the symptoms $y \subseteq Y$ within each of the mutually exclusive and exhaustive diagnosis θ_1, θ_2, and $\theta_w \in \Theta$.

Table 7 shows the beliefs induced on Θ by the individual observation of symptom x_3 or of symptom y_2, respectively. We assume that the symptoms are independent within each disease, hence the General Bayesian Theorem can be applied. The independence assumption means that if we knew which disease holds, the observation of one of the symptoms would not change our belief about the status of the other symptom. The right part of Table 7 shows the beliefs induced on Θ by the joint observation of symptoms x_3 and y_2. The beliefs are computed by the application of relation in Section 3.5. The symptoms, individually and jointly, essentially support $\{\theta_1, \theta_w\}$. The meaning of $bel(\theta_w | x_3, y_2) = 0.27$ merits further explanation. It quantifies our belief that the joint symptoms x_3 and y_2 are caused neither by θ_1 nor by θ_2. It supports the fact that the joint observation is caused by another disease or by a still unknown disease. A large value for $bel(\theta_w|x_3, y_2)$ supports the fact that we might be looking at new disease. In any case, it should encourage us to look for other potential causes to explain the observations.

Θ	$\begin{array}{c}|x_3\\ m\end{array}$	$\begin{array}{c}|y_2\\ m\end{array}$	m	$\begin{array}{c}|x_3,y_2\\ bel\end{array}$	pl
$\{\theta_1\}$	.00	.00	.00	.00	.64
$\{\theta_2\}$	.00	.00	.00	.00	.24
$\{\theta_w\}$	.12	.08	.27	.27	1.00
$\{\theta_1, \theta_2\}$	.00	.00	.00	.00	.73
$\{\theta_1, \theta_w\}$	.48	.32	.49	.76	1.00
$\{\theta_2, \theta_w\}$	.08	.12	.09	.36	1.00
$\{\theta_1, \theta_2, \theta_w\}$	.32	.48	.15	1.00	1.00

Table 7 Left part: the basic belief masses (m) induced on Θ by the observation of symptom x_3 or of symptom y_2, as computed from the Generalized Bayesian Theorem. Right part: the basic belief masses (m) and the related belief function (bel) and plausibility function (pl) induced on Θ by the joint observation of x_3 and y_2, as computed by the application of Dempster's rule of combination on the bbm obtained after observing x_3 and y_2, respectively.

Table 8 shows the beliefs induced on $\{\theta_1, \theta_2\}$ when we condition our beliefs on Θ on the fact $\{\theta_1, \theta_2\}$, or when we have some *a priori* belief on Θ. The results are obtained by the application of the conjunctive rule of combination applied to the *a priori* belief on Θ and the belief induced by the joint observations. The belief functions shown are normalized.

7 CONCLUSIONS

We presented a survey of the transferable belief model, showing its basic properties and pointing to some of its more intricate features. The potential of the model was illustrated by examples taken from problems encountered in information systems. A major advantage of this model lies in its ability to handle problems that involve uncertainty of the kind that is not directly linked to chance or to objective probabilistic systems. In particular, we showed how this model permits applications that group together data obtained from partially reliable sources of information.

$|x_3, y_2$	$m(\theta_1, \theta_2) = 1$		$m(\theta_1) = .3$ $m(\theta_2) = .7$		$m(\theta_1) = .3$ $m(\theta_1, \theta_2) = .7$	
Θ	m	bel_n	m	bel_n	m	bel_n
$\{\}$	.30	.00	.70	.00	.32	.00
$\{\theta_1\}$	.54	.77	.19	.63	.57	.84
$\{\theta_2\}$	.06	.09	.11	.37	.04	.06
$\{\theta_1, \theta_2\}$	.10	1.00	.00	1.00	.07	1.00

Table 8 The basic belief masses (m) and the related (normalized) belief function (bel_n) induced on Θ by the joint observation of x_3 and y_2, and based on three different *a priori* beliefs on Θ: an *a priori* that rejects θ_ω, a probabilistic *a priori* on $\{\theta_1, \theta_2\}$, and a simple support function on $\{\theta_1, \theta_2\}$.

Acknowledgments

This work was supported in part by the CE-ESPRIT III Basic Research Project 6156 (DRUMS II). Additionally, the work of Philippe Smets was supported by the Communauté Française de Belgique, ARC 92/97-160 (BELON), and the work of Rudolf Kruse was supported by the Fraunhofer Gesellschaft Project No. T/R470/NO191/NO407. The authors would like to thank E. Zimanyi for his helpful comments.

REFERENCES

[1] A. P. Dempster. Upper and lower probabilities induced by a multiple-valued mapping. *Ann. Math. Statistics.*, 38: 325–339, 1967.

[2] D. Dubois and H. Prade. On the unicity of Dempster rule of combination. *International Journal of Intelligent Systems*, 1: 133–142, 1986.

[3] D. Dubois and H. Prade. A set theoretical view of belief functions. *International Journal of General Systems*, 12: 193–226, 1986.

[4] J. Gebhardt and R. Kruse. The context model: an integrating view of vagueness and uncertainty. *International Journal of Approximate Reasoning*, 9: 283–314, 1993.

[5] I. J. Good. Subjective probability as a measure of a non-measurable set. In E. Nagel P. Suppes and A. Tarski, editors, *Logic, Methodology and Philosophy of Science*, pages 319–329. Stanford University Press, 1962.

[6] P. Hajek. Deriving Dempster's rule. In *Proceedings of IPMU International Conference on Information Processing and Management of Uncertainty in Knowledge-Based Systems* (Mallorca, Spain, July 6–10), pages 73–75. UIB, 1992.

[7] J. Y. Jaffray. Application of linear utility theory for belief functions. In L. Saitta B. Bouchon and R. R. Yager, editors, *Uncertainty and Intelligent Systems*, pages 1–8. Springer-Verlag, Berlin, 1988.

[8] R. Kennes. Evidential reasoning in a categorial perspective: conjunction and disjunction of belief functions. In Ph. Smets B. D'Ambrosio and P. P. Bonissone, editors, *Uncertainty in Artificial Intelligence 91*, pages 174–181. Morgan Kaufmann, San Mateo, CA, 1991.

[9] F. Klawonn and E. Schwecke. On the axiomatic justification of Dempster's rule of combination. *International Journal of Intelligent Systems*, 7: 469–478, 1992.

[10] F. Klawonn and Ph. Smets. The dynamic of belief in the transferable belief model and specialization-generalization matrices. In B. D'Ambrosio D. Dubois, M. P. Wellman and Ph. Smets, editors, *Uncertainty in Artificial Intelligence 92*, pages 130–137. Morgan Kaufmann, San Mateo, CA, 1992.

[11] J. Kohlas and P. A. Monney. Representation of evidence by hints. In J. Kacprzyk R. R. Yager, M. Fedrizzi, editor, *Advances in the Dempster-Shafer theory of evidence*, pages 473–492. Wiley, 1994.

[12] J. Kohlas and P. A. Monney. Theory of evidence: a survey of its mathematical foundations, applications and computational aspects. *ZOR—Mathematical Methods of Operations Research*, 39: 35–68, 1994.

[13] J. Kohlas and P. A. Monney. *A Mathematical Theory of Hints. An Approach to Dempster-Shafer Theory of Evidence. Lecture Notes in Economics and Mathematical Systems No. 425*. Springer-Verlag, Berlin, 1995.

[14] B. O. Koopman. The bases of probability. *Bulletin of the American Mathematical Society*, 46: 763–774, 1940.

[15] R. Kruse, D. Nauck, and F. Klawonn. Reasoning with mass. In Ph. Smets B. D'Ambrosio and P. P. Bonissone, editors, *Uncertainty in Artificial Intelligence 91*, pages 182–187. Morgan Kaufmann, San Mateo, CA, 1991.

[16] R. Kruse and E. Schwecke. Specialization: a new concept for uncertainty handling with belief functions. *International Journal General Systems*, 18: 49–60, 1991.

[17] R. Kruse, E. Schwecke, and F. Klawonn. On a tool for reasoning with mass distributions. In *Proceedings of IJCAI 12th International Joint Conference on Artificial Intelligence Vol. 2* (Sydney, Australia, August 24–August 30), pages 1190–1195. IJCAII, 1991.

[18] H. E. Kyburg. *Probability and the Logic of Rational Belief*. Wesleyan University Press, 1961.

[19] X. N. Ling and W. G. Rudd. Combining opinions from several experts. *Applied Artificial Intelligence*, 3: 439–452, 1989.

[20] T. H. Nguyen and Ph. Smets. On dynamics of cautious belief and conditional objects. *International Journal of Approximate Reasoning*, 8: 89–104, 1993.

[21] N. Pal, J. Bezdek, and R. Hemasinha. Uncertainty measures for evidential reasoning i: a review. *International Journal of Approximate Reasoning*, 7: 165–183, 1992.

[22] N. Pal, J. Bezdek, and R. Hemasinha. Uncertainty measures for evidential reasoning ii: new measure of total uncertainty. *International Journal of Approximate Reasoning*, 8: 1–16, 1993.

[23] J. Pearl. *Probabilistic Reasoning in Intelligent Systems: Networks of Plausible Inference*. Morgan Kaufmann, San Mateo, CA, 1988.

[24] R. H. Ruspini. The logical foundations of evidential reasoning. Technical Report Technical Note 408, SRI international, 1986.

[25] L.J. Savage. *Foundations of Statistics*. Wiley, New York, 1954.

[26] G. Shafer. *A Mathematical Theory of Evidence*. Princeton University Press, Princeton, 1976.

[27] G. Shafer. Perspectives in the theory and practice of belief functions. *International Journal Approximate Reasoning*, 4: 323–362, 1990.

[28] Ph. Smets. *Un modéle mathématico-statistique simulant le processus du diagnostic médical*. Thesis, 1978.

[29] Ph. Smets. Medical diagnosis: fuzzy sets and degree of belief. *International Journal of Fuzzy Sets and Systems*, 5: 259–266, 1981.

[30] Ph. Smets. Combining non-distinct pieces of evidence. In *Proceedings of NAFIPS North American Fuzzy Information Processing Systems Workshop* (New Orleans, USA), pages 544–548. NAFIP, 1986.

[31] Ph. Smets. Belief functions. In D. Dubois Ph. Smets, A. Mamdani and H. Prade, editors, *Non standard Logics for Automated Reasoning*, pages 253–286. Academic Press, London, 1988.

[32] Ph. Smets. The combination of evidence in the transferable belief model. *IEEE-Pattern Analysis and Machine Intelligence*, 12: 447–458, 1990.

[33] Ph. Smets. Constructing the pignistic probability function in a context of uncertainty. In L. N. Kanal M. Henrion, R. D. Shachter and J. F. Lemmer, editors, *Uncertainty in Artificial Intelligence 5*, pages 29–40. North Holland, Amsterdam, 1990.

[34] Ph. Smets. Probability of provability and belief functions. *Logique et Analyse*, 133/134: 177–195, 1991.

[35] Ph. Smets. The concept of distinct evidence. In *Proceedings of IPMU International Conference on Information Processing and Management of Uncertainty in Knowledge-Based Systems* (Mallorca, Spain, July 6–10), pages 789–794. IPMU, 1992.

[36] Ph. Smets. The nature of the unnormalized beliefs encountered in the transferable belief model. In D. Dubois, M. P. Wellman, B. D'Ambrosio, and Ph. Smets, editors, *Uncertainty in Artificial Intelligence 92*, pages 292–297. Morgan Kaufmann, San Mateo, 1992.

[37] Ph. Smets. An axiomatic justification for the use of belief function to quantify beliefs. In *Proceedings of IJCAI International Joint Conference on AI* (Chambery, France, August 28 – September 3), pages 598–603. IJCAII, AFIA, 1993.

[38] Ph. Smets. Belief functions: the disjunctive rule of combination and the generalized Bayesian theorem. *International Journal of Approximate Reasoning*, 9: 11–35, 1993.

[39] Ph. Smets. Jeffrey's rule of conditioning generalized to belief functions. In D. Heckerman and A. Mamdani, editors, *UAI 93*, pages 500–505. Morgan Kaufmann, San Mateo, 1993.

[40] Ph. Smets. No Dutch book can be built against the TBM even though update is not obtained by Bayes rule of conditioning. In R. Scozzafava, editor, *SIS, Workshop on Probabilistic Expert Systems*, pages 181–204. SIS, 1993.

[41] Ph. Smets. Probability of deductibility and belief functions. In S. Moral M. Clarke, R. Kruse, editor, *ESQARU 93*, pages 332–340. Springer-Verlag, Berlin, 1993.

[42] Ph. Smets and R. Kennes. The transferable belief model. *Artificial Intelligence*, 66: 191–234, 1994.

[43] C. A. B. Smith. Consistency in statistical inference and decision. *Journal of the Royal Statistical Society*, B23: 1–37, 1961.

[44] P. Smith and O. R. Jones. *The Philosophy of Mind, An Introduction.* Cambridge University Press, 1986.

[45] T. M. Strat. Making decisions with belief functions. In *Proceedings of the 5th Workshop on Uncertainty in Artificial Intelligence* (Windsor, Ontario, August 18–August 20), pages 351–360. UAI, 1989.

[46] T. M. Strat. Decision analysis using belief functions. *International Journal of Approximate Reasoning*, 4: 391–418, 1990.

[47] F. Voorbraak. *As Far as I Know: Epistemic Logic and Uncertainty.* Thesis, 1993.

[48] P. Walley. *Statistical Reasoning with Imprecise Probabilities.* Chapman and Hall, London, 1991.

13

APPROXIMATE REASONING SYSTEMS: HANDLING UNCERTAINTY AND IMPRECISION IN INFORMATION SYSTEMS

Piero P. Bonissone

Information Technology Laboratory
General Electric Corporate Research and Development
Schenectady, NY 12301, USA

1 INTRODUCTION

In this chapter we provide a personal perspective of the progress made in the field of approximate reasoning systems and their relevance and applicability to information systems. Within the scope of this chapter, the concept of information systems covers the entire range of Databases (DB), Information Retrieval (IR), and Knowledge-Based Systems (KBS).

Because of space limitations, we will limit the scope of our discussion to cover the most notable trends and efforts in reasoning with imperfect information, i.e., uncertainty and imprecision. The existing approaches to representing this type of information can be subdivided into two basic categories according to their *qualitative* or *quantitative* characterizations of uncertainty.

Models based on qualitative approaches are usually designed to handle the aspect of uncertainty derived from the incompleteness of the information, such as reasoned assumptions [23] and default reasoning [52]. With a few exceptions, these models are generally inadequate to handle imprecise information because they lack any measure to quantify confidence levels [23]. A few approaches in this group have addressed the representation of uncertainty using either a formal representation, such as knowledge and belief [34], or a heuristic representation, such as the theory of endorsements [17]. The formal approach has a corresponding modal logic theory that determines the mechanism by which inferences (theorems) can be proven or believed to be true. The heuris-

tic approach has a set of context-dependent rules to define the way by which
frame-like structures (endorsements) can be combined, added or removed.

We will further limit our presentation by focusing on the development of the
quantitative approaches.

1.1 Uncertainty and Imprecision

Over the past few years, quantitative uncertainty and imprecision management
have received a vast amount of attention from the researchers in the field [58,
37, 13, 20, 29, 14] leading to the establishment of two well-defined classes of
approaches that differ in the semantics of their numerical representation. The
first class deals with *uncertainty*, and the second one deals with *imprecision*.

Uncertainty is typically caused by the lack of information about the world
to decide if a statement about a state of the world is true or false, whereas
imprecision is generally attributed to the granularity of the language used to
make such a statement.

For instance, let S be a propositional statement about a particular state of the
world. S is defined by the assignment of a value x_1 to a variable V, and is
represented as:
$$S : V \leftarrow x_1 \quad \text{(where } x_1 \in X)$$

Using this example, we can define the following concepts:

Objective Probability: the statement S is true, qualified by an objective
probability value p_1 describing the frequency with which S is true.

Subjective Probability: the statement S is true, qualified by a degree of
belief p_1 describing the willingness of a rational agent to accept any of the
two following bets:

- If you pay him $\$p_1$, then he agrees to pay you \$1 if S is true (for
  $p_1 \in [0, 1]$).
- If you pay him $\$(1 - p_1)$, then he agrees to pay you \$1 if S is false.

The first bet represents the belief that the probability of S is not larger
than p_1; the second bet represents the belief that the probability of S is
not smaller than p_1.

(Crisp) Imprecision: the value v_1 is not defined by a crisp number but rather constrained by intervals or disjunctions. These boundaries are hard constraints on the value of V, represented by a characteristic function mapping X into $\{0,1\}$.

Vagueness/Fuzziness: the value v_1 is not defined by a crisp number but rather constrained by ill-defined boundaries. These boundaries are soft constraints on the value of V, represented by a characteristic function mapping X into $[0,1]$.

Inaccuracy: the value x_1 is an incorrect value of V. We have complete inaccuracy if the correct value of V and x_1 are disjoint intervals or different numbers. Partial inaccuracy occurs if the correct value and x_1 have overlapping granules (but the real value is not a proper subset of x_1).

Incompleteness: Lack of constraints on the value to be assigned to variable V, e.g., null value (not available). The characteristic function of the values of V is the universe X.

Inconsistency: No possible set of constraints on the value of V, i.e., the characteristic function of the values of V is the empty set $\emptyset$.

Of course, this paradigm does not cover all the useful concepts related to imperfect information. Concepts that cannot be easily defined using the proposed paradigm include (1) the case in which the null value represents *not applicable* rather that not available (neither the universe of discourse X nor the empty set $\emptyset$ would be adequate choices), (2) ontological uncertainty, (3) indistinguishability, i.e., equivalence due to the scale used (discretization), (4) structural information needed to resolve contradictions that led to inconsistency [ATMS], (5) uncertainty regarding the type or the domain, (6) dynamic value assignments, changing over time (temporal uncertainty, obsolescence, trending, updating), (7) frame of discernment changing over time. We will limit our discussion to a subset of the entire problem.

At the beginning of this section we defined *uncertainty* and *imprecision* as two classes of imperfect information. We argued that uncertainty stems from the lack of information about the world and our need to attach a truth value to a well-defined statement describing the state of such a world. These situations are typically captured by subjective or objective probabilities (and by other probabilistic methods in which some of Cox's axioms have been relaxed). We also claimed that imprecision stems from the coarse or vague granularity of the language used to make such statements. These situations are typically captured by vagueness and fuzziness. Let us now analyze some of the approaches used to handle these two classes of imperfect information.

1.2 Approaches

Among the approaches developed to handle uncertainty we find (objective and subjective) probability theory [3, 2, 21], confidence factors [63], belief functions [59], and possibility theory [26].

These approaches try to estimate the propensity, the credibility, the belief, or the possibility that a statement S (about a state of the world) is true.

Among the approaches developed to handle imprecision we find: interval analysis (for range values) [47], fuzzy sets (for vagueness) [79], and default logic (for incompleteness) [52].

The first two approaches try to bound, with either crisp or fuzzy constraints, the ranges or sets of values that the variable V in the statement S (about the state of the world) can take. Default logic actually tries to define the set of possible worlds (extensions) in which the variable takes a precise value.

We will now describe two approaches. One is the probabilistic reasoning approach, based on probability theory. The other one is the fuzzy reasoning approach, based on the semantics of fuzzy sets and many-valued logics. In this chapter we will illustrate and compare these approaches, and we will conclude with a review of efforts aimed at improving their scalability and real-time performance. Finally, we will also try to evaluate their relevance to information systems.

1.3 Approximate Reasoning Systems: A Possible World View

Reasoning systems must attach a truth value to statements about the state or the behavior of a real-world system. When this hypothesis evaluation is not possible because of the lack of complete and certain information, approximate reasoning techniques are used to determine a set of possible worlds that are logically consistent with the available information. These possible worlds are characterized by a set of propositional variables and their associated values.

As it is generally impractical to describe these possible worlds to an acceptable level of detail, approximate reasoning techniques seek to determine some properties of the set of possible solutions or some constraints on the values of such properties. The previous possible-world interpretation for approximate reasoning systems was originally proposed by Ruspini [53, 54].

A large number of approximate reasoning techniques have been developed over the past decade to provide these solutions. The reader is referred to [4, 50] for a survey. We will now analyze two ot the most common approximate reasoning techniques: probabilistic and fuzzy logic (or similarity) based reasoning.

Probabilistic Reasoning

Probability-based, or probabilistic, reasoning seeks to describe the constraints on the variables that characterize the possible worlds by identifying their conditional probability distributions given the evidence in hand. Its supporting formalisms are based on the concept of set measures, additive real functions defined over certain subsets of some space. Probabilistic methods seldom make categorical assertions about the actual state of the system being investigated. Rather, they indicate that there is an experimentally determined (or believed) tendency or propensity for the system to be in some specified state. Thus, probabilistic methods are oriented primarily toward decisions that are optimal, describing the tendency or propensity of truth of a proposition without assuring its actual validity. Depending on the nature of the information, probabilistic reasoning estimates the frequency or propensity of the truth of a hypothesis as determined by prior observation (objectivist interpretation), or the degree of belief describing the willingness of a rational agent to accept a particular bet based on the actual truth of the hypothesis (subjectivist interpretation).

The basic inferential mechanism used in probabilistic reasoning is the conditioning operation. From a practical computational viewpoint, probabilistic methods suffer from problems associated with the reliable determination of all required joint and conditional probabilities. In complex systems, many variables interrelate in ways that cannot be expressed in terms of simpler interactions. In these cases, the complexity of probabilistic inference is exponential in the size of the largest subgraph into which the system can be decomposed.

Fuzzy Logic Based Reasoning

Conversely, following Ruspini's interpretation of similarity, fuzzy logic based reasoning [79] seeks to describe the constraints on the values of the variables of the possible worlds in terms of their similarity to other sets of possible worlds. The supporting formalisms are based on the mathematical concept of set distances or metrics, instead of set measures. These methods focus on single situations and cases. Rather than measuring the tendency of the given proposition to be valid, these methods seek to find another related or similar proposition that is valid. This proposition is usually less specific and resembles (according to some measure of similarity) the original hypothesis of interest.

The single case orientation of similarity-based techniques makes them particularly suitable for Case-Based Reasoning (CBR). In CBR, it is typically the case that the problem in hand (probe) has never been encountered before. The inference in CBR is based on the existence of cases similar enough (i.e., close enough) to the probe, to justify the adaptability of their solution to the current problem. These techniques are also very suitable to represent the subjective degrees of belief inherent in the knowledge bases used to interpret and understand tactical situations. Typically, these situations have never been encountered before, but the problem domain experts can describe and interpret similar, more generic, prototypical situations.

The basic inferential mechanism used in fuzzy logic based reasoning is the *generalized modus-ponens* [83], which makes use of inferential chains and the properties of a similarity function to relate the state of affairs in the two worlds that are at the extremes of an inferential chain.

It should be noted that there are other interpretations for fuzzy logic semantics, which are not based on possible-world semantics. Of special interest is Zadeh's own interpretation of a possibility distribution "as a fuzzy restriction which acts as an elastic constraint on the values that may be assigned to a variable" [82]. This interpretation, in conjunction with the linguistic variable approach [83], is the basis for the development of numerous fuzzy control applications [72].

As a final comment regarding the proposed typology for approximate reasoning systems, we want to consider those hybrid situations that require the simultaneous representation of probability and fuzziness. Such cases were analyzed by Zadeh in the definition of the probability measure of a fuzzy events [80], and by Smets in the extension of belief functions to fuzzy sets [64].

Given the duality of purpose and characteristics between probabilistic and fuzzy logic based methods, we can conclude that these technologies ought to be regarded as being complementary rather than competitive.

2 PROBABILISTIC APPROACHES

Some of the earliest techniques found among the approaches derived from probability are based on single-valued representations. These techniques started from approximate methods, such as the modified Bayesian rule [30] and confirmation theory [63], and evolved into formal methods for propagating probability values over Bayesian belief networks [49, 50].

Another trend among the probabilistic approaches is represented by interval-valued representations such as Dempster-Shafer theory [22, 59, 45].

2.1 Bayesian Belief Networks

Over the last five years, considerable efforts have been devoted to improve the computational efficiency of Bayesian belief networks for trees and small polytrees and for directed acyclic graphs (influence diagrams) [39, 55].

An efficient propagation of belief on Bayesian Networks has been originally proposed by Pearl [49]. In his work, Pearl describes an efficient updating scheme for trees and, to a lesser extent, for polytrees [43, 51]. However, as the complexity of the graph increases from trees to polytrees to general graphs, so does the computational complexity. The complexity for trees is $O(n^2)$, where n is the number of values per node in the tree. The complexity for polytrees is $O(K^m)$, where K is the number of values per parent node and m is the number of parents per child. This number is the size of the table attached to each node. Since the table must be constructed manually (and updated automatically), it is reasonable to assume that the table will be small. The complexity for multi-connected graphs is $O(K^n)$, where K is the number of values per node and n is the size of the largest nondecomposable subgraph. To handle such complexity, techniques such as moralization and propagation in a tree of cliques [44] and loop cutset conditioning [71, 68] are typically used to decompose the original problem (graph) into a set of smaller problems (subgraphs).

When this problem decomposition process is not possible, exact methods must be abandoned in favor of approximate methods. The most common among these methods are clustering, bounding conditioning [38], and simulation techniques, such as logic samplings and Markov simulations [36]. Figure 1 illustrates a taxonomy of these Bayesian inference mechanisms.

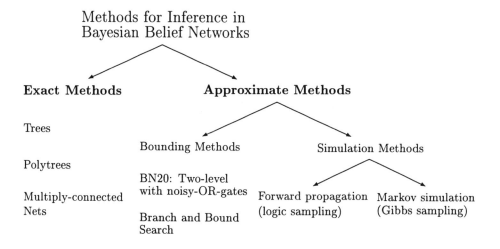

Figure 1 Taxonomy of inference mechanisms for Bayesian belief networks (provided by Max Henrion).

2.2   Dempster-Shafer Theory (Belief Functions)

Belief functions were introduced in an axiomatic manner by Shafer [59]. Their original purpose was to compute the degree of belief of statements made by different sources (or witnesses) from a subjective probability of the sources' reliability.

Many other interpretations of belief functions have also been presented, ranging from functions induced from some probability measure and multivalued mappings [22] or compatibility relations [45] to probability of provability [51] to inner measures [53, 31] to a nonprobabilistic model of transferable belief [66] to random sets [48].

All these interpretation share the same static component of the theory: the Möbius transform that defines a mapping from basic probability assignments (masses assigned to subsets of the frame of discernment) to the computation of the lower bound (belief) of a proposition (a region defined in the same frame of discernment). An inverse Möbius transform can be used to recover the masses from the belief. All these interpretations also share the same definition of the upper bound (usually referred to as plausibility).

More specifically, this formalism defines a function that maps subsets of a space of propositions Θ on the [0,1] scale. The sets of partial beliefs are represented by mass distributions of a unit of belief across the propositions in Θ. This distribution is called *basic probability assignment (bpa)*.inxxBasic probability assignmentThe total certainty over the space is 1. A nonzero *bpa* can be given to the entire space Θ to represent the degree of ignorance. Given a space of propositions Θ, referred to as frame of discernment, a function $m : 2^\Theta \to [0, 1]$ is called a basic probability assignment if it satisfies the following three conditions:

1. $m(\emptyset) = 0$ where $\emptyset$ is the empty set
2. $0 \leq m(A) \leq 1$
3. $\sum_{A \subseteq \Theta} m(A) = 1$

The certainty of any proposition A is then represented by the interval $[Bel(A), Pl(A)]$, where $Bel(A)$ and $Pl(A)$ are defined as

$$Bel(A) = \sum_{x \subseteq A} m(x) \qquad (13.1)$$

$$Pl(A) = \sum_{x \cap A \neq \emptyset} m(x) \qquad (13.2)$$

From the above definitions the following relation can be derived:

$$Bel(A) = 1 - Pl(\neg A)$$

Equations 13.1 and 13.2 represent the static component of the theory, which is common to all interpretations. However, these interpretations do not share the same dynamic component of the theory: the process of updating (i.e., conditioning or evidence combination). This issue has been recently addressed by various researchers [33, 66].

Given the beliefs (or masses) induced by two pieces of evidences for two propositions A and B, Dempster's rule of combination can be used (under assumptions of independence) to derive their combined belief.

If m_1 and m_2 are two *bpas* induced from two independent sources, a third *bpa*, $m(C)$, expressing the pooling of the evidence from the two sources, can be computed by using Dempster's rule of combination:

$$m(C) = \frac{\displaystyle\sum_{A_i \cap B_j = C} m_1(A_i) \cdot m_2(B_j)}{1 - \displaystyle\sum_{A_i \cap B_j = \emptyset} m_1(A_i) \cdot m_2(B_j)} \qquad (13.3)$$

If proposition B is true (i.e., event B has occurred), then $Bel(B) = 1$ and from Dempster rule of combination, we can derive a formula for conditioning A given B:

$$Bel(A \mid B) = \frac{Bel(A \cup \neg B) - Bel(\neg B)}{1 - Bel(\neg B)}$$

This expression is compatible with the interpretation of belief as evidence, and as inner measure. However, this expression is not compatible with the interpretation of belief as the lower envelope of a family of probability distributions. Under such interpretation, the correct expression for conditioning is

$$Bel(A \parallel B) = \frac{Bel(A \cap B)}{Bel(A \cap B) + Pl(\neg A \cap B)}$$

The interested reader is referred to reference [60] for a lucid explanation and an updated bibliography on belief functions.

As for the case of belief networks, a variety of exact and approximate methods have been proposed to perform inferences using belief functions. Typically, the exact methods require additional constraints on the structure of the evidence. Figure 2 illustrates a taxonomy of Dempster-Shafer (D-S) inference mechanisms.

D-S Exact Methods

In the general case, the evaluation of the degrees of belief requires time exponential in $|\Theta|$, the cardinality of the frame of discernment, which is caused by the need of possibly enumerating all the subset and superset of a given set. Barnett [1] showed that when the frame of discernment is discrete and each piece of evidence supports only a singleton proposition or its negation, the computational-time complexity can be reduced from exponential to linear by combining the belief functions in a simplifying order.

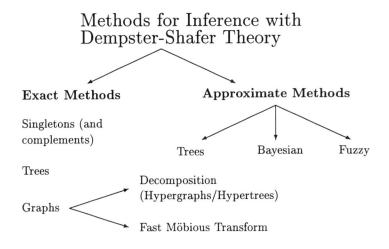

Figure 2   Taxonomy of inference mechanisms for Dempster-Shafer.

Strat [69] proved that when the frame of discernment is continuous and the evidence supports only contiguous intervals along the number line, the complexity can be reduced to $O(n^2)$, where n is the number of atomic propositions, i.e., intervals of unit length.

By imposing a tree structure restriction on the evidence, Shafer and Logan [61] implemented a system that derives exact belief functions. Hierarchical evidence enables a partitioning of the frame of discernment Θ and a great resulting efficiency over the unrestricted domain of size $|\Theta|$. While the unrestricted D-S calculus is NP-complete, the Shafer and Logan algorithm is order $O(nf)$, where $n = |\Theta|$ and f is the branching factor of the tree structure.

Shenoy and Shafer addressed the issue of computing belief functions over an unrestricted graph by creating a hypergraph, decomposing it into smaller subgraphs (via a covering hypertree), and finally using the Markov tree associated with the hypertree to perform local propagations [62].

Another useful algorithm aimed at decreasing the computational complexity of belief propagation is the fast Möbius transform [67], which is the fast Fourier transform equivalent for the Möbius transform described by equation 13.1.

D-S Approximate Methods

There are many approximate methods to efficiently compute belief functions. Because of space constraints we will only cite a few. Using a tree structure restriction, Gordon and Shortliffe [32] propose an algorithm to compute approximate belief functions when different pieces of evidence are relevant to different levels of abstraction in a hierarchy of diseases. A Bayesian approximation in which the probability mass is distributed uniformly among the elements of the subset of Θ has been proposed by Voorbraak [74]. Finally, Dubois and Prade [28] propose a consonant approximation of belief functions that is mathematically equivalent to a fuzzy set.

Decisions with Belief Functions

Belief theory is a relatively new theory and, unlike probability, does not yet have a fully developed decision theory. Initial work in this direction has been proposed by Jaffray [41], Strat [70], and Smets [65].

3   FUZZY LOGIC BASED APPROACHES

Among the nonprobabilistic approaches, the most notable ones are based on a fuzzy-valued representation of imprecision. These include Zadeh's possibility theory and linguistic variable approach [82, 83], and the triangular-norm based approach [56, 25, 5, 10, 11].

The approach proposed by Zadeh is based on the notion that fuzziness is fundamentally different from randomness and, as such, cannot be modeled by traditional probabilistic techniques. The distinction between randomness and fuzziness is based on the different types of uncertainty captured by each concept. In randomness, the uncertainty is derived by the nondeterministic membership of a point (in the sample space) to a well-defined region in that space. The sample space represents the set of possible values for the random variable. The well-defined region represents an event. The region's characteristic function creates a dichotomy in the universe of discourse of the possible values for the random variable: when the point falls within the boundary of the region, it fully belongs to such a region. Otherwise, the point's membership in the region is zero. Probability measures the tendency (frequency) with which such a random variable takes values inside the region.

In fuzziness, the uncertainty is derived from the partial membership of a point (in the universe of discourse) in an imprecisely defined region in that space. The region represents a fuzzy set. The characteristic function of the fuzzy set does not create a dichotomy in the universe of discourse; it maps the universe of discourse into the interval [0,1] instead of the set {0,1}. The partial membership of the point does not represent any frequency. It defines the degree to which that particular value of the universe of discourse satisfies the property that characterizes the fuzzy set.

Because space constraints prevent us from citing the large fuzzy sets literature, we would like to refer the reader to a compilation of selected papers by Zadeh, which provides a chronological description of the evolution of this theory [77].

We will conclude the analysis of fuzzy logic based reasoning by briefly discussing an approach based on many-valued logic operators (triangular norms) and the generalized *modus ponens*.

3.1 Triangular Norm Based Reasoning Systems

Triangular norms (T-norms) and their dual T-conorms are two-place functions from $[0, 1] \times [0, 1]$ to [0,1] that are monotonic, commutative, and associative [56, 57, 10, 5]. They are the most general families of binary functions that satisfy the requirements of the conjunction and disjunction operators, respectively. Their corresponding boundary conditions satisfy the truth tables of the Boolean AND and OR operators.

Any T-norm $T(A, B)$ falls in the interval $T_w(A, B) \leq T(A, B) \leq \min(A, B)$, where
$$T_w(A, B) = \begin{cases} \min(A, B) & \text{if} \max(A, B) = 1 \\ 0 & \text{otherwise} \end{cases}$$

The corresponding DeMorgan dual T-conorm, denoted $S(A, B)$, is defined as
$$S(A, B) = 1 - T(1 - A, 1 - B)$$

$T_w(A, B)$ is referred to as the *drastic* T-norm (to reflect its extreme behavior) and is clearly noncontinuous. By changing one of the axioms of the T-norms [56], we can derive a subset of T-norms, referred to as *copulas*, such that any copula $T(A, B)$ falls in the interval $\max(0, A + B - 1) \leq T(A, B) \leq \min(A, B)$.

In fuzzy logic the conjunction and disjunction operators are the minimum and maximum, respectively (upper and lower bounds of the T-norm and T-conorm ranges, respectively). These operators play a key role in the definition of the generalized *modus ponens.*

These T-norm-based reasoning techniques were implemented in RUM/PRIMO, a fuzzy expert system that was developed by the author in 1987 [11] and further refined in the early 1990s [7].

Knowledge Representation in RUM/PRIMO

Uncertainty is represented in RUM/PRIMO in both facts and rules. Facts represent the assignment of values to a set of propositional variables. Rules are acyclic quantitative Horn clauses in which a conjunct of antecedents implies (to a certain degree of belief) the rule consequent.

Facts are qualified by an uncertainty interval. The interval's lower bound represents the minimal degree of confirmation for the value assignment. The upper bound represents the degree to which the evidence failed to refute the value assignment. The interval's width represents the amount of ignorance attached to the value assignment. The uncertainty intervals are propagated and aggregated by T-norm-based calculi.

Rules are discounted by a degree of sufficiency, indicating the strength with which the antecedent implies the consequent and a degree of necessity, indicating the degree to which a failed antecedent implies a negated consequent.

Inference

Inference in RUM/PRIMO is performed by five uncertainty calculi based on the following T-norms:

$$T_1(a,b) \quad = \quad \max(0, a + b - 1)$$

$$T_{1.5}(a,b) \quad = \quad \begin{cases} (a^{0.5} + b^{0.5} - 1)^2 & \text{if } (a^{0.5} + b^{0.5}) \geq 1 \\ 0 & \text{otherwise} \end{cases}$$

$$T_2(a,b) \quad = \quad ab$$

$$T_{2.5}(a,b) \quad = \quad (a^{-1} + b^{-1} - 1)^{-1}$$

$$T_3(a,b) \quad = \quad \min(a,b)$$

4 CONCLUSIONS

4.1 Real-Time Approximate Reasoning Systems

We conclude this discussion with a few remarks on the applicability of approximate reasoning systems to real-world problems requiring real-time performance. This performance is necessary if we want to guarantee the techniques' scalability from small data sets to large databases. To achieve real-time performance levels, probabilistic reasoning systems need an efficient updating algorithm. The main problem consists in conditioning the existing information with respect to the new evidence: the computation of the new posterior probabilities in general belief networks is NP-hard [18]. A variety of solutions have been proposed, ranging from compilation techniques to shift the burden from run-time to compile-time, to the determination of bounds of the posterior probabilities. In particular, Heckerman, Breese, and Horvitz [35] proposed a decision-theoretic based analysis of computation versus compilation to determine the conditions under which run-time computation is preferable to lookup tables (generated at compile time). Horvitz *et al.* [38] proposed a method to approximate the posterior probabilities of the variables in each subgraph of a belief network. This method, called bounded conditioning, defines the upper and lower bounds of these probabilities and, if given enough resources, converges on the final point probabilities.

Because of its different underlying theory, fuzzy logic based reasoning does not exhibit the same complexity problems as probabilistic reasoning. Most of the efforts aimed at achieving real-time performance from fuzzy logic based reasoning systems have been based on translation and compilation techniques [12, 6] or hardware solutions [19, 75].

Among the compilation techniques, a notable effort is RUMrunner, RUM's run-time system. RUMrunner is a software tool that transforms the customized knowledge base generated during the development phase into a fast and efficient real-time application. This goal is achieved by a combination of efforts: the translation of RUM's complex data structure into simpler, more efficient ones (to reduce overhead); the compilation of the rule set into a network (to avoid run-time search); the load-time estimation of each rule's execution cost (to determine, at run-time, the execution cost of any given deductive path); and the planning mechanism for path selection (to determine the largest relevant rule subset which could be executed within a given time-budget).

Currently there are several hardware solutions to the problem of real-time performance for fuzzy logic based reasoning system. Most of these solutions were inspired by the early research on fuzzy chips by Togai and Watanabe [19, 75]. These chips were used in a variety of applications of fuzzy logic to industrial control.

Fuzzy controllers (FC) [72] represent one of the earliest instances of simple yet effective knowledge-based systems successfully deployed in the field. Their main use has been the replacement of the human operator in the feedback control loop of industrial processes. Their key advantage has been their cost-effectiveness in quickly synthesizing nonlinear controllers for dynamic systems. This technology has enabled us to reduce design cycle time during the development phase by using an interactive computing environment based on a high-level language with its local semantics, interpreter, and compiler. We also achieved efficiency and portability by cross-compiling the resulting FC knowledge bases or nonlinear control surfaces prior to deployment.

Initially outlined by Zadeh [81] and explored by Mamdani in the early 1970s [46, 42], fuzzy controllers applications exhibited their first industrial and commercial growth in Japan almost a decade later [72, 78, 73]. Since then, many Japanese companies have offered consumer-oriented products enhanced by fuzzy controller technology, such as camera autofocus control, automatic transmission control, room air conditioner control, clotheswasher control, and elevator control, to mention a few. With a better understanding of FC synthesis and analysis methodologies and the availability of commercial FC development tools, FC applications have also become more popular in the USA and Europe [9].

4.2   Information Systems

Finally, we want to analyze the applicability and impact of approximate reasoning techniques to handle uncertainty and imprecision in information systems.

Conventional DBs (with Complete and Precise Data)

- We can handle crisp and fuzzy imprecision in query formulation. This can be considered metainformation defining the imprecision/vagueness of the query formulated by the user.

- We can also handle uncertainty (probabilistic or belief) in query formulation (user's goal recognition).

The imprecise or vague query formulation can be captured by extending the Dempster-Shafer formalism to handle fuzzy events with crisp data [64].

In section 2.2 we always considered the query to be a well-defined event, i.e., a crisp set in the frame of discernment. However, it is possible to determine the lower and upper bounds of ill-defined queries (events) that will be represented as fuzzy sets in the frame of discernment. Let us assume that our query is the event B, defined by its characteristic function $\mu_B(x)$, for $x \in \Theta$. Furthermore, let us assume that the (precise) data in the DB is represented by sets A_s containing singletons in Θ. The lower and upper bounds $L(B)$ and $U(B)$ can be computed as

$$L(B) = \sum_{A_s \subseteq \Theta} m(A_s) \times (\bigwedge_{x \in A_s} \mu_B(x))$$
$$U(B) = \sum_{A_s \subseteq \Theta} m(A_s) \times (\bigvee_{x \in A_s} \mu_B(x))$$

Note that if the event B is crisp, i.e., its characteristic function $\mu_B(x)$ only takes value in $\{0,1\}$, the above formulae reduce to the crisp case defined earlier [64].

Clearly, the above formulation holds for DB containing imprecise but not vague data, i.e., crisp-range values or disjunctions. In this case, each range-valued or disjunctive data is still represented by each sets A_s, which now contains a Boolean sets of the points of the frame of discernment.

DBs Containing (Crisp or Fuzzy) Imprecise Data

- We can handle crisp and fuzzy imprecision in query formulation. Again, this is meta-information defining the imprecision/vagueness of the query formulated by the user.

- We can handle uncertainty (probabilistic or belief) in query formulation (user's goal recognition).

By continuing the generalization process, it is possible, based on fuzzy data, to determine lower and upper bounds of ill-defined events. (Imprecise data can be treated as fuzzy data whose characteristic function is defined by a Boolean interval). One possible way to compute those bounds is by using the concept of necessity and possibility measures:

$$
\begin{aligned}
L(B) &= \sum_{A_s \subseteq \Theta} m(A_s) \times N(B \mid A_s) \\
U(B) &= \sum_{A_s \subseteq \Theta} m(A_s) \times \Pi(B \mid A_s)
\end{aligned}
$$

where $N(B \mid A_s)$ is the *necessity measure* of B given A_s, and $\Pi(B \mid A_s)$ is the *possibility measure* of B given A_s.

The necessity measure $N(p \mid d)$ represents the degree of semantic entailment of a pattern descriptor p given a datum d. The possibility measure $\Pi(p \mid d)$ represents the degree of intersection between the same pattern and datum. Thus, the interval defined by $[N(p \mid d), \Pi(p \mid d)]$ represents the lower and upper bounds of the degree of matching between such pattern and datum.

More specifically, let X be the universe of discourse of the pattern descriptor p, and of the datum d; i.e., X is the collection of all the possible values that can be tested by p or that can be taken by d. Let the meaning of the pattern descriptor p be described by its characteristic function $\mu_P(x)$. Let $\mu_D(x)$ be the characteristic function of the datum d. By definition, we have $\mu_P : X \to [0, 1]$ and $\mu_D : X \to [0, 1]$, for all x in X.

Then the necessity measure is defined as

$$
\begin{aligned}
N(p \mid d) &= \bigwedge_x (\mu_D(x) \to \mu_P(x)) \\
&= \bigwedge_x (\max[(1 - \mu_D(x)), \mu_P(x)]) \\
&= 1 - \bigvee_x (\min[(1 - \mu_P(x)), \mu_D(x)])
\end{aligned}
$$

The possibility measure is defined as

$$
\Pi(p \mid d) = \bigvee_x (\min[\mu_P(x), \mu_D(x)])
$$

Notice that $N(p \mid d) = 1 - \Pi(\neg p \mid d)$; i.e., the degree of necessity of a pattern p given a datum d is equivalent to the degree of *impossibility* of the negation of the pattern given the same datum. In the degenerate case in which p and d are crisp sets, defined by Boolean characteristic functions, the above is the same relationship that exists between the necessity and the possibility operators in modal logics; i.e., $\Box(p) = \neg \Diamond \neg(p)$ [40]. These measures were extensively studied by Dubois and Prade [24].

There are several current efforts aimed at extending existing database manager systems and query language (such as SQL) to allow the representation of (fuzzy) imprecise queries. The interested reader is referred to the work by Bosc and Pivert [16].

Information Retrieval and Case-Based Reasoning Systems

■ We can handle crisp and fuzzy imprecision in probe definition/query formulation in both IR and CBR systems.

The use of fuzzy logic in information-retrieval systems is exemplified by the work of Bordogna and Pasi [15]. Their effort is aimed at developing a compound fuzzy representation of documents using linguistic quantifiers. In this specific work, the authors use the ordered weighted averaging operators [76] to create the aggregation functions required to evaluate the document retrieval.

In case-based reasoning, fuzzy logic is typically used in the the computation of similarity metrics for CBR retrieval, as illustrated in reference [8]. In this work, a case is defined as a situation/solution pair, indexed by surface (observed) and abstract (derived) features. The mapping from surface to abstract features, is based on fuzzy predicates and plausible rules implemented in Plausible Reasoning Module (PRIMO). This mapping represents the situation descriptor of the case in a more robust feature space.

The similarity of each abstract feature is computed as the complement of the distance between the fuzzy numbers representing the feature values. The abstract features similarities are aggregated hierarchically according to a semantic taxonomy. The aggregation is based on (weighted) T-norms, averaging operators, and T-conorms [25, 27].

Knowledge-Based Systems

■ We can handle uncertainty and imprecision in rule-based and graph-based reasoning systems.

In section 3.1 we covered the use of fuzzy logic in rule-based systems. However, there is also a wide body of literature covering the representational and inferential issues associated with the propagation of probability values (or degrees of belief) over graphs of different topologies. These graphs could have been manually derived from the problem formulation or automatically derived from compiling rule sets. The interested reader is referred to references [58, 37, 13, 20].

4.3 Final Remarks

In conclusion, we proposed a framework for comparing various aspects of imperfect information, ranging from uncertainty to imprecision and vagueness. We provided a taxonomy of approximate reasoning systems, covering probabilistic, belief, and fuzzy set based approaches, and we discussed some of their inferential mechanisms: *conditioning*, for probability and belief-based systems, *modus ponens*, for the fuzzy-based systems. We focused on the real-time requirements of these systems, highlighting the role of rule compilation for fuzzy logic based systems (both expert systems and fuzzy controllers). Finally, we discussed the extension of query formulation to handle imprecise and vague probes in databases and case-based reasoning.

REFERENCES

[1] J. A. Barnett. Computational methods for a mathematical theory of evidence. In *Proceedings of the 7th International Joint Conference on Artificial Intelligence*, Vancouver, British Columbia, Canada, 1981.

[2] T. Bayes. An essay towards solving a problem in the doctrine of chances. *Philosophical Transactions of the Royal Society of London*, 53: 370–418, 1763. (Facsimile reproduction with commentary by E.C. Molina in "Facsimiles of Two Papers by Bayes" E. Deming, Washington, DC, 1940, New York, 1963. Also reprinted with commentary by G. A. Barnard in Biometrika, 25, 293–215, 1970.).

[3] J. Bernoulli. *Ars Conjectandi*. Basel, Switzerland, 1713. (Reprinted in 1968 by Culture and Civilisation, 115 Avenue Gabriel Lebon, Brussels. Part IV, translated into English, is available in microfiche from the Clearinghouse for Scientific and Technical Information, Washington, DC.).

[4] P. P. Bonissone. Plausible reasoning: Coping with uncertainty in expert systems. In S. Shapiro, editor, *Encyclopedia of Artificial Intelligence*, pages 854–863. John Wiley, New York, 1987.

[5] P. P. Bonissone. Summarizing and propagating uncertain information with triangular norms. *International Journal of Approximate Reasoning*, 1(1): 71–101, January 1987.

[6] P. P. Bonissone. A compiler for fuzzy logic controllers. In *Proceedings of the International Fuzzy Engineering Symposium (IFES-91)*, pages 706–717, November 1991.

[7] P. P. Bonissone, J. Aragones, and J. Stillman. PRIMO: A tool for reasoning with incomplete and uncertain information. In *Proceedings of the Third International Conference on Information Processing and Management of Uncertainty in Knowledge-Based Systems (IPMU-90)*, pages 325–327, Paris, France, July 1990.

[8] P. P. Bonissone and S. Ayub. Similarity measures for case-based reasoning systems. In *Proceedings of the Fourth International Conference on Information Processing and Management of Uncertainty in Knowledge-Based Systems (IPMU-92)*, pages 483–487, Palma, Spain, 1992.

[9] P. P. Bonissone, V. Badami, K. Chiang, P. Khedkar, K. Marcelle, and M. Schutten. Industrial applications of fuzzy logic at General Electric. *Proceedings of the IEEE*, 83(3): 450–465, March 1995.

[10] P. P. Bonissone and K. Decker. Selecting uncertainty calculi and granularity: An experiment in trading-off precision and complexity. In L. N. Kanal and J. F. Lemmer, editors, *Uncertainty in Artificial Intelligence*, pages 217–247. North-Holland, Amsterdam, The Netherlands, 1986.

[11] P. P. Bonissone, S. S. Gans, and K. S. Decker. RUM: A layered architecture for reasoning with uncertainty. In *Proceedings of the 10th International Joint Conference Artificial Intelligence*, pages 891–898. AAAI, 1987.

[12] P. P. Bonissone and P. C. Halverson. Time-constrained reasoning under uncertainty. *The Journal of Real Time Systems*, 2(1/2): 22–45, 1990.

[13] P. P. Bonissone, M. Henrion, L. N. Kanal, and J. F. Lemmer, editors. *Uncertainty in Artificial Intelligence 6*. North-Holland, Amsterdam, The Netherlands, 1991.

[14] P. P. Bonissone and E. Ruspini, editors. *Proceedings of the IEEE International Conference on Fuzzy Systems*. IEEE, March 1993.

[15] G. Borgogna and G. Pasi. Controlling retrieval through a user-adaptive representation of documents. *International Journal of Approximate Reasoning*, 12(3/4): 317–339, April/May 1995.

[16] P. Bosc and O. Pivert. SQLf: A relational database language for fuzzy querying. *IEEE Transactions on Fuzzy Systems*, 3(1): 1–17, 1995.

[17] P. Cohen. *Heuristic Reasoning about Uncertainty: An Artificial Intelligence Approach*. Pittman, Boston, Massachusetts, 1985.

[18] G. F. Cooper. The computational complexity of probabilistic inference using belief networks. *Artificial Intelligence*, 42(2–3): 393–405, 1990.

[19] R. J. Corder. A high speed fuzzy processor. In *Proceedings of the Third International Fuzzy Systems Association*, pages 379–389. IFSA, August 1989.

[20] B. D'Ambrosio, P. Smets, and P. Bonissone, editors. *Proceedings of the Seventh Conference on Uncertainty in AI*. Morgan Kaufmann, San Mateo, California, 1991.

[21] B. DeFinetti. La prévision: ses lois logiques, ses sources subjectives. *Annales de l'Institut H. Poincaré*, 7: 1–68, 1937.

[22] A. P. Dempster. Upper and lower probabilities induced by a multivalued mapping. *Annals of Mathematical Statistics*, 38: 325–339, 1967.

[23] J. Doyle. Methodological simplicity in expert system construction: The case of judgements and reasoned assumptions. *The AI Magazine*, 4(2): 39–43, 1983.

[24] D. Dubois and H. Prade. *Fuzzy Sets and Systems: Theory and Applications*. Academic Press, New York, 1980.

[25] D. Dubois and H. Prade. Criteria aggregation and ranking of alternatives in the framework of fuzzy set theory. In H. J. Zimmerman, L. A. Zadeh, and B. R. Gaines, editors, *TIMS/Studies in the Management Science, Vol. 20*, pages 209–240. Elsevier, 1984.

[26] D. Dubois and H. Prade. *Théorie des Possibilités: Applications à la représentation de connaissances en informatique*. Masson, Editeur, Paris, France, 1985. (Translated as *Possibility Theory: An Approach to Computerized Processing of Uncertainty*, Plenum Press, New York, 1988).

[27] D. Dubois and H. Prade. Weighted minimum and maximum operations in fuzzy set theory. *Information Science*, 39: 205–210, 1986.

[28] D. Dubois and H. Prade. Consonant approximations of belief functions. *International Journal of Approximate Reasoning*, 4(5/6): 419–449, 1990.

[29] D. Dubois, H. Prade, and J. Bezdek, editors. *Proceedings of the IEEE International Conference on Fuzzy Systems*. IEEE, March 1992.

[30] R. O. Duda, P. E. Hart, and N. J. Nilsson. Subjective Bayesian methods for rule-based inference systems. In *Proceedings AFIPS 45*, pages 1075–1082, New York, 1976. AFIPS Press.

[31] R. Fagin and J. H. Halpern. Uncertainty, belief, and probability. In *Proceedings 11th International Joint Conference on Artificial Intelligence*, pages 1161–1167, Detroit, Michigan, 1989.

[32] J. Gordon and E. H. Shortliffe. A method for managing evidential reasoning in a hierarchical hypothesis space. *Artificial Intelligence*, 26: 325–339, 1985.

[33] J. Y. Halpern and R. Fagin. Two views of belief: Belief as generalized probability and belief as evidence. In *Proceedings Eight National Conference on Artificial Intelligence*, pages 112–119, Boston, Massachusetts, 1990.

[34] J. Y. Halpern and Y. Moses. A guide to modal logics of knowledge and belief. In *Proceedings of the 5th National Conference on Artificial Intelligence*, pages 4480–490. AAAI, 1986.

[35] D. E. Heckerman, J. S. Breese, and E. J. Horvitz. The compilation of decision models. In *Proceedings of the the Fifth Workshop on Uncertainty in Artificial Intelligence*, pages 162–173, August 1989.

[36] M. Henrion. Practical issues in constructing a Bayes' belief network. In L. N. Kanal, T. S. Levitt, and J. F. Lemmer, editors, *Uncertainty in Artificial Intelligence 3*, pages 161–173. North-Holland, Amsterdam, The Netherlands, 1989.

[37] M. Henrion, R. D. Shachter, L. N. Kanal, and J. F. Lemmer, editors. *Uncertainty in Artificial Intelligence 5*. North-Holland, Amsterdam, The Netherlands, 1990.

[38] E. J. Horvitz, H. J. Suermondt, and G. F. Cooper. Bounded conditioning flexible inference for decisions under scarce resources. In *Proceedings of the Fifth Workshop on Uncertainty in Artificial Intelligence*, pages 182–193, August 1989.

[39] R. A. Howard and J. E. Matheson. Influence diagrams. In R. A. Howard and J. E. Matheson, editors, *The Principles and Applications of Decision Analysis*, volume 2, pages 719–762. Strategic Decisions Group, Menlo Park, California, 1984.

[40] G. E. Hughes and M. J. Creswell. *An Introduction to Modal Logic*. Methuen, London, United Kingdom, 1968.

[41] J. Y. Jaffray. Linear utility theory for belief functions. *Operations Research Letters*, 8: 107–112, 1989.

[42] W. J .M. Kickert and E. H. Mamdani. Analysis of a fuzzy logic controller. *Fuzzy Set and Systems*, 12: 29–44, 1978.

[43] J. H. Kim and J. Pearl. A computational model for causal and diagnostic reasoning in inference engines. In *Proceedings of the 8th International Joint Conference on Artificial Intelligence*, pages 190–193, Karlsruhe, Germany, 1983.

[44] S. L. Lauritzen and D. Spiegelhalter. Local computations with probabilities on graphical structures and their application to expert systems. *Journal Royal Statistical Society Ser. B*, 50, 1988.

[45] J.D. Lowrance, T.D. Garvey, and T.M. Strat. A Framework for Evidential-Reasoning Systems. In *Proceedings 5th National Conference on Artificial Intelligence*, pages 896–903, Menlo Park, California, 1986. AAAI.

[46] E. H. Mamdani and S. Assilian. An experiment in linguistic synthesis with a fuzzy logic controller. *International Journal of Man Machine Studies*, 7(1): 1–13, 1975.

[47] R. E. Moore. *Interval Analysis*. Prentice-Hall, 1966.

[48] H. T. Nguyen. On random sets and belief functions. *Journal of Mathematical Analysis and Applications*, 65: 531–542, 1978.

[49] J. Pearl. Reverend Bayes on inference engines: a distributed hierarchical approach. In *Proceedings Second National Conference on Artificial Intelligence*, pages 133–136. AAAI, August 1982.

[50] J. Pearl. Evidential reasoning under uncertainty. In H. E. Shrobe, editor, *Exploring Artificial Intelligence*, pages 381–418. Morgan Kaufmann, San Mateo, California, 1988.

[51] J. Pearl. *Probabilistic Reasoning in Intelligent Systems: Networks of Plausible Inference*. Morgan-Kaufmann, San Mateo, California, 1988.

[52] R. Reiter. A logic for default reasoning. *Artificial Intelligence*, 13: 81–132, 1980.

[53] E. H. Ruspini. Epistemic logic, probability, and the calculus of evidence. In *Proceedings of the Tenth International Joint Conference on Artificial Intelligence*, Milan, Italy, 1987.

[54] E. H. Ruspini. On the semantics of fuzzy logic. *International Journal of Approximate Reasoning*, 5(1): 45–88, January 1991.

[55] R. D. Schachter. Evaluating influence diagrams. *Operations Research*, 34: 871–882, 1986.

[56] B. Schweizer and A. Sklar. Associative functions and abstract semi-groups. *Publicationes Mathematicae Debrecen*, 10: 69–81, 1963.

[57] B. Schweizer and A. Sklar. *Probabilistic Metric Spaces*. North-Holland, New York, 1983.

[58] R. D. Shachter, T. S. Levitt, L. N. Kanal, and J. F. Lemmer, editors. *Uncertainty in Artificial Intelligence 4*. North-Holland, Amsterdam, The Netherlands, 1990.

[59] G. Shafer. *A Mathematical Theory of Evidence*. Princeton University Press, Princeton, New Jersey, 1976.

[60] G. Shafer. Perspectives on the theory and practice of belief functions. *International Journal of Approximate Reasoning*, 4(5/6): 323–362, 1990.

[61] G. Shafer and R. Logan. Implementing dempster rule for hierarchical evidence. *Artificial Intelligence*, 33: 271–298, 1987.

[62] P. P. Shenoy and G. R. Shafer. Axioms for probability and belief-function propagation. In R. D. Shachter, T. S. Levitt, L. N. Kanal, and J. F. Lemmer, editors, *Uncertainty in Artificial Intelligence 4*, pages 169–198. North-Holland, Amsterdam, The Netherlands, 1990.

[63] E. H. Shortliffe and B. Buchanan. A model of inexact reasoning in medicine. *Mathematical Biosciences*, 23: 351–379, 1975.

[64] P. Smets. Belief functions. In P. Smets, A. Mamdani, D. Dubois, and H. Prade, editors, *Non-Standard Logics for Automated Reasoning*. Academic Press, New York, 1988.

[65] P. Smets. Constructing the pignistic probability function in a context of uncertainty. In M. Henrion, R. D. Shachter, L. N. Kanal, and J. F. Lemmer, editors, *Uncertainty in Artificial Intelligence 5*, pages 29–40. North-Holland, Amsterdam, The Netherlands, 1990.

[66] P. Smets. The transferable belief model and other interpretations of Dempster-Shafer's model. In P. Bonissone, M. Henrion, L. N. Kanal, and J. F. Lemmer, editors, *Uncertainty in Artificial Intelligence 6*, pages 375–383. North-Holland, Amsterdam, The Netherlands, 1991.

[67] P. Smets and R. Kennes. Computational aspects of the mobius transform. In P. Bonissone, M. Henrion, L. N. Kanal, and J. F. Lemmer, editors, *Uncertainty in Artificial Intelligence 6*, pages 401–416. North-Holland, Amsterdam, The Netherlands, 1991.

[68] J. Stillman. On heuristics for finding loop cutsets in multiply-connected belief networks. In P. Bonissone, M. Henrion, L. N. Kanal, and J. F. Lemmer, editors, *Uncertainty in Artificial Intelligence 6*, pages 233–243. North-Holland, Amsterdam, The Netherlands, 1991.

[69] T. M. Strat. Continuous belief functions for evidential reasoning. In *Proceedings of the National Conference on Artificial Intelligence*, pages 308–313, Austin, Texas, 1984.

[70] T. M. Strat. Decision analysis using belief functions. *International Journal of Approximate Reasoning*, 4(5/6): 391–417, 1990.

[71] J. Suermondt, G. Cooper, and D. Heckerman. A combination of cutset conditioning with clique-tree propagation in the pathfinder system. In P. Bonissone, M. Henrion, L. N. Kanal, and J. F. Lemmer, editors, *Uncertainty in Artificial Intelligence 6*, pages 245–253. North-Holland, Amsterdam, The Netherlands, 1991.

[72] M. Sugeno, editor. *Industrial Applications of Fuzzy Control*. North-Holland, Amsterdam, The Netherlands, 1985.

[73] T. Terano, K. Asai, and M. Sugeno. *Applied Fuzzy Systems*. Academic Press, Cambridge, Massachusetts, 1994.

[74] F. Voorbraak. A computationally efficient approximation of Dempster-Shafer theory. *International Journal of Man-Machine Studies*, 30: 525–536, 1989.

[75] H. Watanabe and W. Dettloff. Fuzzy logic inference processor for real time control: A second generation full custom design. In *Proceedings of the Twenty-first Asilomar Conference on Signals, Systems and Computers*, pages 729–735. IEEE, November 1987.

[76] R. R. Yager. On ordered weighted averaging aggregation operators in multi-criteria decision making. *IEEE Transactions on Systems, Man and Cybernetics*, 18(1): 183–190, 1988.

[77] R. R. Yager, S. Ovchinnikov, R. M. Tong, and H. T. Nguyen, editors. *Fuzzy Sets And Applications: Selected Papers by L. A. Zadeh*. John Wiley, New York, 1987.

[78] S. Yasunobu and S. Miyamoto. Automatic train operation by predictive fuzzy control. In M. Sugeno, editor, *Industrial Applications of Fuzzy Control*. North-Holland, Amsterdam, The Netherlands, 1985.

[79] L. A. Zadeh. Fuzzy sets. *Information and Control*, 8: 338–353, 1965.

[80] L. A. Zadeh. Probability measures of fuzzy events. *Journal of Mathematical Analysis and Applications*, 10: 421–427, 1968.

[81] L. A. Zadeh. Outline of a new approach to the analysis of complex systems and decision processes. *IEEE Transactions on Systems, Man and Cybernetics*, SMC-3: 28–44, 1973.

[82] L. A. Zadeh. Fuzzy sets as a basis for a theory of possibility. *Fuzzy Sets and Systems*, 1: 3–28, 1978.

[83] L. A. Zadeh. A theory of approximate reasoning. In P. Hayes, D. Michie, and L. I. Mikulich, editors, *Machine Intelligence*, pages 149–194. Halstead Press, New York, 1979.

ON THE CLASSIFICATION OF UNCERTAINTY TECHNIQUES IN RELATION TO THE APPLICATION NEEDS

E. H. Mamdani

Department of Electrical and Electronic Engineering
Imperial College
London, UK

1   INTRODUCTION

Computerized information systems are subject to a variety of imperfections and uncertainty; either in the data themselves or in the query designed to access items of information from the system. Meanwhile, a great deal of research work is available on techniques for handling uncertainty. It is clear that these techniques can be exploited for the management of uncertainty in information systems. However, the plethora of available techniques poses a challenge to the designers of information systems as to which technique is best suited to the problem to be managed. This dilemma is familiar to the designers of artificial intelligence (AI) systems. Many system builders have expressed a wish to see research results that would provide a comprehensible classification matrix showing the suitability of each uncertainty techniques to some abstract features of the problem needing uncertainty management. This chapter argues that such a classification is not possible given the present state of research in uncertainty and indeed it is not meaningful to attempt to produce a matrix of the type suggested.

This should not be taken to mean that researchers working on uncertainty techniques have only concerned themselves with their own individual techniques. In fact researchers are often at pains to compare the merits of each other's techniques. There is good literature available surveying uncertainty techniques as well as showing classification of uncertainty techniques. However, surveys, comparisons, and classifications of this sort are usually confined to technical aspects of uncertainty or are concerned with the foundational nature of uncertainty. Classifications dealing with the nature of uncertainty may help an application builder (whether of an AI application or information system application) to understand the nature of uncertainty he is dealing with, but they give little clue as to how to represent the uncertainty in order to exploit the best suitable technique for managing that uncertainty. Similarly, a classification of techniques is based on the way uncertainty is represented but does not show how to obtain the information about uncertainty in the first place.

Below we review some of the many classifications that have been produced before analyzing why a table providing a match between a technique and the domain uncertainty cannot be easily produced. We start by looking at the classification of uncertainty techniques and then go on to discuss the sources of uncertainty. The techniques do not directly match the sources, which leaves a gap creating the dilemma for application builders.

2   ON THE CLASSIFICATION OF UNCERTAINTY TECHNIQUES

The most obvious parameter for classifying techniques is the manner in which the uncertainty is represented; i.e., whether numerical values are used or only a categorical representation is needed [6, 10, 3, 8]. This is not simply a superficial classification, because all these authors, in one way or another, contend that *numerical* representation is used when the information is *uncertain* whereas the *categorical* or *symbolic* representation is used when information is *incomplete or missing*.

Numerical Techniques for Uncertainty

Research on uncertainty techniques has proliferated recently mainly as a result of the extension of artificial intelligence research. Before this happened, handling of uncertainty was the exclusive preserve of probability theory. The advent of newer techniques was, therefore, not at all well received by "Probabilists," who reacted first by pouring criticisms on the new upstart techniques and then by initiating much further work to provide complex technical mechanisms for dealing with problems of uncertainty posed by AI scientists. Fuzzy sets theory and fuzzy logic was one such technique that was derided by "Probabilists;" the certainty factors approach used in MYCIN was another such technique; Dempster-Shafer theory also received its share of criticisms. The response was that all these techniques were in turn made more sophisticated by researchers, and so we had possibility theory and belief functions and so on. All this has happened in the space of a mere 10 to 15 years. The intense arguments have included all manners of comparisons, from detailed foundational issues to comparisons of the axiomatization of the theories, to highly technical matters concerned with differences of the results calculated by one technique as opposed to another. So intense have these arguments been that only those deeply involved with the investigations are in a position to reproduce all the twists and turns of the arguments. Even knowledgeable workers in closely related areas have found it difficult to follow all the arguments.

None of the surveys provide a good understanding of the arguments involved. It is as yet impossible to do this with thorough impartiality so that all parties will agree with what is reproduced. Any such task will inevitably attract criticisms from all sides that their arguments have not been reproduced accurately. This situation gives a low credibility to survey literature. If one must venture a judgment, it seems that the main argument centers on subjective uncertainty. The term *uncertainty* itself is often applied only to techniques using numerical representation. If these numbers cannot be measured with any well laid down procedure (as would be the case say if the numbers represented frequencies of occurrence of events), then they could only be acquired by asking a human to exercise some form of judgment. It seems that much of the argument then concerns how to deal with these numbers. If this is correct, then no amount of discussion that is confined only to technical issues can settle the matter, because the underlying issue is foundational rather than a purely technical one.

Symbolic (or Categorical) Methods for Handling Uncertainty

Symbolic techniques have arisen out of attempts to increase the expressive power of classical logic. Traditionally classical logic can only deal with statements that are TRUE; i.e., both known and believed to be true. It is useless for dealing with statements whose truth is in doubt in any way: e.g., statements whose truth may change over time, statements that *may* be true, statements that can be assumed to be true, etc. It is *either* necessary to expand the vocabulary of classical logic to handle such doubtfully TRUE statements *or* to extend the reasoning ability of the logic.

The latter is the more frequently used approach in AI. In its simplest form the reasoning system is aware that some of the statements it reasons about may not actually be TRUE, and that these may give rise to contradictions in the conclusions drawn. While classical logic would be unable to cope with any form of contradiction, a system with a reasoner that is aware of this possibility can allow recovery from contradictions. Alternatively, some systems allow a direct way of classifying some of the statements among the totality of statements whose truth cannot be guaranteed. These can be treated as assumptions, and only a subset of these assumptions can be expected to be consistent with the statements that are definitely known to be TRUE. Furthermore, there can be more than one such subset of assumptions. The reasoner is then designed to cope with the situation in a reliable way. Such systems exhibit the technical property of *nonmonotonicity* so that as more definitely TRUE information becomes available the conclusions do not grow monotonically but some of them may need retraction.

Instead of making the reasoner wise to deficiencies in the categorical truth of the statements, one may increase the vocabulary of writing the statements, which would allow the expression of the statement as well as its attitude (or modality). The reasoning system also needs to be extended in order to reason about not just the statements that are TRUE, but also their modalities. Unfortunately modal logics have not been used extensively in AI except as a way of analyzing nonmonotonic logics.

Because both the above approaches no longer deal exclusively with statements that are TRUE, there is common approach to understanding their semantics. One can talk about *possible worlds* in both cases as a collection of mutually consistent statements. Clark [3] draws the following conclusions about symbolic techniques in contrast to quantitative ones:

1. Symbolic techniques have a shorter history than quantitative techniques.

2. Symbolic techniques derive inspiration more from patterns of competent human reasoning.

3. Symbolic techniques make fewer assumption about independence and exclusivity and are, therefore, more robust in some circumstances. However, by making stronger assumptions quantitative approaches achieve greater precision in the combination of evidence.

4. Symbolic techniques are more amenable to implementation of metalevel control.

One would need to correct item one in the above list slightly. Modal logics have as long a history as probability theory. They merely have a shorter history of awareness among AI researchers and practically no history of application in AI.

On Nonnormative and other Approaches

There are techniques that do not fit neatly into the above two classifications. Nonnormative systems are those that are primarily motivated by how humans cope with uncertain information. This is a contentious category to have to create and it may be best to call all techniques that do not neatly fit into the above two categories merely "other techniques." In [10] it is stated that

> There is considerable dispute over the value of nonnormative approaches in artificial intelligence as well as other fields. Should we concern ourselves with how people do in fact think, or with how they ought to? On the one hand, attempts to get computers to reason logically or probabilistically have many imperfections. Among these the advocates of nonnormativity would put the counter-intuitiveness of some conclusions. Against this the normative reasoners would argue that the whole point to theories is to guide us when our intuitions fail us.

One such nonnormative approach that received much attention some years ago was Cohen's theory of endorsements [4]. Endorsements are domain dependent heuristics to problems solving containing many forms of uncertainty. The technique tracks the sources of uncertainty through the reasoning process and thus allows intelligent explanation of the support for the conclusions. The approach has fallen from grace recently due to its "lack of method for propagating, combining, and ranking endorsements and hypotheses."

MYCIN [11] is another technique that can be called nonnormative although it essentially propagates numerical values. Other similar techniques are due to Bundy [2] and Fox [5]. We will discuss later in section 4 why such techniques can often be so powerful.

Recently, as a way of reducing computations involved in numerical techniques (and also as a way of combining different types of numerical uncertainties), Parsons has proposed the use of qualitative algebras [7, 13, 9].

There are many other techniques that do not easily fall under the neat classification of numerical (quantitative) versus categorical (qualitative). There are

- essentially numerical techniques that capture more than one type of uncertainty

- numerical techniques that, like modal logics, represent the attitude of the statements

- nonmonotonic systems with numerically weighted assumptions

The list of techniques is apparently endless. It seems that there is no reason why someone should not invent a new technique for dealing with uncertainty and many inadequacies (or perceived inadequacies) of current techniques. The starting point of handling uncertainty cannot therefore be the classification of techniques but the nature of uncertainty to be handled. Furthermore, even when one knows exactly the nature of uncertainty, there is unlikely to be a unique technique that will commend itself.

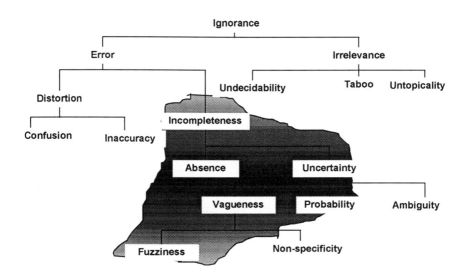

Figure 1   A taxonomy of ignorance.

The reasons behind a classification of the techniques is that they will map onto some taxonomy of different types and causes of uncertainty. Figure 1 is one such taxonomy due to Smithson [12]. There is nothing definitive about this taxonomy; others may wish to classify terms differently. For example, in this figure incompleteness includes both uncertainty and *absence* (a new term) and this new term, absence, is used for the kind of uncertainty that is modeled by nonmonotonic logics. Notice also that only the terms included in the shaded area have some form of techniques available for modeling them.

3   ON SOURCES OF UNCERTAINTY

3.1   Definitions

Many uncertainty technicians (researchers working on techniques) often fall back on an English dictionary to find out what the various English language terms referring to uncertainty mean. Smets (Chapter 8) has provided the result of one such search. Figure 1, though containing fewer terms than Smets, goes one step further and provides a taxonomy of the terms. One of the most interesting observations is that according to definitions produced by Smets the term *fuzzy* is nearer in meaning to nonspecificity than to the term *vagueness* which is the definition that the technicians have traditionally used. This other meaning of fuzzy is a derogatory meaning. It means someone who is woolly, indicating senility or brain damage. Could it be that it is this connotation of the term *fuzzy* that is the reason for fuzzy set theories not having been well received by some researchers? Scientists are not renowned for their competence in the use of a language; but while there is no necessity for technical terms to follow the ordinary usage, a divergence can cause problems. The biggest difficulty normally arises with terms used in numerical techniques, for it is not just the meaning of the term that has to be understood but also the numerical representation of it — the numbers have to come from somewhere, and numerical answers have to be interpreted somehow. Thus

Probability and Possibility

People have difficulty understanding probability at the best of times, but subjective probability is really difficult. Even if one can be pragmatic about the matter and agree to use numbers, one still needs to admit that the numbers are unlikely to be accurate. Hardly any technique makes the use of sensitivity analysis mandatory in such cases. Many of these arguments also apply equally to possibility.

Belief

Belief functions do have an advantage in that they allow a representation of ignorance, but, again, one goes to great length in numeric computation using numbers whose accuracy and validity is extremely questionable. No one has questioned what is to be gained in carrying out lengthy computation with arbitrarily obtained numbers.

Consider a consultation process in which the raw data is gathered by asking someone about his belief in some proposition A to be given in the range 0 to 1. One would be very surprised indeed if the response was "0.67843." Clearly the raw data is never expected to have such accuracy. Most techniques that deal with such highly inaccurate data, however, involve a great deal of computation. Clearly, the computation involved in these techniques is out of proportion considering the accuracy of the data.

Truth

Degrees of truth are one of the worst offenders in this sense. A statement that is TRUE is just what it says: it is *satisfiable* with respect to the state of the world; otherwise it is FALSE. This is a profoundly philosophical matter in which a technician (however competent he may be with playing around with equations) has no automatic right to pronounce that henceforth truth will be a matter of degree unless he first demonstrates equal competence in the field of philosophy. The ideas must have a fair amount of support from the philosophy community, otherwise they are worthless. The ordinary usage of terms such as *quite true* and *perhaps true* or even *maybe* do not immediately indicate that truth is a matter of degree. They are always a shorthand way of saying something like: "I *believe* that if I were to analyze the matter further then it is *likely* that (*possible* that) the statement in question will turn out to be true." Such terms indicate a belief in the likelihood of the outcome of a process of further analysis or further inference or further investigations.

In summary, there are three distinct types of definitions of terms that one needs to be aware of. First, there is definition based on the ordinary usage of the language, which is reflected in dictionaries. Second, there are operational definitions provided by technicians for use strictly within a given technique. Finally, there is definition resulting from deep philosophical reflection and debate. The latter is not merely the result of some abstract (and hence meaningless) activity. All of us, technicians, application builders, as well as philosophers are in the business of dealing with abstractions of one kind or another. Indeed, philosophical reflections are often (unfortunately not always) about profoundly practical matters. In fact, philosophical definitions are closer to what an application builder needs than the offerings of dictionaries and technicians.

Sources of Uncertainty

There are many sources of such uncertainty. While it is impossible to give an exhaustive account of these, some of the key ones that arise in the literature on expert systems are as follows:

- One's *belief* in a given proposition or a piece of knowledge.

- The *likelihood* of a simple, compound, or conditional event.

- The *extent* of a proposition concerning a continuous variable.

- The *imprecision* about any information.

- Any *exception* to a general rule.

- The *mandate* for performing some action.

- The *relevance* of one piece of information to another.

- The interpretation of *missing* or *null* value.

Various features of the sources of uncertainty may also be noted:

- It is not necessary to represent all the previous types of uncertainty as numerical values signifying their degree. Thus, belief, exception, mandate, and relevance may all be expressed as attitudes or modalities of the underlying propositions. However, it is important to reason about not just the propositions but also their modalities.

- Imprecision can be about likelihoods or extents or degrees of beliefs. It may be expressed as upper and lower limits of a variable or as a fuzzy subset of all possible values.

There is a great deal to be said for the classification offered by Henri Prade:

- The essential distinction to be made is between *uncertainty* and *imprecision*.

- Uncertainty is a qualifier of a statement and includes probability and possibility and perhaps also belief. In reasoning, these qualifiers have to be propagated along the inference chain.

- Imprecision concerns disjunction of any kind. Whether logical disjunction of two or more statements, or a range of values or fuzzy values. This is not a qualifier of a statement by the property of the statement itself.

- There is often a trade-off between the degree of uncertainty and the degree of imprecision.

4   BUILDING APPLICATIONS WITH UNCERTAINTY MANAGEMENT

The builder of an application must first begin with a careful analysis of the sources of uncertainty. From what has been mentioned previously, he is likely find greater help from philosophers than from dictionaries and technicians. Long before any technique is chosen to deal with whatever kind of uncertainty, the application builder must be as well aware as possible of the nature of uncertainty, how it can be detected, and the boundaries to be placed upon the methods for treating it; i.e., what can and cannot be said about it. In short, desiderata for techniques for managing that particular form of uncertainty. Bonissone [1] provides a good example of such desiderata that apply mainly in connection with numerical representation of plausible reasoning:

1. Combination rules should not be used on global assumptions of evidence independence.

2. The combination rules should not assume the exhaustiveness and exclusiveness of the hypotheses.

3. There should be an explicit representation of the amount of evidence for an against each hypothesis.

4. There should be an explicit representation of the reasons for and against each hypothesis.

5. The representation should allow the user to describe the uncertainty of any information at the available level of detail (i.e., allow heterogeneous information granularity).

6. There should be an explicit representation of consistency.

7. There should be an explicit representation of ignorance to allow for non-committal statements.

8. There should be a clear distinction between a conflict in the information (violation of consistency) and ignorance about the information.

9. There should be a second-order measure of uncertainty, recording the uncertainty of the information as well as the uncertainty of the measure itself.

10. The representation must be, or appear to be, natural to the user to facilitate graceful interaction, natural to the expert to permit elicitation of consistent weights or reasons, and the semantics of procedures for propagating and summarizing information must be clear.

11. The syntax and semantics of the representation should be closed under the rules of combination.

12. Making pairwise comparisons of uncertainty should be feasible, as these are required for decision making.

13. The traceability of the aggregation and propagation of uncertainty through the reasoning process must be available to resolve conflicts or contradictions, to explain the support of conclusions, and to perform metareasoning for control.

Clark [10] suggests that this list is incomplete, because in practical application other factors need also to be taken into account. It is important, he suggests, that the system gives the "right answers." And this in turn may need additional characteristics to be present within the technique. His concern is that it is not sufficient to know what outcome the system on its own will produce because most systems do not operate on their own but along with human users:

> Here the appropriate level of analysis is not the outcome of the expert system in isolation but of the wider cognitive system composed of the decision maker and the expert consultation system. When a wider perspective is taken, it is clear that the concept of outcome must be given a broader interpretation in terms of the results of consultations between the user and the expert system. This will be affected by factors such as intelligibility of the advice provided, the ability to perform appropriate decision support tasks (such as critiquing user's proposals)m and the nature of system dialogues.

The above is as valid for information systems as for expert systems. Almost every technique ignores the plight of the human user. If the technicians engage in "talmudic" disputations about subtle properties of their techniques, then what hope has any ordinary user?

Only after such desiderata have been fully specified should any technique be chosen. It is unlikely that a single technique will be found to meet all the desiderata specified. It is slightly more possible that several techniques may satisfy all the desiderata. More than likely, some few techniques will meet the majority of key specifications, in which case it is worth considering modifying the technique. It is also worth implementing a completely *ad hoc* technique especially when the intelligibility of an existing technique is in question, for, intelligibility is not worth sacrificing for the sake of the purity of a technique.

While on the subject of *ad hoc* techniques, it is worth remarking that often two quite dissimilar techniques used to characterize a given domain problem yield not-too-dissimilar results, and both techniques may be judged to be acceptable. The main reason this happens is that acceptable results are never entirely dependent upon the technique being used, but are also dependent on the domain knowledge involved and represented within any technique. It is this domain knowledge that is primarily responsible for the results of applying any technique.

5   CONCLUSIONS

Anyone who has followed the on-going research into uncertainty over the past years will attest that last five years have seen a dramatic advance in results in this research and a marked improvement in our understanding of the subject of uncertainty and the techniques used for handling them. However, new techniques continue to be invented. The disputations that continue to take place within the uncertainty research community have indeed provided a better understanding, but as yet they are far from resolving all the key issues.

All the previous discussion presented in this chapter points to the inevitable conclusion that it is naive to want to produce a matrix of techniques against classes of domain applications. It gives the techniques *per se* too high a place in determining the quality of results that are likely to be obtained. The main determinant of performance is always the domain knowledge that is to be represented by any technique, and it so happens that the techniques do not point to a unique way of representing a particular type of knowledge.

Clearly, all these techniques are meant to be *prescriptive* about how humans ought to think when faced with uncertainty and not *descriptive* of how they in fact think. The justification of any prescription has got to be philosophical. The mathematical formulation is just the representation and a model for the essentially philosophical foundations. However, once a mathematical model has been built, then its elegance, tractability, and internal symmetry become an additional justification in itself. The philosophical explanation for it is often a *post facto* justification for retaining the "beauty" of the mathematical model. Purely technical considerations cannot be allowed to outweigh the more fundamental foundational issues. Indeed, such technical criteria are no better (if that) than simple utilitarian criteria that are likely to be advanced by application builders.

The technicians are just that: experts on investigating techniques. By being experts in their own work they have not become better qualified to build applications than the application builders themselves; and they certainly cannot be supposed to have assumed the mantle of philosophers.

Consider a situation in which a clinician is planning to use an uncertainty technique not just to diagnose a patient's condition but also to help him decide what action to take. What is an uncertainty technique proposing to give him? A sounder way of thinking than he is capable of? Does he need to understand all the subtleties of such a technique? If not, then is he being asked to take its workings and results on trust? If yes, then clearly the technicians have to make it understandable by any informed user, which they have as yet failed to do. Is one entitled to tell him, "Look, the answer has had the benefit of two hours of a supercomputer's time, so it is bound to be correct, and you cannot argue with its results."

An understanding of the sources of uncertainty is the main analysis required to build the application for the management of uncertainty in information systems. It is not a bad idea to convert the results of this analysis into desiderata for the management technique. Furthermore, it is a good idea to analyze the total cognitive system including the machine-based part as well as the human user, as often the main source of uncertainty and ambiguity occurs at the interface between the man and the machine: the one source that is almost always ignored and one that has received scant attention from the technicians. Any clever management of uncertainty within the underlying machine-based information immediately evaporates as soon as the ambiguity caused by the man-machine interface is imposed on it. In fact, a majority of the techniques are so clever and subtle that they contribute to this ambiguity by the bucketful. Until this particular problem is fully addressed by the uncertainty research community, a matrix is merely likely to add to the confusion and unwelcome debate.

This is not to say that application builders should not implement uncertainty handling techniques. Indeed, any effort spent on building uncertainty management in information systems is likely to produce a handsome dividend. One possibility definitely worth considering is to use uncertainty technique only within the machine-based part (we can call this reasoning *with* uncertainty) and keep the uncertainty invisible from the human user so he does not have to reason *about* uncertainty. A careful analysis in the course of building an application is likely to require much effort, and one should not be asking for any shortcuts such as a matrix.

REFERENCES

[1] P. P. Bonissone. Plausible reasoning. In S. Shapiro, editor, *Encyclopaedia of Artificial Intelligence*, pages 854–863. John Wiley & Sons, London, 1987.

[2] A. Bundy. Correctness criteria of some algorithms for uncertain reasoning using incidence calculus. *Journal of Automated Reasoning*, 2(2): 109–126, 1986.

[3] D. A. Clark. Numerical and symbolic approaches to uncertainty management in AI. *Artificial Intelligence Review*, 4(2): 109–146, 1990.

[4] P. Cohen. *Heuristic Reasoning About Uncertainty: An Artificial Intelligence Approach*. Pitman, London, 1985.

[5] J. Fox. Knowledge, decision making and uncertainty. In W. A. Gale, editor, *Artificial Intelligence and Statistics*, pages 57–76. Addison-Wesley, Reading, Massachusetts, 1986.

[6] D. Pang, J. Bigham, and E. H. Mamdani. Reasoning with uncertain information. *Proc IEE*, 134, Pt D(4), July 1987.

[7] S. Parsons. On using qualitative algebras in place of meta-theories for reasoning under uncertainty: a preliminary report. In *Proceedings of Drums RP4 workshop*. Department of Electronic Engineering, Queen Mary & Westfield College, Mile End Road, London, 1990.

[8] S. Parsons. *Combined Modes of Reasoning Under Uncertainty*. Ph.D. Dissertation, London University, 1993.

[9] S. Parsons and J. Fox. Qualitative and interval algebras for robust decision making under uncertainty. In M. G. Singh and L. Travé-Massuyés, editors, *Decision Support Systems and Qualitative Reasoning*. Elsevier Science Publishers B.V. North Holland, 1991.

[10] Alvey Project. A survey of techniques for inference under uncertainty (final report). Technical Report IKBS-047, Deptartment of Electronic Engineering, Queen Mary & Westfield College, May 1989.

[11] E. H. Shortliffe. *Computer-Based Medical Consultations: MYCIN*. Elsevier, New York, 1976.

[12] M. Smithson. *Ignorance and Uncertainty: Emerging Paradigms*. Springer-Verlag, New York, 1989.

[13] M. P. Wellman. Fundamental concepts of qualitative probabilistic networks. *Artificial Intelligence*, (44): 257–303, 1990.

A BIBLIOGRAPHY ON
UNCERTAINTY MANAGEMENT IN
INFORMATION SYSTEMS
Curtis E. Dyreson

Department of Computer Science
James Cook University
Townsville Q4811, Australia
curtis@cs.jcu.edu.au

1   INTRODUCTION

This is an evolving bibliography of documents on uncertainty and imprecision in information systems. By uncertainty and imprecision, we mean the representation of and query support for information that is fuzzy, unknown, partially known, vague, uncertain, probabilistic, indefinite, disjunctive, possible, maybe, incomplete, approximate, erroneous, or imprecise. Currently, the bibliography concentrates almost exclusively on database and knowledge-base systems, with few references on other kinds of information systems.

In contrast to other chapters in this book, which anticipate future research directions, the bibliography is a look back at past work. The bibliography is organized into nine sections: survey papers, null value papers, logic and deductive database papers, fuzzy set and possibility theory papers, probability theory papers, query-level papers, schema-level papers, complexity papers, and miscellaneous papers. The sections loosely reflect some topics of past research. Papers that relate to a particular research area are listed in the relevant section. If a paper applies to more than one research area then it is cross-referenced in all the appropriate sections. Since these research topics may be unfamiliar to some readers, we briefly describe the unifying theme of each section.

The survey section lists papers that give an overview of the field, or even a part of the field. Few surveys exist.

The null value section references two kinds of papers. First, this section ostensibly references papers on null values. Much of the research on imprecision in database systems has focused on null values; consequently, there are many papers listed. This section also contains references to papers that are not concerned exclusively with null values but concentrate on "unweighted" information, such as an exclusive-or disjunction of facts or tuples. What these two kinds of papers have in common is that they make no use of numbers, preferences, or weights to handle degrees of uncertainty or imprecision.

Support for disjunctive and indefinite information in logic and deductive databases is also unweighted information, but it is a distinctive enough subset to be given its own section. The logic section also includes work on the application of non-Horn clause and nonmonotonic logics to uncertain and imprecise information management.

Sections 5 and 6 list papers that support uncertain and imprecise information within the framework of fuzzy set or possibility theory and probability theory, respectively. In general, both of these related, yet distinct, frameworks make use of "weighted" information to support varying degrees of uncertainty and imprecision.

The section on query-level papers cites papers relating to approximate querying and data mining. Some of these papers also use probability or possibility theory but are placed here (and cross-referenced to the appropriate section) because they add uncertainty and imprecision to the query rather than to the underlying data.

Uncertainty could also exist in the meta-data, concerning how the data is stored and organized, rather than in the data itself. Papers that address schema-level uncertainty are listed in Section 8. Again, some of these papers adopt fuzzy set, logic, or probabilistic approaches but are listed in this section because of their narrower topic.

Adding support for uncertain and imprecise information is sometimes costly. Research that characterizes the time or space complexity of various approaches appears in the section on complexity.

Finally, papers that defy simple categorization appear in the miscellaneous papers section.

Figure 1 shows a histogram of the papers in the bibliography plotted by the year of publication. The figure indicates that interest in uncertainty management in information systems, as measured by the number of publications, dramatically increased during the 1980s. We suspect that the slight downward trend in the last three years is due to delays in the propagation of publication information.

2 SURVEYS

This section lists the few papers that give an overview of some area in uncertainty management.

[1] Chisholm, P., G. Chen, D. Ferbrache, P. Thanisch, and M. H. Williams. Coping with indefinite and negative data in deductive databases: A survey. *Data and Knowledge Engineering*, 2 (1987), pp. 259–284.

[2] Lakshmanan, L. Evolution of intelligent database systems: A survey. In *Proceedings of SOFTEK 93, Workshop on Incompleteness and Uncertainty in Information Systems*. Montreal, Canada: Oct. 1993.

[3] Motro, A. Accommodating imprecision in database systems: issues and solutions. *ACM SIGMOD Record*, 19, No. 4, Dec. 1990, pp. 69–74.

[4] Motro, A. Imprecision and incompleteness in relational databases: Survey. *Information and Software Technology*, 32, No. 9, Nov. 1990, pp. 579–588.

[5] Motro, A. Management of uncertainty in database systems. In *Modern Database Systems*. Ed. W. Kim. ACM Press, 1994. Chap. 22. pp. 457–476.

[6] Pirotte, A., and E. Zimányi. Imperfect knowledge in databases. RR 92-36. Unité d'Informatique, Université de Louvain, Belgium. Oct. 1992.

[7] Prade, H. Information processing (annotated bibliography). In *Readings on Fuzzy Sets in Intelligent Systems*. Ed. D. Dubois, H. Prade, and R. Yager. Morgan Kaufmann, 1994. Chap. 6.

[8] Stephanou, H. E., and A. P. Sage. Perspectives on imperfect information processing. *IEEE Transactions on Systems, Man, and Cybernetics*, 17, No. 5 (1987), pp. 780–798.

[9] Willis, H. L., J. E. D. Northcote-Green, and H. N. Tram. Computerized distribution planning: Data needs and results with incomplete data. In *IEEE/PES 1986 Transmission and Distribution Conference*. Anaheim, CA: Sep. 1986.

3 NULL VALUES

This section lists papers on null values in database systems and, more generally, papers that make no use of weights or preferences to represent varying degrees of uncertainty and imprecision. Figure 2 shows the publication history for null value approaches. The figure shows that the field is old (for uncertainty management) but continues to be researched.

Related work can be found in

- Section 4—[142, 167]

- Section 5—[212]

- Section 6—[300, 301, 308]

- Section 7—[320]

- Section 9—[347, 348, 350, 353]

[10] Abiteboul, S., and G. Grahne. Update semantics for incomplete databases. In *Proceedings of the International Conference on Very Large Databases*. Stockholm, Sweden: Aug. 1985, pp. 1–12.

[11] Anfindsen, O. J. Multivalued logic and database systems. TR R 41/92. Norwegian Telecom Research, Oct. 1992.

[12] ANSI/X3/SPARC Interim report of the study group on database management system. *FDT (ACM SIGMOD Bulletin)*, 7, No. 2, Feb. 1975.

[13] Atzeni, P., and R. Torlone. Approaches to updates over weak instances. In *Proceedings of the 1st Symposium on Mathematical Fundamentals of Database Systems*. Visegrad, Hungary: June 1989, pp. 12–23.

[14] Atzeni, P., and M. C. DeBernardis. New interpretation for null values in the weak instance model. *Journal of Computer and System Sciences*, 41, No. 1, Aug. 1990, pp. 25–43.

[15] Atzeni, P., and V. De Antonellis. The theory of null values. In *Relational Database Theory*. Benjamin/Cummings, 1993. Chap. 6.

[16] Biskup, J. A formal approach to null values in database relations. In *Proceedings of the Workshop on Formal Bases for Databases*. Ed. H. Gallaire and J.M. Nicolas. Toulouse, France: Dec. 1979.

[17] Biskup, J. A Formal approach to null values in database relations. In *Advances in Data Base Theory.* Ed. H. Gallaire, J. Minker, and J. Nicolas. New York: Plenum Press, 1981. Vol. 1. pp. 299–341.

[18] Biskup, J. A foundation of Codd's relational maybe-operations. *ACM Transactions on Database Systems*, 8, No. 4, Dec. 1983, pp. 608–636.

[19] Biskup, J. Extending the relational algebra for relations with maybe tuples and existential and universal null values. *Fundamenta Informaticæ*, VII, No. 1 (1984), pp. 129–150.

[20] Brudno, V. A. Valuations in incomplete information databases. *Information Sciences*, 47 (1989), pp. 389–398.

[21] Codd, E. F. Extending the database relational model to capture more meaning. *ACM Transactions on Database Systems*, 4, No. 4, Dec. 1979, pp. 397–434.

[22] Codd, E. F. Missing information (applicable and inapplicable) in Relational Databases. *ACM SIGMOD Record*, 15, No. 4, Dec. 1986, pp. 53–78.

[23] Codd, E. F. More commentary on missing information in relational databases (applicable and inapplicable information). *ACM SIGMOD Record*, 16, No. 1, Mar. 1987, pp. 42–50.

[24] Codd, E. F. Missing Information. In *The Relational Model for Database Management: Version 2.* Addison-Wesley, 1990. Chap. 8–9.

[25] Date, C. J. Null values in database management. In *Proceedings of the 2nd British National Conference on Databases.* Bristol, England: July 1982.

[26] Date, C. J. Null values in database management. In *Relational Database: Selected Writings.* Reading, MA: Addison-Wesley, 1986. Chap. 15. pp. 313–334.

[27] Date, C. J. NOT is not 'not'! (notes on three-valued logic and related matters). In *Relational Database Writings 1985-1989.* Reading, MA: Addison-Wesley, 1989. Chap. 8. pp. 217–248.

[28] Date, C. J. EXISTS is not 'exists'! (some logical flaws in SQL). In *Relational Database Writings 1985-1989.* Reading, MA: Addison-Wesley, 1989. Chap. 13. pp. 339–356.

[29] Deshpande, V., and P. A. Larson. An algebra for nested relations with support for nulls and aggregates. Research Report CS-91-16. University of Waterloo, Canada. 1987.

[30] Gadia, S. K., S. Nair, and Y.-C. Poon. Incomplete information in relational temporal databases. In *Proceedings of the International Conference on Very Large Databases*. Vancouver, Canada: Aug. 1992.

[31] Gadia, S., S. Nair, and Y.-C. Poon. Incomplete information in relational databases. In *Proceedings of the International Workshop on an Infrastructure for Temporal Databases*. Arlington, TX: June 1993.

[32] Gessert, G. H. Four value logic for relational database systems. *ACM SIGMOD Record*, 19, No. 1, Mar. 1990, pp. 29–35.

[33] Gessert, G. H. Handling missing data by using stored truth values. *ACM SIGMOD Record*, 20, No. 3, Sep. 1991, pp. 30–42.

[34] Goldstein, B. Constraints on null values in relational databases. In *Proceedings of the International Conference on Very Large Databases*. Cannes, France: Sep. 1981, pp. 101–110.

[35] Golshani, F. Growing certainty with null values. *Information Systems*, 10, No. 2 (1985), pp. 289–297.

[36] Gottlob, G., and R. Zicari. Closed world databases opened through null values. In *Proceedings of the International Conference on Very Large Databases*. Los Angeles, CA: 1988, pp. 50–61.

[37] Grahne, G. Dependency satisfaction in databases with incomplete information. In *Proceedings of the International Conference on Very Large Databases*. Singapore: Aug. 1984, pp. 37–45.

[38] Grahne, G. Horn tables—an efficient tool for handling incomplete information in databases. In *Proceedings of ACM SIGMOD, International Conference on Management of Data*. Philadelphia, PA: Mar. 1989, pp. 75–82.

[39] Grahne, G. The problem of incomplete information in relational databases. Ph.D. Dissertation. University of Helsinki, Finland, Mar. 1989.

[40] Grant, J. Null values in a relational data base. *Information Processing Letters*, 6, No. 5, Oct. 1977, pp. 156–157.

[41] Grant, J. Partial values in a tabular database model. *Information Processing Letters*, 9, No. 2, Aug. 1979, pp. 97–99.

[42] Grant, J. Incomplete information in a relational database. *Fundamenta Informaticæ*, III, No. 3 (1980), pp. 363–378.

[43] Grant, J., and J. Minker. Answering queries in indefinite databases and the null value problem. In *Advances in Computing Research*. Ed. P. Kanellakis. London: JAI Press, 1986. Vol. 3. pp. 247–267.

[44] Havránek, T. An alternative approach to missing information in the GUHA Method. *Kybernetika (Prague)*, 16, No. 22 (1980), pp. 145–155.

[45] Hegner, S. Specification and implementation of programs for updating incomplete information databases. In *Proceedings of the ACM Symposium on Principles of Database Systems*. San Diego, CA: Mar. 1987.

[46] Ho, N. C. Context dependent null values and multivalued dependencies in relational databases. *Bulletin of the Polish Academy of Sciences*, 36, No. 1/2 (1988), pp. 91–91.

[47] Homenda, W. Databases with alternative information. *IEEE Transactions on Knowledge and Data Engineering*, 3, No. 3, Sep. 1991, pp. 384–386.

[48] Hulin, G. Relational databases with marked null values: A new approach. Manuscript M333. Philips Research Laboratory, Brussels. Jan. 1990.

[49] Hurson, A., and L. Miller. Database machine architecture for supporting incomplete information. *Computer Systems Science and Engineering*, 2, No. 3, July 1987, pp. 107–116.

[50] Imieliński, T. Problems of representing information in relational databases (in Polish). Ph.D. Dissertation. Institute of Computer Science, Polish Academy of Sciences, 1981.

[51] Imieliński, T., and W. Lipski, Jr. On representing incomplete information in a relational database. In *Proceedings of the International Conference on Very Large Databases*. Cannes, France: Sep. 1981, pp. 388–397.

[52] Imieliński, T., and W. Lipski, Jr. Epilogue to 'incomplete information in a relational database.' In *Readings in Artificial Intelligence and Databases*. Ed. M.L. Brodie and J. Mylopoulos. Berlin and New York: Springer-Verlag, 1989.

[53] Jaegermann, M. Information storage and retrieval systems with incomplete information. *Fundamenta Informaticæ*, II (1978), pp. 17–41.

[54] Jia, Y., Z. Feng, and M. Miller. A Multivalued approach to handle nulls in RDB. In *Future Database 92, Proceedings of the 2nd Far-East Workshop on Future Database Systems*. Kyoto, Japan: Apr. 1992, pp. 71–76.

[55] Jichao, H. Extending the relational model to deal with null value (in Chinese). *Chinese Journal of Computation*, 10, No. 8 (1987), pp. 449–459.

[56] Kao, M., N. Cercone, and W. Luk. What do you mean "Null"? Turning null responses into quality responses. In *Proceedings of the 3rd International Conference on Data Engineering*. 1987, pp. 356–364.

[57] Keller, A. M., and M. W. Wilkins. Approaches for updating databases with incomplete information and nulls. In *Proceedings of the International Conference on Data Engineering*. IEEE Computer Society. Los Angeles, CA: IEEE Computer Society Press, Apr. 1984, pp. 332–340.

[58] Keller, A. M., and M. W. Wilkins. On the use of an extended relational model to handle changing incomplete information. *IEEE Transactions on Software Engineering*, SE-11, No. 7, July 1985, pp. 620–633.

[59] Keller, A. M. Set-theoretic problems of null completion in relational databases. *Information Processing Letters*, 22, No. 5, Apr. 1986, pp. 261–265.

[60] Kocharekar, R. Nulls in relational databases: Revisited. *ACM SIGMOD Record*, 18, No. 1, Mar. 1989, pp. 68–73.

[61] Koubarakis, M. Representation and querying in temporal databases: The power of temporal constraints. In *Proceedings of the International Conference on Data Engineering*. Vienna, Austria: Apr. 1993, pp. 327–334.

[62] Kouramajian, V., and R. Elmasri. A generalized temporal model. Technical Report. University of Texas at Arlington, Feb. 1992.

[63] Kouramajian, V., and R. Elmasri. Uncertainty in valid time databases, In *Proceedings of the Workshop on Uncertainty in Databases and Deductive Systems*. Ithaca, NY: Nov. 1994.

[64] Laurent, D., and N. Spyratos. Partition semantics for incomplete information in relational databases. In *Proceedings of ACM SIGMOD, International Conference on Management of Data*. ACM Press, 1988, pp. 66–73.

[65] Lerat, N., and W. Lipski, Jr. Nonapplicable nulls. *Theoretical Computer Science*, 46 (1986), pp. 67–82.

[66] Levene, M., and G. Loizou. A domain theoretic approach to incomplete information in nested relational databases. In *Proceedings of the 3rd International Conference on Foundations of Data Organization and Algorithms*. 1989, pp. 439–456.

[67] Levene, M., and G. Loizou. Modeling incomplete information in complex objects. In *Proceedings of the 7th British National Conference on Databases.* 1989, pp. 441–459.

[68] Levene, M., and G. Loizou. Correction to null values in nested relational databases by M. A. Roth, H. F. Korth, and A. Silberschatz. *Acta Informatica*, 28 (1991), pp. 603–605.

[69] Levene, M., and G. Loizou. Inferring null join dependencies in relational databases. *Bit*, 32, No. 3 (1992), pp. 413–419.

[70] Levene, M., and G. Loizou. A fully precise null extended nested relational algebra. *Fundamenta Informaticæ*, 19 (1993), pp. 303–343.

[71] Levene, M., and G. Loizou. Semantics for null extended nested relations. *ACM Transactions on Database Systems*, 18, No. 3, Sep. 1993, pp. 414–438.

[72] Lien, Y. Multivalued dependencies with null values in relational data bases. In *Proceedings of the International Conference on Very Large Databases.* 1979, pp. 61–66.

[73] Linn, F. Missing, and inapplicable values. *ACM SIGMOD Record*, 16, No. 2, Sep. 1987, pp. 18–19.

[74] Lipski, W., Jr. Informational systems with incomplete information. In *Proceedings of the 3rd International Colloquium on Automata, Languages, and Programming.* Edinburgh, Scotland: July 1976, pp. 120–130.

[75] Lipski, W., Jr. On semantic issues connected with incomplete data bases (extended abstract). In *Proceedings of the International Conference on Very Large Databases.* Florence, Italy: Oct. 1977, pp. 491.

[76] Lipski, W., Jr. On the logic of incomplete information. In *Proceedings of the 6th International Symposium on the Mathematical Foundations of Computer Science.* Tatranská Lomnica, Czechoslovakia: Sep. 1977, pp. 374–381.

[77] Lipski, W., Jr. On semantic issues connected with incomplete information databases. *ACM Transactions on Database Systems*, 4, No. 3, Sep. 1979, pp. 262–296.

[78] Lipski, W., Jr. On databases with incomplete information. *Journal of the Association of Computing Machinery*, 28, No. 1 (1981), pp. 41–70.

[79] Lipski, W., Jr. Logical problems related to incomplete information in data-bases. Technical Report 138. Laboratoire de Recherche en Informatique, Université de Paris-Sud, Centre d'Orsay, Sep. 1983.

[80] Lipski, W., Jr. On relational algebra with marked nulls. In *Proceedings of the ACM Symposium on Principles of Database Systems*. Waterloo, Ontario, Canada: Apr. 1984, pp. 201–203.

[81] Liu, K. C., and R. Sunderraman. Applying an extended relational model to indefinite deductive databases. In *Proceedings of the 2nd International Symposium on Methodologies for Intelligent Systems*. Charlotte, NC: Oct. 1987, pp. 175–184.

[82] Liu, K. C., and R. Sunderraman. On representing indefinite and maybe information in relational databases. In *Proceedings of International Conference on Data Engineering*. Los Angeles, CA: Feb. 1988, pp. 250–257.

[83] Liu, K. C., and R. Sunderraman. Indefinite and maybe information in relational databases. *ACM Transactions on Database Systems*, 15, No. 1, Mar. 1990, pp. 1–39.

[84] Liu, K. C., and R. Sunderraman. On representing indefinite and maybe information in relational databases: A generalization. In *Proceedings of the 6th International Conference on Data Engineering*. 1990, pp. 495–502.

[85] Liu, K. C., and R. Sunderraman. A generalized relational model for indef-inite and maybe information. *IEEE Transactions on Knowledge and Data Engineering*, 3, No. 1 (1991), pp. 65–76.

[86] Liu, K. C., and R. Sunderraman. Natural Joins in Relational Databases with Indefinite and Maybe Information. In *Proceedings of the 7th International Conference on Data Engineering*. 1991, pp. 132–194.

[87] Maier, D. Null values, partial information, and database semantics. In *The Theory of Relational Databases*. Rockville, MD: Computer Science Press, 1983. Chap. 12.

[88] Miller, L. L., and A. R. Hurson. Interpretation of null values in database machine architecture. *Microprocessing and Microprogramming*, 26, No. 4, Dec. 1989, pp. 289–300.

[89] Morrissey, J. M., and C. van Rijsbergen. A formal treatment of missing and imprecise Information. In *Proceedings of the 10th Annual ACM SIGIR Conference on Research and Development in Information Retrieval*. 1987.

[90] Morrissey, J. M. Imprecise information and uncertainty in information systems. *ACM Transactions on Office Information Systems*, 8, No. 2, Apr. 1990, pp. 159–180.

[91] Nau, H. W., and H. Wedekind. Die Spezifikation von Nullwerten als Problem einer wissensbasierten Büroautomatisierung. In *Proceedings GI-Fachtagung, Datenbank-Systeme für Büro, Technik und Wissenschaft, Germany*. Zürich, Switzerland: 1989.

[92] Ola, A., and G. Özsoyoğlu. A Family of incomplete relational database models. In *Proceedings of the International Conference on Very Large Databases*. 1989, pp. 23–31.

[93] Ola, A. Modeling of relational databases with exclusive disjunctions. Technical Report. North Carolina State University, 1991.

[94] Ola, A. Relational databases with exclusive disjunctions. In *Proceedings of the 8th International Conference on Data Engineering*. Tempe, AZ: Feb. 1992, pp. 328–336.

[95] Osborn, S. Insertions in a multi-relation database with nulls. In *Proceedings of COMPSAC 81, IEEE Computer Society's 5th International Computer Software and Applications Conference*. Chicago, IL: Nov. 1981, pp. 75–80.

[96] Reiter, R. A sound and sometimes complete query evaluation algorithm for relational databases with null values. Technical Report. Department of Computer Science, University of British Columbia, June 1983.

[97] Reiter, R. A sound and sometimes complete query evaluation algorithm for relational databases with null values. *Journal of the Association of Computing Machinery*, 33, No. 2 (1986), pp. 349–370.

[98] Roth, M. A., H. F. Korth, and A. Silberschatz. Null values in non-1NF relational databases. Technical Report TR-85-32. University of Texas at Austin, Dec. 1985.

[99] Roth, M. A., H. F. Korth, and A. Silberschatz. Null values in nested databases. *Acta Informatica*, 26 (1989), pp. 615–642.

[100] Roth, M. A., H. F. Korth, and A. Silberschatz. Addendum to null values in nested relational databases. *Acta Informatica*, 28 (1991), pp. 607–610.

[101] Sagiv, Y. Can we use the universal instance assumption without using nulls? In *Proceedings of ACM SIGMOD, International Conference on Management of Data*. Ann Arbor, Michigan: ACM Press, 1981, pp. 108–120.

[102] Schöning, H. Praktische Behandlung von Nullwerten—Realisierung im Molekül-Atom-Datenmodell. In *Proceedings GI-Fachtagung, Datenbank-Systeme für Büro, Technik und Wissenschaft, Germany.* Kaiserslautern, Germany: 1991.

[103] Sciore, E. Null values, updates, and normalizations in relational databases. Technical Report. Department of Electrical Engineering and Computer Science, Princeton University, 1979.

[104] Siklóssy, L. Efficient query evaluation in relational databases with missing values. *Information Processing Letters*, 13, No. 4–5 (1981), pp. 160–163.

[105] Tseng, F. S.-C., A. L. P. Chen, and W. P. Yang. Generalizing the division operation on indefinite databases. In *Future Database 92, Proceedings of the 2nd Far-East Workshop on Future Database Systems.* Kyoto, Japan: Apr. 1992, pp. 347–354.

[106] Vassiliou, Y. Null values in database management—a denotational semantics approach. In *Proceedings of ACM SIGMOD, International Conference on Management of Data.* New York: ACM Press, May 1979, pp. 162–169.

[107] Vassiliou, Y. A formal treatment of imperfect information in database management. Technical Report CSRG-123. University of Toronto, Nov. 1980.

[108] Vassiliou, Y. A formal treatment of imperfection in database management. Ph.D. Dissertation. University of Toronto, 1980.

[109] Vassiliou, Y. Functional dependencies and incomplete information. In *Proceedings of the International Conference on Very Large Databases.* Oct. 1980, pp. 260–269.

[110] Wedekind, H. Null values in DBS (in German). *Informatik Spektrum*, 11 (1988).

[111] Weiyi, L. The determining method about the conflict between null constraints and the set of functional dependencies. *Journal of Computer Science and Technology* (English language edition) (China), 4, No. 2, Apr. 1989, pp. 116–125.

[112] Winslett, M. Updating logical databases containing null values. In *Proceedings of the International Conference on Database Theory.* Ed. G. Ausiello and P. Atzeni. Rome, Italy: Springer-Verlag, Sep. 1986, pp. 421–435.

[113] Winslett, M. Updating databases with incomplete information. Ph.D. Dissertation. Stanford University, Jan. 1987.

[114] Winslett, M. A Model-Based Approach to Updating Databases with Incomplete Information. *ACM Transactions on Database Systems*, 13, No. 2 (1988), pp. 167–196.

[115] Yager, R. R. Set-Based Representations of Conjunctive and Disjunctive Knowledge. *Information Sciences*, 41 (1987), pp. 1–22.

[116] Yang, J. D., and Y. J. Lee. A sound and complete query evaluation for implicit predicate which is a semantic descriptor of unknown values. *Information Processing Letters*, 39, Sep. 1991, pp. 283–289.

[117] Yang, J. D., and Y. J. Lee. Characterization of unknown values with implicit predicate. *Decision Support Systems*, 7, No. 2, May 1991, pp. 133–144.

[118] Yazici, A. Representing Imprecise Information in NF**2 Relations. In *IEEE Proceedings of Southeastcon 90 - Technologies Today and Tomorrow*. New Orleans, LA: Apr. 1990, pp. 1026–1030.

[119] Yia, Y., Z. Feng, and M. Miller. A Multivalued Approach to handle nulls in RDB. In *Future Database 92, Proceedings of the 2nd Far-East Workshop on Future Database Systems*. Kyoto, Japan: Apr. 1992.

[120] Yuan, L. Y., and D. Chiang. A sound and complete query evaluation algorithm for relational databases with null values. In *Proceedings of ACM SIGMOD, International Conference on Management of Data*. ACM Press, May 1988, pp. 74–81.

[121] Yue, K. A more general model for handling missing information in relational databases using a 3-valued logic. *ACM SIGMOD Record*, 20, No. 3, Sep. 1991, pp. 43–49.

[122] Zaniolo, C. Database relations with null values (extended abstract), in *Proceedings of the ACM Symposium on Principles of Database Systems*. Los Angeles, CA: Mar. 1982, pp. 27–33.

[123] Zaniolo, C. A formal treatment of nonexistent values in database relations. Technical Report. Bell Laboratories, 1983.

[124] Zaniolo, C. Database relations with null values. *Journal of Computer and System Sciences*, 28 (1984), pp. 142–166.

[125] Zicari, R. Incomplete information in object-oriented databases. *ACM SIGMOD Record*, 19, No. 3, Sep. 1990, pp. 5–16.

4 LOGIC

Logic-based approaches to uncertainty management are common. We do not include references on logics for uncertainty reasoning; such papers are beyond the limited scope of this bibliography. Figure 3 shows the publication history for logic-based approaches. The last ten years have witnessed significant interest in this area.

Related work can be found in

- Section 2—[1]
- Section 3—[43, 47, 81, 82, 83, 84, 85, 86, 92, 93, 94, 115]
- Section 5—[182, 272]
- Section 9—[351, 352]

[126] Brewka, G. Handling incomplete knowledge in artificial intelligence. In *Information Systems and Artificial Intelligence: Integration Aspects*. Ed. D. Kargiannis. Berlin: Mar. 1990, pp. 11–29.

[127] Caseau, Y. Constraints in an object-oriented deductive database. In *Proceedings of DOOD 91, the International Conference on Deductive and Object-Oriented Databases*. Munich, Germany: Dec. 1991.

[128] Chan, E. A possible world semantics for disjunctive databases. *IEEE Transactions on Knowledge and Data Engineering*, 5, No. 2, Apr. 1993, pp. 282–292.

[129] Chaudhuri, S., and P. Kolaitis. Can Datalog be approximated? In *Proceedings of the ACM Symposium on Principles of Database Systems*. Minneapolis, MN: Apr. 1994.

[130] Demolombe, R., and L. Fariñas del Cerro. An algebraic evaluation method for deduction in incomplete databases. *The Journal of Logic Programming*, 5, No. 3, Sep. 1988, pp. 183–205.

[131] Demolombe, R. An efficient strategy for non-Horn deductive databases. *Theoretical Computer Sciences*, 78, No. 1, Jan. 1991, pp. 245–259.

[132] Eiter, T., and G. Gottlob. Complexity aspects of various semantics for disjunctive databases. In *Proceedings of the ACM Symposium on Principles of Database Systems*. Washington, DC: May 1993, pp. 158–167.

[133] Eiter, T., G. Gottlob, and H. Mannila. Adding disjunction to Datalog. In *Proceedings of the ACM Symposium on Principles of Database Systems.* Minneapolis, MN: Apr. 1994.

[134] Esculier, C. Non-monotonic knowledge evolution in VLKDBs. In *Proceedings of the International Conference on Very Large Databases.* Brisbane, Australia: 1990.

[135] Gallaire, H. Impacts of logic on data bases. In *Proceedings of the International Conference on Very Large Data Bases.* IEEE Computer Society Press. Sep. 1981, pp. 272–281.

[136] Gallaire, H., J. Minker, and J. M. Nicolas. Logic and databases: A deductive approach. *ACM Computing Surveys,* 16, No. 2, June 1984, pp. 153–185.

[137] Gelfond, M., V. Lifschitz, H. Przymusińka, and M. Truszczyński. Disjunctive defaults. In *Proceedings of KR 91, the 2nd International Conference Principles of Knowledge Representation and Reasoning.* Cambridge, MA: Apr. 1991.

[138] George, R., A. Yazici, F. E. Petry, and B. P. Buckles. Uncertainty modeling in object-oriented geographical information systems. In *Proceedings of DEXA 92, the 3rd International Conference on Database and Expert Systems Applications.* Valencia, Spain: 1992.

[139] Güntzer, U., W. Kiessling, and H. Thöne. New directions for uncertainty reasoning in deductive databases. In *Proceedings of ACM SIGMOD, International Conference on Management of Data.* Denver, CO: May 1991, pp. 178–187.

[140] Henschen, L. J., and H. S. Park. Indefinite and GCWA inference in indefinite deductive databases. In *Proceedings of AAAI-86.* 1986, pp. 191–197.

[141] Henschen, L. J., and H. S. Park. Compiling the GCWA in indefinite deductive databases. In *Foundations of Deductive Databases and Logic Programming.* Ed. J. Minker. Los Altos, CA: M. Kaufmann, 1986, pp. 395–438.

[142] Hulin, G. A Proof-theoretic perspective of deductive databases with marked null values. Manuscript M273. Philips Research Laboratory, Brussels. Dec. 1988.

[143] Imieliński, T. On algebraic query processing in logical databases. In *Advances in Data Base Theory.* Ed. H. Gallaire, J. Minker, and J.M. Nicolas. New York: Plenum Press, 1984. Vol. 2. pp. 285–318.

[144] Imieliński, T., and W. Lipski, Jr. Incomplete information in relational databases. *Journal of the Association of Computing Machinery*, 31, No. 4 (1984), pp. 761–791.

[145] Imieliński, T. Query processing in deductive databases with incomplete information. TR 177. Rutgers University, Mar. 1986.

[146] Imieliński, T. Automated deduction in databases with incomplete information. TR 181. Rutgers University, Mar. 1986.

[147] Imieliński, T. Query processing in deductive databases with incomplete information. In *Proceedings of ACM SIGMOD, International Conference on Management of Data*. 1986, pp. 268–280.

[148] Imieliński, T. Automated deduction in databases with incomplete information. In *Preprints of the Workshop on Foundations of Deductive Databases and Logic Programming*. Washington, DC: Aug. 1986, pp. 242–283.

[149] Imieliński, T. Incomplete information in logical databases. *IEEE Database Engineering Bulletin—Special Issue on Imprecision in Databases*, 12, No. 2, June 1989, pp. 29–40.

[150] Johnson, C. A. Handling indefinite and negative data in a deductive database. *Data and Knowledge Engineering*, 6, No. 4, July 1991, pp. 333–348.

[151] Kifer, M., and A. Li. On the semantics of rule-based expert systems with uncertainty. In *Proceedings of the International Conference on Database Theory*. Springer-Verlag, 1988, pp. 102–117.

[152] King, P., and C. Small. Default databases and incomplete information. *Computer Journal*, 34, No. 3, June 1991, pp. 239–244.

[153] Ku, C., D. Heung, and L. Henschen. An efficient indefiniteness inference scheme in indefinite deductive databases. *IEEE Transactions on Knowledge and Data Engineering*, 6, No. 5, Oct. 1994, pp. 713–722.

[154] Lakshmanan, V. S., and F. Sadri. Modeling uncertainty in deductive databases. In *Proceedings of DEXA 94, the 5th International Conference on Database and Expert Systems*. Athens, Greece: Sep. 1994.

[155] Lenzerini, M. Type data bases with incomplete information. *Information Sciences*, 53 (1991), pp. 61–87.

[156] Lerat, N. Query processing in incomplete logical databases. In *Proceedings of the International Conference on Database Theory*. Ed. G. Ausiello and P. Atzeni. Rome, Italy: Springer-Verlag, Sep. 1986, pp. 260–277.

[157] Levesque, H. J. The logic of incomplete databases. In *On Conceptual Modeling: Perspectives from Artificial Intelligence Databases and Programming Languages*. Ed. J. Mylopoulos, M. Brodie, and J. W. Schmidt. Berlin and New York: Springer-Verlag, 1984, pp. 165–186.

[158] Lozinskii, E. Computing facts in non-Horn deductive systems. In *Proceedings of the International Conference on Very Large Databases*. Aug. 1988, pp. 273–279.

[159] van der Meyden, R. Recursively indefinite databases (extended abstract). In *Proceedings of the International Conference on Database Theory*. 1990, pp. 364–378.

[160] Minker, J. On indefinite databases and the closed world assumption. In *Proceedings of the 6th Conference on Automated Deduction*. Lecture Notes in Computer Science No. 138. Springer-Verlag, 1982, pp. 292–308.

[161] Minker, J. On theories of definite and indefinite databases. TR 1250. Department of Computer Science, University of Maryland, 1983.

[162] Naqvi, S. and F. Rossi. Reasoning in inconsistent databases. Technical Report ACT-ST-269-89. MCC, June 1989.

[163] Ostermann, P. Interprétation de l'information incomplète en logique modale. In *4ème conférence Bases de Données Avancées*. Benodet, France: 1987, pp. 279–296.

[164] Ostermann, P. Modal logic and incomplete information. In *Proceedings of the 1st Symposium on Mathematical Fundamentals of Database Systems*. Dresden, GDR: Jan. 1987, pp. 181–196.

[165] Ostermann, P. Logiques modales et informations incomplètes. Ph.D. Dissertation. Toulouse, Sep. 1988.

[166] Parsons, S., and J. Fox. A general approach to managing imperfect information in deductive databases. In *Proceedings of the Workshop on Uncertainty in Databases and Deductive Systems*. Ithaca, NY: Nov. 1994.

[167] Reiter, R. Towards a logical reconstruction of relational database theory. In *On Conceptual Modeling: Perspectives from Artificial Intelligence Databases and Programming Languages*. Ed. J. Mylopoulos M. Brodie, and J. W. Schmidt. Berlin and New York: Springer-Verlag, 1984, pp. 191–238.

[168] Reiter, R. What should a database know? In *Proceedings of the Symposium on Computational Logic*. Brussels: 1990, pp. 96–113.

[169] Ross, K. A., and R. W. Topor. Inferring negative information from disjunctive databases. *Journal of Automated Reasoning*, 4, No. 4, Dec. 1988, pp. 397–424.

[170] Royer, V. The Semantics of incomplete databases as an expression of preferences. *Theoretical Computer Science*, 78, No. 1, Jan. 1991, pp. 113–136.

[171] Sakama, C. Possible model semantics for disjunctive databases. In *Proceedings of DOOD 90, the International Conference on Deductive and Object-Oriented Databases*. Kyoto, Japan: Dec. 1989.

[172] Subrahmanian, V. S. Paraconsistent disjunctive deductive databases. In *Proceedings of the 20th International Symposium on Multiple-Valued Logic*. Charlotte, NC: May 1990, pp. 339–346.

[173] Vardi, M. Y. Querying logical databases. *Journal of Computer and System Sciences*, 33 (1986), pp. 142–160.

[174] Vardi, M. Y. On the integrity of databases with incomplete information. In *Proceedings of the ACM Symposium on Principles of Database Systems*. 1986, pp. 252–266.

[175] Williams, M. H., and Q. Kong. Incomplete information in a deductive database. *Data and Knowledge Engineering*, 3, No. 3, Nov. 1988, pp. 197–220.

[176] Williams, M. H., Q. Kong, and G. Chen. Handling Incomplete Information in a logic database. In *UK IT 88 Conference Publication*. Swansea, United Kingdom: July 1988, pp. 224–227.

[177] Yahya, A. and L. J. Henschen. Deduction in non-Horn databases. *JAR*, 1 (1985), pp. 141–160.

5   FUZZY SET AND POSSIBILITY THEORY

Fuzzy set and possibility theory approaches are popular. Figure 4 shows the increasing popularity for handling uncertainty and imprecision in information systems using these approaches.

Related work can be found in

- Section 2—[7]

[178] Andreasen, T., and O. Pivert. On the weakening of fuzzy relational queries. In *Proceedings of ISMIS 94, The 8th International Symposium on Methodologies for Intelligent Systems.* Charlotte, NC: Oct. 1994.

[179] Anvari, M., and G. F. Rose. Fuzzy relational databases. In *Analysis of Fuzzy Information.* 1987. Vol. 2. pp. 203–212.

[180] Arrazola, I., A. Plainfosse, H. Prade, and C. Testemale. Extrapolation of fuzzy values from incomplete data bases. *Information Sciences*, 14, No. 6 (1989).

[181] Baldwin, J. F., and S. Q. Zhou. A fuzzy relational inference language. *Fuzzy Sets and Systems*, 14 (1984), pp. 155–174.

[182] Bandler, W., and L. Kohout. The interrelations of the principal fuzzy logical operators. In *Approximate Reasoning in Expert Systems.* Ed. M. M. Gupta A., Kandel W. Bandler, and J. B. Kiszka. New York, NY: Elsevier Science Publishers, 1985, pp. 767–780.

[183] Bhuniya, B., and P. Niyogi. Lossless join property in fuzzy relational databases. *Data and Knowledge Engineering*, 5, No. 1, Feb. 1993, pp. 122–122.

[184] Bosc, P., M. Galibourg, and G. Hamon. Fuzzy querying with SQL: Extensions and implementation aspects. *Fuzzy Sets and Systems*, 28 (1988), pp. 333–349.

[185] Bosc, P., and M. Galibourg. Flexible selection among objects: A framework based on fuzzy sets. In *Proceedings of the ACM Conference on Research and Development in Information Retrieval.* Grenoble, France: 1988, pp. 433–449.

[186] Bosc, P., and M. Galibourg. Indexing principles for a fuzzy data base. *Information Sciences*, 14, No. 6 (1989).

[187] Bosc, P., and O. Pivert. Some algorithms for evaluating fuzzy relational queries. In *Proceedings of the International Conference on Information Processing and Management of Uncertainty in Knowledge-Based Systems.* 1990, pp. 431–442.

[188] Bosc, P., and O. Pivert. About Equivalences in SQLf, a relational language supporting imprecise querying. In *Proceedings of the International Fuzzy Engineering Symposium.* Yokohama, Japan: 1991.

[189] Bosc, P., and O. Pivert. Some properties of alpha-cuts of fuzzy predicates. In *Proceedings of the 11th European Meeting on Cybernetics and Systems Research*. Vienna, Austria: 1992.

[190] Bosc, P., and O. Pivert. On the evaluation of fuzzy quantified queries in a database management system. In *Proceedings of the North American Fuzzy Information Society*. Dec. 1992.

[191] Bosc, P., L. Lietard, and O. Pivert. Soft querying, a new feature for database management systems. In *Proceedings of DEXA 94, the 5th International Conference on Database and Expert Systems*. Athens, Greece: Sep. 1994.

[192] Bosc, P., and H. Prade. Fuzzy division for regular relational databases. In *Proceedings of the Workshop on Uncertainty in Databases and Deductive Systems*. Ithaca, NY: Nov. 1994.

[193] Buckles, B. P., and F. E. Petry. Fuzzy databases and their applications. In *Fuzzy Information and Decision Processes*. Ed. M. M. Gupta and E. Sanchez. Amsterdam: North-Holland, 1982, pp. 361–371.

[194] Buckles, B. P., and F. E. Petry. Security and fuzzy databases. In *Proceedings of the 1982 IEEE International Conference on Cybernetics and Society*. 1982, pp. 213–226.

[195] Buckles, B. P., and F. E. Petry. A fuzzy representation of data for relational databases. *Fuzzy Sets and Systems*, 7, No. 3, May 1982, pp. 213–226.

[196] Buckles, B. P., and F. E. Petry. Extension of the fuzzy database with fuzzy arithmetic. In *Proceedings of the IFAC Symposium on Fuzzy Information, Knowledge Representation and Decision Processes*. Marseille, France: July 1983, pp. 409–414.

[197] Buckles, B. P., and F. E. Petry. Query languages for fuzzy databases. In *Management Decision Support Systems*. 1983, pp. 241–252.

[198] Buckles, B. P., and F. E. Petry. Information theoretical characterization of fuzzy relational databases. *IEEE Transactions on Systems, Man, and Cybernetics*, SMC-13, No. 1 (1983), pp. 74–77.

[199] Buckles, B. P., and F. E. Petry. Extending the fuzzy database with fuzzy numbers. *Information Science*, No. 34 (1984), pp. 145–155.

[200] Buckles, B. P., and F. E. Petry. Uncertainty models in information and database systems. *Information Sciences*, 11 (1985), pp. 77–87.

[201] Buckles, B. P., F. E. Petry, and H. Sachar. Retrieval and design concepts for similarity-based (fuzzy) relational databases. In *Robotics and Expert Systems 1986, Proceedings of ROBEXS 86: The 2nd Annual Workshop on Robotics and Expert Systems.* Houston, TX: June 1986, pp. 335–343.

[202] Buckles, B. P., and F. E. Petry. Generalized database and information systems. In *Analysis of Fuzzy Information.* 1987. Vol. 2. pp. 177–201.

[203] Buckles, B. P., and F. E. Petry. Towards a fuzzy object-oriented data model. In *Proceedings of NAFIPS 91, the North American Fuzzy Information Processing Society.* May 1991, pp. 73–77.

[204] Chang, S. K., and J. S. Ke. Database skeleton and its application to fuzzy query translation. *IEEE Transactions on Software Engineering*, SE-4 (1978), pp. 31–43.

[205] Chang, S. K., and J. S. Ke. Translation of fuzzy queries for relational database systems. *IEEE Transactions on Pattern Analysis and Machine Intelligence (PAMI-1)*, (1979), pp. 281–294.

[206] Chen, G. A general treatment of data redundancy in a fuzzy relational data model. *Journal of the American Society for Information*, 43, No. 4, May 1992, pp. 304–304.

[207] Cross, V., and T. Sudkamp. Representation and support generation in fuzzy relational databases. In *Proceedings of NAECON 91, the IEEE 1991 National Aerospace and Electronics Conference.* Dayton, OH: May 1991, pp. 1136–1143.

[208] Cubero, J. C., and M. A. Vila. A new definition of fuzzy functional dependency in fuzzy relational databases. *International Journal of Intelligent Systems*, 9, No. 5, May 1994, pp. 441–449.

[209] DiCesare, F., and Z. Sahnoun. Linguistic summarization of fuzzy data. *Information Services*, 52 (1990), pp. 141–152.

[210] Dockery, J. T., and E. Murray. Fuzzy linguistic data bases. An application. *Information Sciences*, 14, No. 6 (1989).

[211] Dubois, D., and H. Prade. *Fuzzy Sets and Systems: Theory and Applications.* New York, NY: Academic Press, 1980.

[212] Dubois, D., H. Prade, and C. Testamale. Handling incomplete or uncertain data and vague queries in database applications. in *Possibility Theory: An Approach to Computerized Processing of Uncertainty.* New York and London: Plenum Press, 1988. Chap. 6. pp. 217–257.

[213] Dubois, D., and H. Prade. The treatment of uncertainty in knowledge-based systems using fuzzy sets and possibility theory. *International Journal of Intelligent Systems*, 3 (1988), pp. 141–165.

[214] Dubois, D., and H. Prade. Processing fuzzy temporal knowledge. *IEEE Transactions of Systems, Man, and Cybernetics*, 19, No. 4 (1989), pp. 729–744.

[215] Dutta, S. Approximate spatial reasoning. In *Proceedings of the 4th Conference on Artificial Intelligence for Space Applications*. Huntsville, AL: Nov. 1988, pp. 95–106.

[216] Dutta, S. An event-based fuzzy temporal logic. In *Proceedings of the 18th IEEE International Symposium on Multiple-Valued Logic*. Palma de Mallorca, Spain: 1988, pp. 64–71.

[217] Dutta, S. Generalized events in temporal databases. In *Proceedings of the 5th International Conference on Data Engineering*. Los Angeles, CA: Feb. 1989, pp. 118–126.

[218] Dutta, S. *Approximate Reasoning with Temporal and Spatial Concepts*. Ph.D. Dissertation. University of California, Berkeley, May 1990.

[219] Fleischman, R. M. *Supporting Fuzzy Logic Selection Predicates on a High Throughput Database System*. Boston, MA: MIT Library, 1991.

[220] Gala, S., D. Chawala, and C. Eastman. Combining fuzzy and nonfuzzy approximate retrieval in a database management system. In *Proceedings of NAFIPS 91, the North American Fuzzy Information Processing Society Workshop*. May 1991.

[221] Haar, R. L. A fuzzy relational data base system. Technical Report TR-586. University of Maryland Computer Center, Sep. 1977.

[222] Hawkes, L., S. Derry, and E. Rundenesteiner. Individualized tutoring using an intelligent, fuzzy, temporal relational database. *International Journal of Man and Machine*, 33 (1990), pp. 409–429.

[223] Kacprzyk, J., and A. Ziolkowski. Database queries with fuzzy linguistic quantifiers. *IEEE Transactions on Systems, Man, and Cybernetics*, SMC-16, 3, May/June 1989, pp. 474–479.

[224] Kacprzyk, J., S. Zadrozny, and A. Ziolkowski. FQUERY III plus. A 'human-consistent' database querying system based on fuzzy logic with linguistic quantifiers. *Information Sciences*, 14, No. 6 (1989).

[225] Kamel, M. S., B. Hadfield, and M. Ismail. Fuzzy query processing using clustering techniques. *Information Processing and Management*, 26, No. 2 (1990), pp. 279–293.

[226] Klir, G. J., and T. A. Folger. Fuzzy sets, uncertainty and information. Englewood Cliffs, NJ: Prentice-Hall, 1988.

[227] Kurutach, W., and J. Franklin. On temporal-fuzziness in temporal fuzzy databases. In *Proceedings of DEXA 93, the 4th International Conference on Database and Expert Systems* . Prague, Czech Republic: Sep. 1993, pp. 154–165.

[228] Lee, D., and M. Kim. Discovering database summaries through refinements of fuzzy hypotheses. In *Proceedings of ICDE, the International Conference on Data Engineering*. Houston, TX: Feb. 1994, pp. 223–230.

[229] Lopez-Permouth, S. R. On categories of fuzzy models. *Information Services*, 53 (1990), pp. 211–220.

[230] Mansfield, W. H., and R. M. Fleischman. A high performance, ad-hoc, fuzzy query processing system for relational databases. In *Proceedings of the North American Fuzzy Information Processing Society*. Dec. 1992.

[231] Matyuta, T. A., V. V. Pasichnik, and A. A. Stogniy. Means for management of relational fuzzy databases—way to merging of systems of data bases and knowledge bases. In *Proceedings of the 1st Symposium on Mathematical Fundamentals of Database Systems*. Visegrad, Hungary: June 1989, pp. 337–346.

[232] Medina, J. M., O. Pons, and M. A. Vila. GEFRED: A generalized model of fuzzy relational databases. *Information Sciences*, 76, No. 1/2, Dec. 1994, pp. 87–87.

[233] Mouaddib, N. Fuzzy identification in fuzzy databases: The nuanced relational division. *International Journal of Intelligent Systems*, 9, No. 5, May 1994, pp. 455–475.

[234] Murthy, S. V., and A. Kandel. Fuzzy sets and typicality theory. *Information Sciences*, 51 (1990), pp. 61–93.

[235] Overton, K., and D. Gaucas. Fuzzy representation for event occurrence, in *Sensor Fusion II: Human and Machine Strategies*. Philadelphia, PA: Nov. 1989, pp. 472–479.

[236] Pedrycz, W. Relevancy of fuzzy models. *Information Services*, 52 (1990), pp. 285–302.

[237] Potoczny, H. On similarity relations in fuzzy relational databases. *Fuzzy Sets and Systems*, 12 (1984), pp. 231–235.

[238] Prade, H. The connection between Lipski's approach to incomplete information data bases and Zadeh's possibility theory. In *Proceedings of the International Conference on Systems Methodology*. Washington, DC: Jan. 1982, pp. 402–408.

[239] Prade, H., and C. Testemale. Generalizing database relational algebra for the treatment of incomplete or uncertain information and vague queries. *Information Sciences*, 34 (1984), pp. 115–143.

[240] Prade, H. Lipski's approach to incomplete information data bases restated and generalized in the setting of Zadeh's possibility theory. *Information Systems*, 9, No. 1 (1985), pp. 27–42.

[241] Prade, H., and C. Testemale. fuzzy relational databases: Representational issues and reduction using similarity measures. *Journal of the American Society for Information Science*, 38, No. 2, Mar. 1987, pp. 118–126.

[242] Prade, H., and C. Testemale. Representation of soft constraints and fuzzy attribute values by means of possibility distributions in databases. In *The Analysis of Fuzzy Information*. Ed. J. Bezdek. Boca Raton, FL: CRC Press, 1987. Vol. 2. pp. 213–229.

[243] Prade, H., and C. Testemale. The possible approach to handling of imprecision in database systems. *IEEE Database Engineering Bulletin—Special Issue on Imprecision in Databases*, 12, No. 2, June 1989, pp. 4–10.

[244] Raju, K. V. S. V. N., and A. Majumdar. Fuzzy functional dependencies in fuzzy relations. In *International Conference on Data Engineering*. Los Angeles, CA: Feb. 1986, pp. 312–319.

[245] Raju, K. V. S. V. N., and A. Majumdar. The study of joins in fuzzy relational databases. *Fuzzy Sets and Systems*, 21, No. 1 (1987), pp. 19–34.

[246] Raju, K. V. S. V. N., and A. Majumdar. Fuzzy functional dependencies and lossless join decomposition of fuzzy relational database systems. *ACM Transactions on Database Systems*, 13, No. 2 (1988), pp. 129–166.

[247] Ramer, A. Data dependencies in fuzzy databases. In *Proceedings of NAFIPS 90, the North American Fuzzy Information Processing Society*. Toronto, Canada: 1990, pp. 258–261.

[248] Rundensteiner, E. A., L. W. Hawkes, and W. Bandler. Set-valued temporal knowledge representation for fuzzy temporal retrieval in ICAI. In *Proceedings of NAFIPS 87, the North American Fuzzy Information Processing Society.* May 1987.

[249] Rundensteiner, E. A., and L. Bic. Towards modeling imprecision in semantic data models. In *Proceedings of the 3rd International Fuzzy Systems Association World Congress.* Aug. 1989.

[250] Rundensteiner, E. A., and L. Bic. Aggregates in possibilistic databases. In *Proceedings of the International Conference on Very Large Databases.* 1989.

[251] Rundensteiner, E. A., and L. Bic. Semantic database models and their potential for capturing imprecision. In *Proceedings of COMAD 89, the International Conference of Management of Data.* Hyderabad, India: Nov. 1989.

[252] Rundensteiner, E. A., L. W. Hawkes, and W. Bandler. On nearness measures in fuzzy relational data models. *International Journal of Approximate Reasoning,* 3, No. 3, July 1989, pp. 267–298.

[253] Rundensteiner, E. A., and L. Bic. Evaluating aggregates in possibilistic relational databases. *Data and Knowledge Engineering,* 7 (1992), pp. 239–267.

[254] Ruspini, E. Possibilistic data structures for the representation of uncertainty. In *Approximate Reasoning in Decision Analysis.* Ed. M. M. Gupta and E. Sanchez. Amsterdam: North-Holland, 1982. pp. 411–415.

[255] Ruspini, E. H. Possibility theory approaches for advanced information systems. *Computer,* 9, No. 2, Sep. 1982, pp. 83–89.

[256] Sheng, R. L. A linguistic approach to temporal information analysis. Ph.D. Dissertation. University of California, Berkeley, May 1984.

[257] Shenoi, S., and A. Melton. Proximity relations in the fuzzy relational database model. *Fuzzy Sets and Systems,* 31 (1989), pp. 285–296.

[258] Shenoi, S., and A. Melton. An extended version of the fuzzy relational database model. *Information Sciences,* 52, No. 1 (1990), pp. 35–52.

[259] Shenoi, S., A. Melton, and L. T. Fan. An equivalence classes model of fuzzy relational databases. *Fuzzy Sets and Systems,* 38, No. 2, Nov. 1990, pp. 153–170.

[260] Shenoi, S., A. Melton, and L. T. Fan. Functional dependencies and normal forms in the fuzzy relational database model. *Information Sciences*, 60, No. 1/2, Mar. 1992, pp. 1–28.

[261] Singer, D. Default data generation in databases of net systems: A fuzzy set approach. *International Journal of Systems Science*, 20, No. 3, Mar. 1989, pp. 385–385.

[262] Sudkamp, T., and V. Cross. Support generation in fuzzy relational databases. In *Proceedings of NAFIPS 90, the North American Fuzzy Information Processing Society*. Toronto, Canada: 1990, pp. 265–268.

[263] Tahani, V. A conceptual framework for fuzzy query processing—a step toward very intelligent database systems. *Information Processing and Management*, 13 (1977), pp. 289–303.

[264] Takahashi, Y. Fuzzy database query languages and their relational completeness theorem. *IEEE Transactions on Knowledge and Data Engineering*, 5, No. 1, Apr. 1993, pp. 122–122.

[265] Tripathy, R. C., and P. C. Sexena. Multivalued dependencies in fuzzy relational databases. *Fuzzy Sets and Systems*, 38, No. 3, Dec. 1990, pp. 267–279.

[266] Umano, M. FREEDOM-O: A fuzzy database system. In *Fuzzy Information and Decision Processes*. Ed. M. M. Gupta and E. Sanchez. Amsterdam: North-Holland, 1982, pp. 339–349.

[267] Umano, M. Retrieval from fuzzy data base by fuzzy relational algebra, in *Proceedings of the IFAC Symposium on Fuzzy Information, Knowledge Representation, and Decision Processes*. Marseille: July 1983, pp. 1–6.

[268] Umano, M. Retrieval from fuzzy data base by fuzzy relational algebra. In *Fuzzy Information, Knowledge Representation, and Decision Analysis*. Ed. E. Sanchez. Oxford, England: Pergamon Press, 1984, pp. 1–6.

[269] Vandenberghe, R., A. Van Schooten, R. De Caluwe, and E. E. Kerre. Some practical aspects of fuzzy database techniques. An example. In *Fuzzy Databases, the 2nd International Fuzzy Systems Association Congress*. Tokyo, Japan: July 1989, pp. 465–472.

[270] Vandenberghe, R., A. Van Schooten, R. De Caluwe, and E. E. Kerre. Some Practical Aspects of Fuzzy Database Techniques. An Example. *Information Systems*, 14, No. 6 (1989), pp. 443–453.

[271] Vasiliadis, S., G. Triantafyllos, and W. Kobrosly. A fuzzy reasoning database question answering system. *IEEE Transactions on Knowledge and Data Engineering*, 6, No. 6, Dec. 1994, pp. 868–888.

[272] Vila, M. A., J. C. Cubero, and J. M. Medina. A logic approach to fuzzy relational databases. *International Journal of Intelligent Systems*, 9, No. 5, May 1994, pp. 449–459.

[273] Vitek, M. Fuzzy information and fuzzy time. In *Proceedings of the IFAC Symposium on Fuzzy Information, Knowledge Representation, and Decision Analysis*. Marseille, France: 1983, pp. 159–162.

[274] Voung, L. T., and H. Thuan. Retrieval from fuzzy database by fuzzy relational algebra. *MTA Sztaki Kozlmemenyek*, 37 (1987), pp. 223–248.

[275] Voung, L. T., and H. Thuan. Relational database extended by application of fuzzy set theory and linguistic variables. *Computers and Artificial Intelligence*, 8, No. 2 (1989), pp. 153–168.

[276] Wang, F., G. B. Hall, and Subaryono. Fuzzy information representation and processing in conventional GIS software: database design and application. *International Journal of Geographical Information Systems*, 4, No. 3 (1990), pp. 261–283.

[277] Wong, M. H., and K. S. Leung. A fuzzy database-query language. *Information Systems*, 15, No. 5 (1990), pp. 583–590.

[278] Yager, R. R. Fuzzy quotient operators for fuzzy relational databases. In *Proceedings of the International Fuzzy Engineering Symposium*. Yokohama, Japan: 1991.

[279] Yang, Q., W. Zhang, C. Luo, and H. Yu. Unnesting fuzzy SQL queries in fuzzy databases. In *Proceedings of SOFTEK 93, Workshop on Incompleteness and Uncertainty in Information Systems*. Montreal, Canada: Oct. 1993.

[280] Yang, Q., C. Liu, J. Wu, and C. Yu. Efficient processing of nested fuzzy SQL queries. In *Proceedings of ICDE, the International Conference on Data Engineering*. Taipei, Taiwan: Mar. 1995.

[281] Zadeh, L. Knowledge representation in fuzzy logic. *IEEE Transactions on Knowledge and Data Engineering*, 1, No. 1 (1989), pp. 89–100.

[282] Zemankova-Leech, M., and A. Kandel. Fuzzy relational data bases—a key to expert systems. Interdisciplinary Systems Research Series. Köln: TÜV Rheinland, 1984.

[283] Zemankova, M., and A. Kandel. Implementing imprecision in information systems. *Information Sciences*, 37 (1985), pp. 107–141.

[284] Zemankova, M. FIIS: A fuzzy intelligent information system. *IEEE Database Engineering Bulletin—Special Issue on Imprecision in Databases*, 12, No. 2, June 1989, pp. 11–20.

[285] Zhang, W., C. Yu, R. Reagan, and H. Nakajima. Context-dependent interpretations of linguistic terms in fuzzy relational databases. In *Proceedings of ICDE, the International Conference on Data Engineering*. Taipei, Taiwan: Mar. 1995.

[286] Zvieli, A., and P. Chen. Entity-relationship modeling and fuzzy databases. In *Proceedings of the 2nd International Conference on Data Engineering*, 1986, pp. 320–327.

[287] Zvieli, A. On complete fuzzy relational query languages. In *Proceedings of NAFIPS 86, the North American Fuzzy Information Processing Society*. New Orleans, LA: 1986, pp. 704–726.

6   PROBABILITY THEORY

Probability theory is much older than fuzzy set and possibility theory, but probability-based approaches to managing uncertainty are rarer. Figure 5 shows the publication history for handling uncertainty and imprecision in information systems using probabilistic methods.

Related work can be found in

- Section 4—[139]

- Section 7—[332, 333]

[288] Barbará, D., H. García-Molina, and D. Porter. A probabilistic relational data model. TR 215–89. Princeton University, Jan. 1989.

[289] Barbará, D., H. García-Molina, and D. Porter. A probabilistic relational data model. In *Proceedings of EDBT 90, the International Conference on Extending Database Technology*. Venice, Italy: Mar. 1990, pp. 60–74.

[290] Barbará, D., H. García-Molina, and D. Porter. The management of probabilistic data. *IEEE Transactions on Knowledge and Data Engineering*, 4, No. 5, Oct. 1992, pp. 487–502.

[291] Brown, D. E., and W. J. Markert. Uncertainty management with imprecise knowledge with application to design. IPC-TR 90-001. University of Virginia, Jan. 1990.

[292] Cavallo, R., and M. Pittarelli. The theory of probabilistic databases. In *Proceedings of the International Conference on Very Large Databases*. Ed. P. Hammersley. Brighton, England: Sep. 1987, pp. 71–81.

[293] Dyreson, C. E., and R. T. Snodgrass. Valid-time indeterminacy. In *Proceedings of the International Conference on Data Engineering*. Vienna, Austria: Apr. 1993, pp. 335–343.

[294] Fuhr, N. A probabilistic framework for vague queries and imprecise information in databases. In *Proceedings of the International Conference on Very Large Databases*. Brisbane, Australia: 1990.

[295] Garcia-Molina, H., and D. Porter. Supporting probabilistic data in a relational system. TR 147–88. Princeton University, Feb. 1988.

[296] Gelenbe, E., and G. Hebrail. A probability model of uncertainty in data bases. In *Proceedings of the International Conference on Data Engineering*. IEEE Computer Society. Los Angeles, CA: IEEE Computer Society Press, Feb. 1986, pp. 328–333.

[297] Kornatzky, Y., and S. Shimony. A probabilistic spatial data model. In *Proceedings of DEXA 93, the 4th International Conference on Database and Expert Systems*. Prague, Czech Republic: Sep. 1993.

[298] Kornatzky, Y., and S. Shimony. A probabilistic object-oriented data model. TR FC 93-04. Ben-Gurion University, May 1993.

[299] Lakshmanan, L., and H. Johnstone. A relational data model for manipulating probabilistic knowledge. In *Proceedings of SOFTEK 93, Workshop on Incompleteness and Uncertainty in Information Systems*. Montreal, Canada: Oct. 1993.

[300] Lee, S. K. Imprecise and uncertain information in databases: An evidential approach. in *Proceedings of the International Conference on Data Engineering*. Ed. F. Golshani. Los Alamitos, CA: IEEE Computer Society Press, Feb. 1992, pp. 614–621.

[301] Lee, S. K. An extended relational database model for uncertain and imprecise information. In *Proceedings of the International Conference on Very Large Databases*. Vancouver, Canada: Aug. 1992.

[302] Pearl, J. *Probabilistic Reasoning in Intelligent Systems*. Palo Alto, CA: Morgan Kaufmann, 1988.

[303] Pittarelli, M. An algebra for probabilistic databases. *IEEE Transactions on Knowledge and Data Engineering*, 6, No. 2, Apr. 1994, pp. 293–303.

[304] Wong, S. K. M., and Y. Y. Yao. A probabilistic inference model for information retrieval. *Information Systems*, 16, No. 3 (1991), pp. 301–321.

[305] Wuthrich, B. A probabilistic query language. TR CS94-8. Hong Kong University of Science and Technology, Mar. 1994.

[306] Zimányi, E. Query evaluation in probabilistic databases. RR 92-01. INFODOC, Université Libre de Bruxelles, Belgium, Sep. 1992.

[307] Zimányi, E. Probabilistic relational databases. RR 92-02. INFODOC, Université Libre de Bruxelles, Belgium, Oct. 1992.

[308] Zimányi, E. Incomplete and uncertain information in relational databases. Ph.D. Dissertation. Université Libre de Bruxelles, July 1992.

7 QUERY-LEVEL UNCERTAINTY

As information systems grow in size, storing terra-bytes of data or more, data mining and approximate querying will become increasingly more important. Figure 6 shows the publication history for query-level uncertainty.

Related work can be found in

- Section 5—[191]

[309] Anwar, T. M., H. W. Beck, and S. B. Navathe. Knowledge mining by imprecise querying: A classification-based system. In *Proceedings of the International Conference on Data Engineering*. Tempe, AZ: Feb. 1992, pp. 622–630.

[310] Aref, W. G., D. Barbara, S. Johnson, and S. Mehrotra. Efficient processing of proximity queries for large databases. In *Proceedings of ICDE, the International Conference on Data Engineering*. Taipei, Taiwan: Mar. 1995.

[311] Buneman, P., S. B. Davidson, and A. Watters. A semantics for complex objects and approximate queries. In *Proceedings of the ACM Symposium on Principles of Database Systems*. Austin, TX: Mar. 1988, pp. 305–314.

[312] Buneman, P., S. B. Davidson, and A. Watters. A semantics for complex objects and approximate answers. *Journal of Computer and System Sciences*, Aug. 1990, pp. 170–218.

[313] D'Atri, A., and L. Tarantino. From browsing to querying. *IEEE Database Engineering Bulletin—Special Issue on Imprecision in Databases*, 12, No. 2, June 1989, pp. 46–53.

[314] Dreizen, H. M., and S. K. Chang. Imprecise database: Imprecise queries and view navigation. *Inf. Sci. Eng. 1*, 1, Jan. 1985, pp. 12–43.

[315] Eastman, C. M. Approaches to approximate retrieval in database management systems. In *Proceedings of NAFIPS 87, the North American Fuzzy Information Processing Society Workshop*. May 1987.

[316] Eastman, C. M. Approximate retrieval: A comparison of information retrieval and database management systems. *IEEE Database Engineering Bulletin—Special Issue on Imprecision in Databases*, 12, No. 2, June 1989, pp. 41–45.

[317] Ichikawa, T., and M. Hirakawa. ARES: A relational database with the capability of performing flexible interpretation of queries. *IEEE Transactions on Software Engineering*, 12, No. 5, May 1986, pp. 624–634.

[318] Kamel, M. S., W. S. Loo, and A. K. C. Wong. Intelligent database query translation. In *Proceedings of the 1988 IEEE International Conference on Systems, Man, and Cybernetics*. Beijing/Shenyang, China: Aug. 1988, pp. 665–669.

[319] Missaoui, R., and R. Godin. A concept lattice approach in data dredging. In *Proceedings of SOFTEK 93, Workshop on Incompleteness and Uncertainty in Information Systems*. Montreal, Canada: Oct. 1993.

[320] Motro, A. Query generalization: a method for interpreting null answers. In *Expert Database Systems*, 1986, pp. 597–616.

[321] Motro, A. Completeness information and its application to query processing. In *Proceedings of the International Conference on Very Large Data
Bases*. Aug. 1986, pp. 170–178.

[322] Motro, A. VAGUE: A user interface to relational databases that permits
vague queries. *ACM Transactions on Office Information Systems*, 6, No.
3, July 1988, pp. 187–214.

[323] Motro, A. A trio of database user interfaces for handling vague retrieval
requests. *IEEE Database Engineering Bulletin—Special Issue on Imprecision in Databases*, 12, No. 2, June 1989, pp. 54–63.

[324] Motro, A. FLEX: A tolerant and cooperative user interface to databases.
IEEE Transactions on Knowledge and Data Engineering, 2, No. 2, June
1990, pp. 231–246.

[325] Özsoyoğlu, G. Synthetic query response construction in scientific databases
with time constraints and incomplete information. In *Proceedings of the
International Conference on Data Engineering*. IEEE Computer Society.
Los Angeles, CA: IEEE Computer Society Press, Feb. 1987, pp. 282.

[326] Rabitti, F., and P. Savino. Retrieval of multimedia documents by imprecise query specification. In *Proceedings of EDBT 90, the International
Conference on Extending Database Technology*. Venice, Italy: 1990, pp.
203–218.

[327] Shin, D. Semantics for handling queries with missing information. In *Proceedings of the 9th Annual International Conference on Information Systems*. Minneapolis, MN: Dec. 1988.

[328] Shum, C. Quick and incomplete responses: The semantic approach. In
*Proceedings of CIKM 93, the 2nd International Conference on Information
and Knowledge Management*. Arlington, VA: Nov. 1993.

[329] Vrbsky, S. V., and Jane W. S. Liu. An object-oriented query processor that
produces monotonically improving approximate answers. In *Proceedings of
the International Conference on Data Engineering*. Kobe, Japan: 1991.

[330] Vrbsky, S. V., and J. W. S. Liu. APPROXIMATE: A Query Processor that
Produces Monotonically Improving Approximate Answers. *IEEE Transactions on Knowledge and Data Engineering*, 5, No. 6, Dec. 1993, pp.
1056–1068.

[331] Vrbsky, S. Approximate: A query processor that produces monotonically
improving approximate answers. Ph.D. Dissertation. University of Illinois
at Urbana-Champaign, 1993.

[332] Wong, E. A statistical approach to incomplete information. Technical Report CCA-80-01. Computer Corporation of America, May 1980.

[333] Wong, E. A statistical approach to incomplete information in database systems. *ACM Transactions on Database Systems*, 7, No. 3, Sep. 1982, pp. 470–488.

[334] Yen, S.-J., and A. Chen. Neighborhood/conceptual query answering with imprecise/incomplete Data. In *Proceedings of the 12th International Conference on the Entity-Relationship Approach*. Dallas, TX: Dec. 1993.

8 SCHEMA-LEVEL UNCERTAINTY

Uncertainty and imprecision can also exist in the schema, that is, in how the data is organized. In some cases, this is a by-product of schema evolution, although the general topic of schema evolution is beyond the scope of this bibliography.

Related work can be found in

- Section 3—[125]
- Section 4—[155]
- Section 5—[286]
- Section 10—[384]

[335] Dreizen, H. M., and S. K. Chang. Imprecise schema: A rationale for relations with embedded subrelations. *ACM Transactions on Database Systems*, 14, No. 4, Dec. 1989, pp. 447–479.

[336] Imieliński, T., S. Naqvi, and K. Vadaparty. Querying design and planning databases. In *Proceedings of DOOD 91, the International Conference on Deductive and Object-Oriented Databases*. Munich, Germany: Dec. 1991.

[337] Imieliński, T., S. Naqvi, and K. Vadaparty. Incomplete objects—a data model for design and planning applications. In *Proceedings of ACM SIG-MOD, International Conference on Management of Data*. Denver, CO: May 1991, pp. 288–297.

[338] Ramirez, R. G., R. Dattero, and J. Choobineh. Extension of relational views to derived relations with exceptions. *Information Systems*, 15, No. 3 (1990), pp. 321–333.

[339] Tanaka, K., M. Yoshikawa, and K. Ishihara. Schema design, views and incomplete information in object-oriented databases. *Journal of Information Processing*, 12, No. 3 (1989), pp. 239–250.

9   COMPLEXITY ANALYSES

Adding support for uncertain and imprecise information is sometimes costly. Research that characterizes the time or space complexity of various approaches appears in this section.

Related work can be found in

■   Section 4—[132]

[340] Abiteboul, S., P. Kanellakis, and G. Grahne. On the representation and querying of sets of possible worlds. In *Proceedings of ACM SIGMOD, International Conference on Management of Data*. Ed. U. Dayal and I. Traiger. San Francisco, CA: ACM Press, May 1987, pp. 34–48.

[341] Abiteboul, S., P. Kanellakis, and G. Grahne. On the representation and querying of sets of possible worlds. *Theoretical Computer Science*, 78, No. 1, Jan. 1991, pp. 159–187.

[342] van Beek, P., and R. Cohen. Exact and approximate reasoning about temporal relations. *Computational Intelligence*, 6 (1990), pp. 132–144.

[343] van Beek, P. Temporal query processing with indefinite information. *Artificial Intelligence in Medicine*, 3, No. 6, Dec. 1991, pp. 325–339.

[344] Dean, T., and M. Boddy. Reasoning about partially ordered events. *Artificial Intelligence*, 36, No. 3, Oct. 1988, pp. 375–399.

[345] Imieliński, T., and K. Vadaparty. Complexity of query processing in databases with or-objects. In *Proceedings of the ACM Symposium on Principles of Database Systems*. 1989, pp. 51–65.

[346] Koubarakis, M. Dense time and temporal constraints with $\neq$. In *Proceedings of KR 92, the 3rd International Conference on Principles of Knowledge Representation and Reasoning*. Oct. 1992.

[347] Lakshmanan, V. S. Query evaluation with null values: Completeness and complexity. In *Office and Data Base Systems Research*. Computer Systems Research Institute, University of Toronto, Toronto, Canada: Sep. 1988, pp. 218–227.

[348] Lakshmanan, V. S. Query evaluation with null values: How complex is completeness? In *Proceeding of the 9th Conference on Foundations of Software Technology and Theoretical Computer Science*. Bangalore, India: Dec. 1989, pp. 204–222.

[349] Libkin, L., and L. Wong. Semantic representations and query languages for or-sets. In *Proceedings of the ACM Symposium on Principles of Database Systems*. Washington, DC: May 1993, pp. 37–48.

[350] Libkin, L. Aspects of Partial Information in Databases. Ph.D. Dissertation. University of Pennsylvania, 1994.

[351] van der Meyden, R. The complexity of querying indefinite information: Defined relations, recursion, and Linear Order. Ph.D. Dissertation. Rutgers The State University of New Jersey—New Brunswick, 1992.

[352] van der Meyden, R. The complexity of querying indefinite data about linearly ordered domains (preliminary version). In *Proceedings of the ACM Symposium on Principles of Database Systems*. San Diego, CA: June 1992, pp. 331–345.

[353] Suchenek, M. A. Two applications of model-theoretic forcing to Lipski's data bases with incomplete information. *Fundamenta Informaticæ*, 12, No. 3, Sep. 1989, pp. 269–287.

10 MISCELLANEOUS

Papers that do not fit neatly into one of the previous sections (or that we have yet to classify) appear in this section.

[354] Atzeni, P., and M. C. DeBernardis. A new basis for the weak instance model. In *Proceedings of the ACM Symposium on Principles of Database Systems*. 1987, pp. 79–86.

[355] Babad, Y. M., and J. A. Hoffer. Even no data has a value. *Communications of the Association of Computing Machinery*, 27, No. 8 (1984), pp. 748–756.

[356] Bhatnager, R., and L. Kanal. Handling uncertain information: A review of numeric and non-numeric methods. In *Uncertainty in Artificial Intelligence*. Ed. L. N. Kanal and J. F. Lemmer. New York, NY: Elsevier Science Publishers, 1986, pp. 3–26.

[357] Bolloju, N Modelling of imprecise and uncertain information. In *Proceedings of COMAD 90, the Conference on Management of Data*. New Delhi, India: Dec. 1990.

[358] Borgida, A. Language features for flexible handling of exceptions in information systems. *ACM Transactions on Database Systems*, 10, No. 4 (1985), pp. 565–603.

[359] Borgida, A., and K. E. Williamson. Accommodating exceptions in databases, and refining the schema by learning from them. In *Proceedings of the International Conference on Very Large Databases*. Stockholm: 1985.

[360] Borgida, A., and D. Etherington. Hierarchical knowledge bases and efficient disjunctive reasoning. In *Proceedings of the 1st International Conference on Principles of Knowledge Representation and Reasoning*. Toronto: May 1989, pp. 33–43.

[361] Borgida, A., R. Brachman, D. McGuiness, and L. Resnick. CLASSIC: A structural data model for objects. In *Proceedings of ACM SIGMOD, International Conference on Management of Data*. June 1989, pp. 59–67.

[362] Bowers, D. S. A database architecture for aggregate-incomplete data. *The Computer Journal*, 27, No. 4 (1984), pp. 294–300.

[363] Brudno, V. A. Estimating the unknown values in a database with incomplete information. *Automation and Remote Control*, 49, No. 1, Jan. 1988, pp. 114–119.

[364] Buneman, P., S. B. Davidson, and A. Watters. Querying independent Databases. *Information Sciences*, 43, No. 1, Aug. 1987, pp. 170–218.

[365] Chandrasekaran, B., S. Mittal, and J. W. Smith. Reasoning with uncertain knowledge: The MDX approach. In *AMIA Congress 82*. Ed. D. A. B. Lindberg. NY: Masson Publishing, 1982, pp. 335–339.

[366] Chatterjee, A., A. Segev, and S. Sheshadri. A partitioning strategy for approximate joins. In *Proceedings of the 1993 Workshop on Information Technologies and Systems*. Orlando, FL: Dec. 1993.

[367] Danforth, S., and P. Valduriez. The data model of FAD: A database programming language. *Information Sciences*, 60, No. 1992, pp. 51–75.

[368] Dayon, B. Reliability of answers to an SQL query. Technical Report. Department of Computer Sciences, Concordia University, May 1990.

[369] de Korvin, A., G. Quichmayr, and S. Hashemi. Identifying precedents under uncertainty. In *Proceedings of DEXA 94, the 5th International Conference on Database and Expert Systems*. Athens, Greece: Sep. 1994.

[370] Demichiel, L. G. Performing database operations over mismatched domains. Ph.D. Dissertation. Department of Computer Sciences, Stanford University, 1989.

[371] Demichiel, L. G. Resolving database incompatibility: An approach to performing relational operations over mismatched domains. *IEEE Transactions on Knowledge and Data Engineering*, 1, No. 4, Dec. 1989, pp. 485–493.

[372] Dignum, F., and R. P. van de Riet. Addition and removal of information for a knowledge base with incomplete information. *Data and Knowledge Engineering*, 8 (1992), pp. 293–307.

[373] Dreizen, H. M. Imprecise database: Representation of imprecise and exceptional conditions via embedded relations. Ph.D. Dissertation. University of Illinois, 1983.

[374] Drescher, P., M. Holena, R. Kruschinski, and G Laufkter. Integrating frames, rules and uncertainty in a database-coupled knowledge-representation system. In *Proceedings of DEXA 94, the 5th International Conference on Database and Expert Systems*. Athens, Greece: Sep. 1994.

[375] Dubois, D., and H. Prade. Incomplete conjunctive information. *Computers and Mathematics with Applications*, 15, No. 10 (1988), pp. 797–810.

[376] Gelenbe, E. Incomplete representations of information in data bases. Research Report No 9. ISEM, Univ. Paris-Sud. 1983.

[377] Gelenbe, E. Incomplete representation of information in databases. In *Proceedings of ICOD-2, the 2nd International Conference on Databases*. Cambridge, England: Aug. 1983, pp. 246–258.

[378] Goodman, I. R., and H. T. Nguyen. *Uncertainty models for knowledge-based systems.* Amsterdam: North-Holland, 1985.

[379] Gunter, E., and L. Libkin. A functional database programming language with support for disjunctive information. AT&T Technical Memo BL011261-931203-47, Dec. 1993.

[380] Gunter, E., and L. Libkin. OR-SML: A functional database programming language for disjunctive information and its applications. In *Proceedings of DEXA 94, the 5th International Conference on Database and Expert Systems.* Athens, Greece: Sep. 1994.

[381] Hou, W., Z. Zhang, and N. Zhou. Statistical Inference of unknown attribute values in databases. In *Proceedings of CIKM-93, 2nd International Conference on Information and Knowledge Management.* Arlington, VA: Nov. 1993.

[382] Hull, R. Relative information capacity of simple relational database schemata. Technical Report TR 84-300. Computer Science Department, The University of Southern California, Jan. 1984.

[383] Imieliński, T., and W. Lipski, Jr. Incomplete information and dependencies in relational databases. In *Proceedings of ACM SIGMOD, International Conference on Management of Data.* Orlando, FL: June 1983, pp. 178–184.

[384] Kent, W. Solving domain mismatch and schema mismatch problems with an object-oriented database programming language. In *Proceedings of the International Conference on Very Large Databases.* Barcelona, Spain: 1991, pp. 147–160.

[385] Kent, W. The breakdown of the information model in multi-database systems. *ACM SIGMOD Record*, 20, No. 4 (1991), pp. 10–15.

[386] Kiessling, W., H. Thöne and U. Güntzer. Database support for problematic knowledge. In *Proceedings of EDBT 92, the International Conference on Extending Database Technology.* Vienna, Austria: 1992.

[387] Kirsche, T., R. Lenz, H. Schuster, and H. Wedekind. Towards a cooperative data model: Uncertainty and beyond. In *Proceedings of ADTI 94, International Symposium on Advanced Database Technologies and Their Integration.* Nara, Japan: Oct. 1994.

[388] Knight, B. Information loss in temporal knowledge representations. *Computer Journal*, 36, No. 2 (1993).

[389] Kratzer, K., and U Schreier. Behandlung von Ausnahmesituationen mit einer Metadatenbank. In *Proceedings GI-Fachtagung, Datenbank-Systeme für Büro, Technik und Wissenschaft, Germany.* Karlsruhe, Germany: 1985.

[390] Lacroix, M., and A. Pirotte. Generalized joins. *ACM SIGMOD Record*, 8, No. 3 (1976), pp. 14–15.

[391] Lefons, E., A. Silvestri, and F. Tangorra. An analystic approach to statistical databases. In *Proceedings of the International Conference on Very Large Databases.* Florence, Italy: Oct. 1983, pp. 260–274.

[392] Leikauf, P. Konsistenzsicherung durch Verwaltung von Konsistenzverletzungen. In *Proceedings GI-Fachtagung, Datenbank-Systeme für Büro, Technik und Wissenschaft, Germany.* Zürich, Switzerland: 1989.

[393] Levene, M. *The Nested Universal Relation Database Model.* Lecture Notes in Computer Science No. 595. Springer-Verlag, 1992.

[394] Levesque, H. J. Incompleteness in knowledge bases. In *Proceedings of the Workshop on Data Abstraction, Databases, and Conceptual Modeling.* Pingree Park, CO: June 1980.

[395] Levesque, H. J. The interaction with incomplete knowledge bases: A formal treatment. In *Proceedings of the International Joint Conference on Artificial Intelligence.* Vancouver, B.C.: Aug. 1981, pp. 240–245.

[396] Levesque, H. J. A formal treatment of incomplete knowledge bases. Ph.D. Dissertation. University of Toronto, Feb. 1982.

[397] Levesque, H. J. A formal treatment of incomplete knowledge bases. FLAIR Technical Report 3. Fairchild Laboratory for Artificial Intelligence Research, Palo Alto, CA, Feb. 1982.

[398] Libkin, L. A Relational algebra for complex objects based on partial information. In *Proceedings of the 1991 Symposium on Mathematical Fundamentals of Database Systems.* Lecture Notes in Computer Science No. 495. Springer-Verlag, 1991, pp. 36–41.

[399] Lim, E., J. Srivastava, and S. Shekhar. Resolving attribute Incompatibility in database integration: An evidential reasoning approach. In *Proceedings of ICDE, the International Conference on Data Engineering.* Houston, TX: Feb. 1994, pp. 154–163.

[400] Lozinskii, E. Plausible world assumption. In *Proceedings of the 1st International Conference on Principles of Knowledge Representation and Reasoning.* May 1989, pp. 266–275.

[401] Mendelson, H., and A. Saharia. Incomplete information costs and database design. *ACM Transactions on Database Systems*, 11, No. 2 (1986), pp. 159–185.

[402] Michalewicz, Z., and A. Yeo. Sets in relational databases. In *Proceedings of the Canadian Information Processing Society.* Edmonton, Canada: Nov. 1987, pp. 237–245.

[403] Michalewicz, Z., and L. J. Groves. Sets and uncertainty in relational databases. In *Proceedings of IPMU 88, Uncertainty and Intelligent Systems.* Urbino, Italy: July 1988, pp. 127–137.

[404] Michalewicz, Z., and K. Chen. Uncertain information in relational databases. *International Journal of Policy and Information (Taiwan)*, 13, No. 2, Dec. 1989, pp. 187–202.

[405] Montgomery, C. A., and E. H. Ruspini. The active information system: A data-driven system for the analysis of imprecise data. In *Proceedings of the International Conference on Very Large Databases.* IEEE Computer Press, 1981, pp. 376–384.

[406] Motro, A. Integrity = validity + completeness. *ACM Transactions on Database Systems*, 14, No. 4, Dec. 1989, pp. 480–502.

[407] Motro, A. Annotating answers with their properties. *ACM SIGMOD Record*, 21, No. 1, Mar. 1991.

[408] Ola, A., and G. Özsoyoğlu. Incomplete relational database models based on intervals. *IEEE Transactions on Knowledge and Data Engineering*, 5, No. 2, Apr. 1993, pp. 293–308.

[409] Orli, R. Modeling data for the summary database. *Data Base*, (1990), pp. 11–19.

[410] Orlowska, M. E. On syntax and semantics related to incomplete information databases. In *Proceedings of the 4th South African Computer Symposium.* Pretoria, South Africa: July 1987, pp. 109–129.

[411] Orlowska, M. E. On incomplete information databases. in *Proceedings of the 4th International Conference on Systems Research, Informatics, and Cybernetics.* Baden-Baden, W. Germany: 1988.

[412] Orlowska, M. E. Two interpretations of queries to incomplete information databases. *South African Journal of Philosophy* , 7, No. 2 (1988), pp. 126–132.

[413] Pawlak, Z. Knowledge and uncertainty: A rough set approach. In *Proceedings of SOFTEK 93, Workshop on Incompleteness and Uncertainty in Information Systems*. Montreal, Canada: Oct. 1993.

[414] Pearl, J. Reasoning under uncertainty. *Annual Review of Computer Science*, 4 (1989–1990), pp. 37–72.

[415] Read, R. A multi-resolution relational data model. In *Proceedings of the International Conference on Very Large Databases*. Vancouver, Canada: 1992.

[416] Read, R. L., D. S. Fussel, and A. Silberschatz. Computing bounds on aggregate operations over uncertain sets. In *Proceedings of the Workshop on Uncertainty in Databases and Deductive Systems*. Ithaca, NY: Nov. 1994.

[417] Sadri, F. Modeling uncertainty in databases. In *Proceedings of the International Conference on Data Engineering*. IEEE Computer Society. Los Angeles, CA: IEEE Computer Society Press, 1991, pp. 122–131.

[418] Sage, A. P. On the management of information imperfection in knowledge based systems. In *Information Processing and Management of Uncertainty*. Ed. B. Bouchon and R. Yager. New York: Springer-Verlag, 1987.

[419] Said, J., V. Alagar, and F. Sadri. Intelligent computations in managing uncertainty in relational database systems. In *Proceedings of SOFTEK 93, Workshop on Incompleteness and Uncertainty in Information Systems*. Montreal, Canada: Oct. 1993.

[420] Schiel, U., and B. Oresotu. Historical data modeling and the logic of precise and imprecise time. *ACM SIGMOD Record*, 15, No. 4, Dec. 1986, pp. 30–31.

[421] Schiel, U. Representation and retrieval of incomplete and temporal information. TR DSC-02/87. Universidade Federal Da Paraiba. May 1987.

[422] Shiri, N., and M. Jamil. Uncertainty as a function of expertise. In *Proceedings od SOFTEK 93, Workshop on Incompleteness and Uncertainty in Information Systems*. Montreal, Canada: Oct. 1993.

[423] Shum, C., and R. Muntz. Implicit representation for extensional answers. In *Proceedings of the 2nd International Conference on Expert Database Systems*. Apr. 1988, pp. 257–273.

[424] Skowron, A. Management of uncertainty in AI: A rough set approach. In *Proceedings of SOFTEK 93, Workshop on Incompleteness and Uncertainty in Information Systems*. Montreal, Canada: Oct. 1993.

[425] Slowinski, R., and J. Stefanowski. Rough classification in incomplete information systems. *Mathematical and Computer Modelling* (Oxford), 12, No. 10–11 (1989), pp. 1347–1357.

[426] Testemale, C. Un système de traitement d'informations incomplètes ou incertaines dans une base de données relationnelle. Ph.D. Dissertation. Université Paul Sabatier, Toulouse, 1984.

[427] Thöne, H., W. Kiessling, and U. Güntzer. Modelling, chaining and fusion of uncertain knowledge. In *Proceedings of DASFAA 95, the 4th International Conference on Database Systems for Advanced Applications*. Singapore: Apr. 1995.

[428] Tzvieli, A. Representation and access of uncertain relational data. *IEEE Database Engineering Bulletin—Special Issue on Imprecision in Databases*, 12, No. 2, June 1989, pp. 21–28.

[429] Warden, A. Into the unknown [database languages]. *Relational Journal* (UK), No. 9, Mar. 1990, pp. 7–12.

[430] Wille, R. Formal concept analysis of incomplete and uncertain data. In *Proceedings of SOFTEK 93, Workshop on Incompleteness and Uncertainty in Information Systems*. Montreal, Canada: Oct. 1993.

[431] Williams, M. H., and K. A. Nicholson. An approach to handling incomplete information in databases. *The Computer Journal*, 31, No. 2 (1988), pp. 133–140.

[432] Yager, R. R. A new approach to the summarization of data. *Information Sciences*, 28, No. 1, Oct. 1982, pp. 69–86.

[433] Yager, R. R. On incomplete and uncertain knowledge bases. In *Expert Systems in Government Symposium*. McLean, VA: Oct. 1986, pp. 96–100.

[434] Yan, Z., and H. Jichao. Data dependencies in database with incomplete information. *Journal of Computer Science and Technology* (English language edition) (China), 3, No. 2, Apr. 1988, pp. 131–138.

[435] Yeo, A. Sets in relational databases. Master's Thesis, Victoria University, Wellington, New Zealand, 1987.

[436] Zhou, N. Representation and processing of uncertain information in relational databases. In *The 10th International Conference on the Entity-Relationship Approach*. San Francisco, CA: Oct. 1991.

Acknowledgments

Our goal is to make a comprehensive bibliography so contributions, corrections, and/or suggestions are both welcomed and encouraged. Please contact the author of this article about any desired changes or additions. We wish to sincerely thank those who have contributed to the bibliography: all the participants of UMIS; especially Ami Motro, Esteban Zimányi, Henri Prade, Patrick Bosc, Alex Borgida, and Roberto Zicari; as well as others in the community; Ole J. Anfindsen, Birgit Boss, Valerie Cross, Angela Dappert-Farquhar, Werasak Kurutach, Leonid Libkin, William Mansfield, and Richard T. Snodgrass. The bibliography is available as a bibliographic database through anonymous ftp at `cs.arizona.edu` (file `bib/incomplete.bib` in bibdb format or file `bib/text/incomplete.bib` in BIBTEX format). It is also available as both a LATEX document (file `bib/incomplete.tex`) and a PostScript document (file `bib/incomplete.ps`). This work was supported by NSF grant IRI-8902707 and by IBM contract #1124.

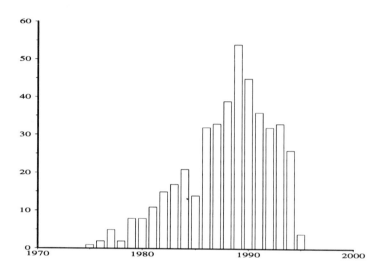

Figure 1   Publication history of every paper.

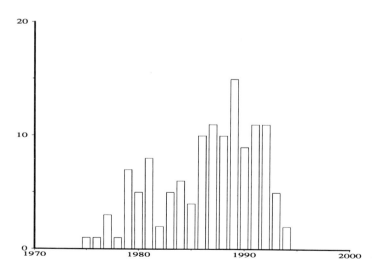

Figure 2   Publication history of unweighted approaches.

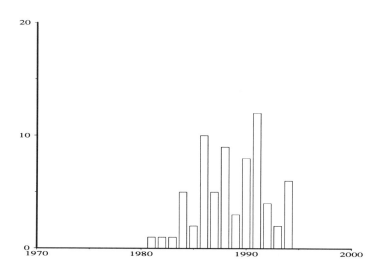

Figure 3   Publication history of logic-based papers.

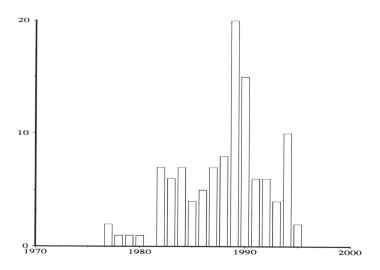

Figure 4   Publication history of fuzzy set and possibility theory approaches.

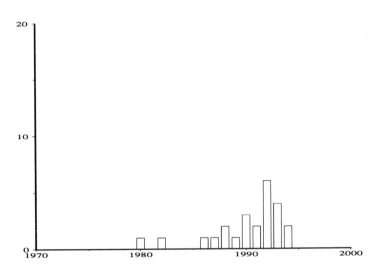

Figure 5   Publication history of probability theory approaches.

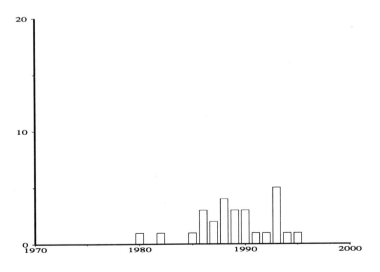

Figure 6   Publication history of query-level papers.

INDEX

W